10/5

P9-AEZ-082

The Second Chinese Revolution

ALSO BY K. S. KAROL

Visa for Poland

Khrushchev and the West

China: The Other Communism

Guerrillas in Power: The Course
    of the Cuban Revolution

The Second Chinese Revolution

K. S. Karol

Translated from the French
by Mervyn Jones

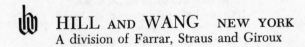 HILL AND WANG NEW YORK
A division of Farrar, Straus and Giroux

Copyright © 1973 by K. S. Karol

Translation copyright © 1974 by Farrar, Straus and Giroux, Inc.

All rights reserved

Printed in the United States of America

Published simultaneously in Canada by
Doubleday Canada Ltd., Toronto

Designed by Gustave Niles

Library of Congress Cataloging in Publication Data

Karol, K   S
The second Chinese revolution.

Translation of La deuxième révolution chinoise.
Includes bibliographical references.
1. China—Politics and government—1949–
             I. Title.
DS777.55.K32413   320.9′51′05   73–91174

CONTENTS

The Second Chinese Revolution

INTRODUCTION

Beyond the Mysteries of China

"This is the second Chinese revolution." It was in these enthusiastic terms that *People's Daily*, the central organ of the Chinese Communist Party, celebrated the Great Proletarian Cultural Revolution of 1966–9.[1] And the Party even pledged itself, in the statutes adopted at its Tenth Congress in August 1973, to engineer in the future a whole series of similar upheavals. Yet until that time, whenever a Communist Party had carried through a revolution, it had hastened to describe any subsequent popular movement as counterrevolutionary. What, then, are we to make of these recurring Chinese revolutions? Whom do they attack? Do they threaten the political domination of the Communist Party that holds power? Or are these emphatic Peking statements conferring the name of revolution on events that in no way deserve it?

These questions have been asked in the outside world ever since 1966, and all the signs show that in China too they still arouse arguments and misunderstandings. *People's Daily*, in the article quoted above, tells us that "many comrades badly failed to

[1] See the editorial from *People's Daily and Red Flag*, "Commemorate the Fiftieth Anniversary of the Communist Party of China," in *Peking Review*, No. 27 (July 2, 1971).

understand the Cultural Revolution when it began"; and the Tenth Congress has denounced the very leaders, such as Lin Piao and Ch'en Po-ta, whom Mao Tse-tung appointed in 1966 to direct the "great mobilization of the masses." To my mind, it is a certainty that this movement did not take the name of revolution in vain. The tens of millions of Chinese who battled during those three years were really putting their individual and collective fate at stake. Moreover, if the form taken by this ordeal was unexpected and baffling, the same cannot be said of the beliefs that impelled the leaders to unleash the storm.

Diverging from the traditions of the Third International, Mao declared in effect that the seizure of power by the Communist Party, while necessary for the transition to socialist society, was not enough to guarantee it. He took the line that the workers and the dispossessed—the masses—must continue their struggle for social and political liberation after the revolution, in order to wipe out step by step the social division of labor and the inequalities formerly established to the advantage of power holders and of those occupied in "dignified" brainwork, and to the detriment of "laborers" forced to carry out orders from above. In terms of China, this amounted to saying that even a very backward country, in the economic sense, should not wait to be modernized before embarking on revolutionary social changes and altering the basic relationships between man and man, in production and in society, as speedily as possible. To be still more precise, Mao envisaged a "socialist path" leading upward from underdevelopment; by following it, a postrevolutionary country could achieve a prosperous modern society already freed from most of the values, the injustices, and the alienating imbalances that mark, both in the West and in the East, societies emerging from an industrial revolution of the traditional type.

Such, beyond argument, is the historic gamble made by Mao's China, and the Cultural Revolution was no more than a dramatic —and doubtless very costly—episode in the struggle to bring it off. I do not claim, by thus stating my basic assumptions at the outset, to justify the fascination and the sympathy that I feel for the Chinese experiment, or to suggest that its success can be taken as certain. I wrote a long book on the subject in 1966, and when I now revert to the fundamental issues, I do so to give fair warning that to write a book on the second Chinese revolution is itself a gamble. For while it cannot be denied that Mao's ideas on the development of China, in contrast to the Soviet model, are highly relevant to us and have already upset many deep-rooted Western notions about the priorities required by socialist construction, it is also true that the Chinese seem to be very little concerned to let the rest of the world share their experiences. The face of China is that of a vast society in the throes of change, capable of taking the risks of an amazing convulsion such as the Cultural Revolution, but reluctant to explain its mechanisms and especially tight with information about its effects. The Chinese leaders are openhanded with statements of their general principles, thus arousing passionate debates about their doctrines and their basic decisions. But, having stirred our curiosity, they generally say that we have no business peeking into their internal affairs and offer us take-it-or-leave-it "explanations" of their political conflicts.

Their accounts are not merely extremely one-sided but also very terse and poorly documented. Four years after the end of the Cultural Revolution, not one book on the subject had been published in China. There is no source material even on famous self-contained episodes, such as the "revolutionary storm" in Shanghai at the end of 1966, or the battles of the Red Guard groups in the universities in 1967–8. Not a single protagonist has come forward as a witness, not a single "rebel" group has written its own history. Never before has a revolution been followed by such a silence. Nor can it be attributed to the inscrutable Chinese character; after their victory in 1949, the Communists wasted no time in putting out accounts of the Long March and the various battles of the heroic era.

In reality, we know quite well why they choose to wait this time. The outcome of the Cultural Revolution is just what has split the Chinese leadership with a violence rare in the history of the CCP. This crisis at the top—which began in 1969 and reached its climax in 1971—led to changes in the ruling team, and many of those who guided the Cultural Revolution are now described as bourgeois careerists, counterrevolutionary double agents, renegades, Trotskyites, traitors, and revisionists. The main targets are Lin Piao, once Mao's designated heir and "closest comrade in arms," and Ch'en Po-ta, chairman of the Central Group for the

Cultural Revolution, who was one of Mao's principal fellow workers ever since the Yenan days. To show that the elimination of the left-wing leaders did not mean an abandonment of the line pursued from 1966 to 1969, the new team that emerged from the Tenth Congress accused the losers of the most unlikely personal crimes and attributed to them political attitudes that were exactly the contrary of those they preached in public during the events in question. This procedure was no novelty in Communist history. But it obviously cannot help to enlighten us about the "anti-Party plot of Lin Piao," still less to tell us what was the real record of the "guilty men" during the Cultural Revolution.

All the same, many people in the West let themselves be convinced that, in September 1971, Lin Piao tried to blow up Mao's train on the Nanking Bridge and that, after failing to assassinate the Chairman, he met his death in a plane crash in Mongolia while fleeing to the Soviet Union. They accepted this version because they had always subscribed to a certain view of the nature of Chinese internal conflicts. In their eyes, acute though these differences were, they were detached from social and political issues and revealed nothing but a power struggle between a few unprincipled and ambitious men. If they feel so sure, let them stick to those easy convictions. But I don't envy the position of anyone who accepts all official statements as sound currency, or places the scornful label of "widower of Lin Piao" on those who venture to ask for evidence and question the guilt of the defeated. I myself am no widower, never having been espoused, and this book aims neither to praise nor to bury Lin Piao. My concern is not to write a pro-Lin or anti-Lin history of the second Chinese revolution, but to make an attempt simply at history, starting from the events and the issues that led to the explosion of 1966 and ending with the situation that is the current outcome of the years of struggles and splits.

Although the Chinese may keep silent or issue brief and contradictory accounts, we now possess enough material to undertake such a reconstruction. In the course of events, serious inroads were made on the official monopoly of information in China, and this reduced to a great extent one of the major obstacles to an independent study. Hundreds of internal Party documents and circulars or directives from the Central Group for the Cultural Revolution, relating to the period from 1956 to 1968, have been published abroad. These massive leaks can doubtless be ascribed to the uncontrolled Red Guard press, but sometimes they can also be traced to a decision on the part of the Party center to release material that the CCP had hitherto kept for its own use alone. Thus we can avail ourselves of many documents whose existence—if not whose content—had certainly been known for a long time. Among these are certain speeches by Mao, dating from the time of the Great Leap Forward of 1958, which are of key importance and enable us to grasp his basic assumptions about postrevolutionary development; the texts, however, had never been published before the Cultural Revolution.

Moreover, the Chinese press and the daily bulletin supplied to the outside world by the New China News Agency represent a mine of information about the three years from 1966 to 1969. The often irritating style of these publications stayed the same as in the earlier period, but this was not true of the content. *Verba volant, scripta manent;* when verbal accounts differ too widely, it is wise to refer as much as possible to what was written at the time of the events. During the period of the Cultural Revolution the Chinese wrote a great deal, and much can be learned from reading them.

The same goes for the Red Guard papers. Often criticized for their well-known bias and naïveté, they nevertheless vividly reflect the political atmosphere of the period and often provide us with valuable and even eloquent data. Finally, we have the accounts of foreigners who lived in Peking or Shanghai or who visited China during this era of "broad democracy." Their writings are often biased in one direction or the other, but they remain interesting, if only because they reveal which aspects of these remarkable events took outsiders by surprise.

However, many gaps in our knowledge remain, and in my chapters on the Cultural Revolution the reader will often meet with guesses based on dubious information, and sometimes with simple admissions of ignorance. To give an example, let me say at once that the record of the Cultural Revolution in the countryside is very scanty—not because the rural world remained untouched, but because we know very little about what really happened. In this context, I confine myself to describing my long interview with

Ch'en Yung-kuei, the moving spirit of the model brigade of Tachai, who has recently become a member of the Political Bureau (Politburo) of the Party. Still, while I am convinced of his good will, I don't believe that he told me the whole story.

How much trust, in fact, should we put in interviews in general, and in accounts heard on the spot, when they are necessarily based on the latest official version? In my view, they throw a certain light on known facts, add extra details, and thus enrich the meaning that we can read in these facts. But I have not sought to put into the mouths of my informants more than they said, and as a general rule I have kept my reporting distinct from my attempts to reconstruct political events. Hence the reader will find six chapters devoted to the political history of the second Chinese revolution, and five postscripts garnered from my travels in China in 1971.

Altogether, I have spent more than six months in that country, traveling widely, before and after the Cultural Revolution. I believe that in the course of my two trips, in 1965 and 1971, I visited more communes, factories, and universities, especially in regions normally closed to foreigners, than my colleagues from the European and American press. If I have decided, not without hesitation, to make a critical and independent study of current theory and practice in Maoist China, rather than to limit myself to a purely descriptive account, my reason lies in my deep belief that, to understand what is happening, we must pay special attention to the great problems that this country has dedicated itself to solving.

"The ideology of the man who plans," Strumilin wrote, "is one of the decisive factors in planning." [2] This applies still more strongly to the man who describes from the outside the plans and results of socialist construction in a society like that of China. This country fascinates me, not as a model or because I expect it to export its revolution, but because it has posed in a fresh way most of the problems of socialism that are ours too. Thanks to China, we have already learned a great deal about ourselves and about European societies that claim to be socialist.

[2] See Czeslaw Bobrowski, *La Formation du système de planification soviétique* (The Hague: Mouton, 1956).

Thus I make no claim to be neutral toward China, and I do not offer an account that can be above the battle or worthy of academic objectivity. But I have tried to take from my friends in the universities a discipline of method that consists of putting quotations in their context, checking dates and facts, telling all the news whether it is good or bad, and conceding to the various protagonists the same measure of political sincerity. I have sought to understand the motives of all concerned and not only of those who are now in power. The reader will judge whether I have kept strictly enough to these rules. But, to bring these preliminaries to a close, I should like to point to another paradox: the CCP continually declares that it is not monolithic and it does not claim to march "with measured stride" in the "direction of history." Mao's thinking gives the lie to the bombastic picture, long displayed in Russia, of a Party that knows everything and never changes its mind. Among the quotations from the Chairman taught in all Chinese schools and workplaces, pride of place is given to the one that explains that in every human community there is always "a Left, a Center, and a Right." Here and there in Mao's writings we even find allusions to the great difficulty experienced by the Left in winning out in these clashes; it comes up repeatedly against the inertia of the Center and the resistance of the Right, buttressed by the social and cultural heritage of the past. In Mao's eyes, this endless struggle extends into the very heart of the Party, where the most progressive wing does not always have the power to make its views prevail.

But if this is so—and it is highly convincing—we should listen at every point not only to the account given by the victors but also to that of the defeated "deviationists." Although it is admitted that the Left may suffer temporary setbacks, none of the ruling groups in Peking ever portrays itself as being on the Right; all of them, all the time, claim to have defeated "right-wing deviations," or trends that pretend to be on the Left but are really on the Right. This contradiction does not make it easier to understand the situation. To overcome it, I think, we must apply to China the very method Mao urged on his comrades more than thirty years ago: "In every matter, a Communist must ask the question *why*; he must reflect carefully and see if everything is truly founded and corresponds to reality. Never must he blindly follow others or demand slavish submission to someone else's opinion." [3]

My Four Months in China in 1965

In 1965 I did not go to China to learn from 700 million people that the Soviet bloc was incapable of creating an alternative civilization to the doomed capitalist societies. No long journey in the Far East is needed to confirm this elementary truth; we can reach our verdict on the spot. For myself, I have been able to make my practical test by living in the USSR for seven years (from 1939 to 1946) and then in France during the 1950's. So my interest in China derived from no such political impulse; it came primarily from the great curiosity, mingled with sympathy, aroused in me by a "revolution of the downtrodden" that refused to revolve in the Soviet orbit. Basically, despite my limited knowledge, I had many preconceived ideas at the time of my first contact with Chinese realities. Like most people on the Left, I supposed that Mao was trying *first of all* to industrialize China, avoiding the excesses of the Russians but accepting the basic principles and the ideological heritage of Stalinism. Anyway, was he not defending Stalin's personality? Had he not tried to force the pace of economic growth in the Great Leap Forward of 1958, like the Russians in the 1930's?

Everything that we knew about China strengthened the belief that the first task of a victorious revolution in an underdeveloped country is to develop it. Alas, industrialization has never been carried through anywhere without sufferings. The most that one could hope for, under these conditions, was that the men in power would not add to the already huge difficulties by their own mistakes and would not extort too high a toll from the generation that built the "material foundations of socialism." Trustworthy witnesses, principally Edgar Snow, assured us that in China the process would be more humane than usual—thanks to Mao, who was averse to using repressive methods. So I expected to find in China an "enlightened Stalinism," freed from the irrational brutality of the Soviet record.

[3] See Mao Tse-tung, "Rectify the Party's Style in Work" (February 1, 1942), *Selected Works*, Vol. III (Peking: Foreign Languages Publishing House, 1965).

What I did find was something else. I traveled with Marc Riboud, who had already been in China in 1957 and who grasped with the eye of the photographer the immense progress achieved since then. He was still more impressed because he had traveled in every country in Asia—and in the Third World—and no other could come anywhere near to claiming such headway. So we listened carefully while our hosts explained their "miracle," achieved in isolation because the USSR had withdrawn its aid and its technicians in 1960. Now, although they claimed to be the guardians of Leninist and Stalinist orthodoxy (and denounced Khrushchev from that standpoint), everything they said was the contrary of all Stalinist theories and methods of growth. For a start, they disowned the priorities of the Soviet model, centered on heavy industry, and also its principles of wide differentials in wages and of individual competition in output. In Chinese factories at the time of my visit, no one even knew the meaning of Stakhanovist emulation or of piecework. This, and a great many other "class" innovations, created an atmosphere I had not expected, for it differed greatly from what I had known during the seven years of my life, from 1939 to 1946, when I worked in the Soviet Union.

Our discoveries in the countryside were no less astonishing. First of all, agriculture was described as the basic element in the economy and not as merely a source of accumulation of capital for industrialization. The people's communes enjoyed an autonomy that seemed to stimulate their efficiency, and extensive opportunity to develop by "relying on their own strength." The stress was put on politics, on "the campaign for socialist education in the rural sector," and the talk everywhere was of changed relationships between individuals, of mutual aid, and of the need to keep on strengthening the collective element. The slogan was already: "In agriculture, follow the model of Tachai," a brigade in a very poor region of the northwest cited by Mao on account of its independent spirit and its exceptionally socialist methods of organizing and sharing work.

I wondered, all the same, whether this outlook had not been imposed on the Chinese Communist Party by circumstances: for example, by the impossibility of making a rigid centralized plan for the growth of an economy exceptionally unbalanced by regional differences and, on the whole, very slightly concentrated. It is no secret that there are at least ten different Chinas and that the northeast (formerly Manchuria) and Shanghai are already in the industrial era, in contrast with, for instance, Szechwan and Yunnan. Our hosts gave us a chance to see this by taking us to visit remote regions and indeed, within these regions, communes laboring under special handicaps. They told us that, in the provinces of Yunnan and Kwangsi, which contain many formerly persecuted national minorities, at the time of the Liberation they had found communities living in every possible form of precapitalist society, from slavery to well-developed feudalism. Nevertheless, from our discussions in the four corners of China, it emerged clearly that the Chinese were by no means making a virtue of necessity, and that their plan of development was based on a systematic and far-reaching general theory, evolved in the course of a special revolutionary experience.

We delved to some extent into this past by visiting historic places, from Mao's native village in Hunan Province to his Red capital, Yenan in the northwest, where the techniques and theories of Maoism were shaped during a period of ten years (eight of these during the war with Japan). What struck me most during these four months of inquiry was the extraordinary egalitarian purpose of the Chinese Communists, their goal of abolishing as quickly as possible the social distinctions inherited from the old order and preventing new ones from being formed over the heads of the masses. "Purpose" was the right word, for no magic wand can get rid overnight of the differences between town and country, between brainwork and manual labor, between the most advanced and the most backward regions. But I repeat that these egalitarian ambitions struck me as extraordinary in the true sense; I had never seen anything like it in the socialist world.

It is in the name of this egalitarianism that the "antirevisionist" political atmosphere was created in the factories and communes; that the span of wages in industry was narrowed; that a huge and ceaseless swap-around of population was instituted; that city dwellers were sent to work for months in the fields; and that an army "like no other army" was—and is—maintained, recruited from the sons of peasants and taking part in every kind of work, as in the heroic age of Yenan. It seemed to me that this orientation paid off, that the Chinese were succeeding where other socialist countries had failed for lack of adequate mass participation. Poor as it was, this China appeared to be definitely better organized and relatively more prosperous than its former allies. The working-class standard of living was still very low, but it was incomparably higher than before and it was improving from year to year. Moreover, the workers did not have to waste their energies in standing in line outside the stores, or in finding ways to keep up with galloping inflation as best they could, or in waging an individual struggle to acquire assets in the official economy in order to engage in black-market activities in the parallel "economy number two." [4] These were essential facts about human life, and the information that I gathered, partly from non-Chinese residents, seemed to me completely convincing on the subject. This orientation also explained some beneficial side effects of importance in social life, such as the decline in crime, the wiping out of prostitution, the extraordinary progress in public health, and the recovery of dignity in everyday behavior—witness the refusal of tips and the absence of servility. All this could not have been imposed by commands or by sermons. It was the social organization that enabled people to transform their old habits. What mechanism of integration had been put to work in People's China to evoke from the citizens this effort at work and this different outlook toward the community and therefore in personal relationships?

The question was hard to answer, for the one thing that was clear to me was that this mechanism was not based on the desire for gain, nor yet on coercion. To understand it, I believe, we must revise many of our ideas about Chinese development. Is it possible, indeed, to go on speaking of the "failure" of the Great Leap Forward, since it was only in 1958 that China opted for its new, and socially very beneficial, methods? Moreover, the Chinese were showing that a definite mode of industrialization in a backward country—Stalinism, in brief—was by no means neces-

[4] "Economy number two" is an expression invented in the USSR during the war to cover all productive or commercial operations carried on outside state control and more or less tolerated. When I revisited Moscow in October 1970 I found that the term is still accurate under contemporary conditions. Today, just as yesterday, an enormous parallel economic sector flourishes.

sary as a way out of underdevelopment. For the first time a post-revolutionary nation was entering a new item in the balance sheet of "the inevitability of Stalinism during the period of weakness in production," which had divided and agitated the Left for decades. And this item carried enormous weight, for the Chinese were countering Russia's historical experience not with a theory but with another experience, on a scale equal to or greater than that of the USSR.

All this gave grounds for very positive conclusions, as I said frankly when I came back. But I preferred to be cautious, for I was aware of the contradictions in the Chinese system and also of the limitations of my inquiry. I will say no more about my Soviet experiences, but I kept myself equally on guard in China, since I was often asked to judge by appearances without having any opportunity to share the life of the man in the street. Nor, at that time, did anyone mention to me the "struggle between the two lines" within the Party, or the existence of a Left, a Center, and a Right; what Mao had said in this connection was brought to light only later, during the Cultural Revolution. The public face of the CCP was united and solid, and also very hierarchical, with Chairman Mao at the head presiding over a team of five vice-chairmen—Liu Shao-ch'i, Chou En-lai, Chu Teh, Ch'en Yün, and Lin Piao.[5] Mao was the focus of a boundless personality cult, which I described as frankly irritating. But this question was closely linked to another—the whole question of the "mass line" methods that were supposed to ensure the genuine and independent participation of the masses in the social and economic development of their country. Through what channels did the masses have a chance to express themselves?

My hosts spoke to me of their austere lives and showed me their calloused hands to prove that, whatever their rank, they all did spells of manual work in factories and on the land. They assured me that they were thus sharing directly in the joys and sorrows of the workers and that they did so in order to "garner the ideas of the masses, concentrate them, and take them back to the masses so that they can be put into practice." [6] In short, they all carried

[5] Another portrait very frequently seen was that of Teng Hsiao-p'ing, the secretary-general of the Party.

[6] See Mao Tse-tung, "Some Questions Concerning Methods of Leadership" (June 1, 1944), Selected Works, Vol. III.

out this vital command of Chairman Mao and thus escaped the "worst danger" for a Chinese cadre:[7] to reveal himself as authoritarian and violate the principle that the proletariat freely supports the general line of the Party. The best way for a Communist to win the trust and respect of the workers, they told me, was to "carry the heaviest burden" in all conditions, also in conformity with a directive from the Chairman.

Being a Communist cadre in Mao's China was clearly no bed of roses. Pledged to a Spartan way of living, punished for the least temptation to exploit their status, obliged to submit to criticism and self-criticism for every sin of omission, these leaders were more like missionaries spreading the gospel among the people than like Party bureaucrats in other socialist countries. According to a story which they told me and which evidently held a symbolic value for them, one distinguished and long-standing cadre had lost the job of deputy minister to which he had just been appointed because, on his first day, he claimed an official car. This revealed that he was not unselfish and that he relied on outward symbols of power to gain authority.

Still, all this did not answer my question about the decision-making power of the masses. The reality was that these modest cadres, devoted to the people and engaging in manual work, nevertheless made all the decisions and were accountable only to their superiors in the Party. Their "good conduct" undeniably influenced the political climate of the country—without it all the speeches about equality and class struggle would not have had any effect. The Party had chosen to manage society by relying on the political mobilization of the masses and was thus obliged to play the part of a teacher rather than simply that of a leader in the traditional style. But it made no bones about its position as the political vanguard and cast itself, in fact, in a more central role than the other power-wielding Communist Parties.

There was another point. In the Soviet-bloc countries, the Party controls everything, including the state administration. But, to

[7] The term *cadre* as used in China has a very specialized meaning. For a detailed explanation, see Franz Schurmann, *Ideology and Organization in Communist China*, 2nd ed. (Berkeley and Los Angeles: University of California Press, 1968), pp. 162–72.

make things look good, it is the usual practice to keep the two systems apart and it is thought proper that the Party secretary should not also be the chairman of the local council. Likewise, in the industrial sphere, factory directors are not necessarily Party members and are very seldom at the head of the Party organization in the factory. In China, since the Great Leap Forward, there has been, on the contrary, a tendency toward fusing the two branches of the executive. In most towns, in 1965, the mayor was none other than the Party secretary. The factory director or the commune chairman was generally the key Party man in the enterprise. Why, I asked, this concentration of jobs? The purpose, it was explained to me, was to enable the proletariat to defend its interests through the medium of its Party and to "put politics in command" everywhere.

The evidence was clear: everything in China was being politicized, and the Party, the political organism par excellence, was "carrying the heaviest burden" in all spheres of social and economic life. The Party alone was considered capable of instilling the proletarian spirit into the masses and securing their active participation in the struggle to bring the great development plans to fruition. By doing so, it candidly assumed all the responsibilities of management and could not, in the event of failure, lay the blame on scapegoats in the state administration (as is sometimes done in Eastern Europe). By the same token, however, might it not expose itself to the harshest kind of criticism, if one day its own doctrines were fully applied and the workers expressed themselves on every possible subject?

After my 1965 visit, I reached two conclusions. Having chosen a different road from the Russians, the Chinese would necessarily arrive at a different form of socialism; and, in a country where political activity is stimulated, where the workers are encouraged toward participation and trained in an egalitarian spirit, the people would sooner or later free themselves from the rigid paternalism of the Party.[8] But I did not imagine that this would happen in the near future, still less that the problem was already being discussed at the top level of the Party itself.

[8] See my China: The Other Communism (New York: Hill and Wang, 1967), p. 22.

The Shock of the Cultural Revolution

Like everyone else, I was caught short by the Cultural Revolution. That a nation in the midst of its development effort, and, moreover, threatened by war on its frontiers, should put itself in a position of risk and accept the hazards of a vast internal conflict—this was something that had never been seen before. Mao, the man who embodied the People's Republic of China and the CCP, encouraged criticism of all the institutions of his state and his Party. The history of the socialist world has no precedent for such a revolution in its framework. No event since the October Revolution of 1917 has upset so many of our habits of thought and our ideas about socialist development.

The Cultural Revolution was equally astonishing in its methods. An indescribable worship of Mao went hand in hand with virulent attacks on many veterans of Maoism. If one adds to this the flood of false reports from the China watchers of Hong Kong, Tokyo, and Moscow, it must be admitted that it has never been so hard to comment on any historical episode. But my experiences in China the year before were of precious assistance in putting events into perspective and at least saved me from formulating the kind of superficial theories that are swiftly refuted by facts.

From the outset I refused to see the Cultural Revolution as a struggle among cliques for the succession to Mao, or as a struggle on Mao's part to regain the power he was supposed to have lost in the later 1950's. The notes I had made in China gave me more reliable clues to the true origin of the new happenings. In the first place, I was not surprised that they had started in the universities, where all the contradictions of the Chinese system are, so to speak, crystallized in a pure state. Throughout the world, access to higher education is a privilege. In China it was reserved for a happy band numbering only 600,000, strictly selected according to the places and resources available. But at the same time it was vital at any cost to prevent these students from turning into new mandarins. To this end, it was necessary to press forward with the political education of these young people and fill them, more than anyone else, with egalitarian and anti-hierarchical principles. Thus, to make them "Red and expert," they were trained in the spirit of anti-authoritarianism and equality, while they were also

kept firmly in hand and hog-tied by a rigid discipline—that of a
university built on the Soviet model, which is even more firmly
structured and hierarchical than a university in the West. There
was a contradiction here, and the authorities knew it, for they said
even to me that this system could not last. But no one seemed in
any hurry to make changes until the day when the student
posters—the *ta tzu pao*—aimed at "reactionary academic authorities" showed that it was too late for a reform handed down from
above. However, the member of the Party leadership in charge,
Liu Shao-ch'i, took the initiative by sending Party work teams to
restore the situation and purge the universities. As will be seen, he
paid dearly for this "authoritarian action," though it had hitherto
been customary in national life.

Here, then, was a sign that standards had changed in China;
what had previously been regarded as normal, or even good, was
now to be condemned. Besides, many of these "Party despots"
who were denounced from the start of the upheaval were known
to me. As the Party's spokesmen on questions of culture, of the
press, or of education, they had explained to me the line that was
in favor in 1965 and extolled its virtues. Thus I knew Chou Yang,
the head of the Central Committee department responsible for
cultural affairs, and most of the power holders in the Peking
newspaper world who were later denounced en bloc as a "black
gang." [9] A leader of the Italian Communist Party even accused
me, with a smile, of having the irritating habit of always seeking
the company of rebels, even in China. But were they really rebels,
and precisely how were they in opposition to Mao?

Comparing their line of talk with new Chinese documents, I
easily grasped the difference, and it concerned a most important
point: the role of the Party in society. To them, as has been said,
the Party was the sole instrument of the dictatorship of the
proletariat and had to control everything. Since the Cultural
Revolution, this notion was deemed revisionist and they were
accused of using it to grab "a part of the powers of the
proletariat" and set themselves up as "despots moving along the
capitalist road."

My hosts had given me another clue when, in the course of my

[9] See my interview with Chou Yang in *China: The Other Communism*, p. 275.

visit, they had discussed the USSR and the origins of "Khrushchev-ism" with me. Our interpretations differed, but I saw that through their attacks on Khrushchev's alleged coup d'état they were tacitly denouncing the methods of Communist Parties that are too much inclined to hand down orders from above, too centralized, and not democratic enough. To forestall the same scenario in China, they stressed the need to watch over the quality of their cadres and their integration with the masses; but, whenever I went back to my notes, I could see evidence that the question of submitting executive power, monopolized by the Party, to organized control by the masses was being raised. Certain minor facts assumed a new meaning in the light of the Cultural Revolution, for they showed that Mao, long before he appeared in Red Guard uniform, had become convinced of the urgent need to subject his Party to a radical test from below. Doubtless the student turmoil had given him a good pretext to speed up events. But was there not an objective justification for his call for an overhaul of the system?

My Return to China in 1971

I was highly delighted to be returning to Peking in the spring of 1971. China had only just reopened her doors to journalists, and I was the first from Europe to secure permission from the Ministry of Foreign Affairs to make a study in depth of the Cultural Revolution. While I was eager to examine on the spot the changes produced by the great upheaval, I also found that the priority with which I was favored had a certain political meaning. Chinese diplomats had never commented on my writings—except to protest in October 1966 because I criticized the cult of Mao's personality—and our contacts had been reduced to a strict minimum until 1970. From then onward, invitations to the embassy became more frequent and my hosts praised the objectivity of my articles in *Nouvel Observateur*. Without going into things more deeply, they promised that, as a "friend of the Chinese people," I should be the first to get a visa to revisit their country. At first I thought that they were merely being polite, but I was forgetting that the Chinese always keep their word.

Now, although I have always followed Chinese developments

with sympathy and opposed farfetched interpretations of the Cultural Revolution, I have not approved of everything and I have never hesitated to put forward my own explanations, which were often in contrast with the official story. The fact that this was accepted and did not deprive me of the status of friend of the Chinese people indicates that the Chinese are not so sectarian as they are made out. In practical terms, my second visit, like my first, was made wholly at my own expense and I thus maintained my full independence.

Even before I reached Peking, while making my first stop at Canton, I felt that I was no longer a stranger in China. I had benefited from the 1965 journey, covering 15,000 miles and a dozen provinces; I was familiar with the welcoming formalities, the customs of my hosts, and everyday life, to say nothing of the Chinese landscape. This time, I did not need to discover the country as a country and I could concentrate on studying its problems—I could listen rather than look.

My first interviews at the Ministry of Foreign Affairs in Peking confirmed that, on the whole, conditions were favorable for me. My hosts, now installed in a modern building, warned me not to be too optimistic; they explained that the process of rebuilding the Party and the administration absorbed the energies of many people in responsible positions and they would not be able to meet me everywhere as in 1965. But I had no wish to tour China from north to south over again. I wanted only to go to certain industrial districts in the northeast and to Shanghai, where the most significant events had occurred, to revisit certain factories and certain universities, to see the changes that had taken place and discuss them with those concerned. In principle the northeast is not open to foreigners, but my hosts promised to get me a travel permit and suggested two other trips—to the famous rural brigade of Tachai, in the northwest, and to Chingkangshan, in the southeast, where Mao had set up his first Red base in 1927 and organized the first units of the People's Liberation Army. Obviously this was bound to add to the value of my inquiry, without diverting me from my main object, the study of the Cultural Revolution.

So everything began under the best auspices. But suddenly, at the beginning of April, a dramatic event drew my attention to

Chinese foreign policy. An American table-tennis team arrived in Peking, accompanied by representatives of the American press. These were the first American journalists to enter China on an official basis, and the event was a world sensation. My friends at the Ministry of Foreign Affairs did not try to play down its importance, but they tried with great seriousness to set it in the framework of "contacts between peoples" and made a long justification of Sino-American friendship on that level. By their account, the presence of these American citizens was quite natural; at the recent table-tennis tournament at Nagoya they had taken the initiative in expressing a wish to visit China; and there was no reason for a refusal because, in the Chinese view, this request showed that "the American people, unlike their government, was renewing the best traditions of friendship with the Chinese people." Any effort to get beyond this explanation was obviously pointless, so I did not press my hosts. In group discussions in factories this version was repeated to me word for word; but a few workers, when questioned off the cuff, admitted that they had been a little surprised by the arrival of American guests.

Then, toward the end of April, during a stopover at Shanghai on my way back from Chingkangshan, some friends gave me a still more surprising piece of news. *Life* had published the interview given by Mao to Edgar Snow. In it, Mao had said that Americans of the Left, the Center, and the Right would soon be able to come to China; Nixon himself would be welcome, whether in his capacity as head of state or simply as a tourist. This statement, given great publicity by foreign radio stations, was already known to my official hosts. Once again, they set themselves to prove to me that it was in the tradition of good relations between the two peoples—no more than that.

But, in addition to the disclosure of what was already called "Ping-Pong diplomacy," the Snow interview contained a real bombshell. Mao had explained to his American friend that the cult of personality, inevitable to a certain extent in any society with hierarchical features, had in effect been necessary during the Cultural Revolution to encourage the masses to dismantle the Party bureaucracy; unfortunately, it had also set up false standards for the decision about the succession, and now it should be reduced to correct proportions. As Mao said, the Red Guards had reached the point of judging the political convictions of leaders and militants by the number of portraits of the Chairman, plaster statues, and "other junk" with which they were surrounded. This had to stop.

I am almost sure that Mao had spoken in the same terms, three months before he met Snow, at the meeting of the Central Committee in September 1970. How else could one explain the fact that people I met, even in the provinces, knew several statements and anecdotes from the interview well before it was published? For instance, to illustrate a certain lack of sincerity in earlier years, of which he "strongly disapproved," Mao told Snow the following symbolic story: "Someone, while saying that the struggle should be carried out by reasoning and not by coercion or force, actually gave the other fellow a kick under the table and then drew back his leg. When the person kicked asked, 'Why did you kick me?' the first person said, 'I didn't kick you. Don't you see my foot is still here?'" This tale of the kick was told me in identical words in several places, and everyone seemed to have known it by heart for quite a while.

This severe attack on the methods of the Cultural Revolution by the man who had done most to inspire it had, it seemed to me, one advantage. At last one could openly discuss a question that had hitherto been taboo for Chinese officials. I was all the more glad of this because the question of the cult had in earlier years been a source of tension, even of discord, in most of my talks with Chinese spokesmen. In 1966, though it was not their policy to comment on writings by foreigners, they had made some fairly bitter remarks about passages in my earlier book criticizing the excesses of the cult of Mao. Since then the cult had grown to extravagant proportions. In accordance with Lin Piao's directive, the whole of China had been transformed into "a vast school of the thought of Chairman Mao." Though we knew that the teaching in this school was radically different from the Russian curriculum at the time of the cult of Stalin, we still found it hard to cheer at this way of "unifying the 700 millions of China" through hero worship. Once Mao himself had reached the conclusion that the abuse of this method was harmful, I had hopes that this question—a basic factor in any estimate of the Cultural

Revolution—would be open to full discussion, from which "foreign friends" would not be excluded.

But my hosts in Peking had no intention of interpreting Mao's interview in this way. True, they relaxed their previous discretion and were more willing to enter into the problems of the past, but this was only to let me into the story of the "ultra-Left" plot of 1967, which had caused havoc in the Ministry of Foreign Affairs, stained the image of China for the world, and almost led to a counterrevolutionary coup. This affair was, however, of great importance. I eagerly took notes and then tried to compare them with what was already known in the West and with the slender documentation that I had brought with me. Most of the facts that were thus brought to light—such as the premeditated arson at the office of the British chargé d'affaires in August 1967, or the attacks on Ch'en Yi[10]—proved at the least, to my mind, that a certain type of doctrinal hysteria had led some young (and not so young) people into unbridled sectarianism and claimed unnecessary victims. But my hosts did not take that view; "it was not a matter of sectarianism," they repeated patiently to me, and came back to their story of the plot. To get around the difficulty, I suggested a compromise between their point of view and mine: the frenzy of sectarianism had led certain militants, and even leaders, to engage in concerted secret activities and hence, objectively, in plots. Not at all, they replied. "Your approach produces nothing but confusion; these people acted wrongly on purpose under the orders of the arch-traitor Liu Shao-ch'i. Yao Wen-yuan[11]showed in September 1967 that they claimed to be on the Left while they were really on the Right and that they spread universal distrust in order to fish in troubled waters." All right; but in that case could they give me the names of the guilty men and more detailed information on the whole record? "Inquiries are not yet complete," my hosts replied prudently, and promised to reveal further details at a suitable time.

It followed that, in the meantime, anyone might be suspect. As soon as a leader ceased to appear in public—and this was often

[10] Ch'en Yi (1901–72), vice-premier and minister of foreign affairs since 1958.

[11] Yao Wen-yuan, literary critic before the Cultural Revolution and now a member of the Politburo of the CCP.

the case—the question at once arose whether he should be regarded as involved in the "plot." Was a new showdown happening at the top level? During one of my first meetings at the ministry, I had been intrigued by the reaction to my request for an interview with Ch'en Po-ta: "What do you want to discuss with him? Why do you think he is competent to speak to you about the Cultural Revolution?"—and so forth. This caution inevitably suggested to me that the number four of the Party was on the skids. Was it really surprising that a foreigner, authorized to make a study of the Cultural Revolution, should wish to meet the former chairman of the Central Group, the very man who had directed it? Since my hosts stopped short of saying that he was implicated by the "inquiry into the 1967 plot," the conclusion was that his fate—like that of other former leaders—was still under debate in high places. Of course, it was unthinkable that the same applied to Lin Piao; my hosts had explained to me that the aim of the "plotters of the May 16 Group" (this was their official label) had been to drive a wedge between Chairman Mao and Vice-Chairman Lin Piao; not daring to attack the former, they gunned for the latter. Am I to imagine that these "fanatics" were attacking their own leader? Yet the postdated account given by the Chinese "revealed" that Lin Piao was the chief of the conspiracy.

However, it is not my concern to contrast these talks in the spring of 1971 with later events, which must surely have taken my friends by surprise. At the time of my visit, I simply had a feeling that I was confronted with two Chinas. There was the China of the people, which I was warmly invited to see—as I shall describe—and which on the whole gave me pleasant surprises. And there was the China of the summit, from which rumors emanated of unprecedented conflicts that were hard to interpret, but by which one was bound to be fascinated. "For the time being, you must study the Cultural Revolution on the grass-roots level," one official told me; and he went on to add, carried away by sincerity, that events at the top level had many mysteries that he himself did not expect to understand for years to come. I believe that he felt rather sorry for me, thinking of the difficulties I was to meet in writing my book, but he was also indicating to me in an elegant fashion that I must "rely on my own resources"—in the words of the Maoist slogan—in seeking to disentangle the skeins of history. I did not yet know how sound this advice was; but I began to suspect that my task would be more arduous than I had at first expected.

A China of Two Political Levels

If there is one thing that is hard to grasp quickly in a foreign country, after a relatively short absence, it is the extent of material progress that has been achieved. We also know that revolutionary periods are not normally favorable to rapid economic growth. In the case of China between 1966 and 1969, it was already considered a notable success that it was able to keep production going at the necessary pace in essential fields, and no economic miracles were to be expected during these stormy years. In other words, the material conditions of the Chinese people had not radically changed between 1965 and 1971; I could add nothing much to my earlier book by giving another account of the standard of living, the income distribution, food supplies, wages, and prices. Besides, the values that governed social organization and the methods of development had, in my view, stayed the same as before. The farming communes and factories in the China of 1971 seemed to me fairly similar to those that I had visited six years before, at least in the basic organization, which displayed the distinctively Chinese priorities—"politics in command," be "Red and expert," "Red" counts for more than "expert."

What, then, had changed since the "great upheaval"? When I put together the accounts given to me by the rank and file, I should say, in essence, that the Cultural Revolution enabled them to get a greater mastery of doctrine, and therefore to apply it with greater knowledge and effectiveness. Sometimes I politely disagreed when my hosts tried to convince me that the doctrine itself had been forged in the course of events; they usually admitted that this picture was exaggerated and shifted to ground where they felt more secure. "Back in 1965 we told you about the triple alliance of workers, cadres, and technicians, and about the principle of manual work for all cadres, but what happened in practice was quite different from the present day, and our thinking has advanced thanks to the experiences of the Cultural

Revolution." After which, they showed me how this new "spiritual force" took effect in greater productive experimentation, in "material force," which enabled them to achieve after the ordeal many things that had been impossible before.

These more factual expositions, backed by detailed examples, soon convinced me that China in 1971 was in a sense a vast laboratory of the road to socialism, in which many projects launched at the time of the Great Leap, and later suspended, were being renewed. In general, the country was visibly increasing the dynamism of its different development. Besides, one of the sectors that was vital to the future of society—education—had been overhauled from top to bottom, and Chinese universities now bear no resemblance to those of Western nations or of the Soviet bloc. In all this there was rich material for a thorough study of the general line that had been established during the Great Leap of 1958, and notably strengthened since that time by the "qualitative jump" in the consciousness of the Chinese people during the Cultural Revolution.

This being so, how did the rank and file see the battles that had enabled them to make this jump? No one concealed from me that the ordeal of the Cultural Revolution had been hard. During that time, in a sense, China looked at herself in the mirror, which suddenly reflected all the contrasts remaining in society despite the abolition of private ownership of the means of production. My hosts, more inclined to self-criticism than to boasting, told me freely how "broad democracy" had revealed to them the scale of bureaucratization, the persistence of old habits, abuses of authority echoed by obedience, the existence of new and subtle social distinctions. Thanks to this mobilization, reaching tens of millions of people, everyone had been able to recognize his own "dark side" and to learn at the same time how to set about defending his rights under the dictatorship of the proletariat. It was then made clear to me that this mutual criticism had often been violent and partisan and that, instead of merely attacking ideas and methods, it had at times taken the form of direct and physical attacks on individuals, which had led to injustices and unnecessary conflicts.

These accounts, although they were very similar and featured too many quotations from Chairman Mao, always struck me as exciting and even moving. In effect, they showed me the drama of a society marked by the heritage of a terrible past, yet confessing its inability to destroy it down to the roots. The Chinese masses, filled with egalitarian ideas through a decade of campaigns of socialist education, had wound up when the hour struck for "rebellion" by seeing every official as the usurper of a power that belonged by right to them; and, at the same time, it was clear that they had not been able to abolish all inequalities. So they had to choose, in the heat of the moment, between a great range of plans and of men. They had to distrust "false ideas," but also to beware of distrust itself, for this would have made it impossible to win back the "good" cadres and leaders and carried a risk of smashing the social mechanism before it could be replaced by a system that could work more or less smoothly. If passions and enmities arose in such a situation, it was no wonder. That these sometimes degenerated into blind violence seemed to be an established fact and, in a way, natural. This revolution was no tea party, either for the rank-and-file rebels or for those who sought to direct and guide it.

Paradoxically, all my discussions in factories and universities led me to the conclusion that—despite the advice I had received to study the events of 1966–9 at the grass-roots level—the Cultural Revolution could be understood only through an analysis of the interaction between the pressure from below—the mass movement—and the splits that it caused at the top, in the "proletarian headquarters," as it is officially called. It was no use asking a Shanghai worker, or even a senior provincial official, in 1971 why the original plan (announced in the "sixteen-point decision" of August 1966) for the creation of "permanent mass organizations designed to function for a long time" had not been carried through and had been modified several times. Only those who belonged to the proletarian headquarters or moved in its orbit were equipped, thanks to their overall view of the situation, to formulate policies designed to canalize a movement that was so hard to control. It was quite natural that they disagreed about the solutions, and there was no need to look for magical explanations and "plots" in order to understand that some urged a renewal of the struggle while others tried to find a safer way out. They alone could tell us on what foundations they based their analysis at this or that stage, and how they reacted when their plans led to unexpected consequences.

By the end of my journey I also understood why, after the Cultural Revolution, the men who had launched it found the utmost difficulty in remaining united and in finding a way to pursue the venture in another form, when the great mass movement was on the ebb. But, before we reach that stage, we must patiently reconstruct the course of ideas that gave birth to the Maoist scheme of continuous revolution, to the break with the Soviet model, to the great debate within the Party about the Party itself, then to the Cultural Revolution and its reverberations. For me, the history of the second Chinese revolution is far more estimable, and also more dramatic, than the official versions—formulated while the political struggle was still going on—that are offered to us today. Perhaps only a friend from the outside world, who is not forced to take sides in the internal conflict, can attempt a critical and impartial piecing together of these events. In any case, I believe that what I have said about my journey in China demonstrates the spirit and the equipment with which I have written this book.

CHAPTER ONE

Which Revolution?
Which Socialism?

The Soviet Lessons

In the full flood of the Cultural Revolution, in the fall of 1966, someone asked Mao during an enlarged work meeting whether the old slogan "Learn from the Soviet Union" had not been a poisonous plant nurtured for too long in China. The posters of the Red Guards that reproduced this question did not say who had asked it, but it is easy to see what he meant. Everything imported from the USSR was then suspected of revisionism, and many leaders were suddenly compelled to justify their old pro-Soviet speeches. Mao had decided to clear them all, flatly declaring that no one need be ashamed of having been trained in the Soviet school. He himself had learned everything he knew from the revolution of October 1917 and the Soviet struggle to "build a great and splendid socialist state." Future generations should take inspiration from the same example. "As the Soviet Union is dominated by revisionists, do we still have to learn from it? Yes . . . Far from ignoring them, we can regard them as our 'negative' teachers and draw lessons from them." [1]

A revealing answer, which is eloquent of Mao's feeling that he

[1] Jerome Ch'en, *Mao Papers: Anthology and Bibliography* (New York: Oxford University Press, 1970), p. 39.

and his revolution belong to the international movement founded by the Bolsheviks, because they led him to the theory of Marxism and gave him an international perspective of revolutionary struggle. Before the "rifle shots of October," he was only a rebel confined to the limited sphere of his humiliated country; after his adherence to Communism, he and his comrades ranked among the makers of the greatest revolution of our times, which has liberated one-fourth of mankind. Without the analytical equipment that he owed to the Bolsheviks, and without the worldwide solidarity shown by Communists during decades of common struggles, victory in China would have been impossible, and Mao has said so more than once. In 1966 he simply added that the past shared by Communists can never be wiped out, for they still feel its effects even after the breakup of their former solidarity. Each Party follows the fortunes of others and sees in them a warning for itself, glimpsing the dangers and contradictions that are taking shape on its own horizon. Since their fate is thus linked for better or worse, Mao refuses to renounce or even modify the allegiance of his Party to the great tradition of the Communist movement, or to regard the USSR as a power just like any other.

For their part, the Russians, despite the pragmatism and the retreat from ideology of recent years, still take pride in the part they once played in the Communist International and thus see themselves as fathers of its Chinese branch. Moscow publishes studies on the Russian advisers in China in the 1920's—notably Borodin and Blücher—and on the Soviet contribution to the founding and struggles of the CCP.[2] Stalin is the great missing figure in these works; his ghost merely haunts their closing pages, which laconically record the premature and highly unnatural deaths, in the late 1930's, of most of the Russians who played a part in the period. But the fact that they did not survive the great

[2] The most important of these works are: G. V. Efimov, *Problemy novoi i noveishei istorii Kitaya v Sovetskoi istoriografii, 1945–1946* (Vestnik Leningradskovo Universiteta, Vol. XXI, No. 2, 1967); A. I. Cherepanov, *Zapiski voennovo sovetnika v Kitae* (Moscow: Izdatel' stvo Nauka, 1964); R. A. Mirovitskaya, *Pervoe desyatletie* and *Leninskaya politika SSSR v otnoshenii Kitaya* (Moscow: Izdatel' stvo Nauka, 1968); A. F. Osetrov, *Sovetskii narod-revolyutsionnomu Kitayu* (Moscow: Izdatel'stvo Nauka, 1967); and also V. Duchenkin, *Ot soldata do marchala* (Moscow, 1966) (a biography of Marshal Blücher).

purges clearly does not affect either their virtues or those of the "collective leadership" of the Communist Party of the Soviet Union and the Comintern, which—according to this myth—went on functioning in spite of everything and spared no efforts to help the Chinese comrades. Since Mao too, in his writings, recognizes the part played by the USSR and "all the revolutionary forces on a world scale" in the consolidation of his revolution, the Russian version is echoed by the Chinese themselves. Thus the Soviet reader has grounds for believing in the monstrous ingratitude of the Maoists when, instead of seeking happiness in the great socialist family, they embarked in the late 1950's on a disastrous path to bring misery on themselves and injure their benefactors.

Most historians are puzzled both by the complacency of the Russians and by the astonishing moderation of the Chinese. Generally, after each split in the Communist world, the dissident Party blames Moscow for its misfortunes, including those caused by its own errors.[3] Had the Chinese wished to do so, they would have been obliged to invent nothing and could have drawn arguments from sources that are both varied and irrefutable. Some of the misfortunes they endured through Moscow's fault are a matter of public record, notably the dramatic events of the 1920's, which were watched by credible witnesses, led to big debates in the Comintern, and inspired many political and literary works, from Harold Isaacs's *The Tragedy of the Chinese Revolution* to André Malraux's *Man's Fate*.[4]

So there is no doubt that the Chinese Communists paid dearly for the blunders of the "general staff of the world revolution," which sat in Moscow and failed to grasp the revolutionary dynamic of their society. This harmed the Soviet Union too, for it

[3] For instance, the Communist parties of both Yugoslavia and Albania did not hesitate to throw open on a considerable scale the records of their relations with the USSR before they broke away, respectively, in 1948 and in 1961. Even the leaders of some Communist countries that have not broken away—the Poles in 1956 and the Cubans in 1967—have made revelations through private channels about their disputes with the Russians during periods when their relations with Moscow were tense.

[4] See also *La Question chinoise dans l'Internationale communiste* (Paris: Editions EDI); and, above all, Isaac Deutscher's biographies of Stalin and Trotsky.

stood in need of uprisings in the East to reduce its isolation and undermine the strength of Western capitalism. But all that it knew how to do was to suggest to the Chinese (or impose on them) strategies and alliances drawn from its own history. Thus the CCP was advised to help the nationalist bourgeoisie to carry out a "democratic revolution" (even merging itself into the Kuomintang) and to take as its own priority work among the urban proletariat, which, in a second phase, would carry out a socialist and truly working-class revolution. Its efforts were to be concentrated on the big cities, those working-class islands in a society still more backward than Czarist Russia. The outcome of this policy is well known and appalling: in April 1927 Chiang Kai-shek, the official ally of the CCP and honorary member of the leadership of the Comintern, massacred tens of thousands of Communists in Shanghai. In December of that year a similar massacre in Canton put an end to the short-lived attempt to set up a revolutionary commune in this other stronghold of the Chinese working-class movement.

After this catastrophe, Chinese Communism made a fresh start in the remote villages of Chingkangshan and other outlying regions, basing itself this time on the strategy of Mao: an alliance between the proletarian vanguard and the vast masses of bitterly exploited peasants, the creation of permanent support bases, and the formation of a Red Army for a prolonged revolutionary war in the countryside. Mao's plan was not evolved merely from a recognition of the defeat in the cities; in working it out, he had made a detailed analysis of the uniqueness of the Chinese situation and the political and social characteristics of this huge country, virtually devoid of central administration and plagued by the *Jacqueries* of wretched peasants.[5] These peasants, whose numbers were greater than the whole population of Europe, were starved of land and crammed into a cultivable area representing barely 10 percent of the nation's territory. It was in this bottomless reservoir, according to Mao, that the Communists should recruit and politically educate their troops, rather than giving battle in cities dominated by imperialism and its allies.

[5] See Mao Tse-tung, "Class Analysis of Chinese Society" (March 1926) and "Report on an Investigation of the Peasant Movement in Hunan Province" (March 1927), *Selected Works*, Vol. I.

But this line aroused no enthusiasm among leaders trained in Moscow and appointed by the Comintern to guide the CCP. It was regarded as contrary to the Leninist tradition and loaded with dangers. Was there not a risk that the proletarian vanguard and its army would lose their class characteristics and their Marxist purpose, through living for decades among the peasantry and imbibing its individualist and superstitious outlook? True, the underground leaders in Shanghai and their Comintern advisers accepted the victories achieved by Mao. But, in order to check his alleged adventurist and peasant tendencies, they kept pressing him to make attacks on towns that were more or less within reach of his army, and regularly condemned him to defeat in hopeless battles. Far from being hailed as the savior of the CCP or "the best Chinese pupil of Stalin," Mao was so distrusted by his superiors that in 1934 he was living under supervision in the Red Republic of Kiangsi that he himself had founded three years before.[6] His mentors had to suffer another setback before he finally got into the clear, became the undisputed leader of his Party, and succeeded in having his revolutionary strategy adopted for good.

We know little about these episodes in the early 1930's because they took place in outlying regions and attracted little publicity. But such knowledge as we possess, including official history, gives a definite picture of the difficult relationship between emergent Maoism and the international Communist movement and shows how long the position of Maoism within that community remained precarious. The agreement that was ultimately reached between Mao's Party and Stalin's Comintern had neither parallel nor precedent in the Communist world. To a great extent, it was determined by the actual situation; these forces were fighting on such totally different fronts that they could work only on their own, giving moral support to each other rather than coordinating their actions. In a sense, the relationship was already that of two allied states of unequal strength, which explains why the Chinese

[6] See John E. Rue, *Mao Tse-tung in Opposition, 1927–1935* (Stanford, Calif.: Stanford University Press, 1966). I myself am not wholly convinced by the account given in this book (also dubious for other reasons) that describes Mao as under arrest in 1934, a few months before the Long March. But it has since been followed frequently in other studies.

occupied a junior position while also enjoying greater independence from Moscow than other Communist Parties.

Historians are convinced that, despite Stalin's tolerance—tinged with mistrust of the CCP—Mao stored up many legitimate grievances against him. The echoes of some of these arguments resounded for a long time in foreign ears. We also know that Stalin confessed, with a humility that he seldom showed, that he had given the Chinese bad advice in the last phase of their civil war and that they had not followed it.[7] During the Cultural Revolution we heard the version of this episode given by Mao at a private meeting in 1962, and it was clear that he had not minced his words. Here and there in official Peking documents, as we shall see, bitter notes are struck. In 1965 Chou En-lai talked to me about the futility of the Comintern and the way in which the Russians had used foreign Parties to serve their selfish purposes, making it clear that he could, someday, reveal a great deal on this subject.[8] As a survivor of the Shanghai massacre, Chou had been involved with the history of the Comintern long before Mao and much more deeply than Mao. But it was precisely Mao who did not wish to bring the past into the argument with the USSR on present-day issues. He insists on castigating only the CCP leaders who followed the bad advice from the Russians and the Comintern, not those who gave it.

Why this generous attitude, which gives us no help in disentangling the threads of the past? As things now stand in Russia, it is of no benefit to whitewash Stalin, who is no longer

---

[7] Yugoslav evidence is given by V. Dedijer in *Tito Speaks* (New York: Arno, 1972 [reprint of 1953 ed.]) and also in other writings by the same author and other Yugoslav leaders.

[8] As an aside in the interview he gave me in 1965, Chou expressed his skepticism about the value of the Comintern by recalling: "To begin with, there was the First International, which we all honor as the pioneer of the workers' movement, although it did not know how to bring about a revolution. Then there was the Second International, numerically stronger and apparently better organized. But during its term no revolution took place, and it was only after it broke up, during World War I, that the great October Revolution in Russia occurred. Later there was the Third International. There again, no sign of any revolution; but after its dissolution in 1943 a whole series of revolutions followed, among them the Chinese revolution, and more recently still, that in Cuba." (See my earlier book, *China: The Other Communism*, p. 63.)

denounced by anyone but is omitted from history. The Maoists might have followed the example of Soviet historians and made a retort to them on their own ground, by ignoring the fallen leader and listing the misfortunes that the CCP incurred thanks to the allegedly collective and farsighted leadership of the Communist Party of the Soviet Union (CPSU) and the Comintern. After all, since the Chinese Communists have been accused of ingratitude, they might well recall the martyrs of Shanghai, Canton, and various other disasters brought about by those Comintern envoys on whom praise is heaped in their native country. That would have been both a legitimate polemical argument and a useful contribution to historical truth.

But Mao refuses to do it for reasons which are not purely tactical, and which can be ascribed rather to his conception, as a teacher, of the past links with the USSR and of the history of Communism in general. He seeks to bring out the positive elements of the past, in order to explain to the Chinese that this phase of their history ushered in a new age for them and was both necessary and indispensable. Year One for a strong and self-respecting China is 1917; and, according to Mao, a Chinese who had fought from that date for the liberation of his country could succeed only to the degree that he mastered Marxist theory and was conscious of solidarity with his comrades all over the world fighting on the same side of the barricades. The nationalist tone that is cheerfully ascribed to the Maoists is completely absent from this interpretation. Far from seeking possible ancestors of Chinese Communism among various utopian rebels, Mao repeats in all his writings that the Chinese people could never have made a revolution without the theory that they owe to Marx, Engels, and Lenin.[9] Indeed, "Maoism" is a forbidden word in Peking, because of the risk of implying that it is a specifically Chinese "ism," whereas in reality the "thought of Mao" is only a contribution to a universal doctrine and an adaptation of it to Chinese conditions.

Is it justifiable, however, to pass over the crises endured by the

[9] The great German Sinologist Joachim Schickel maintains in his book *Groose Mauer, Grosse Methode, Annäherungen an China* (Ernst Klett Verlag, 1968) that there were many utopian socialists in nineteenth-century China whose works had a considerable influence on the evolution of Mao and his comrades.

Chinese Communists vis-à-vis the rest of the Comintern? Some analysts of Mao's thinking declare ironically that, having for so many years defended his strategy as in line with orthodox Marxism-Leninism, he finally convinced himself of the total identity of his line and Stalin's. But the facts in no way bear out this barely serious theory; Mao's record is one of continuous disobedience rather than submission to Moscow. If he went on claiming to be a pupil of the Soviet school, it was above all to highlight the independent use that he had made of the knowledge he had acquired. On that point there could never be any doubt, even at the time when other Communists believed that only Stalin could tell them what strategy and tactics to use. In China, as far back as 1945, it was said, on the other hand, that Mao was the best authority on the theory needed by the Chinese revolution; and moreover (doubtless with his approval) that his contribution would be of service in all ex-colonial countries where similar conditions existed. If Mao and his comrades had no doubts on the matter at that time, when speaking this kind of language was somewhat risky, it is hardly likely that they have any now.

Thus the Chinese version of relations with the USSR before the onset of de-Stalinization pays no tribute to Stalin's infallibility or to the Soviets' ability to guide revolutions throughout the world. It is far more subtle and appears to tend, paradoxically, to illustrate Togliatti's theory of unity in diversity. For, according to the Maoists, the CCP has always "walked on its own legs" and framed its own policy, for which it took complete responsibility. It admitted no foreign interference and did not intervene in the affairs of other Parties; but, whenever the opportunity arose, it hit at the enemy in tune with them, in solidarity, without ulterior motives or selfish calculations. What preserved the cohesion of the international movement was the cement of ideology; all the Parties, steering by the same Marxist compass, helped one another by their discoveries and innovations in the struggle and thus gave lasting strength to their fundamental unity. We know that the CCP believes today in this nonstructured internationalism, so it is naturally attributed to the past to show how much it achieved in other periods.

The trouble with this retrospective and educational version of international Communist unity is that it jars with the outcome of which we are aware—the Sino-Soviet split and the violent enmity between the former partners. If unity between the two greatest Communist Parties of the world, rooted in solidarity and strengthened by theory, leads in the end to a split on this scale, what is to happen to weaker movements that "march separately and strike together"? The more you idealize the cooperation of the past, the less you can convince anyone that it is valid for the present and the future. Worse: by praising it so much, you find yourself unable to explain its failure in a concrete and glaring case such as the Sino-Soviet break. In point of fact neither Peking nor Moscow can explain this, and they take refuge in all-purpose answers to get out of the difficulty—"Khrushchev's betrayal" for the former, "Mao's sudden craziness" for the latter. But no evil careerists could have brought about the overnight cracking of the powerful ideological cement. The ship of solidarity was wrecked on hidden reefs—a triumph for the irony of history.

In reality, the Sino-Soviet question cannot be reduced to isolated elements, such as the degree of independence enjoyed by Mao's Party or the offense given by Soviet interference in its affairs. Many factors played a part, and primarily that of the internal development of the USSR, over which neither the Chinese nor other Parties had any influence. At first they were obliged to judge by appearances—it is thus that Mao believed himself to be marching in the same direction as Stalin while in fact taking an entirely different road—and then, face to face with results, they saw a brand of "socialism" that was peculiarly unattractive and nevertheless claimed to be a model. But this time their allies lost no time in raising an outcry about Chinese innovations, not because Khrushchev was less tolerant than Stalin, but because the content of the divergence had become too central, challenging a principle that was far more important than the tactics of fighting the common enemy.

Whether they are aware of it or not, this Sino-Soviet split has its roots in a long history: that of the Maoists, emerging from a different kind of revolution, and that of the Russians, with whom the Chinese were bound sooner or later to have a fundamental reckoning. My aim here is to reconstruct the framework within which Maoist ideas took shape before and during the big split. We shall thus be able to understand why the Chinese reacted quite

differently from other Communist states or parties to the crisis of
the 1950's in the Soviet bloc, and how they built up their own
model of development. This is the number-one problem, at the
root of all the others with which China is grappling today.

Mao and Stalin: The Distant Allies

On January 6, 1935, at Tsunyi in Kweichow Province, Mao
Tse-tung became Mao Chu-hsi—Chairman Mao—for the rest of
his days. An enlarged meeting of the Party Politburo, by giving
him this title, gave him the supreme Party authority, which he still
holds. The anniversary of this event is duly celebrated in China,
and during the Cultural Revolution Tsunyi was invaded by
crowds of young pilgrims, in the same way as Shaoshan (Mao's
native village) and Chingkangshan. Thus, for official historians, the
1935 meeting represents a decisive turning point in Mao's career
and in the destinies of the Chinese revolution. But, in conformity
with present-day attitudes, it is described as the private business
of the Chinese Communists, on which no outside influence could
or should have been exerted. In its independence, the CCP made
its choice to meet its own needs and is proud of that choice, for
subsequent events showed that it was right.

Foreign historians, however, are still hungry for facts on the
subject, if only because the records and the list of participants of
the Tsunyi meeting have never been published. They also wonder
what was the basis of the CCP's independence, since it had
subscribed at its foundation, like all other Communist Parties, to
the twenty-one conditions of the Comintern, and among other
things had recognized the latter's right to choose or replace its
leaders. In fact, search as one may in the annals of the world
Communist movement, one finds no precedent for the Tsunyi
meeting and no other Chairman Mao.

The election of Mao was "legalized" ten years later by a CCP
Congress, but the mystery about this business is how it could have
occurred and how it could have been immediately accepted by
Stalin's Comintern. Even today, despite the slackening of Communist discipline, it is not easy to become the leader of a major
Communist Party without Moscow's approval. In 1935, in the age
of constant vigilance, such matters were indeed no joke, and

Stalin put his trust only in leaders whom he knew personally and had himself chosen. Mao had never set foot in the USSR before becoming Chairman, and after 1935 he showed no impatience to do so. Stalin, therefore, had never met him, or read his writings. This, by the way, was mutual; according to Ch'en Po-ta, Mao did not begin to study the works of the Soviet leader until 1937.[10] We can only conclude that the Chinese Communists declared their independence unilaterally on January 6, 1935, and that, for this reason, their history came to diverge from that of all other Parties belonging to the Third International.

In reality, it had already begun to diverge in 1927, when the survivors of the political and military disasters of the earlier period joined Mao and enlisted in his long war of liberation. From then on, Communist cadres were trained by his side in armed battles and in the entire life of "special Chinese conditions," while leaders trained at the University of Toilers of the East in Moscow no longer contributed anything more than a top coating, applied artificially to this increasingly robust and flourishing body. Historians have adopted the habit of calling Mao and his team "the Kiangsi faction," which greatly annoys the Chinese—"Chairman Mao has never been the leader of a faction." Whatever the subtleties of nomenclature, the Chinese can make out a good case; the faction was composed of others, of the "twenty-eight Bolsheviks" trained in Moscow, headed by Wang Ming (Ch'en Shao-yü) and Po Ku (Ch'in Pang-hsien), or of the Shanghai and Peking underground leaders (who in any case gradually rallied to the Kiangsi Republic). Up to 1935, power was in the hands of the twenty-eight because of the structural oddity that allowed the Comintern to designate leaders according to its own standards, to apply a policy it laid down. In China this system was a resounding failure, for if there is one thing that absolutely cannot be guided by remote control, it is a revolutionary war. Besides, theoretical training in a Moscow university can never suffice to make a good guerrilla leader.

The Tsunyi meeting drew the lessons of these experiences. It

[10] See Ch'en Po-ta, *Stalin and the Chinese Revolution* (Peking: Foreign Languages Publishing House, 1950). This essay, in honor of Stalin's seventieth birthday, also appeared in the USSR in *Bolshevik* (No. 17, September 1950), but without the passage explaining Mao's delay in studying Stalin's works.

was held at the beginning of the Long March, between two
battles, when the Red Republic of the Southeast was changing
itself into a sort of wandering republic, on the move through the
provinces of China. Then more than ever it needed a leader who
could inspire confidence and a united and capable commanding
team. Respect for formalities and concern for ruffled feelings
abroad no longer counted, in crucial conditions endangering the
very survival of the Party and its army. Mao had gained the
support both of those who led his troops, the Communist fighters
who had lived with him since Chingkangshan—Chu Teh and Lin
Piao among others—and of most of the leaders who had been his
superiors in the hierarchy, such as Chou En-lai, but who had given
him their enduring support (as the future showed).[11] So to the
question "Why did the USSR accept this unilateral change in the
Chinese Communist leadership?" the answer is simple and
obvious: there were no other worthwhile Communists in China.

True, the Comintern could have disavowed them and urged a
handful of loyalists to start from scratch and rebuild a truly
proletarian Party in the big cities dominated by Chiang Kai-shek
(with whom the USSR had just established a new modus vivendi).
But this solution was neither realistic nor necessary. This violation
of the rules in China did not threaten to create a precedent,
because no other Party was in a position to copy it. Besides, the
Maoists did not take pride in their disobedience; they declared, on
the contrary, that they were the most faithful comrades and
admirers of the USSR. So the best course was to clap the telescope
to the blind eye, to come to terms, and to keep a willing and
apparently effective ally in this huge and amorphous subcontinent
of China.

As for Stalin, he tried to avoid getting too much involved, and
this was not simply from reluctance to hurt Chiang Kai-shek's
feelings; sizing up Mao's revolutionary war, he did not scent

[11] In an interview that he gave me for *Il Manifesto* (Rome, No. 1, June 1963)
Edgar Snow said: "Chou has a rather special history. In 1934–5 he was in fact the
top man in the Party and the army, and the election of Mao was in a sense a defeat
for him. But Mao brought it off, and Chou, seeing that Mao had the support of all
the essential revolutionary organizations, no longer defied him and did not claim to
assert himself in an independent way in the sphere of ideology, where the
Chairman is the master."

heresy so acutely as did his enemy Trotsky,[12] but he did nevertheless smell it. In terms of theory, the Maoist strategy could not be reconciled with Lenin's teachings and was particularly suspect in Russia, where it was easily identified with the old ambitions of the populists (*narodniki*) and the Socialist Revolutionaries whom Lenin had fought in his day. In practice, the position and status of the new Maoist republic could not be put into the right slot. In this period of the People's Front and of anti-war and anti-Fascist alliances, the Chinese Communists alone carried rifles on their shoulders. They had a firmly defended territory, which no one could enter without permission, they made their own propaganda, they invited journalists like Edgar Snow at their own discretion, they told their story of the amazing epic of the Long March; and legends surrounded their leaders—Mao, Chu Teh, P'eng Teh-huai, and others.[13] True, they did not claim to have a sovereign socialist state, but nevertheless they were the legal and established rulers of a region of China, like the Italian Communists in Emilia today. In short, despite their great admiration for the USSR, they inevitably posed many problems for the Kremlin, which prudently held aloof to a certain extent.

The Soviet presence in Mao's Yenan Republic, between 1937 and 1947, was therefore barely perceptible and purely symbolic.

[12] On Trotsky's skepticism, indeed hostility, toward Mao's revolutionary war, see Isaac Deutscher, "Maoism—Its Origins, Background and Outlook," *Socialist Register* (London: Merlin Press, 1964), reprinted in *Ironies of History* (New York: Oxford University Press, 1966), pp. 106ff. "Trotsky bluntly ruled out the possibility of the consummation of the Chinese revolution without a previous revival of the revolutionary movement among the urban workers. He feared that Maoism, despite its Communist origin, *might* become so completely assimilated with the peasantry as to become nothing but its mouthpiece, that is the champion of the small rural proprietors. If this were to happen, Trotsky went on, Mao's Partisans, on entering the cities, might clash in hostility with the urban proletariat and become a factor of counter-revolution." This, Deutscher says, explains the anti-Maoism of dogmatic Trotskyites.

[13] Chu Teh was as legendary a figure as Mao, and his life story was given to the world by Agnes Smedley in her famous book *Battle Hymn of China* (New York: Knopf, 1943). Both she and Edgar Snow, in his *Red Star over China*, devoted long chapters to the life of P'eng Teh-huai, which was rich in drama. As a child, he had almost been condemned to death by a family court for having offended his grandmother. Miraculously saved by an uncle, he went to make a brilliant career; and, according to Agnes Smedley, he was the real brains of the Chinese Red Army.

No important guest from the USSR was ever welcomed there; no military advisers were sent, even during the war against Japan. Moscow was a distant well-wisher, occasionally publishing eulo- gistic articles in the Comintern's house journals, or inviting a few leaders who had been wounded in battle to come to the USSR for treatment or convalescence (for instance, Lin Piao at the end of the 1930's). As for Mao, the envoys whom he sent to Moscow to represent his Party were leaders in disgrace whom he wanted out of his way, such as Li Li-san—not the best of advocates to plead his cause to the Comintern or to Stalin.

This strange relationship, warm in words and remote in deeds, had considerable practical consequences. The Chinese Commu- nists were "walking on their own legs" without Soviet crutches and had to rely on themselves to find new solutions to equally new problems. Their life style took shape during testing years while they had to build the Red Army, stir up guerrilla war behind the Japanese lines, organize a new type of administration in liberated or half-liberated districts, stimulate production to meet their needs, and spread their ideas by means of the "mass line." The cadres of the Long March were joined during this decade by thousands of young Chinese who, deserting the corrupt regime of Chiang Kai-shek—with its seat at Chungking—learned how to live in self-contained communities and fight in an army without ranks, the most egalitarian that the world had ever seen. Moreover, to put an end once and for all to old inbred ideas, Mao launched a "great rectification campaign" between 1942 and 1944, which pushed them into adopting collectivist values and, according to some accounts, can be compared with the future Cultural Revolution.[14]

All this happened quite openly, without the faintest criticism from the USSR. It was only a step to draw the deduction that Stalin approved, and the Yenan generation seems to have taken the step without hesitation. The Chinese Communists saw Russia as a super-Yenan, yet more heroic in that it was bearing, from

[14] A remarkable book on this period has recently been produced by Mark Selden, *The Yenan Way in Revolutionary China* (Cambridge, Mass.: Harvard University Press, 1972). Selden speaks for the new generation of American Sinologists and is among the founders of their association, the Committee of Concerned Asian Scholars.

1941, the heavy burden of the war against Fascism; it was inspired by the same principles, and these contributed to its victories. To be on the same side of the barricade as these brave fighters for socialism, to share their vision and their internationalist outlook, was a first-rate moral inspiration. This fully explains why the Chinese were so attached to—and are now so nostalgic about—their identification with the Soviet people. But there was more to it than that.

After the Grand Alliance was welded during World War II, Soviet protection provided the CCP with a trump of no little significance. The United States set up official contacts with it and sent a standing military mission to Yenan. Chiang Kai-shek was no longer in a position, as in the past, to renege on his agreements with Mao or launch a new campaign against the "Red bandits." The Communists had full status as allies, and even a special reputation for integrity and fighting spirit. This definitely eased their task and gave them elbowroom for action. The proof of this is obvious: at the end of the war with Japan, they were in practice governing 100 million people in the provinces of the north, the northeast, and the mid-south, not to mention their old stronghold around Yenan in the northwest. And, in bringing them to the end of the long period of battles and sacrifices, it was the USSR that had dealt the final blow to the Japanese invaders, which raised in Chinese eyes both its own prestige and that of its Chinese Communist comrades. So the Maoists had good reason to feel grateful to the Soviet Union; their complete independence went along with a real attachment.

Yalta

The Maoists seem to have escaped, because of their special relationship, the heart searchings that other foreign comrades went through during this period. For China, 1937 was the year of all-out war against Japan and not of the great purges in the Soviet Union. From then on, the struggle against Asia's greatest military power eclipsed other concerns, including those that might have arisen in 1939 from the unexpected signature of the Nazi-Soviet Pact. This point is worth noting; the Chinese seem to think today that Communist Parties in Europe could have taken up the same

attitude that they did—could have understood the political
necessities of the USSR and stuck unflinchingly to the anti-Nazi
struggle at home. This argument is all the more comprehensible
because, according to Mao (in a speech made at Yenan in 1943, at
the time when Stalin closed down the Comintern), the International had never intervened in the affairs of his Party since 1935
and had therefore never complained about the CCP's anti-Japanese line during the sensitive period of German-Soviet cooperation.[15] But would the Comintern have been equally tolerant if
Stalin had made a pact with Tojo's Japan in 1939?

Be this as it may, some clouds nevertheless gathered in the
Sino-Soviet sky during the "happy" period of the wartime
alliance. Trouble arose, very discreetly, when Stalin explained
Mao's aims to his new allies and intimates from the United States.
By his account, the Chinese Communists were not real Communists so much as agrarian reformers, hoping merely to modernize
their country by democratic methods. In point of fact, the USSR
was trying to reassure its British and American allies of the
moderation of its protégés, not only in China but all over the
world. These were the years of "Browderism" in the United States
and in Latin America, years when nationalism took priority over
class struggle in most of the Communist Parties and indeed in the
Soviet Union. It seems, however, that Mao was displeased by this
watered-down picture of his revolution—especially since he
learned of it indirectly, through the press of the United States or
of Chiang's China.

The situation began to deteriorate during the awkward year of
negotiations between the Communists and Chiang, after the
victory over Japan and before the outbreak of civil war at the end
of 1946. American mediators, who were extremely active, regu-

[15] This speech, made by Mao on May 26, 1943, is not included in his *Selected
Works*, but has been published in Stuart Gelder's *The Chinese Communists*
(London: Gollancz, 1946), p. 169. It should also be pointed out that, in several of
Mao's speeches in the years 1939–41, he discussed the probability of the entry of
Britain and the United States into the war against Japan. To prepare his comrades
for an alliance with these nations and stress its positive character, Mao explained
their relatively progressive ranking in the capitalist world. But at that time, in the
USSR and in many Communist Parties, the rule was—in obedience to the terms of
the Nazi-Soviet Pact—to avoid any such remarks, or indeed to make open attacks
on the nations that were fighting Fascism.

larly passed through Moscow before tackling the problems with the Chinese themselves, and they got from Stalin and Molotov increasingly definite assurances about Mao's good behavior. The White Paper published by the State Department in 1949 is revealing—and sometimes comical, for its authors were quite convinced that Stalin decided everything. But it is an established fact that the Russians were urging their Chinese comrades to behave nicely. Mao himself, in 1962, went so far as to say that "they tried to stop us from making the revolution in China." [16] But why should Stalin, the "leader of the world revolution," have been dubious about revolution in China, the very country where it had seemed to be within reach since the earliest years of the Third International?

The reason generally advanced is Stalin's respect for the Yalta agreements, but this theory is not very convincing. He never hesitated to interpret these vague agreements about the zones of influence of the Great Powers in the way that best suited him. First and foremost a cautious statesman, he did not move his pawns at random and he was reluctant to take responsibility for a

---

[16] These remarks were made in an unpublished speech by Mao at the tenth plenary session of the Eighth Party Congress, on September 24, 1962. Many extracts from this speech, including the call "Never forget the class struggle," were published almost at once, but the passage that follows was evidently considered so confidential that it was revealed only during the Cultural Revolution, and even then seems to have been bowdlerized. Mao devoted a whole section of his speech to Sino-Soviet relations, and the following sentences seem to be the conclusion:

> The roots for [the conflict] were laid earlier. The episode occurred a long time ago. They [the Russians] did not allow China to make revolution. This was in 1945 when Stalin tried to prevent the Chinese revolution by saying that there should not be any civil war and that we must collaborate with Chiang Kai-shek. At that time we did not carry this into effect and the revolution was victorious. After the victory, they again suspected that China would be like Yugoslavia and I would become a Tito.
>
> Later on, I went to Moscow to conclude the Chinese-Soviet Treaty of Alliance and Mutual Assistance (February 14, 1950) which also involved a struggle. He [Stalin] did not want to sign it, but finally agreed after two months of negotiations. When did Stalin begin to have confidence in us? It began in the winter of 1950, during the Resist-America Aid-Korea campaign. Stalin then believed that we were not Yugoslavia and not Titoist.

This extract, copied on Red Guard posters, was then published in various Western newspapers. See *The New York Times*, March 1, 1970.

break with his powerful former allies; but on the whole, when he could secure a gain without arousing a conflict, he went ahead and did so.

Neither reluctance to offend Chiang's American patrons nor fear of having on his flank a revolutionary China that could be too independent was the motive for Stalin's caution. The fact is that in 1946, just as in 1927 and 1935, he did not believe in the soundness or the prospects of Mao's strategy. To his mind, the Communists should have returned to the cities, discontinued their armed peregrinations in remote regions, and made use of the partial democracy of postwar years to strike roots in the working class and prepare for a future—and distant—battle for socialism. This advice was unlikely to find favor with the Maoist leaders, even though they also were averse to taking the initiative in starting civil war. Mao went to Chungking in September 1945, accompanied by the United States ambassador and mediator, Patrick Hurley, and signed a "discussion protocol," if not an agreement, with Chiang. On his return, he explained to his overimpatient comrades that negotiation often provides an opportunity to maneuver with the enemy and to gain ground.[17] But never for a moment had he considered dissolving his army in return for Kuomintang promises about democracy and legality.[18] He had not changed a scrap of his method of advancing to power from the countryside. After years of sacrifice and political indoctrination during World War II, peasant revolt was bursting out all over China in a far more explosive way than in 1927; and this time it was not without allies in the cities, among those who had lost all their illusions about Chiang's progressive tendencies. Above all, the Red Army was abundantly tested in battle and enormously stronger than in the Chingkangshan days. To sum up,

[17] See Mao Tse-tung, "On the Chungking Negotiations" (October 17, 1945), *Selected Works*, Vol. IV. This article was often republished and used as a text in China in 1971-2, when negotiations with the United States were restarted and when the virtues of negotiation had once more to be demonstrated to skeptical comrades.

[18] In their attacks in 1963 on Thorez's French Communist Party and Togliatti's Italian Communist Party, the Chinese reproached these Parties for failing to act as the Chinese had themselves acted at the end of the war and for making the French and Italian Resistance units give up their weapons. See "The Differences Between Comrade Togliatti and Us," *Peking Review*, No. 1 (January 4, 1963).

the political situation bore out the correctness of the strategy that Mao had followed for two decades, and it showed the absurdity of giving it up to return to the old line of the Comintern that was so inappropriate in China.

What had changed since the 1920's was the nonmandatory nature of Soviet advice. When they disobeyed Stalin in 1946, the Maoists convinced themselves by hindsight that things had been the same in the past, when in reality the CCP had been directed by Comintern emissaries. Actually, Stalin had in the old days been the manipulator of the attempted revolution in China and the man responsible for it, whereas after the war he was merely seeking to wash his hands of a plan in which he had no confidence and which he could not control. That was a big difference—but it was not the only one.

Over the years the Soviet Union had become a great military power, enjoying tremendous prestige from its victory in World War II, and its mere presence on the Asian scene was a help to the Maoists even if it supplied them with no weapons. Chiang, convinced that the Russians were doing as much for Mao as the Americans were doing for him, made it his foremost aim to cut the lines of communication between the USSR and the Communist regions. This led him to commit his best troops, all from the south, to semi-Arctic Manchuria, where they were doomed to total defeat. His American advisers warned him against this colossal strategic blunder, but in vain, for it arose from a political obsession, from his notion of a monolithic Communist world committed to mutual aid in all circumstances. The irony of fate ensured that, through the Manchurian collapse, he gave Mao's Red Army far more modern weapons than the USSR had ever been willing (or able) to supply. In January 1949 Mao entered Peking in an American-made jeep, followed by a long column of tanks of the same origin.

In his speeches of gratitude to the USSR, Mao stressed that he would have been unable to consolidate his victory without having the great and powerful Socialist bloc behind him. He thus appears to have been convinced that the United States would have intervened more directly in the Chinese civil war but for fear of Soviet reprisals, particularly in Europe, where the Russians were in a stronger military position and could count everywhere on the help of Communist Parties. The Americans, however, were scarcely likely to plunge into a large-scale land war in Asia two years after the battles of the Pacific, unless through a miscalculation (which we saw in Korea).

In December 1949, two months after the founding of the People's Republic, Mao went to Moscow for the first time in his life. The remarkable length of his stay—nine weeks—was enough to show that he and Stalin had a great deal to say to each other. But despite the eventual outcome, a treaty of friendship and mutual aid, we have no grounds for believing that they really understood each other. Indeed, the concrete pledges made by the USSR were curiously modest; the $300 million credit granted to China was a drop in the ocean of her needs. Beyond that, there were only vague words. Stalin did not even seem inclined to restore the Chinese territory (Dairen and Port Arthur) that he had provisionally annexed.

Fifteen months before greeting Mao, Stalin had excommunicated Tito's Yugoslavia and shown that he preferred a Socialist bloc that was smaller but well disciplined and committed to lining up undeviatingly with the USSR. Would Mao's China adjust itself to the requirements of its best ally? Experts who knew Mao and his comrades tended to answer in the negative and ascribed the first difficulties between Moscow and Peking—which appeared to be purely latent—to China's refusal to become a satellite. This earned them a very bad press, especially in Peking, where even a "friend of the Chinese people" like Edgar Snow was suddenly declared persona non grata. Today Chinese feelings are easier to understand; Stalin strongly suspected Titoite tendencies in the CCP, and the Chinese had to convince him of the contrary by severely rebuking independent friends who were involuntarily feeding his suspicions.

Mao himself confirmed this in his 1962 speech, when he described the bad advice given by Stalin on the eve of the civil war and revealed the latter's reluctance to sign the treaty of alliance and aid.[19] China had to undergo the test of Korea before becoming a revolutionary partner acceptable to the demanding Russian leader. That test was costly to the Chinese and was certainly not willingly undertaken.

[19] See note 16, this chapter.

The Korean Ordeal

If there is one thing we can be sure of about the Korean War, it is that China, condemned for causing it, had nothing to do with it. On June 25, 1950, the two Korean governments—the Communist one at Pyongyang and the anti-Communist one at Seoul—accused each other of armed aggression, each charging that the other's troops had advanced into its territory. Almost immediately the North Koreans were condemned by the U.N. Security Council, which, in view of their military successes, automatically deduced that they were responsible for starting hostilities. This conforms to the logic that "he who defends himself best must be the aggressor"; in any case, all the evidence shows that the North Koreans would have been condemned whatever happened, because they had fallen—this is the most likely theory—into the trap skillfully dug by the United States.[20]

The speed and scale of the American riposte proved from the outset that it was not entirely improvised. In a pathetic call to the "Free World," President Truman charged on June 27, 1950, that "the Communists have gone from the stage of subversion to that of armed world conquest" and asked for an intensive and worldwide reply. There was no longer any question of listening to the North Korean or Chinese version of events or of attempting mediation. The aggressors were to be punished by a combined United Nations force commanded by General Douglas MacArthur, the famous victor of the Pacific campaigns in World War II. On July 2, 1950, a week after the opening of hostilities, United States troops landed in Taiwan to protect the sole legitimate government of China—Chiang Kai-shek's. Moreover, the United States pledged itself to restore his authority in mainland China and swore, in the words of Secretary of State Dean Acheson, never to recognize Mao's government because it had been established by "force and violence" and was outlawed by the civilized and Christian world. The discriminatory measures taken by the United States against Mao's regime, through the Battle Act, were even stricter than those against Germany and Japan in

[20] See I. F. Stone, *The Hidden History of the Korean War* (New York: Monthly Review Press, 1952).

World War II; they involved penalties against any citizen who had acquired, anywhere in the world, products made in China. All this implies that United States aims in the Korean operation clearly went beyond Korea itself.

Why was Mao's China placed in the dock rather than Stalin's Russia, the other neighbor of Communist Korea? Would it not have been more logical to charge Moscow rather than Peking with plotting this "global aggression"? The People's Republic of Korea had been set up at the end of the world war with the help of the USSR, which still had a military mission there, while there had never been a Chinese presence in Pyongyang. But we need not meditate on the verdict obtained at the United Nations by the Americans in the absence of the Soviet delegate, who inexplicably chose to boycott the crucial Security Council meeting rather than use his veto. All the evidence points to an American assessment that the People's Republic of China—not yet a year old—might well fail to survive the ordeal of this war, while the USSR was too strong to be harmed by it.

The aims of South Korea's allies became yet more obvious in the fall of 1950, when the military situation changed decisively in their favor. General MacArthur then forgot that his instructions, in theory, were to repel the aggressor and declared that his aim was the complete liquidation of the Communist regime in Korea. Warned by the Chinese that they would send in volunteers if the American forces crossed the Yalu River, MacArthur imagined that he could see a heaven-sent opportunity to teach them a lesson and press his march of victory as far as Peking. If we can trust documents in the hands of the Chinese, he even had plans to invade the USSR from the Far East, but these were doubtless contingency plans rather than operational intentions. In fact, we know that the Pentagon never for a moment underestimated the strength of the Soviet Army and was wary of coming up against it in a ground battle. On the other hand, scant respect was paid to this barefoot Chinese army of peasant irregulars, who would surely never dare to cross swords with the famous United States Marines and their allies from the world's advanced nations.

The month of November 1950 saw the painful eye opener for the Americans. The Chinese "steamroller" wreaked havoc among the overfed and oversupplied American troops, despite protection from the sea and air. It was the end of a legend, and before long the end of the legendary General MacArthur, when he was refused permission to use atomic weapons against the "Chinese sanctuary." In July 1953, General Mark Clark signed an armistice in the name of the United Nations, an event on which he commented bitterly in his memoirs: ". . . I gained the unenviable distinction of being the first United States Army commander in history to sign an armistice without victory." [21]

But the young Chinese Republic had paid a heavy price for this victory. It was banished from the world stage for a long time, and its hopes of getting into contact with the opposing bloc and developing trade exchanges vanished. Stalin no longer needed to worry about the Titoite tendencies of the Chinese, knowing that they were too dependent on the USSR and could turn to no other country. Thanks to the Korean War, he was also able to slam down the Iron Curtain on Eastern Europe and consolidate, by his own methods, those people's democracies which still appeared too unstable and too open to foreign influences. Even if he had not fomented this war, he had gained something from it, and the same could not be said for China. It was also a legitimate question why the Soviet Union had done nothing to dissuade MacArthur from the Yalu offensive and had never thought of sending its own volunteers into Korea.

The Chinese did not reopen these issues during their polemics against Russia, but in a letter to the CPSU of February 29, 1964, this significant passage occurs:

> It must be stressed that China used the credits granted by the USSR in 1950 to buy war material, most of which was used in the war to resist American aggression and aid Korea. The Korean people carried the heaviest burden and suffered the greatest losses in this war. The Chinese people also made great sacrifices and bore considerable military expenses. The CCP has always considered this an internationalist duty for the Chinese people and nothing to boast about. We repaid the Soviet credits with interest, in the form of commodities which made up a considerable part of our annual exports to the Soviet

---

[21] General Clark's book, *From the Danube to the Yalu* (New York: Harper & Brothers, 1954), was on show in the Military Museum in Peking, as I described in *China: The Other Communism*, p. 335.

Union. Thus even the war material supplied to China during the struggle to resist American aggression and aid Korea was not a free gift.[22]

Slipped in among other attacks on the methods of Soviet aid in the Khrushchev period, these few sentences prove that Soviet behavior was no different in Stalin's time. The certainty is that, by making the Chinese carry the burden of the Korean War, Stalin made them the target of all the hatreds of the Cold War. Communist China, underequipped and suffering, just emerging from a twenty-year revolutionary war, had to face a foreign enemy, as in the past did the young Soviet Republic. But this time, instead of the fourteen nations that attacked Soviet Russia without much energy, China was at grips with the greatest military power in the world, supported by the United Nations.

Mao and the Crisis of 1956

The beginning of the post-Stalin era was marked by a certain ambiguity in Sino-Soviet relations, but on the whole was favorable for China. Soon after Stalin's death in March 1953, the armistice negotiations in Korea—which, contrary to Chinese wishes, had been dragging—were very quickly brought to a conclusion, and this was seen as a sign that the USSR had stopped creating obstacles. At about the same time, Russia agreed to joint industrial undertakings and at last returned Port Arthur and Dairen to China, in compliance with promises that Stalin had made with no apparent intention of implementing them. In addition, Stalin's death happened to coincide with the launching of China's first Five-Year Plan. The Russians expressed their willingness to aid its success by revising the existing agreements and advancing additional credits.

From 1953 onward, while Soviet equipment poured into China, confidential reports on the burdensome legacy of Stalin also quickly reached that country. In Moscow this was a period of

[22] See "Letter of the Central Committee of the C.P.C. of February 29, 1964, to the Central Committee of the C.P.S.U.," *Peking Review*, No. 19 (May 8, 1964). The text of this letter can be found in several books, notably Jean Baby, *La Grande Controverse sino-soviétique* (Paris: Grasset, 1966).

interregnum, and the new leaders were cautiously trying to link their prestigious Chinese ally with their struggles for the succession to Stalin. They visited Peking one after another, with a frequency and enthusiasm never known before. In 1954, Khrushchev and Bulganin were the first to make the pilgrimage, in order to warn Mao against their chief rival, Malenkov, and his inclination to unprincipled concessions. Later, Molotov went to Peking to charge Khrushchev with the same ghastly crime. The Chinese had an inside view of the arguments within the Kremlin, which were to culminate in 1956 in the Twentieth Congress and, a year later, in the complete victory of Khrushchev, who in June 1957 wiped out the "anti-Party group" of Molotov, Malenkov, Kaganovich, and Shepilov.

The Soviet Union had in fact opened a ledger that was all the more disturbing because, since the death of Lenin, the leaders of the Communist Parties—and especially the rank and file—had never been encouraged to take a critical, discriminating, and detached view of their own history, the history of the International, and the process of socialist construction. Hitherto, everything had been presented as a series of glorious triumphs proceeding inevitably from correct decisions. All difficulties had been ascribed to outside enemies and their agents. With the Twentieth Congress, the picture changed. The comrades suddenly saw that not a genius but an evil old man was at the head of the USSR in the years following the October Revolution and the death of Lenin. Mistakes had been committed, and crimes too. Questions germinated. To what extent had these mistakes and crimes blemished the entire achievement? What guarantees could be obtained to prevent the recurrence of similar deviations?

At this time the eyes of the whole Communist movement turned to China, embodiment of the second great socialist revolution. What position would it take on the Twentieth Congress? Would it approve Khrushchev's new policy, or would it support the comrades who had been shocked by the denunciation of Stalin's crimes, seeing the matter as an injustice and, moreover, as a threat to the Communist heritage? Above all, what would be its attitude to the changes at the top level of the CPSU?

So it was not only the Russians who traveled to Peking. After Khrushchev's thunderbolt at the Twentieth Congress, Communist delegations from Eastern Europe often knocked at Mao's door to tell him of their past troubles and present difficulties. The Poles, who had witnessed a bloody strike at Poznan in June 1956, were the first to seek the backing of their Chinese comrades.

What did Mao say about this? According to the Polish leaders who met him, he was very annoyed by Khrushchev's method of presenting the fraternal Parties with a fait accompli in the shape of his "secret speech." This was an abuse of power, for he had no right to take a personal initiative in a problem of such importance to the whole Communist movement. Besides, Mao found the content of the speech inadequate, lacking in any serious analysis, and therefore likely to do harm to Communists everywhere. Khrushchev's scandalous conduct had shown his arrogance and his ambition; and Mao encouraged the Poles to resist with determination all interference by the CPSU in the affairs of their Party. He seems even to have given them a written promise to take their part against the USSR if the latter tried to exercise political and military pressure on Poland. Gomulka is said to have produced this letter from Mao during the dramatic talks with Khrushchev in October 1956.[23]

The prestige of the CCP was thus at its zenith; all Communist Parties, or nearly all, seemed to share Mao's feelings about the secret speech. Even the loyal French Communist Party declared that "the explanations given so far about the errors of Stalin, their causes, and the conditions in which they occurred are unsatisfactory"—though from a defensive reflex in relation to its own rank and file rather than a concern for historical truth. Thorez therefore preferred to allude to a "so-called secret speech" and criticize only the vague references made in the public report.[24] In Italy, Palmiro Togliatti took a more forceful line in his interview with the journal *Nuovi Argumenti*;[25] rather than seeking to soften the impact, he aimed to bring out the full lessons in terms of

[23] See K. S. Karol, *Visa for Poland* (London: MacGibbon and Kee, 1959).

[24] It should be noted in this connection that the secret speech has never been published in any Communist paper. Its official text appeared in *The New York Times*, June 4, 1956.

[25] In the issue of June 13, 1956, Togliatti answered questions in this journal, edited by Alberto Moravia. The text has often been reproduced in the Italian Communist press, notably in *Rinascita*, No. 35 (September 6, 1968).

political significance ("a different and national road to socialism") arising from the revelation of Stalin's crimes and mistakes. At the Eighth Congress of the Italian Communist Party, Togliatti succeeded in his operation of "overhaul within continuity." Meanwhile, one of the most respected intellectuals of the Party, the classical scholar Concetto Marchesi, exclaimed from the platform: "Tiberius, one of the greatest and most maligned Roman Emperors, had an implacable accuser in the person of Tacitus, the Empire's best historian, while Stalin, less fortunate, has only Nikita Khrushchev."

In reality, it was of no great significance that the secret speech had not been fortified by an adequate Marxist analysis. What conclusion was to be drawn from this charge? That the denunciation of Stalin was baseless, or that it must be followed through by deeper explanations concerning the whole of Soviet society? And what was the Chinese view on this essential point?

Chinese public statements continued to be highly Delphic and often disappointing for foreign comrades. Mao did not altogether approve of the Twentieth Congress, but he did not condemn it either. He seemed to be worried by Soviet tendencies toward "Great Power chauvinism," but also by nationalist trends in the other countries of the Communist bloc. He gave a warm greeting to the solemn promise made by the USSR on October 30, 1956, to withdraw its troops from the people's democracies, but a few days later he endorsed the Soviet intervention against the rebels in Hungary. If we must rely on published documents, his two essays "On the Historical Experience of the Dictatorship of the Proletariat" [26] cast little light—particularly the second, which followed the Polish crisis and the Hungarian tragedy—and attempt merely a cautious balance between criticisms of Stalin and praise for his constructive work in the USSR. Especially, they reflect the anxiety, then general in the Communist movement, not to aggravate a crisis that was threatening to get out of control.

In September 1956 the CCP called its Eighth Congress at short notice. Delegations from many countries came to Peking and

[26] These appeared in the *People's Daily* on April 5 and December 29, 1956, "on the basis of discussions held during enlarged meetings of the Politburo of the Central Committee of the CCP," and were later published as a pamphlet by the Foreign Languages Publishing House (Peking, 1959).

listened to a restrained debate, in which—as in other Parties, but with better reason—the Chinese were primarily concerned to show themselves innocent of the "irregularities" that had marked the history of all Communist Parties during the period under review. They did admit that their congresses had not been held regularly—that is, every four years—as the rules provided, the last having been held at Yenan in 1945. Apart from that, Liu Shao-ch'i managed to prove very skillfully that the principle of collective leadership had always been respected in China, owing to the genius and personality of Mao, who had been its strongest upholder and had put the "mass line" into practice for many years. However, the reference in the rules to the commanding role of his thought was prudently dropped, in conformity with the wishes of Mao himself. Thus the CCP was aiming to blunt the sharp corners. Most of its congress was devoted to the Second Five-Year Plan, due to begin two years later—a good way of filling up the agenda without saying anything.

In November 1957 Mao made his second visit to Russia and took part in another meeting of the leaders of Communist Parties in Moscow. In theory, they were there to celebrate the fortieth anniversary of the October Revolution, but in reality this was the pretext for a major secret conference—the most important since the congresses of the Comintern. The surrounding atmosphere appeared happy, for the spectacular triumphs of Soviet sputniks had wiped out the demoralization of the year before.

Mao was received by the Communist family with exceptional honors, as *primus inter pares*. In public, he was showered with praise on every possible occasion; in private, the Russians signed an agreement with him on cooperation in nuclear science, with the aim of quickly making China an atomic power, which was obviously out of the question for other allies. As for Mao, he caused some astonishment, especially for the "little countries" such as Poland and Hungary, by proposing the inclusion in the final resolution of a paragraph on the leading role of the CPSU in the Communist movement. All the signs showed that the barometer of Sino-Soviet relations was set at fair.

The Russians now tell us that Mao's smiles concealed a deliberate wish to provoke his hosts and set himself constantly against their plans and hopes. By this account, he congratulated them on the success of the sputniks only in order to push them toward a war with the United States, hoping to pull chestnuts out of this holocaust of fire. The Chinese have since published Mao's speech at the Moscow conference, and it shows that he flatly ruled out the possibility that a socialist nation could start a war or be the first to use nuclear weapons. Nevertheless, according to the Russians, the doctrine that "the East wind triumphs over the West wind" means that the Eastern bloc should attack the Western. Besides, the charges of warmongering that the Soviet leaders have incessantly made against their Chinese comrades, first privately and then publicly, date from this time. Worse still: Mao is said to have wanted the two super-powers to destroy each other, while keeping his own country out of the battle. In reality, according to the Russians, he had already decided at this period to break with the USSR.

In Peking, the men who accompanied Mao on his journey speak with indignation today of the arrogance of the Russians, who shamelessly paraded their revisionism. Their heads had been turned by the sputniks; and, believing that they had at last become internationally respectable, they took pride in the praises sung by the sirens of imperialism to lure them onto the rocks of unprincipled coexistence. By the Chinese account, Mao confined himself to reminding the Russians of the promises of the October Revolution and their duty to stick to its principles in their internal and international policy. But he had few illusions on the effectiveness of this appeal, for he saw that the leading group in Moscow was hopelessly contaminated by bourgeois ideas and temptations. His visit convinced him that socialism in the USSR could not be reborn except in opposition to Khrushchev and his men.

At first glance, the confidential accounts from the Chinese bear out those from the Russians, to the extent that they confirm that Mao had no further hope of reaching an understanding with the leaders in the Kremlin. But can we deduce from these accounts— inevitably influenced by later events—that in 1957 the Chinese leader had no belief in the possibility of coming to terms with the USSR? All precedents indicate that, whenever he doubted the wisdom of the line put forward by the Russians, he nevertheless chose to temporize and look for practical solutions within his own

Party, hoping that his ideas would triumph in time because of his own successes and the disastrous results of the incorrect line. Such had been his tactics in the later 1920's and up to the victory of his revolution; and, as we have seen, this method had always enabled him to get, if not the eager agreement, at least the prudent solidarity of the Kremlin, and sometimes its retrospective congratulations.

Mao's conduct in the late 1950's seems to have been inspired by these principles and probably these calculations. He was well aware of the scale of the crisis in Eastern Europe, glaringly revealed in 1956. His first concern was what was to be done to avoid such things happening in China. As is not the case with all the Chinese propaganda that now finds nothing in the 1956 events but Khrushchev's personal guilt and seizure of power, Mao was seeking at the time to unearth their objective causes. In the two essays devoted to the interpretation of Soviet history mentioned above, this effort is only very faintly reflected. On the other hand, it is the main theme of two documents that are basic landmarks in Mao's thinking about his own society and, in general, about society in the course of change. In his famous essay "Contradictions Among the People," [27] Mao postulates a dialectical process that sometimes takes shattering forms during the development of postrevolutionary society. What kinds of contradiction emerge? How should one react to them? What are their mechanisms and causes? This essay, very well known in the West, was at first interpreted as a theoretical contribution to the Khrushchev line, as was the Hundred Flowers campaign launched at roughly the same time.[28]

As we shall see, they were nothing of the kind. Western Communists, after the Twentieth Congress had made them aware that the taking of political power in the USSR and the East European countries had not been enough to resolve all social problems and unify these societies—as Stalinist ideology had led them to believe—drew the conclusion that these contradictions

[27] The complete text of this speech and essay appears in Mao Tse-tung, "On the Correct Handling of Contradictions Among the People" (February 27, 1957), *Four Essays on Philosophy* (Peking: Foreign Languages Publishing House, 1966), pp. 79–133.

[28] On this campaign, see K. S. Karol, *China: The Other Communism.*

should be given formal political expression; the regime should be liberalized, natural laws of development should not be violated, revolutionary "voluntarism" should not be imposed on objective social mechanisms. Mao drew precisely the opposite conclusion: if society is disunited, one should not bow to this situation during a long period of material construction, but on the contrary accentuate the revolutionization of social relations that had brought about divisions in the past and continued to produce them. How could this be done? Was it enough to restore a political dialectic, or should a true class struggle be launched again? And, if so, what shape could it take on the level of material construction of socialism?

Two months after the Twentieth Congress, Mao explored this theoretical problem with a combination of outward caution and intellectual boldness, in a document that was revealed to the outside world only at the time of the Cultural Revolution—his speech "On the Ten Great Relationships." [29] This document, taken together with the evidence about the problems raised by Mao during his 1957 visit to the USSR, leaves no doubt regarding his convictions. In his eyes, the source of the trouble was in the model of development put into force in the USSR. The remedies proposed by Khrushchev and his followers were drawn from the logic of that model and accentuated those of its aspects which Mao found most questionable. Hence he considered them not merely useless but dangerous. Could the Chinese, however, merely wait and see, and hope that Soviet policy would change when it led to failure? Could they, with impunity, tackle their own development problems in a different spirit? Much later, in 1963, in a polemical letter to the CPSU, Mao disclosed that he had foreseen that Moscow would react badly to his innovations and had prepared for the worst. It was no longer a question of a tactical divergence but of the very definition of socialism made in Moscow or Peking. The big split had begun.

[29] The text of this speech, made by Mao in April 1956, was again distributed to all Party organizations in China in November 1965 and was then published in the paper of the Red Guards in the Economic College of Peking, December 22, 1966. In Europe it appeared in the Italian journal *Il Manifesto*, No. 5 (May 1970).

A Left-Wing Way Out of Stalinism

The growth rate of the Chinese economy was 14 percent a year during the First Five-Year Plan, worked out with Soviet assistance, and the industrial sector made the most remarkable progress. Indeed, for the first time in history, industrial production bulked larger than agriculture in the Chinese national income. If the country could keep up the same pace for fifteen or twenty years, China would fairly quickly become a major modern industrial power. Such was the aim of Sino-Soviet cooperation, and most of the long-term credits were earmarked for a continual increase in deliveries of Soviet industrial equipment. Thus it appears that Soviet experts have an easy task today; by extrapolating the figures of the First Five-Year Plan and multiplying them in geometrical progression for ensuing years, they can prove that in 1967 or at the latest 1972, at the end of the third or fourth plan, China—thanks to the USSR—should have had a strong and prosperous economy. Mao could have created a reign of plenty in his country simply by letting things take their course and keeping quiet, instead of quarreling with the USSR and endangering the projects established by Soviet planners for China.

Many economists in the West, captivated by the magic of statistics, have been convinced by this logic. Yet in Eastern Europe, where the policy of Five-Year Plans has been in force for a long time, a disillusioned proverb runs: "Statistics are like prostitutes—they cater to everyone's desires." In fact, all these countries have chalked up statistical triumphs as startling as those of China during her period of happy cooperation with the USSR. But, little by little, they all began to utter repeated complaints about the striking imbalances of their economies, about the blunders of their planners, about popular discontent, and about the moral and political crisis of society. One has only to read what the Poles said in 1956 about "economics on the moon," or the Czechoslovaks twelve years later about the dead end they had reached, to grasp the correctness of this proverb that warns us against overclever growth-rate figures.

So the real question is not why the Chinese refused to keep quiet, but why they were the first in the Socialist bloc to realize that they would benefit from taking another path. If it is true that, with Soviet help, China was able to get a system of centralized planning functioning very rapidly, and to create a fairly efficient statistical network employing about 200,000 people, it was, on the other hand, unable to plan according to its own wishes, or to buy factories of its own choice from the USSR.

Having developed in an unbalanced way, the Soviet Union could export only the surplus from sectors to which it had in the past given priority. It was useless to ask it for equipment for the chemical industry—for instance, for the manufacture of fertilizers—because this industry was nonexistent in the USSR and was only just beginning to develop (with misfortunes that are no secret) in the Khrushchev period. Moreover, even the priority branches of the Soviet economy bore traces of their special kind of growth, based on the fulfillment at any cost of quantitative production targets. The USSR had steel plants to sell secondhand, but of the 1946 model. Having been in great need of heavy machinery, the Russians had developed its production on a large scale, but it was suitable for export only to uncritical allies. By supplying them with such equipment, the Russians transferred their technological obsolescence to these countries. Into the bargain, the latter were compelled to pay at world market prices, as if they were getting completely modern products. Sooner or later, and privately or publicly, all Communist countries have complained of being exploited by the USSR. The Chinese behaved with discretion for a long time and counterattacked only in 1964, when they pointed out that they had never received any aid, but had paid to the last kopeck not only for the equipment but even for the advice of their Soviet comrades. By their account, they actually paid even the expenses of Soviet journalists in the Korean War.[30]

[30] *Pravda* of July 14, 1963, drew up a balance sheet of Soviet aid to China. The CPSU's newspaper stated: "The USSR has given China 198 industrial enterprises in the form of aid and contributed to the building of 88 other projects." The *People's Daily* replied on February 29, 1964: "China has received aid from the USSR, but the latter in turn has received corresponding aid from China. No one can claim that Chinese aid to the USSR has been insignificant or unworthy of mention. Here are some examples: by the end of 1962, China had supplied the USSR with cereals, vegetable oils, and other foodstuffs to a value of 2,100 million new rubles [about $2,310 million] . . . In the same period, we supplied to the

But here again, the main point is not to work out whether Sino-Soviet trade was more valuable to the USSR or to China. Some writers have quite truly reminded us that China had no access to other markets, whether to sell or to buy anything.[31] The Chinese were prepared to go on buying from the USSR, but the latter cut off supplies in 1960 for political reasons and then, when the situation had become irreversible, complained because they could no longer sell their industrial surplus goods to the ungrateful Chinese.

Soon after his triumphal entry into Peking, in a speech on the twenty-eighth anniversary of the CCP in June 1949, Mao modestly declared that his Party had learned only one thing—how to wage a revolutionary war.[32] For everything connected with "the heavy task of economic construction," he felt that he was unequipped and recalled, as a consolation, that the Bolsheviks in their day had been no better prepared and had learned as they went along. In reality, Mao's Party was not so devoid of experience as he said. It had managed more or less extensive Red territories for over twenty years and, thanks to this practical record, had settled on at least two permanent guidelines. First, having no real state machine, it must base its relationship with the masses on seeking a genuine consensus on as broad a scale as possible (through consulting the people, bringing the greatest possible numbers into decision making, welcoming individual and group initiative, maintaining contact between rulers and ruled). Second, the peasants, who made up the overwhelming majority of the population, must not be sacrificed. So, when they had to take over the administration of the whole country and not merely of villages, the Maoists tried to stick to these rules in reckoning their resources and deciding their investment priorities. On no account

USSR mining production and metals to a value of over 1,400 million new rubles. Among these products, many were raw materials indispensable to the development of the most advanced branches of science and to the manufacture of rockets and nuclear weapons."

[31] Several comparative studies have been published in the United States, notably O. Hoeffding, *Sino-Soviet Economic Relations* and *Communist China's Foreign Trade* (Santa Monica, California: Rand Corporation, 1971).

[32] See Mao Tse-tung, "On the People's Democratic Dictatorship" (June 30, 1949), *Selected Works*, Vol. IV.

could they envisage a development of which the peasants would pay the cost, nor could they allow social inequalities to widen during the long period of the effort of industrial production. In the CCP's decisions, transformations in the rural sector were always given priority over all others; it was only after land reform was successfully put through that the renovation of the industrial sector was taken in hand and the Five-Year Plan launched in 1953. Similarly, the formation of cooperatives in 1955 preceded the definitive socialization of private enterprise in industry and trade.[33]

Now, it is clear that these priorities conflicted with the logic of planning based on Soviet aid and led from the outset to serious disagreements. The record on this period has never been laid open because it is certainly full of internal arguments and hesitations. A system of management copied from the Soviet pattern was unacceptable on principle, but at the same time it could provide a temporary solution. After all, despite their exceptional history and their experience in the Red regions, the Chinese Communists had been through a twofold education; they had also grown up in the shadow of Stalin's Russia, accepting its mental yardsticks and being influenced by its orthodoxy. They were thus exposed to the temptations of all controllers and were not automatically shocked by what they heard from Soviet advisers about the need to rule by decree during a limited period and postpone the tackling of delicate social problems. Moreover, when they learned after 1953 of the disasters that had occurred in certain branches of the Soviet economy, some of them may have been tempted to delay, for instance, collectivization of land; and the conflict on this issue, in 1955, was particularly sharp.[34]

Nevertheless, the conviction grew that they must neither wait nor copy the USSR. Evidence of this was soon forthcoming and was to become overwhelming, for the CCP began to change its policy from 1956, as if already aware that it was on the wrong track. To be sure, they did not embark lightheartedly on the

[33] See Lisa Foa and Aldo Natoli, "On the Origins of the Cultural Revolution," in Il Manifesto (Paris: Éditions du Seuil, 1970).

[34] The Foreign Languages Publishing House, Peking, published in 1960 a collection of documents "On the Problem of Agricultural Cooperation," introduced by Mao himself and recording the discussions of this period.

search for new directions. The illusion that the USSR, during its struggle for industrialization, had blazed a path for all its allies was one that had cheered the Maoists before their ascent to power and was hard to abandon. To seek another development pattern meant setting themselves questions that were difficult to answer in the context of a backward country, scarcely freed from colonial domination, and hoping like any such country for social peace and a little more prosperity. Had the Soviet model been able to satisfy such hopes, the Chinese would surely have "kept quiet"—not in order to become a Great Power in twenty years' time, but to keep the binding promise that "the revolution will give everyone something more than before." But when experience had shown that to copy this model was to aggravate injustices and create a rift between proletarian state power and the masses, hesitation was no longer possible. The Russians themselves revealed in 1956 that, to make the peasants pay a "tribute" and to impose discipline on the new working class during industrialization, they had resorted to Draconian methods and set up labor camps, whose existence now ceased to be a mystery. In China, starting from an immeasurably lower level, what degree of terror would be needed to obtain comparable production successes? Had there not already been strikes and discontent in 1956, although, according to Mao, excesses had been avoided even when the Soviet model was being followed?

From all the accounts now given by the Chinese of their experiences with Soviet technicians (who were sometimes expert enough but never very Red) it is clear that it was not the Party leaders alone who recognized the need to take another path, and that this choice was not dictated by nationalist motives. The Chinese are certainly proud of having managed, after the Russians left in 1960, to ensure the functioning of plants of which they even lacked the blueprints, these having all been taken away by advisers recalled to the USSR. But they remember these years with bitterness and disappointment, not with the satisfaction of people who found a way to get by on their own. They also claim to have realized, well before it was obvious, that the Soviet economy was not working properly and that Khrushchev's high-flown promises—according to which "Soviet production per capita would overtake and surpass that of the United States by

1965"—were mere boasts designed to deceive the Soviet workers.

Indeed, we can well imagine Mao's reaction when he saw Khrushchev relying on the reclamation of huge virgin lands in Asia to increase his country's inadequate agricultural output. Mao, with his realism and his profound knowledge of the countryside, knew that schemes of this kind bore witness not to resourceful boldness but to fantasy and irresponsibility. A few years later, during the great controversy, Mao offered to send Chinese experts to the USSR to put a little order into its farming sector. In 1965, another high-ranking leader said to me in a joking mood that the Soviet virgin lands were like Khrushchev's head—unproductive. What would have become of China if, after twenty years of Five-Year Plans, it had found itself in such a situation in this vital sector? Even if there had been no other motive, this would have been quite enough to lead China to seek a different development model.

The "Ten Great Relationships"

The First Five-Year Plan was not yet completed (it was in its fourth year), and less than two months had elapsed since the Twentieth Congress, when Mao, in April 1956, gave his Party a report entitled "On the Ten Great Relationships." This document, unpublished at the time, is now known to us thanks to the Red Guards, who gave it wide circulation. At the time of the Cultural Revolution, whose aim was to give a fresh impetus to the Maoist line, it was revived as a major fount of truth.

In this report, Mao enters for the first time into the fundamental problem of balances and imbalances in Chinese society and elaborates his conclusive answer to the questions posed by the Twentieth Congress. His Ten Great Relationships—we could also call them the ten great contradictions that China had to deal with—are the following. The first are relationships, or contradictions, of structure—in other words, they affect investment priorities and aims:

1. between heavy industry, light industry, and agriculture;
2. between the industries of the coastal regions and those of the interior of China.

The next leads us into another category, although it is still a matter of investment priorities, between a productive and a nonproductive sector:

3.   between economic construction and national defense.

Then there are contradictions between social forces:

4.   between the state, production units, and producers;
5.   between central and local administration;
6.   between the Han (ethnically Chinese) people and national minorities;
7.   between the Party and non-Party people.

Then two great relations or contradictions between tendencies:

8.   between revolution and counterrevolution;
9.   between that which is right and that which is wrong.

Finally:

10.   between China and the rest of the world.

Mao's choice of classification enables us to understand the hallmark of his intellectual approach: problems of structure are firmly linked with problems of superstructure—political, historical, and indeed moral (such as the idea of revolution and the idea of right and wrong). This synthesis is required to develop his basic theme: the rejection of development through distinct phases (first material progress, then in other spheres) and through privileged sectors (first heavy industry, and the rest later) in favor of an advance of the whole country, which must progress harmoniously and at the same pace, through a gigantic effort of social, political, and productive unification. He therefore rejects any decisions that would carve new differentiations on a society already only too harshly marked by imbalances between various regions of the country, between various social groups, between the center and the outback, between the political and the social spheres—all inherited from centuries of exploitation and backwardness.

Mao recognizes clearly that this line is exceptional; he announces at the outset that his aim is to spare China the mistakes "made by other socialist countries." However, he launches no direct attack on the principles that guided socialist construction in these countries, first and foremost the sacrosanct assumptions about the priority of heavy industry. On the contrary, he adopts a remarkably devious attitude, declaring that these principles are indeed inviolable but that they should be applied quite differently if they are to be understood in the spirit and not merely in the letter. So he does not believe in absolute priority for heavy industry over agriculture or light industry, but makes his exposition in the guise of defending the traditional principle: "Do I mean that heavy industry should no longer play the guiding role? No, it must play this role. . . . Do I intend to replace it by another key sector? No, it remains the key sector." But only a great advance of agriculture and light industry will produce the rapid accumulation of funds needed to secure the progress of heavy industry. Here is the crux. "Do you or do you not want to develop heavy industry? Do you want it seriously or are you paying lip service to it? If you are paying lip service, you will sacrifice agriculture and light industry. If you want it halfheartedly, you will reduce investments in agriculture and light industry. But if you want it seriously, devotedly, you will rely on the development of agriculture and light industry, to get more consumer goods and a faster accumulation of funds."

Thus the classical principles of industrialization are intact, but Mao argues in the name of realism for a radically different investment policy that will give agriculture its "rightful place," pursue a "right" fiscal policy toward the countryside, and establish a "right" relationship between the prices of agricultural and industrial products. Without delving into theoretical discussions, he simply refuses to see the countryside reduced to the role of manpower reservoir and source of enforced accumulation for industrialization.

He uses the same logic to defend consumer industries and, later on, the industries of the coastal provinces: "Certainly we must build industry where it has not hitherto existed, but if you want to do it seriously and not to pay lip service, you will preserve the importance of established industry in the coastal provinces." According to him, socialist growth does not impose arbitrary decisions against the interests of allegedly less productive classes, but demands an effort in every sector, each according to its own dynamic. "To achieve all the goals of socialist construction in the broadest, speediest, and most economical manner, all forces must be mobilized." This slogan was soon to be heard again in China, at the time of the Great Leap Forward.

The sections of "On the Ten Great Relationships" devoted to economics have recently been interpreted in a surprising way. It has been said that they reveal an antimodernist orientation on Mao's part, a nostalgia for the Yenan days and an attachment to primitive aspects of the countryside. The interpretation is unjustified; Mao deplores, in every context, the backwardness of the Chinese countryside and explains that it would be both unjust in a humanitarian sense and inefficient to wish it to persist, for any reason. Other commentators find Mao showing a preference for development based on massive use of labor power rather than on investment in the most productive techniques. He is said to have opted for so-called labor-intensive rather than capital-intensive methods. In point of fact, already in 1956 Mao is showing his deep mistrust of this style of development (though not yet calling it the capitalist road), because it does not represent the best method of increasing productive forces, particularly in a socialist country. As he sees it, China should make use of industrial machine methods and master technology, but control them and make them serve its needs, both material and political.

For this reason, after discussing contradictions in the economy, he goes on to the problems of political society. Here too he urges a considerable overhaul, in both a quantitative and a qualitative sense. Nonproductive expenses provide the bridge from one theme to the other. Does China need to arm herself? Certainly, Mao answers, because she has many enemies. Does she also need nuclear weapons? Perhaps, he says with rather more skepticism, although "in the past we did not even have aircraft or heavy artillery, and yet we beat Chiang Kai-shek when we were eating millet and fighting with rifles." But, he continues, "if you seriously want a nuclear arsenal, you must reduce military and administrative spending and strengthen economic construction." He finds it "intolerable" that the expenses of the army and the state make up 32 percent of the national budget, and demands a rapid and drastic reduction. Then he goes on to his own sphere, that of the Party, and starkly declares that the CCP apparatus should be reduced by *two-thirds* of its existing staff.

So his hostility to "unproductive spending" cuts deep, but his arguments show that the reduction of waste is not his only aim. He does not want the state, the army, and the Party to become "distinct bodies," overgrown institutions battening on the country and choking the initiative of the masses. Ten years before the Cultural Revolution, he is already pointing out that the problem of institutional "forms and methods" is inseparable from that of the material development of the country. One cannot demand further efforts from the masses, says Mao, unless they are given more power and allowed to express themselves. China needs to be unified; but, to achieve this, those who hold central power must redistribute it throughout society.

Next, coming to problems of "revolution and counterrevolution" and of "that which is right and that which is wrong," he argues in favor of discussion and tolerance, of persuasion, of the dialectic of flexible relationships in which nothing is permanently gained or irreparably lost. "It is important to distinguish between those who are wrong and those who are right, but those who are wrong today may redeem themselves tomorrow. Are not people who have had typhus the best immunized against that disease?" Everything should be done by a communal effort, based on free consent and designed to awaken the creative energies of the whole of society. The so-called advanced sectors should not grow fat at the expense of those who are more backward, but should draw on their own resources and help others to rise to their level. The political vanguard justifies its existence by moving among the masses, living in the same way, and giving up its privileges, whatever they may be.

"Politics in Command"

This is, then, Mao's first sketch of a method of development contrasting with those of his allies—dating from his "Ten Great Relationships" speech of April 1956. But this report was not made public, and thus its importance was not grasped in the West at that time. Moreover, attention was focused on tragic events in Europe, from the Polish unrest to the Hungarian rising. Then— whether because Mao chose to move cautiously or because the scope of his grand design was not clear even to his comrades—few people guessed at the significance and impact of a policy that can be summed up in this question: how to find a left-wing solution to the crisis that awaits a changing society. The West, in fact, read and understood only those Chinese statements which could be placed in the ideological context of the debate then developing in Eastern Europe. The Eighth Congress of the CCP, though observed with interest, turned out to produce nothing new, and Mao did not advance on that occasion the fundamental ideas of his Ten Great Relationships. Curiously, all the basic issues were deferred to a second session of the same congress held a year and a half later, and no one seemed to be greatly surprised by this procedure.

Yet Mao's second essay "On the Historical Experience of the Dictatorship of the Proletariat" (published, as I have said, in December 1956) did contain critical comments on the Soviet model that ought not to have been overlooked. The West saw in it chiefly a circumspect criticism of the Stalin era, in line with that made by other Communist Parties, and no one commented on a remarkably sharp and dry phrase condemning all policies that copied the USSR: "The whole experience of the Soviet Union, including its essential experience, is linked with very definite national peculiarities, and no other country should copy it to the letter . . . To make an undiscriminating copy of the successes of the Soviet Union—not to mention its failures—can lead to failures in other countries." At that time, of course, all the people's democracies were stressing the need to avoid servile imitation of the USSR. But it must be stressed that the Chinese formulation, worded with great care, ascribed even the essentials of the Bolshevik experience to national peculiarities, gave a categorical warning against copying even its successes (let alone its failures), and thus reduced the value of the Soviet model to zero and showed China's intention to follow a completely independent path.

The speech on the Ten Great Relationships also gives us a better understanding, by casting a new light on it, of Mao's February 1957 essay "On the Correct Handling of Contradictions Among the People." As has been said, this was very well received abroad; it was admired for its apparently liberal aspects and for its subtle analysis of the complexity of a changing society. Overwhelmed by the revelation of Stalin's methods, Western Communists hastened to stress that Mao was rightly denouncing administrative methods as useless in ideological contests: he was saying that forbidding the expression of certain ideas has never succeeded in rooting them out but has often led to the opposite result. Moreover, Marxism and "good ideas" in general cannot be fostered like hothouse flowers, sheltered from debates and arguments. Mao adopted for his own purposes the old Chinese proverb: "Let a hundred flowers bloom, let a hundred schools of thought contend." Because of this slogan, he was claimed in Eastern Europe as "the supreme anti-Stalinist," despite his own reluctance to be thus classified. In the West, he was praised for being unique, among Communists holding power, in trying to advance an analysis of socialist systems instead of merely attacking the defects of Stalin's character.

But foreign observers failed to see that, by stressing the objective aspects of contradictions in postrevolutionary societies, Mao shifted the emphasis from the methods employed by state power at the institutional level to the entire social dialectic and therefore to the class struggle—a concept that the Left in the West, by this time, saw only as the justification used by Stalin and Stalinists for repression.[35] Mao saw it, on the other hand, as the fundamental mechanism of development; this is why a total misunderstanding grew up at this period between Mao's European admirers and his own thinking.

This misunderstanding was intensified when the Hundred Flowers campaign was cut short in China, to be replaced by violent onslaughts on "rightists" who had criticized the Party too much and from the wrong standpoint.[36] Suddenly everyone started to talk about Mao's somersault and his inability to "liberalize" his regime. Actually, far from intending merely to urge administrative tolerance ("let everyone think as he wishes"), Mao was pointing out to fraternal Parties—as in his speech on the Ten Great Relationships—the need to resolve contradictions by

[35] The theory of "the intensification of class struggle during the building of socialism" had been used by Stalin solely to justify his policy of police repression against "enemies of the people."

[36] The "anti-rightist" campaign did in fact, in 1957, directly follow the Hundred Flowers campaign.

radicalizing the revolution ("let everyone express himself so that false ideas can be unmasked and defeated"). Thus he was transferring the problem of social conflicts from the level of the superstructure to that of social and productive relationships.

Deeply convinced that this was the right road, he lost none of his optimism because of the mediocre results of the Hundred Flowers campaign, as we see from some words addressed to the Party in the summer of 1957: "We want to create a political situation that is centralized but democratic, disciplined but free, ideologically coherent but individually happy, dynamic and alive. . . . The relationship between the Party and the masses is like that between the fish and the water. *If this is not so, the socialist system can be neither created nor developed.*" Mao carried this conviction to Moscow in the autumn of 1957, but he met with no welcome for ideas of this kind; Communists were then divided, some favoring a trend toward social democracy and others a return to Stalinism, and both policies evaded social radicalization. No wonder, then, that he came back disappointed and that the Russians remembered his visit with, to say the least, mixed feelings.

After his return to China, a short tour of the provinces seems to have proved to him that conditions were ripe for change and that the masses were feeling new needs that created the possibility of far-reaching upheavals. Taking account of all these factors, he submitted for discussion in the Party, in January 1958, a curious document drawn up with the help of Liu Shao-ch'i, "Sixty Points on Methods of Work." [37] By failing to indicate which passages he wrote and which were written by Liu, Mao kept the China experts busy. The distinction is not really very hard to trace even for a nonexpert, for Mao's hand is recognizable wherever we find a historic—almost timeless—vision of social movement and its fundamental dialectic.

The Western reader is also taken aback by an extraordinary mingling of concrete, detailed directives with purely theoretical points. The Sixty Points are a minutely precise listing of what the Party should do in the course of the Great Leap Forward—which was launched in 1958—and of how it should intervene at every

[37] See Jerome Ch'en, *Mao Papers.*

level in the huge country, all these preparations being systematically classified in the Chinese style. But they also lay down what should be the qualities and the ultimate aims of the Party. Thus point 56 is devoted to the importance of fertility stimulants in pig breeding, and point 59 to the best way of surveying forests—and suddenly, with no transition but a fresh paragraph, point 60 is about Mao's decision to give up the Chairmanship of the Republic. After an insipid point 20 on the value of inspection among the provinces, point 21 abruptly raises the question of "continuous revolution," and point 22 that of "politics in command and the need to be Red and expert."

"Politics is our soul and our commander in chief," Mao writes here, striking out at those who give priority to purely economic or technical construction. "Those who concern themselves neither with ideology nor with politics, on the plea of being busy in other ways, are bound to lose all sense of direction and, moreover, any value as economists or technicians." Everyone, at all levels of society, must "integrate politics and economics," for without this no solutions can be found that will serve the building of socialism. There is no dichotomy between "Red" and "expert," since the two must go together in a socialist society. What goes for society as a whole also goes for every worker; progress at every level must be determined at the same time by political advances and by mastery of technique. All this involves constant struggle through the overall praxis of the broad masses.

"Making the revolution," Mao proclaims, "is like making war: after each battle won, it is necessary to prepare at once for the next, without taking time out to congratulate oneself." The idea of building socialism in a harmonious manner, without conflicts, is an idle dream, for the very development of society implies a struggle—continual progress from imbalance (which is the rule) to a balance that is always relative and temporary. This theory of imbalance is far-reaching with Mao and shows that, for him, the true essence of history is change and the destruction of stability, not only at present but in the future. "Imbalance is the universal and objective rule"; it is the mainspring of a cycle that leads society, each time the cycle revolves, to a higher stage of development. The Party itself is only an instrument, involved in but not governing this dialectical process of continuous revolution. If it does not correctly grasp the nature of each imbalance-balance-imbalance cycle, it is in danger of checking the cycle instead of spurring it on, and of succumbing to sclerosis and losing all usefulness.

In early 1958 Mao did not yet believe that the CCP could slow down the implementation of his plans, even though he was already pointing to the ambiguity of its social role, subordinated to the contradictions of historical development. He relied strongly on its ability to stimulate the Great Leap Forward and to adjust itself. To ensure this, he demanded that every leader, whatever his responsibility, should "behave like an ordinary worker, listen patiently to the arguments of others, take account of their opinions, and never regard a criticism as a personal insult." Thanks to the democratic and egalitarian attitude of its cadres, the entire Party would renew itself. As he saw things then, eight years after the establishment of the new regime, a split between the cadres and the masses did not seem to be an immediate danger and could be averted by the participation of all, side by side in solidarity, in the struggles of the Great Leap Forward. This, indeed, was one reason why he wanted these struggles to begin in the near future.

Taking Power and the Destruction of Capitalism

Mao's writings on the Great Leap were not divulged outside China, but his words of command were known; besides, the project began to go into effect under the eyes of thousands of Soviet witnesses, working in the Chinese economy. From 1958 it was therefore clear that China had embarked on a totally distinct and apparently heretical path. The USSR did not omit to announce officially to all who cared to listen that the Chinese enterprise violated the rules of "scientific" socialist construction (we shall see later that Khrushchev considered such a heresy to be intolerable). Knowledge therefore spread of this Maoist attempt to find a new development pattern and, in time, everyone had heard that Mao wanted a "Red and expert" China and was putting "politics in command" to achieve a "continuous revolution."

However, this experiment was greeted by almost the entire Left either with incredulity or with deep mistrust, which persists today even among those who claim to be revolutionaries. This negative reaction suggests certain reflections.

The reproach generally made to Mao was that he had sacrificed material progress on the altar of his egalitarian obsession—permissible in itself but unrealistic in a still underdeveloped country. By favoring ambitious schemes of new social organization, rather than concentrating on growth, he was reverting to the pre-industrial or anti-industrial notions of the Fourierist phalanstery, or had even become a precursor of Western advocates of "zero growth." Thus he had turned his back on every scientific conception of socialism and Communism to reveal himself as a modern peasant-utopian. Was it not indeed a delusion to try to create an egalitarian society in the midst of poverty, when all Marxist doctrine depicted Communism as the reward for a tremendous advance in human and productive wealth?

Those who put this question did not often try to make a deep study of Maoist conceptions of development, for they are convinced that there is little scope for innovation in this crucial sector. Here, it seems to me, we touch on the basic origin of the gulf between the Marxist tradition of the Second and Third Internationals in Europe and the Chinese revolution (in particular, as will be seen, the Cultural Revolution). That gulf is so deep that neither the evidence of crisis in the socialist nations of Europe nor the failure of attempts to remedy it since the Twentieth Congress has sufficed to vindicate the Maoist effort in the eyes of Western socialists or to gain its acceptance as a historic new solution.

Yet a revision of our ideas about the methods that guided socialist construction in the USSR appears to be a necessity. Even the pro-Soviet wing of the Left no longer denies that the societies of Eastern Europe have ceased to correspond to the visions of Marx and Lenin, that they are not progressing toward the withering away of the state, toward the abolition of inequality, or toward that profoundly transformed and truly free civilization which is the goal of any socialist revolution.

What, then, are the causes of these Soviet shortcomings, as outside friends delicately call them? They can no longer be attributed to underdevelopment, for the USSR is now a major industrial power. They cannot be blamed on the cult of personality—no cult surrounds Brezhnev or his counterparts in the people's democracies—or on the hardships of the world situation, for nobody now believes that the USSR is threatened by an anti-Communist crusade. Is socialism impossible? Or were past Soviet mistakes so far-reaching as to impose profound handicaps on the advance of the new society? In that case, precisely which mistakes? Everyone, including allies of the USSR, readily admits that mistakes were made. But everyone limits them to the strictly political sphere, to a method of governing, a conception and use of power, known as Stalinism. Few people ask whether the error was not deeper, involving certain fundamental choices on the *economic* side too of the building of the postrevolutionary society. On this point, oddly enough, the Left never ponders; while used to tracing the crises of capitalist societies to their structural foundations, it does not even dream that the same approach might usefully be applied to socialist societies. It is accepted beyond question that Stalin went wrong, but only on the level of his methods; the development model that he chose for the USSR was basically correct. This assumption seems never to be disputed, even by his most implacable accusers.[38]

But was it really correct? Can it be considered the only possible and viable method of transition from capitalism to socialism in a relatively backward country? Is it certain that Mao, by discarding it, cut himself off from the "scientific" socialism of Marx? What are the fundamental criteria that decide whether a path of transition to socialism can or cannot achieve that transition?

In this argument, the stakes are so high that it can lead only to a confrontation in an ideological world as rigid as that of the Communist movement; nor is the temperature likely to be lowered by a ransacking of the classics to illuminate the question. As we know, Marx did not hamper himself by making too many forecasts—by what he called "cooking for next week." But he made one point clear: after the political revolution (the seizure of

---

[38] See the recent book by Roy Medvedev, *Let History Judge: The Origins and Consequences of Stalinism* (New York: Knopf, 1972), which endorses all the objectives while condemning the methods used.

power) a start will at once be made on reversing the characteristic tendency of capitalism, that is, the relentless dehumanization of man—robbed of his land, his working tools, his product, and his very identity—which extends to stripping him bare and condemning him, as a proletarian, to total alienation. From the outset, the victorious revolution puts into action mechanisms directed toward "increasing domination by the direct producers over their living conditions and thus, in the first place, over their means of production and their products." In simpler language, men become masters of themselves both as producers and as citizens, thanks to a better form of common social organization. But how can these counter-tendencies, designed to abolish man's alienation, subjection, and separation from his work and from society, be put into operation? So far as political relationships go, both Marx and Lenin were very precise: through the revolution, the working class cannot confine itself to taking power in the sense of transferring to its own hands the apparatus of the bourgeois state. It must also completely destroy this state machine, because it is strictly designed for the rule of the bourgeoisie and cannot be used as an instrument of the new society, even in the phase when the working class in turn exercises its domination over the old exploiting classes (the dictatorship of the proletariat). The proletariat, by its very nature, must rely on different mechanisms, such as the abolition of the delegation of power and the right of recall, to create an entirely different relationship between society and the apparatus of government—in short, what Marx saw in the Paris Commune and Lenin in the soviets.[39] In other words, the state will from the outset cease to be divided from the masses in the manner of the old state, the executive committee of the exploiting minority. Lenin, as we know, was especially uncompromising on this subject, rejecting the "revisionist" interpretations of Marx made by the Second International, which inclined after the turn of the century toward gradualist solutions, ironically described by Lenin as "evolution through rest." In the early 1960's, the Chinese attacked Khrushchev and the Western Communist

---

[39] See Karl Marx, *The Civil War in France* ("The political instrument of the enslavement of the proletariat cannot be used as an instrument of its emancipation"), and V. I. Lenin, *The State and Revolution*.

Parties on the same lines, charging them with relapsing into the social-democratic groove of a "peaceful road to socialism." They were consequently losing sight of the fact that the bourgeois state is not neutral, that it is the executive committee of the bourgeoisie, and that all its institutions were devised and shaped to meet the latter's needs to dominate society and exploit the wage earners. So this state must be entirely replaced by "the proletariat organized as a ruling class." [40] This means a form of power exercised by the huge majority, until the day when Communism has been achieved and the state in any form, even proletarian, has become unnecessary.

Thus there can be no possible misunderstanding about the definition of the type of state that characterizes the phase of socialism. But things are more complicated when we leave the scene of political superstructure for that of structure—that is, the mode of production, which, according to Marx, gives birth to the entire system of relationships between men. To what extent should the revolution destroy the production mechanisms inherited from capitalism and clear the way, not only for a somewhat more equitable social order, but for a radically different mode of production capable of creating true equality among mankind in contrast to the inequality and dispossession generated by the old system? The question is sharpened by the fact that, unlike earlier socioeconomic systems, socialist forms of production cannot develop or even take shape within capitalism. True, capitalist economic growth lays the material foundations of the new society and creates the working class that will bring it to fruition. But neither socialist relationships nor a socialist mode of production can develop within, or on the fringe of, the old system (unlike the early capitalist enterprises, which could be born within feudal society). The proletarian revolution does not come to crown a partially achieved social process, needing only a political consecration to complete its flourishing. In this sense, conditions are never absolutely ripe for social upheaval under capitalism. No doubt this is why Lenin was so insistent on the subjective and planned aspect of the revolution; it cannot come to birth alone, like a ripening fruit.

[40] Lenin, *The State and Revolution.*

But it also follows that the proletariat, after its victory, does not at once possess all the instruments needed to free society from the slavery of necessity and alienation. To start with, it must keep the old mode of production and transform it by degrees, while continuing to make it work in order to supply the workers with essential goods. The first of these transformations is self-evident: to put an end to private property in means of production and thus abolish the main obstacle to the channeling of economic growth toward social purposes. As we know, all revolutions since 1917 have strictly followed this policy and have expropriated the possessing classes without much delay in the field of industry, finance, and even distribution. Property in land and in the farming sector in general, being to a great extent precapitalist, has presented more complex problems arising from specific conditions in each country. At all events, no difficulties on the theoretical level are raised by the expropriation of the old owners.

On the other hand, the question is more tricky when it is a matter of other changes required to abolish the capitalist mode of production. For the latter is not identified only with free enterprise and the property system. It is also characterized by its particular form of accumulation—the levying of surplus value from the labor of the workers—and by the totality of social relationships, within and outside the factory, serving this purpose. Marx analyzed precisely this special form of exploitation, whose scale and effects were without precedent; it arises from a completely new civilization, never having existed before the bourgeois Industrial Revolution that scattered everything in its advance.

In fact, it brought a profound change to the relationships between man and his work, man and the product of his work. Whereas in the precapitalist period (and to this day in small-scale farming and craft work) the producer is the owner of the land or of his working equipment, under capitalism he is deprived of both. All he has left is his labor power, which he sells to the capitalist; but the latter derives profit from his work by paying him only part of its value. Capitalism is thus based on a twofold process whereby man is dispossessed both of his means of working (which he no longer owns) and of the product of his work (which no longer concerns him). Capital is accumulated, reproduced, and increased through the appropriation by the capitalist of unpaid labor, of surplus value.

Society is thus divided between the property owners and a mass of men who—as had never before been the case—owned nothing but their hands and their ability to work. And even this was becoming steadily depersonalized. For, as industrialization grew, the alienation of the worker increased; in the old workshops, most of the workers could still understand and partly control the processes in which they were engaged, but in a big modern factory the machine decides the rhythm of production. The workers work together "only in the sense that they are brought together by an external will and intelligence," which in the last analysis is the machine, or fixed capital. "It is not the workers," Marx stresses again, "who have united to pursue a project conceived by them; it is the industrial process, this living monster, that is the subject of production." The worker is only an "isolated living accessory," unable to dominate the process to which he is subjected.[41]

The same goes for the technician and, to a certain extent, even for the factory manager, also ruled by the productive cycle and by the mechanisms of accumulation that govern it (even though their position gives them power over others and makes them alienated men and oppressors at the same time). Now, the more vast and concentrated is the productive enterprise, the more fragmented is the worker's task. Hierarchical rules and the division of labor, ever more rigid and unnatural, emphasize more and more his role as an "isolated living accessory" and put objective limits on his will.

The whole of capitalist society is regulated by this power mechanism of alienation, which demands the increasingly rigid and stratified division of social roles. It puts its stamp deep on both the productive system as a whole and the productive resources it creates. Now, the paradox of the victorious revolution is that the working class overthrows the political power of the bourgeoisie at a stroke, but cannot—at the risk of completely destroying the apparatus of production—immediately overthrow the structure or the economic and technical instruments of

---

[41] Karl Marx, *Grundrisse der Kritik der politischen Ökonomie*, Vol. IV: *Ursprüngliche Akkumulation* (Berlin: Dietz Verlag, 1953), p. 374.

capital, or the division of labor on which they are based. Since they must continue to produce, the workers must continue to be workers, subordinated to the productive rhythm of the factory; they must even produce more, for the revolution sets free increased needs. They cannot do without the machine they have inherited. But if they continue to use it, changing only its ownership, do they not risk contaminating the new society? As long as economic growth is based on this system, will it not be necessary to preserve the fragmentation of work, the social division of labor, hierarchy, and inequality? How can an instrument that spawns injustices be used for the total liberation of mankind and the breaking of social barriers?

The working-class movement, which made its breakthrough in the great industrial nations of Europe in the late nineteenth century, should logically have come to grips with this question. But its founders, Marx and Engels, while they described the dominating character of capitalist society, did not explain in detail how the proletariat, liberated by the revolution, could completely abolish the process of alienation and create its own mode of production.[42] Marx indicated this was indeed the historic task of the working class and declared that, for this reason, the Communist revolution is qualitatively different from all other revolutions; it aims at the destruction of the whole mode of living, of work as it has hitherto been conceived, and therefore of classes, a destruction that demands the transformation even of the class that brings it about (the proletariat).[43] But we also know that he thought of the revolution as the culmination of a gigantic social crisis

[42] In *History and Class Consciousness* (London: Merlin Books, 1972), Georg Lukacs posed in general terms the question: How can the proletariat, which Marx conceived as the pure object of alienation, turn its negative status into positive, become the subject of revolution, and found a new civilization? This book, when first published in German in 1922, was proscribed by the Comintern. It is only in recent years, after the Chinese breakaway, that the social aspects of postrevolutionary transformation have become the theme of wider debate, owing in particular to the contribution of Charles Bettelheim and of the school of Marxists specializing in the problems of the Third World. See the letters in the first section of Paul M. Sweezy and Charles Bettelheim, *On the Transition to Socialism* (New York: Monthly Review Press, 1972).

[43] See Karl Marx and Frederick Engels, *German Ideology* (New York: International Publishers, 1970), Chapter 1.

engendered by the contradiction between the social relationships of capital and the productive forces it had created; beyond a certain point, capitalism is crippled because it no longer stimulates the totality of social production and cheats society out of its already existing capabilities; it increases wealth but imprisons men in the shackles of its system of exploitation, which it prevents them from mastering. From this conception—of capital's absolute inability to resolve this contradiction or others arising from it—the Second International drew its evolutionist theory, according to which the productive system would in the end inevitably liberate itself from capital.[44] Even the part of the working-class movement that did not accept this hopeful forecast adopted the theory that productive forces were neutral, if not good, and they were identified on the whole with the economic structure. It followed that the concept of a capitalist mode of production was reduced to a very limited significance; as generally used, it came down more or less to the system of private property in the means of production.[45] So Marx was interpreted in inside-out style, and the problems of transition were not explored on the theoretical level.

Moreover, in real life, the young October Revolution scarcely had time to devote itself to the definition of concepts. As soon as the Bolsheviks saw the vanishing of their hopes that the revolution would spread across Europe—and we must recall that for a long time they thought this indispensable to their own prospects—the number-one problem facing them was to save their beleaguered state, the only socialist state. How could they achieve self-sufficiency in the production of essential goods and be sure of a rapid and reliable means of accumulation? This became a matter of life and death for them.

But the early years soon showed how difficult it was to control this process in the conditions of underdevelopment that obtained in the USSR. During the civil war the Bolsheviks learned some

[44] In the twentieth century there was a very keen debate on this question within the Left (in which Rosa Luxemburg, among others, joined) around the issues of inevitable collapse and the tendency of capital toward catastrophe.

[45] A remark by Lenin about state capitalism as the final phase of development, after which there would be only socialism, was interpreted in the same way: that the pure and simple replacement of state power would be enough to ensure the end of class divisions in society and the "social" nature of production.

bitter and costly lessons, primarily that an economy so slightly concentrated as theirs could not be controlled and directed by purely political means. Their appeals and orders, in the period of "War Communism," met with little response from the huge mass of small producers in the towns, to say nothing of the countryside, which was still at a semipatriarchal level. By enforcing their commands through requisitions and other coercive methods, they half-paralyzed production; this gravely compromised the state of affairs in the political sphere too. In 1921, with the military danger dispelled, Lenin therefore decided on the New Economic Policy, which restored legality to private enterprise and the free market. The aim was to gain time for the regime to prepare its own economic instruments for the next phase, which would be planned. His slogan of *reculer pour mieux sauter* therefore meant that the jump would be propelled by economic incentives and no longer simply by political decrees.

There was inevitably a keen debate on the methods required to create a system of centrally planned development, the more so because Lenin did not long survive the launching of the NEP and the Bolsheviks no longer had a supreme arbiter. Nevertheless, despite their serious internal disagreements, they all had a more or less similar outlook on the subject of economic development. They saw the expansion of postrevolutionary society as synonymous with industrialization, and this meant an effort to reach the level and the growth rate of the advanced nations of the West. The disputed points concerned the kind of policies and production mechanisms that would best plan this growth. The problem of socialist relationships within these mechanisms was not even glimpsed, for the Bolshevik leaders were convinced that the vital transformation had already been achieved in industry because it was no longer in private hands, and, anyway, that a final transformation of social relationships could only be a later stage, after the "building of the material foundations" of socialism.

Priority was therefore given to the construction of large-scale machine industry, regarded as basic. It was clear that, to begin with, it was necessary to accept the modern system of organization of work found in the major industrial countries. Lenin himself, toward the end of his life, studied the American Taylor system and other advanced techniques of production. As for

Trotsky, after 1920 he argued with conviction for authoritarian as opposed to collective factory management. The fact that this model of large-scale machine industry was the outcome of the specific capitalist mode of production, which was the condition of its functioning, did not seem to worry the Bolsheviks. First of all, this was because they were convinced of its objective necessity; the Industrial Revolution had led to the triumph of capitalism, but it had, in the eyes of the Marxist thinkers of the Second and Third Internationals, an intrinsic value as a "neutral" phenomenon, to be applied to other purposes than those of capital. Second, the political framework had changed; in the USSR, the state was no longer the executive committee of the bourgeoisie but, so to speak, that of the working class, whose interests it defended. Once the exploitation of man by man was impossible, discipline and subordination for the workers took on a totally different meaning.

This aspect of the problem, and indeed the contradiction that it implied, was discussed during the last free debate held by the Bolsheviks, which concerned the system of accumulation. Where and how were the resources to be found to invest in industry? Evgeny Preobrazhensky, an old comrade of Trotsky and an adversary of Stalin (though Stalin finally settled the argument in his favor in 1927) made no bones about saying that "primitive socialist accumulation"—a term that Lenin disliked—could be achieved only through surplus value taken from the workers and taxation of the countryside ("our colonies," as he put it).[46] The obvious, and to some extent inevitable, contradiction in a changing society was softened by an ideological device: the working class was still exploited, to be sure, but by itself, passing "from the stage of object to that of subject of exploitation." Requiring the peasants to provide the manpower and resources to industrialize the country was no new invention either, for capitalism had done the same at the time of its birth in England, and Marx described this phenomenon as "the brutal robbery of the countryside." In the USSR it was more tactfully called "the transfer of resources from the nonsocialist to the socialist sector"

[46] Preobrazhensky developed this theory in *The Fundamental Law of Socialist Accumulation* (Vestnik Kommunisticeskoj Akademii, VIII, 1924), which, with certain changes, became a chapter in his key work, *The New Economics* (New York: Oxford University Press, 1965).

(the land being still in private hands, whereas industry was nationalized).

Certainly, just as the levying of surplus value by the state was to lead to an overall enriching of society, so the "robbery" of the nonsocialist sector was to be carried out in a different way. Only the rich peasants, or kulaks, were to be dispossessed—those who had been spared by capitalism and whom the Soviet state had no reason to protect, since they had virtually dictated the prices of farm products to the country during the NEP. And the poor peasants would be helped to form collective farms. In the first phase, no doubt, price policy would favor industry to the detriment of agriculture, but in a later phase the new industries would supply the countryside with the necessary equipment to make a radical change in its habits of life and work, and this would lead to a firm alliance between workers and peasants. Here too, as in the case of social relationships within industry, the transformation was to be made in two stages: first the peasants would pay a "tribute" to industrialization, then they would be paid back and raised to such a level that the distinction between town and country would be wiped out, as well as the distinction between work in industry and in farming.

The development scheme that emerged from the debates of the 1920's envisaged a series of priority breakthroughs to unite society around the economic pole of the major industries. The making of a new balance for the whole social organism and the transformation of all social relationships were put off to a later stage. But, as soon as it got under way, this process of industrialization acquired its own dynamic and persistently aggravated the inequalities and dispossessions characteristic of the mode of the production that had always governed large-scale machine industry. In the effort to develop productive forces of this kind, there was no choice but to impose the rigidly hierarchical relationships and social distinctions that flowed from them. And since it was no longer possible to depict this system as temporary, in contrast with the essence of long-term revolutionary aims, it had to be justified and praised, a task to which Stalin proved equal.

He announced, therefore, that socialism was incompatible first with *uvravnilovka* (leveling downward), then with *ravnost* (equality), and finally with anything that might be harmful to labor discipline, to specialization, to the status and authority of directors, and so forth. And so industrialization went along with a continual weakening of the egalitarian working-class ideology, which was gradually replaced by a doctrine of promotion familiar in other parts of the world. It was said abroad that this poverty-stricken ideology reflected Stalin's willingness to adapt Marxist theory to the level of the semiliterate mass of peasants flocking into the towns after the great onslaught on the kulaks that had spread ruin in the countryside. He was said to be the right man for the situation, not the Bolshevik veterans imbued with Western Marxist culture, because he knew how to understand and discipline these millions who were at last being introduced to modern industrial civilization. In reality, Stalin was brutally expressing requirements imposed by production relationships, and sticking a "socialist" label on the old principles of organization of giant factories with the highest rate of accumulation. He was the prisoner of this process as much as its moving spirit.

When the record was surveyed after Stalin's death, his successors took pride in having won the epic battle of industrialization and denounced the excesses of the repression that had accompanied it. The breakthroughs envisaged as the first phase had clearly been achieved, but there was no longer anyone around to suggest the second phase or even to remember that it had been the original intention. The new working class had emerged in fragmented condition from the race for individual rewards instituted since the First Five-Year Plan, a race all the more harmful in that it had stimulated rivalry and the worst kind of selfishness in a period of extreme poverty. The peasants had never recovered from the blows inflicted on them during "primitive accumulation" and were relying on their private plots of land, hoping that, by passive resistance on the collective farms, they would at least get full civil rights.[47] As for the higher social groups, those who had managed to attain commanding positions in the established hierarchy, they were certainly not likely to risk what they had gained by calling for a transformation of social relationships.

[47] Soviet peasants still do not possess internal passports, which would allow them to leave the countryside at will and move to the towns.

In this manner, the development pattern designed to unify society had, on the contrary, divided it into layers cut off from one another, even more sharply than in countries where divisions are made "only" by money. Paradoxically, in these "socialist" societies the action of the powerful state machine helps to complete and speed up the stratifications that still follow from inequalities in earnings and social status. Each "more essential" group gets not only higher wages but also privileges that are carefully allotted and designed to increase its qualities of initiative and its social prestige. There is a whole range of distinctions in housing, in weekend homes, in special shops, in clinics and rest homes, not to mention cars of a size corresponding to rank.

As can be seen, all the deferred problems were abandoned by the roadside. The survival of imperfect social relationships, inherited from the capitalist mode of production, which could not vanish simply because of the seizure of political power, is no longer considered to be temporary; the system perpetuates its mechanism, its hierarchy, and its individual roles. Wage labor— that is, labor as a commodity, the basic characteristic of the capitalist mode of production and reproduction—remains, and with it a significant feature of capitalism, the distinctions between manual and intellectual work and between workers and peasants. The governing class, even though not aware of the fact, behaves like a new bourgeoisie, based not on ownership but on "management"; hence its enduring tendency toward bureaucracy and its real remoteness from the masses. Hence, finally, its profile as a traditional state, as a government face to face with the governed, which in no way resembles the ideal of proletarian democracy, of the Paris Commune or the soviets, and appears as a power system strictly and rigidly structured from the top down.

Such are the facts; and, to tell the truth, neither the USSR nor the satellites hide them any longer. Their factories—founded by the state and belonging to it—may not be the daughters of capital, but they are surely its nieces, and therefore they entirely accept the ideology of capitalist productivity. When a society bases its development on this mechanism of accumulation, without taking any steps that might attempt to correct the structure and logic of the capitalist mode of production along the way, the latter must win out, because it will eventually fashion the whole working of society to meet its needs. The durability and strengthening of the state in its classical repressive form, the stifling of all working-class power arising from below, the rigid division between rulers and ruled—all these phenomena, which are at the root of political tensions in the Eastern European countries, can thus be seen as no special vice of Communist bureaucracies, nor as the handiwork of a despot like Stalin; they are, in plain terms, the legal superstructure of a system that, in its social foundations, remains alienated and alienating.

I shall not go into the details of how far this sociopolitical system in the Soviet bloc resembles the capitalist system of production ruling in the West, and how far they diverge. Clearly there are differences, and it would be interesting to make a study of them. The most obvious—it recurs in all the debates in Eastern European countries—is that these countries do not follow to the end the tendency of their production system toward the restoration of classical market mechanisms. On the one hand, the dynamic of their economy, being what it is, should lead them to give complete autonomy to those enterprises which are most profitable and most able to compete in the "socialist" market, and hence to adapt production and prices to the spontaneous requirements of the market according to the law of supply and demand (while liquidating the least competitive). On the other hand, those who wield political power are not prepared to go that far, for these measures would lead to a reaction of self-defense from the workers and other adversely affected categories, who renounced power in return for a range of material safeguards that they regard as permanent gains from the revolution, such as full employment (now endangered only in Yugoslavia), a welfare system, and a certain level of wages. Now, the Eastern European countries are in no condition to accept an "open political dialectic" as it exists in the West; a direct clash with the workers, as occurred in Poland in 1970, was a warning to them and they fear that this policy could throw them off balance. Hence the constant hesitations, since 1956, between the temptation to create a satisfied market through "classical" mechanisms—and thus meet the new demands of the middle classes—and the need for firm political stability. This is reflected in the seesaw between concessions to the economic "reformers" (that is, the advocates of setting free the spontaneous trends of development) and compromises with the state bureaucracy.

These societies cannot entirely revert to the past (since, by definition, they cannot permit a free expression of the class struggle again), but it is time to understand why they are in this position. When we look for the cause of the deadlock, perhaps we shall find it in the "non-neutrality" of the development pattern chosen in the 1920's, because of inexperience and under the pressure of necessity. What Mao Tse-tung realized in the second half of the 1950's was that it is necessary at all costs to control the deep and inevitable tendency to perpetuate the capitalist mode of production, which the revolution inherited from the past and is compelled to use. And this must be done without destroying the productive apparatus, but by using it while defeating its logic, bending it to priorities other than its own, taking as the aim from the outset—not in a later phase—that growth should speed up and not retard the social revolution.

In practice, Mao regarded the primary rule of industrialization —to subject everything to the demands of the most productive sector and accumulate on this basis—as rotten. In his scheme, he assigned an equal role to all sectors, notably to agriculture. He scrapped another law: the big factories were not to receive the greatest investment; every productive unit was to acquire equal dignity, the stress being put on the labor of 700 million Chinese, in the cities and the countryside, working together and seeking to keep up the same pace. Third, so long as the forms of capitalist exploitation (the taking of surplus value) persisted—and they could not be wiped out for a long time, until the transition to true Communism—ideological and egalitarian counter-pressures must be set in motion, within and outside the factory, at least to prevent the hierarchy of the technical division of labor from being translated directly into distinctions of social status to the detriment of the workers.

But to take one's stand on these three priorities meant changing the model, rejecting the laws and the logic of the pattern of industrialization known hitherto—that is, the capitalist model. It was to query all "neutrality," all "objectivity," all "necessity." It was to reject the concept of progress historically linked to it in the West; and this rejection caused a profound jolt to Western thought. In fact, it was to put the accent on what Marx called destruction rather than on continuity. In political terms, it was the great "voluntarist" human choice of liberty and equality, of Communism "in command." Thus Mao's grand design of balanced development was expressed in practice by his theory of successive imbalances on the social level, for to unify society means to begin by destroying its old and new divisions. It was therefore the end of all expectations of gradual and peaceful development—the continuous revolution, in which the seizure of power is only one step forward. It was a break not only with the ideas of most of the Communist Parties after the Twentieth Congress, but also with a profound and implicit tradition which, in Europe, had always enabled the subjectivism of the Third International to coexist with the objectivism claimed by the Second, and which had led since the death of Lenin to that oscillation between Stalinism and social democracy from which the Communist Parties and the socialist countries—except for China—were patently unable to escape.

The Great Leap . . .

Village steel plants—that bold and quickly abandoned experiment—became for many outsiders the symbol of the Great Leap Forward, and naturally of its failure. Did this not prove that it was impossible to devise a mode of industrialization other than that which the world had known since the bourgeois Industrial Revolution? By trying to make steel amid the fields, the Chinese had simply made their peasants waste millions of hours of work, not to mention the waste of raw material, which was often provided by the iron tools of these same peasants. The Russians made equally persistent capital out of this episode, but dwelt more on the disasters wreaked by Maoist innovations in the industrial sphere. Their experts looked on, powerless, at the launching of this experiment involving millions of people, who suddenly started to break the most elementary industrial rules in the hope of simplifying, improving, and transforming their products. According to these witnesses, the Chinese workers, egged on by agitators, had no respect for anything and cared nothing for the central plan, not to speak of the quality or value of their output. As a result, thousands of simplified machines piled up in the warehouses. After a couple of years of such fruitless efforts, the Chinese economy would simply collapse. Here was a still more conclusive proof that, if you try to break the objective laws of development, if you replace competence by working-class improvisation, you invite setbacks on the material level and harm the interests of the workers themselves.

By now Eastern Europe has produced a whole literature on this theme, and as one may imagine, it does not pull any punches.[48] But it must be admitted that the Chinese eased the task of their detractors by publishing, at the end of 1958, truly astounding statistics on the results they had obtained and recognizing later that the figures were exaggerated. In December 1958 the plenary session of the Central Committee of the CCP announced that, in a single year, the total value of industrial and agricultural output had risen by 70 percent, whereas it had risen by only 68 percent in the whole of the preceding five-year period. Steel production was said to have jumped from 5.35 million to 11 million tons, machine tools from 28,000 to 90,000 units, and coal from 130,000 to 270,000 tons. But the truly breathtaking miracle was claimed in agriculture, where the output of cereals had gone up from 185 million tons in 1957 to 375 million tons—in other words, had doubled, something that nature seldom permits.[49] At the celebration of the tenth anniversary of the revolution, in October 1959, the Chinese were already changing their tune; for instance, the 1958 harvest was down to 250 million tons, a much more plausible figure.[50] This statistical trickery was certainly of no help in understanding the Great Leap, and the climax was that the Maoists recognized this and drew the farfetched conclusion that they should publish no more statistics at all.

[48] In Poland, to give one example, the following (involuntarily amusing) studies on China have recently appeared: W. Kanski, *Zarys rozwoju gospodazczego Chinskiej Republiki Ludowij, 1949–69* (Warsaw: Ksiaika Wiedza, 1971), and S. Zyga, *Chinska Republika Ludowa, 1945–1970* (Warsaw: Wiedza Powszichna, 1971).

[49] Central Committee statement, December 1958; see *Documents of CCP Central Committee* (Hong Kong: Union Research Institute).

[50] See the collection entitled *Ten Glorious Years* (Peking: Foreign Languages Publishing House, 1960).

Of course, these premature victory communiqués were meant chiefly for internal consumption, to stimulate emulation among productive units that were being called upon to make unprecedented efforts of inventiveness and reorganization. But in other countries, where statistics are used to make objective judgments and not to spur on the workers, the Great Leap was inevitably seen as an extraordinary economic forcing of the pace, a dash made by an underdeveloped country that has decided to put everything at stake to escape from its backwardness. Other socialist countries had shown a similar impatience in the sphere of production, and the Chinese seemed to be following rather than diverging from their example. Even their decision to produce steel everywhere, including the countryside, appeared to confirm that they were even more ruled by "King Steel" than their Soviet comrades had once been. So everything combined to strengthen observers in the belief that they were watching an old movie and need pay no special attention to Chinese innovations in the system of management.

However, these innovations were given as much space in the Chinese press as the triumphant figures on production results. It was in 1958 that articles appeared in China denouncing "absurd rules" in industry, and very clearly aimed at the hierarchical system based on the social division of labor. It was from this time onward that directors and technicians in industry were deprived of their social prestige and ceased to represent an authority that the workers ought to respect because of abilities beyond their reach. In this experimental movement on the scale of millions of people, stress was laid for the first time not only on the fact that the workers were indispensable because of the unity of the production cycle, but also on their practical knowledge, which, combined with their class spirit, made them supremely "Red and expert."

But the key to the program was the people's communes. In a country where the land had already been collectivized, in 1955, it was suddenly decided to create in the villages a new form of organization, sought by the peasants themselves, enabling them to live in a still more collectivist manner and to diversify the very nature of their work. Moreover, each commune was given powers in the spheres normally reserved to the state, such as education, armed militia, and others. Nor was it accidental that the name of people's commune was chosen for this new organism and explicit allusions were made for the first time to the social plans advanced by the Paris Commune.

"Among the ten steps laid down by Marx and Engels for the period of the dictatorship of the proletariat," wrote *Red Flag* in September 1958, "the two most important are 'to combine industry and agriculture by seeking to eliminate distinctions between town and country' and 'to combine education and material production.' Comrade Mao Tse-tung has said that we must systematically organize industry, agriculture, trade, education, and defense in the great communes that will form the basic units of society. In these communes, industry, agriculture, and trade will serve the material interests of the people, culture and education will reflect its spiritual life, and the armed forces will protect its material and spiritual achievements."

The state did not give up its task of coordinating all these efforts among the communes and other basic units, but it gave them such powers that it appeared possible to speak of a first major step toward the withering away of the state. True, the Chinese press did not at that time raise the institutional problems that were to come forward with the Cultural Revolution, and referred to the Paris Commune rather as the model of a many-sided organization of work and of new social relationships. Nevertheless, the emphasis it put on the decision-making power of the workers, and on their equal rights in production and in social experimentation, amounted to an unprecedented change and foreshadowed nothing less than making it possible for all men to assume control of their work and win a better share of its fruits.

In October 1959, on the occasion of the tenth anniversary of the People's Republic, there was born somewhere in China an entirely new industry—at Taching ("Great Celebration"). The industry was oil, a raw material that China had always lacked and had luckily discovered at the end of the 1950's. Although the exact location of the oil fields has been kept secret for strategic reasons, we were soon told that they were in a very poverty-stricken region and that the pioneers of this new industry had decided to put waste land into cultivation in order to supply their basic needs. Filled with egalitarian spirit, they announced that at

Taching there would be not even an armchair, as a symbol that no one would enjoy privileges or possess even the most modest visible signs of authority. Thus, little by little, developed a remarkable kind of industrial sector, in which concentration in large units was avoided and everyone was engaged in both the extraction and the refining of oil and in farming at the same time. "Learn from Taching" became a motto, written in Mao's own calligraphy and broadcast throughout China.

But is it true that, despite these exemplary experiments, the plans of the Great Leap did not succeed and the Chinese economy was virtually wrecked by the beginning of 1960? The failure of certain undertakings, such as village steel production, is obvious, and one cannot be very convinced by the argument used by some defenders of China that millions of Chinese, thanks to these miniature steel plants, were introduced to hitherto unknown techniques. They could have raised their level of knowledge in a better way by making more useful things, such as cement and fertilizers, two major local industries that have survived and are now progressing with great efficiency. Besides, the originators of the Great Leap have themselves admitted that, in haste to be "always in the lead," many communes adopted methods on the basis of inadequate experience, which were not taken up elsewhere without scrutiny. We also know that the central leadership and Mao himself have taken part of the blame for these mistakes and confessed to an inability to coordinate such a general advance on all fronts of the economy.

But to go from this to the conclusion that everything collapsed is a step that it would be wiser not to take. Looking back, many Western economists speak of a setback rather than a defeat and state that, despite an undeniable drop in production in the three years 1960–2, the economy did not collapse and central planning did not vanish. In fact, even temporarily abandoned projects were restarted and became the basis for a very firm economic advance, most obviously in agriculture, where an unbroken ten-year sequence of good harvests cannot be attributed solely to luck with the weather. The remarkable projects in irrigation and water conservation, and the creation of a whole infrastructure to improve the soil and the quality of seeds, were not completed in time to prevent the disasters of 1959 and 1960, but bore fruit later

and enabled Chinese agriculture to progress at a rate of 4 percent
a year (according to foreign estimates), which is double the
growth rate of the population and explains the continuous rise in
food supplies.

We also know that in 1960 there was the "Russian disaster" and
China was suddenly deprived of all Soviet supplies, including oil.
At that time her own oil industry not only was embryonic but did
not have the required equipment to develop. China had no
factories making drilling equipment, let alone refineries. A few
prototypes were doubtless imported from the West through Hong
Kong, but essentially they were redesigned and put into production in Shanghai and the northeast, in such quantities that China
now exports oil.[51] We might also reflect on the example of nuclear
power, which, despite the absence of Soviet aid, has developed
much faster than any experts predicted—and that precisely
during the difficult years. Other evidence, too, shows that China
never collapsed and never gave up her policy of balanced
investment, which enabled her to limit the damage during the
hard years and to progress steadily after them.

But these examples should not be interpreted, as they have
been by some skeptics in the West, to prove that China too
adopted the model of priority breakthroughs and that, instead of
favoring heavy industry, it made sacrifices for the sake of oil or
nuclear weapons. For in practice it was not a case of decisions
aimed at long-term accumulation but of solutions that were forced
on her; oil had to be developed to escape the stranglehold of
foreign exporters of this vital material, and to eliminate a
bottleneck that threatened to paralyze the whole economy.
Moreover, the planners of the Great Leap never claimed that they
were abandoning all priorities in development policy and allowing
the masses to decide for themselves on the direction of the
economy. This would have meant giving up planning, whereas the
Chinese aim is rather to create a planning system that is more
effective because it is less rigid and is closer to the realities of each
productive unit. It is in this light that we should interpret the
decision to decentralize management and to entrust most of the

[51] In 1971 China produced 25 million tons of oil, more than its own domestic
consumption, which is still held down because of the low level of mechanization.

enterprises to local, district, or provincial authorities. If we can believe the statistics from this period, Peking kept direct control of only 27 percent of enterprises, compared to 46 percent before the Great Leap.

What, then, were the principles of the policy of "readjustment and consolidation" that followed the first surge of the Great Leap? Certain measures, dictated purely by circumstances, did not basically change the orientation of the country. For example, the fact that a large number of blue-collar and white-collar workers, who had come from the rural regions in the preceding years, were now sent back to the countryside was the result of a readjustment enforced by the closing of many projects that should have been completed with Soviet aid. The change in the system of the communes can be regarded as more permanent, for they were reduced in numbers and subdivided into production brigades and teams that, because of their size, could not have the same ambitions or the same diversity as before. But the degree of autonomy that had been granted to them was not revoked, even though this caused serious political problems at the time when the tide ebbed (as we shall see later on).

Likewise, in the industrial sector, where piecework had been abolished during the Great Leap, there was no question of restoring it or of starting an individual race for productivity, although collective bonuses for teams were introduced. Directors and technicians in Chinese factories did not regain the privileges they had enjoyed during the period when the Soviet model was in force; but there was a stress on discipline, and for a short period this seemed to eclipse the stress on collective experiment and "double participation" (of the workers in management and of the cadres in productive work). All this was greatly called into question during the Cultural Revolution, for these measures were said to have been inspired by the "general staff" of Liu Shao-ch'i, because of his desire to give orders from above and prevent the masses from fully managing their own affairs.

Taking a closer look at the Chinese record during this period—including the statistics, which are dubious but instructive—we observe above all that the slogan "Experiment in everything" was as binding on the leaders as on the masses. The project that had been launched was not very far advanced, except for its basic inspiration, defined by Mao in his speech on the Ten Great Relationships and in the Sixty Points. In one of these points he said that it was better to keep the existing Five-Year Plan rather than to fix new quantitative targets and leave it to practice to decide to what extent it was possible to progress on all fronts. Now, the old plan provided for the importation of new factories from the USSR, and in August 1958 and February 1959 China had signed two important agreements for the purchase of Soviet equipment to the value of 1,126 million rubles, as though intending to industrialize in the old way and the new way at the same time. As a result, the numbers of jobs in various sectors were increased—both as planned and in an improvised manner—so that the total of industrial workers rose in a single year from 9 million to 25 million, a record never equaled in any country in the world. There was a similar spectacular jump in technical schools, where the number of students rose in a year from 778,000 to 1.47 million.[52] It is unlikely that these decisions, which had to be revised later, were taken without the knowledge of Mao or that his team indulged in wild ambitions without him. I find it more accurate to conclude that Mao and his team knew where they wanted to go, but not necessarily how to make the journey. Every reform, it is sometimes said in the West, is a leap in the dark. That is even more true of a break on the scale represented by the Chinese new departure of 1958. But we know today that after their leap the Chinese never retraced their steps. Rather, they have continued to advance in the direction of their choice, while drawing lessons from their experiments. This is why the Great Leap was an irreversible turning point in their history.

. . . and the Great Split

The Great Leap was a turning point, too, in China's relations with the USSR. After 1958, the deterioration of relations between Moscow and Peking moved with unexpected speed. At the time, it was explained chiefly by Chinese displeasure with Khrushchev's international initiatives and in particular his attitude toward the United States, crowned by his pilgrimage to Camp David in

[52] See *Ten Glorious Years.*

September 1959. But in hindsight we can understand more clearly that the conflict between the Big Two of the Socialist camp was not limited to this thorny question of Soviet foreign policy. Everything that had shocked the Soviet experts who had been in China during the Great Leap caused a still greater scandal in the Kremlin. For the first time, a socialist country was not simply refusing to adopt the Soviet model but was in open opposition to it; and even if Mao did not shout this from the rooftops, no one missed the significance of his challenge.

Khrushchev, it is true, chose a somewhat unusual way of showing his indignation. In December 1958 he took U.S. Senator Hubert Humphrey into his confidence and compared the Chinese experiment to the War Communism of the early years of Soviet Russia. By this he meant that it was a voluntarist scheme and doomed to inevitable failure. According to Khrushchev, everything that the Chinese were doing, including the people's communes, had been tried in Russia in his young days, so he felt himself to be an authority on the subject. So he made fun of Mao's political childishness and declared that the one country that could speak seriously of the transition to Communism was the USSR, not China. The Soviet Union possessed the material basis for this aim, while Mao was merely chasing phantoms in his backward country.

Khrushchev's public speeches were naturally less explicit, but adopted the same tone. In all his arguments for patience and respect for economic laws there were barbs directed at the originators of the Great Leap Forward. Since he expounded his outlook on the transition to Communism to audiences in the Soviet Union and the satellites in very simple terms, he ended up with unfortunate formulations that the Chinese found wounding. "It's not a bad thing," he said, "to support the theories of Marx with ham and butter. If your stomach is empty, it's sometimes hard to understand Marxism-Leninism. But if you have a nice apartment, good food, and good culture, you'll say, 'I'm in favor of Communism too.'" After this exhortation to the Czechs, who are very keen on ham, came his famous sally to the Hungarians—great goulash eaters—on the merits of "socialism with goulash." The recurrent theme was always the same: we must begin by ensuring better living standards and increasing productivity, and the rest, which you can call Communism if you like, will follow automatically.

The Chinese felt that they were the targets of all these remarks about empty stomachs, and not because they had any inferiority complex regarding the level of consumption in Eastern Europe. In their thinking, it is just those who are poorest and have been most exploited who hope most ardently for revolutionary changes and are filled with the purest class spirit, not the elites who have nice apartments. Scandalized, the Maoists replied to Khrushchev in 1959, anticipating the ninetieth anniversary of Lenin's birth, with a sermon on the class struggle and the dictatorship of the proletariat. In their pamphlet "Long Live Leninism," they used quotations from Lenin aimed against the reformists of the Second International to prove that Khrushchev's outlook was purely social-democratic—no small insult for a Soviet leader. Moreover, the quotations were not torn out of context, and Moscow could hardly deny that Lenin had indeed written in *The State and the Revolution* that the dictatorship of the proletariat is indispensable during the whole socialist phase in order to destroy the political and social remnants of capitalism.

The Chinese document was, however, much more suited to realities in their own country, where the Great Leap was causing a complete upheaval, than in the USSR, where the mere phrase "dictatorship of the proletariat" had become a synonym for the police repression of the Stalin period. For Soviet readers, the Chinese slogan of "politics in command" seemed to imply an increase in the power of political bosses by legalizing their freedom—already excessive—to act as they pleased. In the Leninist protestations of Peking, Russians heard an echo of their own past, not a proof that the Chinese were trying to avoid following the same path.

True, the institutions of the socialist countries did not in any case make it easy for a genuine debate to begin on the great options in the building of socialism. But the communications barrier between the Russians and the Chinese did still more to hide their deeper intentions, even at the level of public opinion. China and the USSR used the same language, the same formulations, but their citizens did not give the same meaning to the words and so both could only be shocked by what they read.

Paradoxically, therefore, on either side of the long frontier along the Amur River, the two peoples lined up unanimously in serried ranks, facing in opposite directions without any risk of internal division. China and the Soviet Union, as states, had every interest in standing shoulder to shoulder to confront the Western bloc; but insofar as they represented two social experiments, radically different and both claiming to be socialist, they were less and less inclined to tolerate each other. Socialism cannot, in fact, be fitted into a variety of types of socialism, each based on different values and principles. Since China refused to renounce her ideas, even after the ebbing of the first wave of the Great Leap, and the USSR stood firm on its own priorities, the dynamic of their evolution inexorably carried them further and further apart.

Nevertheless, neither Moscow nor Peking underestimated the historic gravity of the split in prospect. Unable to alter their internal decisions, they tried at least to synchronize their watches to act together on the international scene. In early 1960 they therefore agreed to call a conference of Communist and Workers' Parties of the whole world, in order to work out an anti-imperialist line acceptable to all. The meeting in Moscow, in November 1960, apparently produced this welcome result and the eighty-one parties adopted a unanimous resolution. But the reconciliation was only apparent, for the conference had not even been intended to tackle the problems at the root of the threat of a Sino-Soviet split. Moreover, even in reaching this vague doctrine of anti-imperialist policy, the Russians and the Chinese clashed with unprecedented sharpness in private sessions, in the presence of their dismayed foreign comrades. So everyone felt that the intensity of this argument could not be explained merely by the subject under discussion, and that—behind the disagreements on the importance of revolutionary wars or peaceful ways to socialism—the Russians and the Chinese held diametrically opposed views on every important problem. It was therefore vain to hope that they would interpret the "resolution of the conference of eighty-one parties," based as it was on ephemeral compromises, in the same fashion. Indeed, the two protagonists in the great controversy used it chiefly as a source of ammunition to accuse each other of betraying the spirit and the letter of this agreed doctrine.

In these venomous exchanges, the USSR was shown to be more vulnerable because it alone was taking part in the great game of world politics—China being excluded from the game by the West—and every setback that it underwent exposed it immediately to stinging criticisms from Peking. Thus, after his misfortunes during the Cuban crisis of October 1962,[53] Khrushchev found himself accused by China of both adventurism and capitulationism; and when, in 1963, he nevertheless decided to sign a treaty with the United States and Britain on the nonproliferation of nuclear weapons, Peking announced that he had broken all the rules of the Socialist bloc and could no longer ask his partners for any respect. In fact, Peking not only published its own twenty-five-point platform for the international working-class movement but began to encourage the formation of Marxist-Leninist groups within or on the fringe of its brother Parties. Since new bilateral discussions at Moscow led to nothing, Khrushchev reached the conclusion that only a world conference of Communist Parties could compel the Chinese to keep quiet or could, if necessary, excommunicate them. The chief ideologist of the Politburo, Mikhail Suslov, thereupon drew up a complete report on the Chinese deviation, to be presented first to the Central Committee of his Party in February 1964, and then to the proposed world conference.

This Soviet charge sheet against China clearly traced the origin of the Maoist "aberration" to "the orientation of the Great Leap Forward." According to the Soviet theoreticians, this "gross violation of the management principles of socialist economies" had plunged China into such difficulties that, in order to get out of them, she had ended by stirring up international adventures and hoping for nuclear war. Accused of "petty-bourgeois revolutionism," according to a famous formulation of Lenin's, the Chinese leaders were denounced by Suslov for their lack of steadiness, their tendency to rush from one extreme to the other, and their ideological incoherence deriving from their nonproletarian origins. He concluded: "Yes, comrades, it must be said frankly: the burden of the political views of the CCP is on many points a

[53] See K. S. Karol, *Guerrillas in Power* (New York: Hill and Wang, 1970), pp. 249 ff.

repetition of Trotskyism, which was rejected long ago by the international revolutionary movement." [54]

Suslov's formula was at once copied by other Soviet ideologists, who competed to analyze the mainly peasant and intellectual composition of the CCP, which was said to be the cause of "Chinese neo-Trotskyism." The tone of voice rose incessantly, and it was soon announced in Moscow that "never in the history of the working-class movement has a 'Left' deviation been as dangerous as this." [55] Next, the official journal of the CPSU, *Partiinaya Zhizn*, explained how such deviationists should be treated in a worldwide movement based on the Leninist principle that the minority should bow to the decisions of the majority: "The Party that finds itself isolated or put into a minority on an important question should conform to the view authorized by the majority, carry out a self-criticism, and revise its mistaken positions from top to bottom." [56] This was the only course still open to the Chinese if they wished to escape excommunication.

Mao's reply was forceful, but above all ironical and almost mocking. Making derisive use of the old Soviet habit of proceeding by ukase, he began by reminding them that the USSR has no right to call any international Communist conference or to summon anyone before this tribunal. Nor does any rule in the Communist movement provide, according to Mao, that a Party in a minority must allow its policy to be decided by others. He declared, on the contrary, that questions involving the principles of Marxism-Leninism cannot be decided by majority vote. "The day when you call together your splitting conference, you will put your feet into your grave."

But, while refusing to take part in a conference, the Chinese explained in a series of documents what they would have said there. The ninth of these, "On Khrushchev's Phony Communism and Its Historical Lessons for the World," [57] makes a very detailed

[54] Suslov's report, delivered at the Central Committee meeting of February 1964, was published in *Pravda* (April 4, 1964).

[55] See Leonid Ilyitchev in *Kommunist*, No. 11 (July 1964).

[56] See *Partiinaya Zhizn*, No. 11 (June 1964), and abridged version of this article in *Pravda* (June 3 and 4, 1964).

[57] Text in *People's Daily* (July 13, 1964), reprinted in *Peking Review*, No. 29 (July 17, 1964).

attack on the internal state of affairs in the USSR. According to this document—which was drawn up by Teng Hsiao-p'ing and edited by Mao, and from which the Cultural Revolution was to draw many quotations—a new bourgeoisie had assumed power in Moscow, usurping the rights of the proletariat and enforcing its own revisionist doctrines. This was possible only because the socialist revolution had not been pressed through to the end "in the spheres of politics, economics, ideology, and culture." Property owners, old and new, had succeeded in raising their heads and imposing their laws on the workers, who were exploited as under the old regime. The chief blame fell on Khrushchev, for whom "the working-class struggle for Communism is not a struggle for the total emancipation of that class and of all mankind, but a struggle for a plate of goulash. . . . In his heart there remains not the slightest trace of scientific Communism, but a society of stupid and frightful bourgeois. . . . He has reduced relationships between men to money relationships and stimulated individualism and egotism. . . . He has once again lowered manual work and given honor to privileges drawn from the appropriation of the fruits of the toil of others."

Replying to the Russians on the question of "the violation of the Leninist principle of material self-interest" in China, the document declares that the prolonged and massive recourse to material incentives in the USSR had encouraged the polarization of classes, had always worked to the benefit of a privileged minority, and had created the danger of a restoration of capitalism. At the end, the CCP launched "an alarm call to all socialist countries, including China, and to all Communist and Workers' Parties, including the CCP," so that they should rise up against this tragic restoration in Lenin's native land. This call was curious in its form, since it was addressed to its own author and was moreover accompanied by an urgent fifteen-point program whose content is equally surprising. For all the measures it proposed were related to the internal Chinese situation and bore witness to Mao's determination to launch a new battle in the class struggle in China. In fact, these fifteen points were the advance program for the Cultural Revolution, and they were already discussed from this viewpoint within the Chinese Communist Party. To the outside world, this document showed simply that China would not give up its

continuous revolution or its mode of development, and that no
international conference could blunt its determination. What
weight, indeed, could the verdict of a disorganized and powerless
Communist organism have, against the prestige of a reality such as
China?

Some Parties, among them the French Communist Party, did
not consider this question because of their loyalty to the USSR,
and also their aversion to whatever was to the left of them. But
others, especially in Asia, and beginning with the Communist
Party of North Vietnam, flatly refused Khrushchev's invitation.
Others again, which were scarcely to be suspected of leftism—
such as those of Italy, Rumania, and Poland [58]—saw with
apprehension that to formalize the split with China would be to
create a precedent, which the Soviet Union might use in efforts to
reorganize the Communist movement under its aegis. This was
not a prospect that they could cheerfully accept, even if Moscow
went on promising to respect their autonomy.

To resolve the dilemma, Palmiro Togliatti, one of the few
survivors of the leadership of the Comintern, dramatically revived
his formula of unity in diversity and pleaded that nothing
irreparable should be done. While siding with the USSR on the
essence of the matter, he urged tolerance of Chinese diversity as
an expression of the special conditions of that society. Let each
Party shape its socialism as best it could, without excommunicating others, and let everyone give priority to the anti-imperialist
struggle, the more so because the United States was intervening
with impunity in Asia and 1964 was a year of escalation in
Vietnam. Shortly before his death at Yalta, Togliatti embodied his
appeal in a memorandum to Khrushchev that is regarded as his
political testament.[59] Five years later, a similar appeal for unity
was contained in the testament of Ho Chi Minh, another
prestigious veteran of the Comintern and leader of a country
admired throughout the world for its resistance to the greatest of
the world's military powers, the United States. But even this
moving appeal went unheard; China and the USSR help the

[58] Later, the Scandinavian Communist Parties, that of Spain, and that of Britain
also showed their strong reluctance.

[59] Toglialli's memorandum was published in *Rinascitatti's memorandum was
published in Rinascita*, No. 39 (1964), and in *Le Monde* (September 4, 1964).

Vietnamese, but each on its own account, because they no longer consider themselves to be engaged in a common battle and do not belong to the same camp.

However, neither Mao—nor still less the USSR—was ever excommunicated by any world Communist conference. Khrushchev fell on October 15, 1964, two months to the day before the date he had fixed for the Moscow gathering. His successors did not manage to fulfill his plan until five years later, in June 1969. Meanwhile, the Cultural Revolution took place, and relations between the CCP and the Parties linked to the USSR were broken of their own accord.[60] But another event, in 1968, the invasion of Czechoslovakia by the armies of the USSR and its five allies in the Warsaw Pact, shook even the most loyal Communist Parties of the West. Their leaders agreed to attend the Moscow conference only on condition that they would not be made to approve of this normalization in Eastern Europe or of the break with China. So neither was mentioned in the final resolution, as if this silence could wipe out an awkward reality that had jolted the Communist movement. Most of the Communist Parties continue to talk about the Socialist bloc "with the strength of more than a billion men and women," pretending not to know that People's China, which provides two-thirds of this strength, denies that the bloc can be called Socialist and charges her former allies with crimes and betrayals.

CHAPTER TWO

Origins of
the Cultural Revolution

The Inevitability of Contradictions
within the Party

Ever since Mao assumed the chairmanship in 1935, the Chinese
Communist Party had faithfully observed this rule: the internal
discussions that led to the working out of a new political line
were, at the end of the process, brought to public knowledge. Far
from hiding the divergences that had emerged in these discussions, the CCP took them completely for granted and explained,
often in a dramatic tone, that they reflected in the sphere of the
Party the real and inevitable contradictions of a society divided
into classes. Thus it declined to present itself as monolithic,
infallible, and always firmly unanimous—a rare attitude among
Communists at the time.

Moreover, the violence of the language to be found in reports of
these debates indicated such sharp disagreements that one might
have expected them to lead, time after time, to changes in the
leadership. Nothing like this happened. Indeed, while the opposing views were frankly publicized, the names of those who had
upheld one or another policy were never mentioned. The Maoists
seemed to believe that opinions were expressed *through* the
protagonists in the drama, because these opinions existed and had

to come out; hence those who became the spokesmen could not be held to blame, still less punished. The point was not to denounce them, but to show clearly how the correct line had won out amid the struggle against mistaken ideas. The detailed exposition of deviations that had been overcome served an essentially didactic purpose, not that of settling accounts among rival groups.

Innumerable illustrations of this method can be found in the resolutions of the Central Committee between 1935 and 1965. There were disagreements over coming to terms with the Kuomintang during the anti-Japanese war; over land reform— should it be more or less radical?—in the final phase of the civil war; over the pace of nationalism when Communist power reached the big cities; and, sharpest of all, over the pace and methods of collectivization of the land in 1955. Again, in 1959, it was said that rightists considered the Great Leap Forward and the communes to be premature, while leftists underestimated the obstacles in the path of carrying out the general line. Finally, in 1962, at a crucial Central Committee meeting, it was found necessary to denounce the errors of a "right wing" that had made too many concessions to free enterprise in the countryside during the difficult years (1959–61) and to recall the essentials of the class struggle and the "different" pattern of development.

No one was unaware that Chinese policy was worked out, as Mao put it, "not peacefully, but through discussions and in conflicts." He even declared, "If there were no contradictions, and political struggles to overcome contradictions, in the Party, the Party's life would come to an end." On the other hand, he thought that any personification of the discussions would be harmful. As early as Yenan he had explained, "We must put the emphasis, not on the personality of certain comrades, but, analyzing the circumstances in which their mistakes were made, on the social, historical, and ideological background . . . in order to clarify ideas and unite our comrades." [1] This was the only way to "cure the sickness and save the man" and to ensure the free circulation of ideas among the cadres.

[1] Both quotations are from Mao Tse-tung, "Our Study and the Current Situation" (April 12, 1944), *Selected Works*, Vol. III (Peking: Foreign Languages Publishing House, 1965), pp. 163–78.

But, of course, the method could be employed only on two conditions: (a) the divergences on each issue must not harden into lasting tendencies, into real factions that might organize themselves to secure the victory of their viewpoint in the future; (b) leaders whose proposals had been rejected must give complete support to the view of the majority—or of Mao, the supreme arbiter—and it was out of the question for them to carry their disagreement to the public arena. Only through the observance of these rules of discipline and discretion could the leaders of the CCP benefit from the undeniable privilege of free discussion among themselves.

Now, at the time of the Cultural Revolution in 1966, Mao decided that all Communists, whatever their merits, should submit to a complete scrutiny, not in their own organization but in front of the people. This was indeed dramatic, and it was still more dangerous because of the risk that the traditional solidarity of Communists might recoil violently upon them. For why had they covered up, for such a long time, for comrades with mistaken ideas? Why had they hidden from the masses a number of facts about the "struggle between two lines" within their ranks? Had they not all, implicitly, been accomplices of the upholders of the "bourgeois path" whom they had not publicly denounced in their time?

These questions, and many others, were to arise inevitably from this sudden change of method. But Mao, and a good part of his team, considered that not to upset things involved a far graver risk: the risk of seeing China develop in the same fashion as the USSR.

Mao's Method

At the root of Mao's method was his absence of sectarianism, his tolerance, and his rejection of repression as alien to the aims and means of the revolution. All experts, even the least suspect of being Maoists, agree on this, and they are amply supported both by witnesses and by quotations from the Chairman. This champion of the most radical breaks with the past has constantly repeated in his writings: "Above all, we must not cut off heads, for they merely grow again like cabbages." [2] In all circumstances, he urged his followers to allow an opponent to express himself, to convince him calmly, and thus to win back the great majority of those who had simply been in error.

The Chinese method was suited to Mao's position. It was feasible only because of his status in the Party—above the warring sides—his undisputed prestige, and also the homogeneity and the exceptionally solid links of solidarity uniting his team. But, in a sense, the contrary was equally true. The CCP method contributed vastly to increasing Mao's prestige and welding the leading group together.

Edgar Snow, who knew Mao from the old days in Yenan, gave this description of him:

> His method of bossing the Party was not overt but indirect and subtle. He spent hours conferring with various committee members, sounding out their views and reconciling them with his own. After he had talked to each of them individually, and was sure of a consensus, he then stated his own opinion as a synthesis. He certainly believed in his own star and destiny to rule. But he was relaxed, natural and unaffected in his personal relationships. He built confidence and trust by his loyalty to those who were loyal to him. He was also magnanimous to those who disagreed with him. Those who fought against him and his ideas would in time lose influence, but they were not purged or physically destroyed on the scale of Stalin's personal rivals.[3]

Very fond of discussions, Mao could always find a subject of conversation, but he was never peremptory or pompous with the people he was talking to. He said to Snow one day, "In the great river of human knowledge many things are relative, and no one can grasp all truths." While keeping calm during discussions to the point of appearing indifferent, he was nevertheless generally very certain of his point of view, especially when basic problems were involved.

"Your cave has grown a lot," Snow remarked when he met Mao a quarter of a century later at his residence in the Imperial City,

[2] Mao Tse-tung, "On the Ten Great Relationships" (quoted above, p. 65).

[3] Edgar Snow, *Journey to the Beginning* (New York: Random House, 1957), p. 167.

in the heart of Peking.[4] But he felt that Mao had not changed. He was still the leader who stood above the battle, seeking to work out the right political line, confident of convincing his comrades in debate, and therefore feeling no need for authoritative measures to impose his point of view. Besides, he was sufficiently detached from the machinery of government to remain the guide, the ideological source of inspiration, and the lucid critic.

To sum up, through these long years of battles Mao played a role comparable to that of Lenin among the Bolsheviks, but he was able to adopt a much less interventionist style because he could rely on a numerous and effective team, proved in years of joint work.

There is also plenty of evidence about the specific characteristics of what is called abroad "the Long March generation of Communists." China experts have noted a certain homogeneity in the recruitment of the Maoist team, initially composed of young intellectuals of peasant or petty-bourgeois background, politically awakened by the confused nationalist stirrings of post-imperial China, then attracted by the rigorous radicalism of Russian Bolshevism. Some of these men became Communists while studying in Europe—these include Chou En-lai, Ch'en Yi, and Chu Teh; some got their political training in Sun Yat-sen's short-lived republic in Canton, others again in Moscow; but almost all of them completed their education with arms in their hands, first as allies of the Kuomintang, and after 1927 at Mao's side in the liberated zones of Kiangsi. It has been said that the Long March brought this education of Communist China's political cadres to perfection, and that no other test could have generated such feelings of solidarity and comradeship. This, indeed, seems to be the reason why they apparently offered no chances to anyone who might have tried to divide them, either before the 1949 victory or during the great controversy with the USSR in the late 1950's. No other Communist Party has ever managed to wage such a violent argument against the Russians without undergoing internal splits. In this respect, too, the CCP is unique.

The stability of the Maoist team has thus become proverbial.

[4] See Edgar Snow, *The Other Side of the River* (New York: Random House, 1961).

For the first seventeen years of its existence, the People's Republic of China was in practice governed by the same men. Only one of the historic leaders, Kao Kang, fell by the wayside, in 1954. The news of his dismissal and his suicide was made public only a year later, but the statement, virulent though it was, gave no information about the nature of his deviation.[5] The chief causes for reproach were his suicide, which made it impossible to win him back, and the fact that he had never explained to his comrades the reasons for his disagreement. The fall of Kao Kang, in any case, led to no other changes at the top level, and some aspects of this episode are still mysterious.[6] Later, in 1959, it was possible to note that the working out of the new line had been underlined by an important change in the command of the army, with Lin Piao replacing Marshal P'eng Teh-huai. But no personal attacks were made against the former minister of defense, and—on the evidence of friends of mine—the appointment of Lin Piao to this post was made public only in 1962, and then in an indirect manner, with the press giving him the title of minister as if he had always held it. All the evidence shows that a demoted leader was handled in China in such a way as to leave him the possibility of an honorable return to posts of high responsibility. Thus the Long March generation showed in power, as in opposition, that it knew how to settle its differences in a highly civilized manner, in contrast to what went on in other Communist countries, and seemed destined to preserve its unity to the end of the road.

Indeed, the most worrying problem in the middle 1960's appeared to be that of the succession. Was not the long maintenance of the same governing team hindering the advance of new cadres? And how could one expect that the next

[5] Kao Kang, born in 1902, founder of the Red base in Shensi to which Mao led his troops after the Long March, and one of the principal leaders in the Yenan period, was given responsibility for Manchuria in 1946 and became chairman of the State Planning Commission in 1952. He was relieved of his duties in 1954—together with his "accomplice," Jao Shu-shih—and committed suicide. The news was made public in April 1955.

[6] During his time in the northeast and later at the State Planning Commission, Kao Kang had many dealings with the Russians, and it is generally thought that he supported their methods of development. This theory is advanced, especially, by Franz Schurmann in *Ideology and Organization in Communist China* (Berkeley, California: University of California Press, 1966).

generation would be of the same caliber as these veterans shaped in unparalleled political battles? During my stay in China in 1965, this problem of generations often came up in private conversations. A year before that, I was told, Mao had made a speech at a Congress of Communist Youth, and although the text was not published, a few quotations came out here and there that showed his great concern over the political quality of the generation of his heirs. It could not have been foreseen then that he would find in the youth the revolutionary dynamism that answered his prayers, and would hail it as an example to the old guard itself. The spark that touched off the gunpowder of the Cultural Revolution came from the students. And at first it was believed that they were merely trying to follow in the path of their elders, who had entered the struggle through the student movement of May 1919.[7]

Mao All-Powerful? Mao in the Minority? Mao Alone?

"All those who have tried to repress the student movement in China have ended up badly." This warning of Mao's to leaders in the Party machine and the state, during the first phase of the explosion, summed up a whole doctrine, which did not merely concern students. In fact, this explosion had been prepared in a certain political and moral atmosphere that had existed for some time. In demanding that the youth should be allowed elbow room, Mao was expounding in public what he had already said in private meetings of the Central Committee, namely, that the Party could not escape the revisionist infection—which had already reached its ranks—and should, in its own interests, welcome rebellion in good time and profit from it instead of trying to repress it; for one could be sure that, sooner or later, it would break out again and could end by sweeping the Party away. It is also certain that Mao himself saw to it that the Party did not start a process of repression and that none of its members evaded salutary criticism. But he did not indicate to the masses who represented the

[7] On May 4, 1919, the students of Peking invaded the Legation Quarter to protest against the Treaty of Versailles, launching a nationwide movement in which almost all the founders of the CCP took part.

"healthy wing" of the Party and who should be got rid of, any more than he opened up the records of old discussions in his general staff. Lin Piao summed up Mao's philosophy in a quotation, widely circulated in 1966 and 1967, declaring with both pride and humility that all Communists "should regard themselves simultaneously as a particle of revolutionary force and as a target of the revolution." [8]

A striking formula, unthinkable in the mouth of a leader of any ordinary socialist country. But in China it did not jar and was wholly consistent with the theory and even the practice of Maoism. Not to mention the rectification campaign in Yenan, which had been a kind of miniature Cultural Revolution, Mao's record abundantly showed this conviction that relations between rulers and ruled were in danger of becoming too oppressive, and that the balance between the Party and the masses should be upset from time to time, lest the system should degenerate and the revolution go back to its starting point. We need only read his essay on contradictions, or the "Sixty Points on Methods of Work," to grasp the sources of the general inspiration of the Cultural Revolution. Moreover, the documents of this period, beginning with the Central Committee's solemn resolution of August 1966, speak for themselves. They show that Mao, now an old man, had decided to stir up this agitation in society, believing, not without reason, that his presence as an arbiter would ease its development and, in case of need, limit the damage. We shall see later that he could step on the brake as well as the accelerator, as he did at the end of 1967, to save as much as possible from this unprecedented and in many respects dangerous experiment.

Any other explanation of Mao's motives and conduct seems to me fallacious. The Red Guards, through their distrust of all other leaders, created the image of a Mao who stood alone, surrounded by bureaucrats who were influenced by the Soviet line or were simply traitors. Western writers have claimed that Mao had virtually lost power since 1959 and had been reduced to a mere figurehead while his "revisionist" rivals held a majority in the Central Committee, until the student revolt gave him an unex-

[8] This quotation is found in a great many documents in late 1966 and 1967. See *Peking Review* and the New China News Agency's *New China Notebooks*.

pected opportunity to isolate them and regain the upper hand. But these legends are devoid of factual proof. Even the Red Guard posters never hinted at Mao's being deprived of power or put in a minority. The sole foundation for the myth is Mao's resignation as Chairman of the Republic in April 1959; but irrefutable documents show that he had been asking his comrades to relieve him of this honorific post since 1957, before the launching of the Great Leap Forward, not in order to withdraw from activity but to intervene more actively in political life. Nor has he cared to resume the Chairmanship since Liu Shao-ch'i's deposition during the Cultural Revolution, and it is still vacant.

Similar unfounded interpretations have been made of the Central Committee sessions of 1959 and 1962. Allegedly, Mao was rescued by Liu Shao-ch'i and Chou En-lai, who seized the chance to impose their own policy, namely, the gradual reestablishment of the standards of the Soviet development model. But is it true that, in the difficult years that followed the Great Leap, China reverted to Soviet theories of growth and abandoned the distinctive features of her own model? The record shows just the opposite. In the excitement of the 1950's, when the Chinese attacked every possible task at the same time, they still gave the impression of being obsessed by "productionism." Later, in the phase of consolidation (when Mao was supposedly in a minority), they dotted the i's so emphatically that it is impossible to ignore the priority they gave to social changes and their violation of the entire logic of the Soviet pattern. It was at this time, too, that their polemics against the USSR ceased to concentrate on anti-imperialist strategy and frankly raised the taboo questions of original sin in the Soviet record. It was also in 1963, on the eve of the break with the USSR, that the Chinese people were urged to take Lei Feng, the complete antithesis of Stakhanovite man, as a model. For this ex-soldier, bursting with virtues and fine sentiments, concern for production was far less important than helping his comrades and thereby creating egalitarian and brotherly relationships. During these years, too, cadres began to take part in manual work; anti-hierarchical slogans were launched to support the "campaign of socialist education"; and the criticism of the sacrosanct teaching system, which prepared the ground for the Cultural Revolution, was initiated.

Other detailed facts show that, during the period when Mao was allegedly powerless, the "majority" took international decisions that followed his line and not their own. In fact, no foreign analyst has ever questioned that the documents on the controversy with the USSR and the break with that country faithfully reflected Mao's ideas. We also know from Soviet accounts that on February 10, 1965, Mao, surrounded by the whole of his directing team, refused the offer of an ideological truce with the USSR and so informed Kosygin, who had come to Peking for the purpose. And we know from Japanese Communist sources that in March 1966 it was Mao who settled the thorny question of joint aid to North Vietnam, and his followers implemented his decision without flinching. All these facts rest on known dates and documents whose authenticity has never been questioned.

But the logical pit into which all these theories fall is most manifest when we examine Mao's conduct during the Cultural Revolution. A "humiliated" leader, when he at last gets the chance to take his revenge, hastens to hold up to popular execration the names of those who had scorned him. But when Mao mentioned the names of his chief "enemies," Liu Shao-ch'i and Teng Hsiao-p'ing, at the conference of October 1966, it was to ask that all the faults of the general staff not be laid at their door. We know of no words of his attacking those who had allegedly supplanted him, while many of his speeches pleaded, as always, for tolerance and stressed that the reshaping of institutions then under way should not necessarily imply the dismissal of directing cadres (still less of those who implemented policy). To be sure, he said that power was at stake—but not his own power, which no one had ever challenged. It was a question of the abusive power of institutions, which had to be restored to the masses as far as possible. His slogan "Open Fire on Headquarters" has a meaning that goes far beyond the commonplace idea of revenge; it was not a matter of recovering a lost personal power, but of launching a struggle against the "dark side" inherent in everyone. The aim of the struggle was a fundamental cleanup of the institutional framework, not the elimination of leaders who had become too powerful.

In my chapters on the Cultural Revolution, I shall try to analyze the degree of success achieved by Mao's ambitious scheme. But let us first dismiss the superficial theories that in fact obscure the origin and scope of this great movement. And among such theories I include those of Chinese propaganda, which throws the spotlight on the "treason" of Liu, cast as Mao's chief adversary.

The Charge Sheet against Liu Shao-ch'i

"Traitor, renegade, and strikebreaker"—when they speak of Liu Shao-ch'i today, the Chinese drop their habitual calm. Their aggressive tone is all the more surprising in that they charge the man with too many sins, mostly contradictory and often without proof. He is said to have been the instigator of all deviations, both Right and Left, and his strategy was to stay in ambush in the Party leadership waiting for Mao's death, in order to seize power as Khrushchev did in the USSR. But if this was his game, he ought to have been as discreet as possible instead of—as the accusation goes—openly opposing all the Chairman's plans for forty-five years, from the miners' strike in Anyuan in 1922 until his overthrow by the wrathful masses in 1967.

But visitors, as they listen to this anathema, grasp that Liu Shao-ch'i is nothing more than the dialectical antithesis of Mao's line—a disembodied negative symbol. Thanks to the didactic value of displacement, the real man has been overshadowed by the policy that must be repudiated. What he actually did in the past no longer matters, any more than his present fate. He has been merged with an idea; he is the image of the mistakes made by the revolution, of the dangers that surround it, of the deviations that it must avoid. No one dreams of demanding his punishment by human justice, because no court can root out false ideas by giving its verdict. To eliminate them once and for all, everyone must "take power in his head," to cite the splendid exhortation of the Cultural Revolution.

In the China of 1965, Liu basked in a minor personality cult, infinitely more discreet than Mao's but closely linked to it. Born in the same district of Hunan Province, in the same type of well-to-do peasant family, five years younger and educated in the same high school at Changsha, he could truthfully be depicted as one of the Chairman's oldest and closest comrades. In Changsha, in the little house where Mao and his first wife, Yang K'ai-hui, had lived in the 1920's, photos of the young Liu were prominently displayed as if he had been part of the family. In Yenan I was shown the neighboring caves that the Chairman and the vice-chairman had occupied in the years of the rectification campaign before the Seventh Party Congress in 1945.[9] Experts abroad, too, considered that the personalities of Mao and Liu were complementary, and that their Hunanese solidarity made understanding between them still easier.

Liu was said to have supplied Mao with the practical administrative talent in which the latter was a little wanting, being so continually preoccupied with working out great ideas and the right political line. The vice-chairman of the CCP had learned the art of organization in the best of schools—in the University of Toilers of the East, in Lenin's Moscow in 1921, and later in underground activity in the heart of the great Chinese working-class centers.[10] Mao had summoned him to Yenan in 1937 because he needed men of this type to take charge of the Party machine, still too much influenced by the dogmatic methods of the former leaders. Edgar Snow's first wife, Nym Wales, met Liu in the Red "capital" at the end of 1937. She found him rather colorless, very reserved in character, admitting to a vague title as a specialist in questions of work. Certainly he had neither the charm of Chou En-lai, nor Chu Teh's legendary fame as a "Red Napoleon," nor P'eng Teh-huai's forthrightness, nor the reputation of being Mao's alter ego like the shy and smiling Lin Piao. Called from the outer world to join this Long March team, he was a sort of gray eminence in the sensitive sphere of the Party machine.

In 1939 Liu collected his lectures on the Party in a little book called *How to Be a Good Communist*.[11] During the Cultural

[9] See my *China: The Other Communism* (New York: Hill and Wang, 1967) for more details.

[10] Liu was also the organizer of the great student demonstration in Peking in December 1935. It was he, too, who secured Edgar Snow's pass to travel to meet Mao in Pao An in 1936.

[11] In Chinese it is called *On the Perfecting of a Communist*, but in foreign-language editions it is still *How to Be a Good Communist* (Peking, 1964). The 1941 edition also includes a supplementary essay, "On the Party," of which some extracts were reprinted. See Stuart R. Schram, "The Party in Chinese Communist Ideology," *China Quarterly*, No. 38 (1969).

Revolution, many quotations from it were used to show that, ever since that time, he had sought to make Communists into "docile instruments" by demanding blind obedience to orders from higher bodies, however crazy these might be: "Subordinates must obey their superiors absolutely; superiors must be obeyed even if they are wrong." Moreover, he regarded Communists as a vanguard imbued with immutable truth, for he said: "The Party must struggle against backward ideas and the backward state of the masses." Finally, as a third "absurdity," he declared: "In our Party, the policy is to put the stress on unity, on the maintenance of good relationships, and on joining together. They [the leaders] must watch over the members like parents."

To these quotations, the Red Guards opposed Mao's words on the right to rebel, even virtually on the right of the rank and file to free will ("No question involving the principles of Marxism-Leninism can be decided by majority vote" [12]), and thus deduced a fundamental and long-standing divergence between the two leaders. Foreign experts also recognized, although with some reservations, that Liu's ideas on the role and organization of the Party had always been far more rigid and traditional than Mao's. Despite this, when taken as a whole Liu's book cannot be interpreted in such a one-sided way. Its tone is not alien to the Yenan spirit. One need only note that Liu admitted that the Party and its leaders could make mistakes. Outside China, no Communist dared to say that in 1939. Then, like Mao, Liu observed that the very concepts of democracy and centralism are contradictory and that, to make an organization work on the basis of democratic centralism, one must employ a light touch and avoid authoritarian tendencies from the top. When he said that all superior orders, even if mistaken, must be carried out, his purpose was to show that a Communist should never cut himself off from the proletarian collective body, outside which he is powerless; while he stays in it he can hope to put the situation right, as Liu proved by several examples. What actually emerges from all this is that Liu was a "man of the Church" and that his firm belief was: "There is

[12] We have seen that this dictum of Mao figured in his reply to the Russians regarding the world conference of Communist Parties and the attempt to put the Chinese in a minority and by this means force them to change their policy.

no health outside the Party." But this "Church" was nevertheless strongly marked by the Yenan atmosphere.

Liu had never been a rebel. He had climbed all the steps on the Party ladder, without mishaps, according to the rules of internal promotion. Mao, on the other hand, knew well from personal experience that it was sometimes necessary to disobey one's superiors in order to save the hopes of the revolution, and that one could even become Party Chairman by doing so. He found what he needed, however, in this collaboration with Liu, whose promotion he ensured at Yenan. The rules of democratic central-ism, so brilliantly defended by Liu, would easily have allowed Mao, had he wished, to alter his comrade's manuscript or even forbid its publication. After all, he was number one in the Party, while in the Yenan period Liu was not even a member of the Politburo or the Secretariat. Why, then, did he put such trust in this machine man and tacitly approve his emphasis on discipline? Setting aside their affinity as fellow Hunanese (there were many others in Yenan), we must conclude that in Mao's eyes the Party could have no other structure than that described by Liu. He regarded democratic centralism as Churchill regarded democracy —the worst possible system except for all the others. Besides, the Party "walked on two legs"; alongside its own machine, Mao based his activity on the great force that the People's Army represented, both as a secular arm and as a mass movement solidly rooted in the population. Finally, we should bear in mind that the CCP, despite its considerable autonomy, belonged to the Comin-tern, and that Liu's theoretical statement reached the limits of permissible deviation. It follows that Liu-ism, as it is now called, was a legitimate component of the Yenan movement and not a foreign body.

Liu, at all events, moved on to further distinctions. He was put in charge of the northern liberated areas, and his success earned him a public tribute at the Seventh Party Congress in 1945, where he was chosen to make the second report after Mao.[13] And his report caused some stir. He was the first to declare that the CCP

[13] The tribute to Liu for his underground activities, contained in the resolution of April 20, 1945, on "Certain Questions of Our Party History," appeared in the first edition of Mao's *Selected Works*, Vol. IV, but not in the present edition.

was guided by the thought of Mao; that the Chairman had the great merit of integrating the universal truths of Marxism with the practice of the Chinese revolution; and, on top of this, that, thanks to Mao, "the CCP is not only the pioneer but also the leader and ideological guide of the anti-imperialist and anticolonial revolutions of Africa and Asia." [14] In short, Liu was the founder of the cult of Mao in China, and also the first to claim a worldwide role for the CCP.

The two statements were linked in Liu's mind because he never separated Mao from the Party, seeing their total identification as a source of strength for both. This point too was disputed in the Cultural Revolution, when Mao's thought was no longer regarded as the monopoly of a specific institution. These words of Liu's were then quoted against him: "In our Party there are no special privileges for individuals, and we tolerate no leadership that is not exercised in the name of the organization. Comrade Mao is the leader of the whole Party, but he too obeys the Party. . . . We are all obedient to the Party, to its Central Committee, to its truth, and not to individuals. . . . Marx, Lenin, and Mao Tse-tung did their work well and stood for truth. It is for this reason that we should obey them." [15] But in the context of the 1940's, when no one yet dreamed of revolutionary voices from the masses outside the Party, what strikes one is that Liu accorded the right to be obeyed only to Marx, Lenin, and Mao, leaving out the leader to whom Communists of the whole world gave their first obedience at that time—Joseph Stalin. Was this mere forgetfulness, or a discreet way of stressing that Mao, as the founder of Asian Marxism, was the best guide to revolutions in what we now call the Third World?

We can be sure, at all events, that Mao found less to worry him in Liu's writings than did the Soviet comrades. On all the evidence, they had little liking for the austere and unbending number two of the CCP. From 1949 the publication of certain articles by Liu in the Cominform journal *For a Lasting Peace, for a People's Democracy*, aroused very grave objections in Moscow. The conviction grew by degrees in "well-informed" Eastern

[14] See Stuart R. Schram, *Mao Tse-tung* (London: Penguin, 1966).
[15] See Schram, "The Party in Chinese Communist Ideology," *China Quarterly*.

European circles that Liu was a sort of whole-hogging Maoist with strong anti-Soviet leanings. His antipathy to Khrushchev was notorious and was easily explained by the contrast between the two men, the gravity of the one jarring with the informality of the other. In any case, it was the Russians who gave Liu the nickname "the Red monk" (though this monk had been married five times) and persisted in describing him as a man with whom one could not come to terms, who carried Mao's line to the extremes of aberration. By their account, when Mao wanted an understanding with the USSR he sent the flexible Chou En-lai; when he wanted to show himself intransigent, he entrusted negotiations to Liu.

What cannot be seriously maintained, we can be positive, is that Liu was opposed to the personality cult—a proposition dear to the Russians at the present time—and that Mao was particularly angered by this (doubtless through vanity). It is equally frivolous to suggest that this "pure Leninist" rose in revolt against Mao's line at the time of the Great Leap, and to seek evidence in speeches made well before that policy was launched. Not only did Liu take part in drawing up the famous Sixty Points that were the charter of the Great Leap, but he also gave the main exposition of them at the second session of the Eighth Party Congress in May 1958.[16] So it is useless to make a selective search among his writings and speeches with the aim of turning him into an "anti-Mao," more concerned with collective leadership and allegiance to the USSR than with loyalty to his own Party. Nor is it credible that Mao, knowing his ideas, should have trusted him to direct the audacious policy of the Great Leap—still less to conduct the delicate negotiations with the USSR in 1960 (during the conference of the eighty-one Communist Parties in Moscow) and in 1963 (through his colleague Teng Hsiao-p'ing) at the time of the last bilateral meeting between the two Parties.

To sum up, a reading of Liu's works shows him as a Party man first and foremost, not as an opponent of Mao's authority and, above all, not as an admirer of Khrushchev's Russia. One could even argue that he was, because of his character and his convictions, the most severe in condemning the relaxation of

---

[16] See *Documents and Resolutions of the Eighth Congress of the CCP* (Peking: Foreign Languages Publishing House, 1959).

discipline in the Soviet Union and the most flatly opposed to its "liberal reforms." Thus his conflict with Mao could not have arisen from his preference for the Soviet model. On the contrary, it must be explained within the framework of the specifically Chinese model, worked out with his collaboration at the time of the Great Leap. If Liu became anti-Mao, it was solely because he disagreed with the Chairman about the methods required to make this policy a success. But this disagreement emerged only in the course of the 1960's, during episodes that can be understood only in the context of the "Chinese road to socialism."

The Great Struggle in the Countryside, 1962–6

Two of these episodes were widely publicized in China: the "four cleanups" campaign and the "great struggle in the intellectual sector." On the first, we have a great deal of material, at least regarding the aims of its initiators, and we can grasp its origins without too much difficulty.

The implementation of the Chinese watchword "centralized direction and delegated management" implied from the outset that two conditions had to be fulfilled. The Party had to centralize the new plans and inspire the rank-and-file units, and the latter had to run their own affairs effectively. The relationship was dialectical, since the Party drew its own inspiration from the experiences of the masses of workers, who represented the vital social agent in the transformation of society. Could this practice, tested in the Red bases of the Yenan period, be simply extended to the whole country and to 700 million people when the Party again took up its mass line during the Great Leap? In fact, two elements had changed, and one of these was the Party. In 1947, two years before victory, the CCP could be justifiably proud of the size of its membership. It was the largest in any country where Communists were still in opposition, and its 3 million members could not be suspected of joining out of careerism, for they ran a great risk of ending up as their comrades had in Shanghai in 1927. So the Party then consisted of a devoted and well-knit vanguard, remarkably numerous for a party that was not in power (the

Russian Bolsheviks had only about 20,000 members in 1917), and full confidence could be felt in its potentialities. But in 1958, at the time of the Great Leap, the Party had 20 million members, all of whom could not be of the same caliber and some of whom might abuse their power.

Liu said that he saw nothing wrong with people joining the Party to become officials. In his view, there were advantages for both sides in this new type of contract: for the man of ambition in search of promotion, and equally for the Party. In the cities especially, thanks to these recruits, it could install an administration that was effective and well under control, capable of organizing the population and keeping in constant touch with its problems. But the essential China was the 550 million peasants, making up 80 percent of the population, and there—considering the thin spread of its members, the relative autonomy of the communes, and the often considerable distances—the Party would meet with greater difficulties in ensuring the good conduct and efficiency of its cadres.

So, when the first review was made after the Great Leap and the three "difficult years," all the leaders concentrated their attention on the situation in the countryside. Mao spoke about it in January 1962 at an enlarged Central Committee conference and, paradoxically, he insisted on the need to increase democracy at the grass roots: "In our country, if we do not completely extend the system of democracy among the people and in the Party, we cannot have a true proletarian centralism either. Without a very high level of democracy there cannot be a high level of centralism, and without the latter we cannot create a socialist economy." [17] The paradox was only apparent; in Mao's eyes, the sole effective control was from below. He did not believe that a purge could be advantageously carried out if it started from the Party center. In September 1962 he said loud and clear: "Do not forget the class struggle." In other words, it was necessary to revive the fighting spirit of the poor peasants and stimulate their desire to rebel against bad managers. This did not mean reverting strictly to the Yenan methods, but finding new techniques adapted to the

[17] See *Documents of the CCP Central Committee, September 1955 to April 1969* (Hong Kong: Union Research Institute, 1971), p. 202.

situation. Hence the idea of "associations of poor peasants and of the lower strata of middle peasants."

As for the general situation, the Central Committee showed itself to be anything but optimistic. "In certain communes the former landlords and rich peasants have succeeded in corrupting the cadres by various methods, and have in fact usurped the leadership by penetrating even its highest bodies. They have restored the feudal laws of clans and are using religion to fool the masses," we read in a resolution addressed to all communes. More, this trend toward restoration was described as almost natural; it was explained both by the grip of "old ideas" on many minds and by the ineffectiveness, or even the complicity through weakness, of a great number of lower-level cadres. The poverty caused by natural disasters and the need to encourage at all costs the most productive elements—not necessarily the most devoted in the political sense—had unleashed the "spontaneous tendencies toward capitalism in the countryside." We can understand, therefore, that the Party shared Mao's view and wished to call a halt to "peaceful coexistence in the countryside," and to reactivate the class struggle in favor of the poor and "semi-poor" peasants by giving them the necessary political weapons for this new battle. The growth of democracy in each brigade, it considered, could serve only the traditionally dispossessed, for they obviously had the greatest grievances against the status quo, and the greatest social ambitions. If things had not gone well hitherto, and had even worsened in some communes, the reason was inadequate contact between the cadres and the masses for lack of an independent organization of poor peasants. It was on the basis of these ideas that a new crusade was launched in rural China.

In May 1963 Mao personally drew up the ten-point directive on the "four cleanups" campaign.[18] The preamble to this document is to be found in his works in the form of an essay, "Where Do Correct Ideas Come From?"[19] All his polemical verve was

[18] "Decision of the Central Committee on Certain Problems of Work in Rural Areas," May 20, 1963, published in *Documents of the CCP*, p. 735.

[19] Mao Tse-tung, "Where Do Correct Ideas Come From?" (May 1963), *Four Essays on Philosophy* (Peking: Foreign Languages Publishing House, 1966), pp. 134–6.

mustered against those who make decisions at the top and are incapable even of explaining how they reached these decisions, as if their ideas "came down to them from heaven." A little further on, in a part of the essay that was not immediately published, Mao quoted a poor peasant of Hunan Province as saying that men of his social class, when they were not organized, were like scattered pearls and lost their value. They must therefore organize and ensure their control over management as a whole, but must avoid setting up a parallel structure to that of the Party, with its own paid functionaries. Instead of taking the place of the existing managers, the masses must obtain full information, check on everything, and take part in everything, even in the private meetings, conferences, and committees of the officials. Thus they could clean up the "four corruptions" that had crept into the account books, the warehouses, the reports to the state, and the allocation of work points.[20] The aim was to eliminate these four "unhealthy" points, but by the action of the masses themselves and not by coercion from above.

In general, only a few "guilty" cadres were to be replaced, and the weapon of criticism was to be used not to fight all the managers but to enlighten their thinking and restore their links with the community. Mao's instructions were as imaginative as they were definite: "Go out to the fields with light equipment. . . . Let the masses wash the hands of the cadres who have got dirty and give them a warm bath. . . . Make all the secretaries of Party committees join in productive work. . . . Clean with a fresh breeze and a soft rain." This socialist education was designed to revive the class spirit of the poor peasants and their allies, who were by their nature the best social agents of the revolution. They must be allowed to speak up; and, for a start, they must remind younger people of their "family tree" as exploited toilers and of the sufferings endured under the old regime. Fifteen years after the founding of the People's Republic, the methods of Yenan were thus honored again, including the famous bitter speeches, which were considered particularly revolutionary because they told the story of those who had acquired the worst grievances under the old order.

[20] In official language, the four spheres to be "cleaned up" were accounting, inventories of stocks, utilization of public property, and registration of work points.

But how could the former poor peasants be distinguished now from other groups? All sorts of people were to be found among the "newly rich," including the poorest of yesterday. In the new proletarian associations, who should be admitted and who should be excluded? As if these problems were not complicated enough, others arose from the material progress of the brigades. Was it not obvious that those who earned most were also those who contributed most to the enrichment of the community? Was it not better to depend on the middle peasants than on the poor, if the former were the most effective in the realm of production?

The center worked overtime to deal with this avalanche of questions. The ten-point directive of May 1963 was followed in September by "ten corrected points," a year later by the "revised version of the ten corrected points," and finally in January 1965 by "twenty-three points on socialist education in the rural areas." The documents were subjected to much discussion, and each seems to have come from a different hand—the first from Mao, the second from Teng Hsiao-p'ing, the third from Liu. The last, again written by Mao, is said to have been the origin of his break with Liu.

The two 1963 documents are generally regarded as complementary. They highlight for us the astonishing complexity of this Chinese peasant universe, equally striking because of its material backwardness and its surprising political dynamism. The picture comes alive, for instance, when we read a long passage in an official document concerning, among other things, "cadres who have committed the error of eating too much" and who must reimburse their comrades for this "unlawfully consumed" food.[21] Further on, we read that no charges should be laid against those who have become rich without injuring the community and the state, but this tolerance must be related to the relative meaning of the word "rich." Concretely, it means "those who have bought a bicycle" or "those who eat less frugally."[22] Yet in this world which is barely above subsistence level there are discussions of "the best way to use philosophy as a keen weapon in the hands of

[21] Resolution of September 1963, in *Documents of the CCP*, p. 775.

[22] According to a definition attributed to Liu, a rich peasant is one who has three horses, a plow, and a cart. See *People's Daily*, September 5, 1967, reprinted in *New China Notebooks*.

the masses," and everyone is urged to detect the main contradiction in each situation (as distinct from secondary contradictions) so as to promote the class struggle and the struggles for production and for scientific experiment.

We find in the "ten corrected points": "Comrades who use a strictly political yardstick to decide the social origin of a peasant are behaving in an unscientific manner, for they arbitrarily exclude from their class many poor peasants who are ideologically confused and temporarily influenced by old ideas and superstitions." Minute details follow on how to treat peasants who were poor at the time of the creation of the cooperatives in 1955, and why the slate should be wiped clean of minor irregularities that some of them may have committed by speculating on the market to help their parents, or simply because they believed in good faith that a little commercial activity was not against proletarian principles. Likewise, a distinction should be made between those who have "made a small fortune" but agree to stop speculating and those who reveal themselves as hardened speculators; between peasants who are simply religious and those who use religion to press for the restoration of clan laws and to corrupt the masses. Long passages are devoted to the treatment of children of landlords and rich peasants, distinguishing between young people who are too much influenced by their family background and others who, having now imbibed correct ideas, should not be ostracized and made to pay for the crimes of their parents.

The May 1963 directive, attributed to Mao, includes explanations very much in his style about the methods to be used in the political debate of the "four cleanups." "No cadre should evade criticism or limit the right of the rank and file to free speech; on the contrary, he should be the first to encourage this criticism. But every criticized cadre should have a chance to defend himself; the masses should establish by democratic discussion whether his arguments are correct; they should guard against any attempt at coercion and give no credit to confessions obtained by coercion; it is strictly forbidden to strike people or to use corporal punishment in any disguised form. . . . Corrupt elements or thieves who have committed serious offenses should be brought to justice with the consent of the masses and may be condemned only by legal process."

In September 1964, fifteen months after the start of the "four cleanups," Party headquarters decided to step on the accelerator. "Work teams" were sent all over the place; they dismissed existing managers and actively sought complaints from the masses. Why did Liu take this initiative? He explained in the self-criticism he made in October 1966. Essentially, as he saw it, the movement developed inadequately when it was left to itself. The "four cleanups" campaign had in fact reached scarcely a third of China's villages.[23] Liu's own wife, Wang Kuang-mei, who had moved in on the brigade at Taoyuan (Tangchan District, Hopeh Province) from November 1963 to April 1964, was the first to reach the conclusion that the method of "from above" was the only possible one and should be brought into general use.

It was not the first time that the Party had sent experienced cadres to "help" the peasants in this way. But this time the intervention was not to Mao's liking, though he did not condemn it at once. In fact, this initiative could have appeared leftist, since it aimed to crack down on the cadres who oppressed the masses, but it was later said to be rightist because it prevented the masses from making their own "rebellion" and replaced the defective cadres by another type of cadre equally immune from control.

The Insurmountable Divergences

Of course, from the time that I arrived in China in 1965, people talked to me about the socialist education campaign in the rural areas. As this phrase carries a definite meaning for us, I was expecting a straightforward propaganda effort, more intensive than usual, among the peasants. My informants never defined the specific character of the "four cleanups," nor did they tell me of the uncertainties about the relationships between cadres and masses in each brigade. But when we visited the "October" commune near Nanking, we saw the peasants gathering in a large school hall, and Marc Riboud, interested in getting group photographs, asked if we could go there too. It was in fact a

[23] China has about 74,000 communes, including on the average ten production brigades, each of about twenty teams. Each of these is a unit with its own responsible management, which brings the number of cadres at the basic level to about 10 million.

meeting of the Association of Poor and Medium-Poor Peasants. As might be expected, the meeting was as calm as it could be, since the presence of strangers undoubtedly inhibited any polemical clashes. Our host, the commune chairman, was very hospitable but extremely vague about the aims and role of the association.

Back in Peking, in the course of my interview with Chou En-lai, I asked him how all these slogans about the intensification of the class struggle in China should be interpreted. Did they not somewhat resemble the slogans in vogue at a certain period in Stalin's Russia? Chou suggested that we should leave Stalin out of it ("Stalin's appraisals of the Russian internal situation were often varied") but was more definite about China. "It is a fact, therefore," he said, "that former landowners and middle-class elements exist. The influence of the practices of the old society remains alive enough. Even among those who have done well in the new society there are some who submit to this influence and take part in illegal speculation. It is this which gives birth to new middle-class elements. Marxists must not ignore these facts if they do not want such people to commit sabotage and corrupt others." [24] But Chou also assured me that in China to fight does not mean to repress; Communists fully understand that correct political ideas cannot be imposed by decree or force. "With us, everything is done by persuasion, in accordance with the directives of Chairman Mao."

But who was to be persuaded, and how? I saw several films in Peking that I found curious. One of them tells the story of a demobilized soldier who returns to his thoroughly proletarian family and sees his brother, a brigade cadre, very friendly with the former landlord and involved in suspect activities. Thanks to the cadre's passivity, not to say corruption, the former rich men have slyly regained control of the village and organized gambling houses where young men spend their nights playing cards. Only the puritanism of the official movie screen prevents the scene from going further, but one can guess that this village has still worse haunts of perdition. Be this as it may, the ex-soldier has several clashes with his brother, but his efforts to bring the latter back to the right road through persuasion are apparently in vain. He then

[24] See *China: The Other Communism*, p. 452.

starts to organize the young poor peasants, half in secret, for the idea of appealing to the higher authorities or to the security services does not even seem to occur to him. Of course, he triumphs in the end. Thanks to the ideological battle that he wages, the young men desert the gambling houses and set traps for the old landlords and the corrupt cadres to catch them red-handed in illegal activities (in point of fact, selling on the free market fertilizers that should go to the commune). The soldier's brother is pardoned at a meeting of the peasants, who bear in mind that he has been the victim rather than the beneficiary of all these swindles.

However, if we are to believe the revelations of the Cultural Revolution, at the time that I saw this film the villages of China were living under a "white terror" exerted by Liu Shao-ch'i's work teams. *People's Daily* wrote on September 6, 1967:[25]

> Chairman Mao laid down in the ten-point directive principles of correct policy for the "four cleanups" movement, which led to a great success. His line aimed at solving an extremely important problem and making the revolution under the conditions of the dictatorship of the proletariat. . . . The "Chinese Khrushchev" felt mortal fear and implacable hatred for this great revolution and strained every nerve to oppose it. He put forward a reactionary bourgeois line, "Left" in appearance but Right in reality, and sent his wife Wang, a bourgeois element, into the Taoyuan brigade to turn it into a tragic testing ground for his policy. Moreover, usurping the name of the Central Committee of the Party, he took care to formulate a so-called Taoyuan experience and ordered it to be popularized throughout the country. This was a plot hatched according to a well-prepared plan, to usurp the power of the Party and of the State.
>
> The "Chinese Khrushchev" cynically altered the character of the "four cleanups" movement, claiming that the main contradiction was "between honesty and dishonesty in the four problems concerned." He sidetracked the general direction of the struggle in order to strike at a great number and protect a small handful. By declaring that it was necessary to "solve problems as they exist," he found pretexts to attack cadres and commune members, repress the revolutionary masses, and lead the "four cleanups" movement on to a disastrous path. According to him, it was necessary to "rely on selected activists to accumulate information from secret contacts." This meant that he

[25] See *New China Notebooks*, No. 244 (September 7, 1967).

was bitterly opposed to using Chairman Mao's method of class analysis, that he set himself violently against the masses, in order to form factions and to recruit cowards and renegades into the service of his clique, thus creating conditions for the restoration of capitalism. Thanks to this plot, political power in the Taoyuan brigade fell into the hands of bad elements who set up their own kind of fascist rule, while the former poor peasants, the lower stratum of middle peasants, and the revolutionary cadres were attacked and persecuted. Here was a living model for the hundred percent restoration of capitalism. It is not hard to understand that China's Khrushchev wanted to spread experiments like that of Taoyuan to the whole country, to realize his dream of forcing our socialist country to retreat and change its color. . . . Inquiries made in various brigades reveal that poor peasants and middle peasants of the lower strata are bringing charges full of tears and blood against the crimes of China's Khrushchev.[26]

After this, it is worth quoting the words in which Liu admitted his mistakes in his self-criticism of October 1966:

In 1964, I called many provincial leaders to Peking to find out how the situation in the rural areas was developing, and I gave too much credit to their verbal reports. I was convinced by them, without a further check, that the "four cleanups" campaign was not intense or profound enough and that it was even meeting with failure. I thus made a gross error of judgment, and I underestimated the effects of the class struggle on improving the political situation and on agricultural and industrial production. Besides, I thought that the mass meetings desired by Chairman Mao were inadequate, which amounted in reality to a negation of his thought. . . . I put too much trust in the results of Comrade Wang Kuang-mei's experiment, which I thought positive, whereas it was mistaken. This led to a confusion in my mind and hence to my deviation, which was Left in appearance but Right in substance. My mistakes were later corrected when Chairman Mao personally presided over the enlarged meeting of the Politburo in January 1965, at which the twenty-three points on the socialist education campaign in rural areas were adopted. But I recognize that my conduct in the preceding years shows that I had forgotten the

[26] On September 6, 1967, the army newspaper published still more precise allegations about the "crimes" of Madame Wang, based on its own inquiries. It seems that she dismissed the former Party secretary Wu Chen, "a relatively good cadre," and replaced him by Kuan King-lung, who had "infiltrated into the Party" since 1954 and was the son of a broker.

whole theory that our Party had succeeded in acquiring through decades of class struggle.[27]

How did this episode—limited, after all—put an end to decades of good understanding between Mao and Liu? The "four clean-ups" campaign seems to have highlighted a divergence between these two leaders dating from 1949. For Mao, not only was the Yenan line to be maintained but it should cut even deeper after victory, and he was firmly convinced that the masses had a greater and more conscious desire than before for profound changes. For Liu, in the new postrevolutionary framework, realities had altered so much that it was no longer possible to rely on the spontaneous enthusiasm of the masses. The peasants were no longer spurred on by hunger and no longer faced an obvious class enemy. The Party, and only the Party, could see to the necessary changes, preferably without repression but also without weakness. In a sense, Mao was right to see Liu's evolution as the traditional change that turns a revolutionary organizer into a brilliant administrator, justifying his own skepticism and his taste for efficiency by unproven objective circumstances. Seeing how his deputy behaved during the "four cleanups," he became convinced that such a man, at the head of the new Party machine, could never regain the enthusiasm and freshness of the "heroic" period—and this at a time when a search for original techniques of mobilizing the masses was not less urgent than before, but more so.

But the problem was not to be solved simply by dismissing Liu. Beyond his personality, it was his "organizational line" that had to be fought—and on this point Chinese documents of the Cultural Revolution appear coherent and convincing. Mao had now to make a frontal attack on this line to stimulate the upheaval he desired. This he did when he decided to appeal to the masses in January 1965; and he put into the twenty-three-point resolution a paragraph that, to say the least, is unusual in Communist Party documents:

> The essential thing in the present movement is to purge persons who hold positions of authority in the Party but follow the capitalist road. This is necessary to develop and consolidate the achievements of

[27] Liu's self-criticism never appeared in the official press, but it was widely circulated in Red Guard papers and its authenticity is generally regarded as definite.

socialism in the cities as much as in the rural areas. Leaders who take the capitalist road hide behind the scenes, but in certain cases they also appear in the foreground.[28]

Addressed primarily to the peasants, to encourage them to settle their problems with the cadres, this resolution could only undermine the authority of the Party as such. Those leaders who hid behind the scenes could be found only in Peking, or at least in regional Party offices, not in the villages. Humble peasants had little chance of meeting them but, by knowing of their existence, could be more challenging toward their representatives—in the first place, toward work teams composed of strangers to their villages. Liu had probably figured this out, and it was for this reason that he was no longer on the same wavelength as Mao.

Another striking point in this remarkable document is number 20, which urges "all communes and brigades to learn from the People's Liberation Army four great democratic attitudes, and to practice democracy in politics, democracy in production, democracy in financial affairs, and democracy in military affairs." Here, too, there was a return to a slogan of the heroic era, when the way of life, work organization, and behavior of the Red soldiers were held up as an example to the peasants (and later to the town dwellers) in liberated areas. But, sixteen years after the foundation of the People's Republic, could these historic watchwords evoke the same response as in the past? Would the masses understand that they must "rebel against oppression" even when it was exercised by representatives of the Communist Party?

The presence of the work teams in the villages produced no noteworthy incidents, and the Associations of Poor and Medium-Poor Peasants did not succeed in raising the banner of challenge as Mao could have wished. The movement he was ready to support did not get off the ground in the countryside. But the explosion was nevertheless set off in the end by echoes of these divergences, mingled with a campaign for simplifying the Party's cultural policy in the cities. In present-day accounts of the origins of the Cultural Revolution, the episode of the "four cleanups" and Mao's twenty-three-point resolution are only an overture, prepar-

[28] See "Resolution on the Problems Raised by the Socialist Education Movement in Rural Areas," *Documents of the CCP*, pp. 824 ff.

ing the listener for the trials of strength around the Party that
were to spread in the cities from the fall of 1965 onward. But here
again the whole context must be reconstructed.

The Dilemma in the Superstructure

One element in this context—perhaps the most difficult to
grasp—concerns the role of culture and of the intellectuals. In
fact, to the degree that Mao pursued a remolding of the
development model, in a Communist and egalitarian sense, and
sought to transfer a share of power to the rank and file and give
the initiative to the masses, the problem of the ideological
unification of the country became more and more urgent. A
strictly centralized system, relying on an effective repressive
organization, can quite well dispense with consent: it lays down
its aims and that is all. But Mao could not be content with this if
he wanted China to be changed by the Chinese themselves. This
was not so much because of "democratism," but because his idea
of change was strictly linked to that of a steady withering away of
the central power of the state, parallel with the taking of direct
responsibility for certain affairs by mass organizations.

Now, this delegation of power to the masses requires the
guarantee of firm cohesion and a strong consensus on the subject,
without which it leads purely and simply to a fragmentation of
society, especially in a country so vast and backward as China.
"All power to the soviets" implies that the soviets are in complete
agreement on fundamental policies. And this cannot come
about—in China still less than in the USSR—without a continual
transfusion of political culture, without what is described by
Communists as an "ideological struggle" and by the West,
somewhat contemptuously, as "indoctrination."

Mao knew all about this. "When you want to change the
regime, you first prepare opinion," he has said. And if there was
one Party department of which Mao seemed to take a poor view,
it was precisely that concerned with propaganda and culture. At
every opportunity, he directed sarcastic remarks at it. At the 1962
Central Committee meeting, when the new offensive in the
countryside was decided on, Mao demanded that these inadequacies in the ideological sector be remedied. The two themes were

linked because, in order to revive the class struggle in the countryside, the poor peasants and their allies had to be given better ideological weapons. Besides, if the relaxation of the preceding years had allowed the old rich to impose their selfish ideas and their clan laws, the blame clearly belonged to the Party for being unable to counter these pernicious influences. It was necessary to declare war on all this. The director of the Propaganda Department, Lu Ting-yi, was promoted and entered the Party Secretariat. His deputy, Chou Yang (whom I met in 1965), was also given enhanced powers to get a grip on the cultural sector and the intellectuals.

Here a delicate nerve was touched. While the ideological training of the masses was a question of efficiency, involving merely the Party's skill in making them aware of their real situation in society, with the intellectuals things were not so easy. With regard to culture, the masses could be considered more or less virgin soil, but the intellectuals were anything but a "blank sheet of paper." In the field of ideas, this distinctive social group was the richest in knowledge and the most capable of criticism, communication, and influence. How could the country be unified unless the intellectuals were deeply attached to the major plans of the revolutionary vanguard, since they were the very people with the ability and the duty to develop and put across these plans? In the West, indignation is sometimes heard at this utility function that revolutionary societies frankly require from culture. But in reality, whether they like it or not, intellectuals always express and serve a certain pattern of values, of society, and therefore of politics.

In China this was no new idea; Lu Hsün, the most famous of progressive writers, had said, "All literature is propaganda." Under the old regime many writers, sometimes without being Communists, had taken the cause of the Communist Party to be their own, and it had the assistance of the huge majority of the cultural community. But after its victory, things deteriorated. The honeymoon ended when many intellectuals found that they and the Party had different ideas on what the new China should be like. On its side, the Party noted bitterly that its fellow travelers were seeking to influence public opinion on their own account, taking advantage of the prestige it had given them. Moreover, the intellectuals split into two blocs. The Party members generally became full-timers in the cultural machine, while those who stayed outside were increasingly inclined to challenge the right of this machine to deal with their problems. There followed a certain number of clashes, and then some purges (such as the one that hit the prominent writer Hu Feng in 1955),[29] which poisoned the atmosphere. In the Hundred Flowers period in 1957, when the Party invited everyone to speak freely, it was overwhelmed by criticisms of the "liberal" kind, far more widespread and sharper than it had expected. It reacted, and called a speedy halt to this outcry; instead of replying to the arguments, it reaffirmed the principle of authority and launched a great campaign against the "rightists." After this slightly traumatic experience, a rather curious modus vivendi between the Party and the intellectuals was established. Distinguished university scholars and other specially valuable creative people were guaranteed a kind of immunity in their specialized spheres, while more committed writers joined the Party to defend the line without any more yearnings for criticism. Apparently there were advantages all around, and both categories enjoyed a privileged position despite the great difference in their functions.

Mao alone could not reconcile himself to this state of affairs, akin to what had been established in Eastern European countries. This peaceful coexistence in the cultural sector seemed to him even more unhealthy than the kind that prevailed in the villages. Did it not mean that the Party itself was sanctioning inequality to the advantage of "those with knowledge"? And what was the point of this knowledge if it did not serve the great social process of transforming China? Convinced that a great many scholars and creative minds could still take the plunge and enlist in the service of a revolutionary plan, as in the Yenan days, he first attacked those who had discouraged them by administrative measures, or had simply proved unable to create the right climate for "a class struggle in the intellectual sector." Here he followed his principle that the only way to escape from backwardness, political as much as ideological or social, was by a straight showdown between the basic tendencies at work among the people.

[29] On the purges in intellectual circles, see *China: The Other Communism.*

But it was probably no accident that the Hundred Flowers experiment had not produced this happy outcome. The class struggle among intellectuals was perceptibly less clear than, say, in a village or a mixed social environment where old production relationships and their effects are found alongside new ones and present an explicit contrast. All the intellectuals, by virtue of their status, belonged to a fairly solid and relatively privileged social group that was cut off from the masses, if only by this "knowledge." So the contrast could be defined only on the level of ideology; as there was no social mechanism by which divergences could be measured, there was always a risk that discussion would be resolved by an appeal to orthodoxy and end in a wholly bureaucratic fashion. Yet how could the masses themselves be brought into a debate whose terms were often very remote from their experience? A discussion between the intellectual and the common man can easily turn out badly. Either the common man listens without perceptibly influencing the intellectual, or else he somehow grasps that the latter is a privileged person, belonging to another sphere if not another class, and brushes him aside.

It was a question, in fact, of the weighty heritage of the social and technical division of labor, which no revolution can swiftly resolve. So long as intellectuals exist as possessors of a knowledge beyond the reach of the masses, difficult problems of alliance—and, beyond that, integration—will continually arise, both in relation to the masses and in relation to the Communist Party, which is a "collective intellectual" in that it is the vanguard directing the social process. Mao, averse to a mere alliance and aiming at a true integration, attempted with the intellectuals what he had tried with the technicians: he urged them to join the people on the level of daily life, to go out to the fields and take part in manual work. Most of them agreed, but, as the Cultural Revolution was to show, this changed neither their status nor, apparently, their outlook. When they were asked to go among the people and imbibe the ideas of the latter, they went off without grumbling to spend a few months on the communes. But when it came to discussing the results, they proved to be very cautious (an effect of the Hundred Flowers fiasco) and chose to withdraw into their specialized spheres and discuss ancient history in preference to current politics.

Thus, a month after Mao's appeal at the Central Committee meeting of September 1962, a large cultural conference assembled in Shantung. But there was no question of a "four cleanups" campaign. There was a passionate discussion about Confucius, the social ambiguity of his teachings, and his influence on the development of ancient China. Some regarded him as the defender of the slave-owning nobility and hence as a reactionary; others saw him rather as the spokesman of the rising classes, and therefore a progressive; others again as a reformer, favoring gradual changes. Professor Liu Chieh declared that in any case, thanks to Confucianism, China had developed in a radically different manner from the Western world and that consequently a division into historical periods, similar to that made for Europe, is not valid for China. In September 1963 a still more agitated debate arose over the historical virtues or defects of Li Hsiu-ch'eng, the last general of the Taiping peasant revolt in the nineteenth century. Some held that he was a traitor because he had surrendered to the enemy; others claimed him as a revolutionary hero, who had employed this ruse to save the hopes of the peasant rebellion and paid for it with his life.

Was it true that these theories—apparently remote from the present day—implied a great many allusive criticisms of Mao's line and even of Marxism itself? In any case, Mao took a dim view of this kind of abstruse controversy. Once again, in a directive dated December 12, 1963, he expressed his displeasure with the Communist authorities and demanded that there should be less talk about personalities of the past and more about the current situation. Another leader, K'o Ch'ing-shih—member of the Politburo and mayor of Shanghai—weighed in to suggest a reform of the opera and the theater and gave impetus to a radical change in their repertory.[30] After this it seems that things calmed down, as though time were needed to digest this innovation.

But the truce was short. On June 27, 1964, Mao promulgated a fresh directive, still more explicit and threatening, in which he declared that the cultural associations and most of their publications were utterly inadequate, and accused the men in charge of

[30] K'o Ch'ing-shih died in April 1965.

behaving "like bureaucrats and great lords." [31] More than this: when he received a delegation of teachers from Nepal, who came to express their admiration for China's educational system, he replied in an offhand way that they should by no means imitate it, because it was bad, traditional, stupidly hierarchical, and based on ridiculous ideas about examinations and the study of abstract documents. These were strong words; and the question of a radical reform of education was abruptly put on the agenda. Then, to give another turn of the screw, Mao poked fun first at the Ministry of Public Health and then at the Ministry of Culture. He suggested that the former should be renamed "Ministry of Health for City Lords," because most of the doctors were devoting themselves to the urban population and not to the 80 percent of Chinese who lived in the countryside, and the latter should be the "Ministry for Alien Personalities of Outworn Times." [32]

Such an outburst of sarcasm could not be ignored, especially since it was a striking novelty in the traditional argument between Communist Parties and intellectuals. Mao was resolutely changing the terms of the question; he was no longer concerned with the content of ideas, or with the lukewarm militancy of writers and artists, so much as with the social distinction arising from a status that traditional cultural institutions—even after the revolution— continued to promote. By doing so, they dug a deep gulf between the intellectuals and the masses and ultimately set them in opposition. What, in addition, was the meaning of his attack on the teaching system? Never, in any Communist country, had anyone doubted that the schools should select an intelligentsia, or questioned the role and the special status of the latter in society. Mao was the first to make a frontal assault on the problem of the division of social groups arising from the division of labor, and to suggest abruptly to the Party a solution that clearly proved difficult to understand. Still, the Party reacted with promptness and discipline. Great problems call for great remedies, and a commission of five leaders of the highest rank (known as the Group of Five) under the chairmanship of P'eng Chen, the mayor

[31] See "Two Instructions Concerning Art and Literature," Peking Review, No. 23 (June 2, 1967).

[32] See Lin Piao's report to the Ninth Party Congress in April 1969, in New China Notebooks and other publications.

of Peking, and assisted by many experts, was entrusted with the preparations for what, from that time on, was called the Cultural Revolution. In May 1965 a strong man, Hsiao Wang-tung, took over the Ministry of Culture. Political commissar of the army's Nanking region, Hsiao had no great opinion of his new ministry, to judge by his remarks published during the Cultural Revolution: "This ministry is rotten; all the administrative chiefs on the level of departments and bureaus are contemptible mangy sheep who have even corrupted the drivers, the workmen, the technicians, and the cooks. . . . With fellows like that, the Cultural Revolution would never succeed if it lasted for a hundred years." [33]

However, if the task of cleansing these Augean stables was heavy, Hsiao claimed that he could make a sound job of it and, on July 13, 1965, he made a highly optimistic provisional report to the Group of Five. In that month of May 1965 I had been able to observe a similar optimism when I met Chou Yang, the man chiefly affected by all these shifts of personnel and probably among those who had suggested them. His picture of the situation was not too black, although he admitted that he was meeting many problems, of which the biggest was this: "The great majority of our intellectuals . . . are mostly of middle-class or lower-middle-class origin and do not have the integrity of the proletarian class. . . . Today a minority among them, 20 percent at the most, have succeeded in assimilating the dialectical method and know how to use it to analyze and to create." [34] So the problem was once again on the level of consciousness; Chou Yang could only hope that, thanks to a campaign of education, larger strata of intellectuals would be reached by the proletarian ideology of which, at present, the Party and its machine was the best and perhaps the sole repository. Until the intellectuals became "Red and expert," he and his colleagues would in perfectly good faith remain as the only judges of the proletarian quality of each piece of writing. They were sure of themselves, they were confident of being the indispensable guardians of Mao's doctrine, they were convinced that nothing fundamental had to be changed, and they had no idea how close they were to the precipice.

[33] See "Hsiao Wang-tung, the Counterrevolutionary, Is Unmasked," a report from the New China News Agency in September 1967.

[34] See *China: The Other Communism*, p. 279.

They were "Liu's men," it is generally said today, but this is an outrageous simplification. In fact, the great majority of propaganda and culture officials had earned their political spurs at Mao's side in Yenan. For instance, Lu Ting-yi, the director of this challenged department, had worked throughout the anti-Japanese war in the propaganda sector of the army, so he was not directly dependent on Liu Shao-ch'i. Chou Yang, a cog in the machine since the 1930's, was first and foremost an official, and he would not have hesitated a second, if called upon by Mao, to launch a vindictive campaign against anyone, Liu included.[35] He had, incidentally, been the first, in December 1963, to advance the formula of "one divides into two," the dialectical law justifying the formation of "Marxist-Leninist" groups in foreign Communist Parties.[36] All progress is made by means of these divisions, he said, and at every stage of the history of the working-class movement the truly revolutionary wing must break the rules and attack the leadership that has become bourgeois. But the idea that he might belong to that kind of leadership never occurred to him. He and the other officials in the Ministry of Culture, in fact, could grasp everything that Mao wanted to do, except his casting doubt on the divisive social principle of which they, like all Party cadres, were to some extent the beneficiaries. Hence, while they were ready to join enthusiastically in hunting down "bad ideas," the deeper aim of Mao's move was alien to them—for how could the very principle of intellectual separateness be abolished? The differentiation of social roles was inherent in, and re-created by, the school system as the source of all intellectuality, and the idea of rejecting it was a profound challenge to the hierarchical principle; the Peking students understood Mao perfectly, and he understood them perfectly, in 1966. Nor is it astonishing that this old man, capable of dreaming of a Communist society and staking everything to bring it to birth, should thus join hands with a developing

[35] In the 1930's Chou Yang had organized the Writers' United Front in Shanghai, based on a conciliatory program designed to have a widespread appeal. This earned him some scornful remarks from Lu Hsün, who was never a Party member but disliked making concessions. In the Cultural Revolution, Lu Hsün's sallies against the creators of the United Front were much used to condemn Chou Yang.

[36] See Chou Yang, *Speeches*.

social group, with the young students who, in their transient situation, were still malleable and open-minded. Mao's words struck home to them, as to their counterparts in Berlin, Rome, and Paris. The Party machine, rendered deaf by its training and its position, was unable to listen; being itself an institution, convinced that its destiny was to govern, it was already divided from the masses whom it sincerely wished to serve.

So, by 1965, everything came inexorably back to this point: a change in the mechanisms of society must imply a change in the mechanisms of the Party. Here too, as in the case of Chou Yang, it was not necessary to be blind or conservative in every respect to disagree on the methods and the proper limits of the change. Liu Shao-ch'i, for example, was by no means convinced of the miraculous immunity of the Party. He had more than once expressed his doubts as to the quality of a Party 80 percent of whose members had joined since its victory and were at a political level that left much to be desired.[37] He was still more pessimistic about the political potential of the masses, who in his opinion were not ripe for independent action. But, according to him, to put the situation right it was enough to improve the Party and untiringly teach its members "how to be good Communists," by following his manual, which was republished in 1962. Only then could this steeled vanguard effectively help the masses to solve their problems. When he was asked for advice on the best way to cleanse the sensitive sector of culture and ideology, he could only suggest the solutions he had already advanced during the campaign of socialist education in the rural areas.

Since January 1965 he had been aware that Mao did not believe in the correctness of his method, even though the latter had not forbidden him to carry his experiment through to the end. How many of the directing team knew about the disagreement between the two leaders? Doubtless Mao no longer showed the same confidence in his vice-chairman, but apparently he had not revealed his feeling that their ways would soon have to part. To judge by appearances, the two men were acting in complete

[37] See Liu Shao-ch'i, "Speech Delivered at the Meeting in Celebration of the Fortieth Anniversary of the Founding of the Communist Party of China," *Peking Review*, Nos. 26 and 27 (July 7, 1961).

harmony. I remember that on May 27, 1965, a few days before I left China, the main newspapers of Peking reported on the front page that during the previous summer Chairman Mao and Vice-Chairman Liu had swum together in the artificial lake (a reservoir near the Ming tombs) in the outskirts of the city: "On the diving board, they chatted with a group of young people, exhorting them to swim and struggle against the elements so as to become vigorous revolutionaries." [38]

This aquatic demonstration of solidarity was doubtless designed to reassure everyone. But it did not prevent the two supreme leaders from being faithful to themselves and heading for diametrically opposed solutions to the basic problem whose urgency both seemed to recognize: how could China avoid the mechanism of degeneration that had struck the USSR?

An Army Unlike Any Other

The Chinese "shout of alarm" against the pseudo-Communism of Khrushchev came at the same time as the "four cleanups" campaign and the struggle in the cultural sphere. This was no coincidence. Documents on the internal struggles, then little known abroad, tell us a great deal about the reasons for Chinese anxiety. Surveying the record of seven years of "continuous revolution" that began with the Great Leap Forward, the leaders in Peking were obliged to recognize that their society had not yet crossed the threshold of minimum safety, beyond which a "quiet restoration" in Soviet style would be impossible. The dominance of proletarian ideas was not yet assured, the politicalization of the masses was inadequate, the "spontaneous tendency toward capitalism" persisted in the rural areas. All this showed that a "Chinese Khrushchev" would have no difficulty in finding a social base among old and new privileged groups and among the politically apathetic for his eventual bid at restoration. It was also known that the institutional framework in China, as formerly in the USSR, was made to measure for such an attempt to put things into reverse. The top level of the Party still held all the decision-making levers, while the proletarian militants had no

[38] See "Mass Swimming," *Peking Review*, No. 23 (June 4, 1965).

means of organizing and resisting in the event of a change of line. In these circumstances, it can be understood that the Chinese leaders had good reason to worry about the unpredictable "revisionist coup" after Mao's death, and the latter wanted to act in time and use his tremendous power to take long-term preventive measures.

Communists had been haunted by the specter of a restoration of capitalism since the day when they took power in Russia in October 1917. The Bolsheviks felt themselves vulnerable because they represented only a limited vanguard and had strikingly concentrated all power at the peak of the political pyramid. Greatly influenced by the history of the French Revolution, they were particularly afraid of a Russian Bonapartism—the more so because their Red Army, strongly structured, would have been quite capable of crushing the Party's civilian leadership any day. This anti-Bonapartist obsession was a permanent feature in the thinking of Soviet leaders from Lenin to Khrushchev. It will be recalled that in 1957 the latter, emerging as undisputed victor in the struggle for the succession to Stalin, at once found it prudent to send Marshal Zhukov, the too prestigious and therefore too dangerous army chief, into retirement. However, no Bonaparte has appeared in half a century of Soviet history, punctuated only by battles between civilian leaders. Khrushchev did in the end fall victim to a palace revolt in the Kremlin, but the military men were not involved.

The Chinese never had any obsessions about their army, but they clearly understood, because of Soviet precedents, that the danger of a "revisionist" political setback could come only from the Party, and in particular from its commanding heights. If the revisionist time bomb were already planted anywhere—which was hypothetical, but possible—it must be in the headquarters, because it was only there that the explosion could bring a triumph. In a country like theirs, no former landlord, embittered counterrevolutionary, or rightist bourgeois intellectual could be a political force threatening the regime. At worst, such "bad elements" could influence unstable cadres in villages or factories, but this would not enable them to impose on the Party a line opposed to its aspirations. But the Party itself could change the line whenever it pleased and, moreover, was not even obliged to give its reasons. Its leading group could bring in a new policy overnight, while claiming that it was continuing to build socialism.

Yet how could one go about defusing a bomb planted in the very heart of the institution that was regarded as indispensable by everyone, including Mao? All the splits that, in normal times, would have meant no more than temporary divisions between Left, Center, and Right—such as the CCP had known so often—were suddenly accentuated to a danger point because of this dramatic question mark against the Party. Was not a symptom of authoritarianism, such as the tendency to give orders from above during the "four cleanups," a sign that some people already had guilty leanings toward usurping power? Was not their inability to give impetus to the class struggle in the cultural sphere a mere pretense? There was material here for deep divisions, leading even to the crystallization of solid groups confronting one another far more sharply than in ordinary debates. In fact, the Chinese leaders seemed to be in a vicious circle. To be secure against an ultimate Khrushchevist coup, they had to speed up the pace of the transformation of society and thus rely still more on the Party. But, by thus giving it the green light for vigorous action, they were strengthening the Party's uncontrolled power over society and increasing the risks that the revisionist time bomb would go off at headquarters.

As a way out, Mao had proposed to set up control from below, and the Associations of Poor and Medium-Poor Peasants were intended to provide the model. But the experiment was inconclusive, because the Party had not known how (or had not wanted) to get these "controllers" from the masses genuinely organized and allow them elbowroom for independent action. It was clear that, being what it was, the Party could not behave otherwise, and therefore it could not be counted on to inspire real mass political activity. But could that project be made a reality without the Party—which meant, implicitly, against it?

This brings us to the origins of the future "Lin Piao affair." The man who made a positive reply to the thorny question of the possibility of letting the masses speak for themselves was decidedly Lin Piao. He did so, moreover, by taking his stand on tangible evidence, for he had been concerned for years with the ideological unification of Chinese youth in the army, of which he was the chief. Today one is given to understand in Peking that he had deliberately misled Mao in order to secure promotion and ease the task of his "leftist" accomplices. But in any Communist Party there is an unmarked boundary between permissible alliances in debate and factional activity. It is regular form to accuse the leader of the losing side of guilty intentions and of factionalism. Can it be said, however, that back in 1965–6 Lin Piao represented a trend of his own, distinct from Mao's? Was he really further to the left than the Chairman, or did he become so during the Cultural Revolution? Is not an attempt being made, in hindsight, to divide him from Mao and destroy the too widely spread image of their inseparable links? These questions must obviously be placed in a whole historical context, and they involve at the outset some consideration of the army's role in the Chinese Communist movement.

The People's Liberation Army is certainly like no other army, and if we had a richer vocabulary we might do well to stop calling it an army and suggesting analogies with conventional military forces. We can state, in any case, that no other army has required from its soldiers, ever since its birth, the "five obligations and two rights" (explained in the postscript to Chapter 6), and has tried so consistently to become a political as well as a military body. Soviet Russia, for a time, had its Red Guards, who were very political-ized and elected their own officers, but as early as March 1918 the Bolshevik Party gave Trotsky the job of organizing a regular and centralized modern army, fully hierarchical and making use of Czarist officers who were skilled in the art of war. Neither Trotsky nor the other Bolshevik leaders ever considered forming a specifically proletarian army and working out tactics suited to its capacities. The founder of the Red Army stated clearly, "On the lowest technical and cultural level [it is impossible] to create an essentially new strategy more highly developed than that reached by the most civilized armies among the capitalist vultures." [39]

Mao was thus the first to create a totally new kind of army and invent a different way of fighting, and this in a country more backward than Russia. In fact, he contrived to make use of the

[39] See Leon Trotsky, "The Path of the Red Army" (May 1922), quoted in *Que faire?*, Paris, Nos. 3–4 (1970).

injustices arising from China's cultural and technical backwardness for his political purposes, and to rely on the human factor, on
the need of the poorest classes to liberate themselves by fighting.
And, ever since the distant days of Chingkangshan, he had not
only built up this new type of army but had primarily given added
depth to its character as a political body, rooted in the masses,
sheltered by them, and capable of drawing them little by little
into the struggle. Every effort had been made to "ideologically
unify" the commanders and soldiers, to forge a thousand links
between them and the people and thus raise the cultural level and
political understanding of the latter.

More than this: almost all the leaders of the CCP were trained
in this school, or spent highly instructive periods in it during the
Long March or the war with Japan. Chou En-lai, whom nobody
pictures nowadays in army boots, reminded Edgar Snow in 1970
that when they had first met, in 1936, he was wearing a uniform,
commanding troops, and acting as vice-chairman of the Military
Revolutionary Committee responsible for all fronts. Most of
Chou's comrades could have made similar claims, for every one of
them wore the grass green of their proletarian army at one stage
or another of his career. And, because of these experiences, they
all learned that the backward world of the villages was fermenting
with inexhaustible political and military potentialities, amply
sufficient to hold at bay the powerful technical machine of the
Japanese Army (and later the Kuomintang Army, equipped by the
United States) and to change Chinese society from top to bottom.

But, to make use of this discovery, the Chinese Communists
had to subject themselves to a collectivist and Spartan mode of
life "among the people," and to make their army a great
laboratory of social knowledge. Their peasant recruits showed
them the realities of the rural world, enabling them to measure
how far this world could be adapted to new ideas and to predict
the possible rhythm of its transformation. Mao's soldiers did not
merely swim among the people like a fish in water; they also
colored the water red by their very presence.

After the victory of 1949, the question of the army was once
more the focus of the attention of the Chinese Communists. In
1950 it had to fight in Korea, outside its "natural" territory, which
presented a fresh problem. Moreover, many Soviet military

advisers came to Peking, all covered from neck to waist with medals well earned on the battlefields of World War II. It was hard not to pay heed to these comrades surrounded with the aura of victory. They unanimously declared that China henceforward would need a proper army, suitably equipped, solidly disciplined, and ready for all contingencies, including service abroad. Their arguments convinced Marshal P'eng Teh-huai, minister of defense and commander in chief of Chinese forces in Korea; we can assume that his practical experience on this front counted for something too. This veteran of Chingkangshan, who had several times rebelled against the orders of the "Comintern" leadership of the CCP in the early 1930's, ended up in 1955 by introducing into the Chinese Army ranks copied from the Soviet pattern and turned his ministry into a straight equivalent of the one in Moscow. Incidentally, this was the period of the First Five-Year Plan, carried out with Soviet aid, and the minister of defense was not alone in following the Soviet model.

Lin Piao and the 700 Million Grains of Sand

But the experiment in imitation did not last long, and China's return to her own sources of inspiration began, as though by chance, with a switch in the military sphere. Little is known of this debate in 1956–7, but we are well aware of its outcome, including the changes in army leadership. In May 1958, at the second session of the Eighth Party Congress, two simultaneous announcements were made: the start of the Great Leap Forward and, in a special resolution, the promotion of Lin Piao to Party vice-chairman. From that day, the most Maoist of the ten marshals was in reality number one in the People's Liberation Army. P'eng Teh-huai remained minister until August 1959, but he devoted all his time to leading military missions abroad or conducting semiprivate inquiries in the provinces.[40] In a regime where "the

---

[40] P'eng led the Chinese military mission to the Eastern European countries from April 14 to June 13, 1959, and according to certain Western sources he used this opportunity to have a secret meeting with Khrushchev in Albania. After his return he seems to have spent three weeks on a tour of China. See *The Case of P'eng Teh-huai* (Hong Kong: Union Research Institute, 1969).

Party commands the gun," a Party vice-chairman in charge of military affairs matters a hundred times more than a minister of defense who does not belong to the supreme executive organ of the Party, and who has moreover been defeated on the question of the correct line.

Of course, Lin Piao was not yet *the* vice-chairman, but one of five men enjoying this status, some of them more important than he. But his portrait was already to be seen everywhere—the strange picture of a marshal who wore neither the uniform of his rank nor medals, his look fixed and grave, his face sickly and almost sorrowful. In 1959, he succeeded P'eng as vice-premier and minister of defense. P'eng had not resigned himself to his defeat in the army and had tried, during the Great Leap, to hit back on another front by criticizing the communes and even making an alliance with Chang Wen-t'ien (alias Lo Fu), the last survivor of the "twenty-eight Bolsheviks." This earned him a rebuke from Mao of unusual violence, final dismissal, and the infamous labels of "rightist" and "careerist."

As for Lin Piao, he seldom showed himself in public. At regular intervals there were rumors in Hong Kong that he had been dismissed or even that his death would shortly be announced. He was known to be ill, never really cured of his war wounds—he had been under treatment in the USSR between 1938 and 1941—and probably obliged to take frequent breaks from work for health reasons. However, so far as we know today, Lin never fell into disfavor, nor was he compelled to rest. He sometimes avoided official ceremonies because he was too busy with his basic work in the army. During these years of so-called eclipse, he once again made the army into "a great school of the thought of Mao Tse-tung," and found out how receptive Chinese youngsters in postrevolutionary conditions were in practice to the methods that had been proved in the heroic era. Once again, too, he set up a whole system of small industrial and farming enterprises, enabling the army to supply its own needs as it had when besieged by the enemy; and, as in the old days at Yenan, he organized artistic units and lectures on the theater and on culture. In short, while apparently keeping in the shadows, he made the army a major center of political attraction, which drew into its scope many enthusiasts for the mass line, including Chiang Ch'ing [41] and the group of "Young Turks" from Shanghai, headed by Chang Ch'un-ch'iao and Yao Wen-yuan.

The prestige of "Chairman Mao's soldiers" was in any case becoming enormous—as I observed in 1965—and in certain respects it far surpassed that of "ordinary" Communists in civilian clothes. A Party member at that time was, in the definition given by Liu Shao-ch'i, a "supplementary cadre." In his neighborhood or factory, his job was to hold periodical consultations with his comrades, who had been picked out as he had been, and to help those in authority to solve problems. This made him important and gave him access to decision-making centers, but did not always add to his popularity. He was "among the masses," but he no longer altogether belonged to the masses because of his vague function as an extra official. No such barrier cut off a soldier from the workers whom he had come to help. In a factory or a commune he was not required to settle any particular problems— he did that only in his barracks; he did not take part in meetings with the higher-ups; and nothing distinguished him from his temporary fellow workers. Besides, he was completely disinterested; he came along only when he was needed and asked for nothing in return. In leisure time, he sometimes spoke of his family tree traced back to poor peasants and helped town dwellers to understand "his China." According to the spokesmen I met in 1965, the model soldier Lei Feng deserved well of the Communist cause not only because of his daily good deeds but also because he helped the country to become aware of its overall problems.[42]

Certainly, to enter the army—this school of correct political thought—it was not enough to be of the right social origin. An annual age group in China consists of at least fifteen million young men, and the army cannot take them all. So Lin Piao was making his experiment in ideological unification with human material that was selected at the outset. But his conclusions, at the dawn of the

[41] In fact, Madame Chiang developed her cultural theories in 1969 at forums organized by the army.

[42] Personally cited by Mao as an example to the nation, Lei Feng has been since 1963, and posthumously too, the perfect illustration of Maoist altruism. I have told his life story in *China: The Other Communism*, pp. 245–50.

Cultural Revolution, were nevertheless definite: if brought into full contact with the doctrine, the masses were perfectly capable of making good revolutionary use of it and acting in a unitary and socialist way. Hence his famous declaration: "China is a great country of 700 million people and needs a unified thought. Only when we are united by the thought of Mao Tse-tung can we act in unity. A great country like ours would still be a scattering of disconnected grains of sand had it not possessed a unified thought. Only the powerful thought of Mao Tse-tung can ideologically unify our entire people." [43]

These sentences sum up a whole program that needs no gloss. But it is useless to stress its exaggerated and religious aspect without remembering that China had been warned by Mao since 1964 that, unless she succeeded in reviving the class struggle, "only a short time will pass, perhaps a few years or a decade, a few decades at the most, before a counterrevolutionary restoration *inevitably* occurs on a national scale, the Marxist-Leninist Party becomes a revisionist party, a fascist party, and the country changes color. Let our comrades reflect well on the danger that lies in this situation!" [44] This amounted to saying that the methods hitherto employed would lead to certain defeat, to a disaster on the Soviet scale. The authoritarian rap over the knuckles that the Party at once gave, by intervening in the countryside in force, earned it still more severe rebukes from Mao. Liu's "innovations," in Mao's eyes, came from the stock of methods already tested and found disastrous. It was necessary to head firmly in another direction, seek unprecedented forms and techniques of popular mobilization, and invite the masses to criticize the "dark side" of the regime and of all who benefited under it. Lin Piao's program was completely in line with the perspective envisaged by Mao. At the most, its distinctive feature was optimism as to the possibility of introducing, in a unifying manner, the new and indeed unprecedented form of relationships between governors and governed.

Lin Piao certainly stood for a trend that had always existed in the CCP and had always been seen as legitimate. But this does not

[43] See *Peking Review*, No. 52 (December 26, 1966).
[44] See Lin Piao's speech to the Ninth Party Congress, in *Documents of the CCP*.

mean that it had been organized for a long time and was a kind of party within the Party. One of the striking facts about the Cultural Revolution is that the classification of Chinese Communists made in the West—into those from Yenan, those from the underground in "white" areas, soldiers, or civilians—ceases to provide a key to the line taken by this or that leader, to unexpected promotions for some and the sudden fall of others. We have to accept that, even on the eve of this unusual period and in the face of unprecedented dangers, old links were broken and each man made up his own mind in relation to a problem that had never arisen so sharply.

Let us take the example of Ch'en Po-ta, who is now depicted as a long-standing accomplice of Lin Piao or even as the brains behind him. This professor of philosophy, coming from a poor peasant family and a graduate of the Sun Yat-sen University in Moscow (in the late 1920's), was one of the few leaders who never wore an army uniform or worked in the "sector of the masses." It is said in the West that at Yenan he was Mao's political secretary, but Chinese sources do not confirm this. His writings from this period are in the same vein as those of Liu Shao-ch'i and Ch'en Yün and are devoted, moreover, to the same problems of Party organization. He lavished much effort on proving that Mao had reached the same theoretical conclusions as Stalin without having read the latter's works; and, as may be imagined, this contribution to the history of the working-class movement was not much appreciated in Moscow, nor is it very valuable. To judge by his Yenan record, Ch'en Po-ta was more predestined to become a "great cultural despot" than Lu Ting-yi, who was working in the same sphere, but in uniform.

However, after accompanying Mao on his two trips to Moscow, Ch'en Po-ta took an unexpected direction. At the time of the Great Leap, his name appeared beside that of Lin Piao. The same session of the Eighth Congress that raised the latter to a vice-chairmanship made Ch'en the editor of a bimonthly journal, *Red Flag*, launched with great publicity. Was this a coincidence, or the start of a collaboration between Lin and Ch'en under Mao's patronage? All we know is that Ch'en was among the first, at the time of the Great Leap, to discover the Paris Commune and its themes of the abolition of the social division of labor and of

freedom through equality. After this period in the limelight, Ch'en
seems to stand aside from the great debates. He was certainly not
an ordinary citizen—as he liked to call himself, apparently—for
he had a seat in the Politburo (as an alternate member) and was
vice-chairman of the Academy of Sciences. Besides, he had his
team on *Red Flag*, where he trained a number of future leaders of
the Cultural Revolution (all leftists, and dismissed in the course of
time). But it is a big jump to deduce from this that he was plotting
with Lin Piao.

On the basis of verifiable information, we can only say that in
the atmosphere created by Mao's warnings Ch'en Po-ta and many
other Communists, young and old, reached the conclusion that
the Party as an institution was the barrier preventing the masses
from absorbing the thought of Mao and expressing themselves "in
the superstructure" in a proletarian fashion. The Party therefore
had to stop playing this harmful role, and to this end it was
reasonable to try to put the masses in direct contact with doctrine,
in accordance with Lin Piao's plan. This was also the best way to
defuse the revisionist time bomb planted somewhere near the top
of the Party, and to forestall, for good, attempts at the usurpation
of power. Finally, if all revolutionary potentialities were really
concentrated below, among the people, why keep to the old
system of lessons handed down from above? But did not this
theory owe everything to the statements of Mao himself about the
revolutionary aspirations of the masses and their ability to destroy
old ideas by engaging in class struggle?

In any case, the rise of Lin Piao's star in 1966 was proportional
to the decline of Liu Shao-ch'i's, and the latter no doubt observed
the fact even in matters of detail. In January 1965, on the thirtieth
anniversary of Mao's accession to the Chairmanship of the CCP at
the Tsunyi conference, a commemorative stamp, widely circulated in the country, showed Mao and Lin—and only these
two—discussing plans for the battles to be waged during the Long
March. Liu had also taken part in the historic 1935 meeting, and
his disappearance from the picture was surely not accidental.

Moreover, on June 1, 1965, all the ranks in the Chinese Army,
introduced in 1955, were abolished. From now on there would be
no marshals, generals, or officers; the People's Army would be
completely egalitarian. To tell the truth, even before this I had

never been able to see the difference between an officer and a private, for it seemed to me that they were all dressed modestly and democratically in their outsize uniforms and straw shoes. But the change was regarded as highly important, and the deputy editor in chief of *People's Daily*, Chen Chun, gave me the reason of his own accord:

> In Chairman Mao's famous phrase, an army is only really effective when its relationship to the people is that of a fish to water. But only a profoundly democratic and egalitarian army can stay close to the people, helping them in their labors and living with them. The threat that hangs over our country has increased recently as a result of American aggression in Vietnam and the treason of the modern revisionists. A great debate was therefore organized in our army, and after several months of discussion at all levels the decision was made to strengthen even further the bonds between the army and the people by abolishing rank and giving soldiers an even more intensive political education.[45]

Now, this intensive education was based on the Little Red Book of quotations from Chairman Mao, produced by Lin Piao himself and first used in the army as an experiment in the perspective of the Cultural Revolution. Here was the vital weapon for the ideological unification of 700 million Chinese.

The Explosive Spring of 1966

Was there an attempt at a Khrushchev-style coup d'état in China, or did Lin Piao altogether invent it "because history, for him, is reduced to a series of palace revolutions and does not follow from the class struggle"? [46] Here we are at the heart of the episode that was to spark off the Cultural Revolution and to bring in its train, though very much later, the indictment of the "crooks of the Liu Shao-ch'i type"—meaning Lin Piao.

In the simplest terms, the episode can be summed up thus: in the months of September and October 1965, in the course of two enlarged meetings of the Politburo attended by leaders of the

[45] See *China: The Other Communism*, p. 317.
[46] This charge was made by Radio Shanghai on November 24, 1972. See *China Quarterly*, No. 53 (1973).

Party's regional bureaus, Mao spoke about the forthcoming Cultural Revolution (although no one knew what it would consist of) and, as an example of the ideological struggle to be waged against "old ideas," made a criticism of the pseudo-historical writings of the deputy mayor of Peking, Wu Han,[47] a non-Communist who had made a specialty of allusive literature. The Group of Five, made responsible for this new battle, took careful note but decided on no concrete measures. On November 10 a Shanghai Young Turk, Yao Wen-yuan, published an attack on the accused historian in his local paper, *Wen Hui Pao*, without consulting the Peking authorities, who were sheltering Wu Han. P'eng Chen, leader of the Group of Five, telephoned the paper to deplore this lack of Party spirit. But he accepted the fait accompli and had Yao's article reprinted in Peking, as if to minimize the importance of the incident. Wu Han was then taken to task in the Peking press by one of his best friends and promptly made a self-criticism, admitting that he had "forgotten the class struggle."

The Group of Five met again in February and drew up a program for concrete action with the help of about ten experts, including Wang Li of *Red Flag*. This document again spoke of the struggle that had to be waged against bourgeois scholars, such as Wu Han, to ensure the dominance of proletarian ideas and prevent a Soviet-style "restoration." The plan, finally presented by P'eng Chen himself, stressed the importance of this struggle,

[47] Wu Han, a specialist on the Ming dynasty, had become a fellow traveler during the war with Japan, when he was teaching at Kunming. After the foundation of the People's Republic, he became a professor at Peking University and continued to be very active in cultural politics, but without joining the Party. Made deputy mayor, he was treated with great respect as an academic celebrity, and in this capacity he was even on personal terms with the highest leaders. In 1961 he published a play, *Hai Jui Dismissed from Office*, about the misfortunes of an honest mandarin in 1559 who came to the defense of the peasants in the region of Suchow and vainly begged the Emperor to listen to his good advice. Hai Jui's pleas were no more acceptable to the Ming ruler than those of P'eng Teh-huai were to Mao, and both were dismissed. All the evidence shows that the author's aim was to criticize this recent dismissal, not to discuss the historical merits of the sixteenth-century figure. But in 1961 this intervention, clearly disinterested, in the affairs of the leading group attracted little attention and was not treated as a scandal. Some years later, Mao cited it to show the political character of the writings of people who claimed to be scholars wholly concerned with studies of historical personalities.

which had gone awry in the USSR, and explained that it required
large-scale preparation by Communist intellectuals, who would
have to defeat their ideological opponents by determined argument. "Discussions should not be limited to political questions," it
declared, "but should go broadly into the various academic and
theoretical issues that are relevant." [48] To conclude, it repeated
Mao's old directive on the need to "encourage expression, give
free scope to the public voice, so that everyone may venture to
speak, criticize, and discuss." Thus the Cultural Revolution was
seen here as a sort of new Hundred Flowers campaign, reserved in
the first place for intellectuals.

One of the members of the Group of Five, K'ang Sheng,[49]
declined to approve of this report. But P'eng Chen, "using the
most infamous methods and acting in an arbitrary manner, abused
his power and hastily put this document into circulation throughout the Party, usurping the name of the Central Committee." [50]
Neither Mao nor Lin nor the other leaders knew of this circular,
presented as an official Party document. Nor does it seem,
incidentally, that Liu was any better informed, and it is known
that he took no part in the private discussions that followed,
because he then left for an official visit to several Asian countries.
After his return a series of new consultations took place about
P'eng Chen's conduct and the content of his document. Finally
Mao personally intervened on May 16, 1966. He dissolved the
Group of Five and appointed a new Central Group for the
Cultural Revolution, composed of eighteen leaders and presided
over by Ch'en Po-ta. More than this, he made his contribution to a
new Central Committee circular, and now he took the gloves off:

[48] See *Documents of the Great Proletarian Cultural Revolution* (Hong Kong:
Union Research Institute, 1968), p. 7.

[49] K'ang Sheng, born in 1903, a member of the Politburo in 1937, greatly assisted
Mao in the rectification campaign in Yenan in 1942–4. After the victory he worked
in Shantung Province but held no posts on the very top level in the Party machine,
despite his Politburo rank. He was reputed to be a specialist on problems of
organization, but nothing precise is known of his activities during these years. In
contrast, during the Cultural Revolution he distinguished himself as one of the
outstanding leaders and became number five in the Party. In theory he still holds
this rank today, though his absence from the political scene seems to indicate that
he is no longer active.

[50] This criticism of P'eng Chen's document appears in the preamble to the
"Circular of May 16."

We must criticize the representatives of the bourgeoisie who have infiltrated into the Party, the government, the army, and cultural circles. . . . Above all, we must not put any trust in them by placing them in directing positions in the Cultural Revolution. Many of them have been in these positions and are still there, and this creates the greatest danger. . . . Certain others, for example individuals of the Khrushchev type, still benefit by our confidence, they have prepared themselves to be our successors, and they are now in our midst.[51]

This very clearly changed the objective of the Cultural Revolution. The target was no longer Wu Han or any other professors, but the leadership of the Party itself. The Party machine, indeed, was described as a collection of "great despots who read neither books nor newspapers, who lack all knowledge and have no contact with the masses, but who usurp the name of the Party, show themselves to be arbitrary, and give orders to others." As a supreme sarcasm, this peremptory document was sent to "all district committees and all Party committees in cultural institutions and in the army," together with the circular of the wretched P'eng Chen, so that these bodies could "judge which of the two documents is right and make it known what they think." The calmness of the discussions may well be imagined.

But, even before delivering this blow at the "despots . . . who lack all knowledge," Mao had, on May 7, sent a programmatic letter to Lin Piao to express approval of his work in the army, "this great school where men are trained on the political, military, and cultural level while they also undertake agricultural and subsidiary production and manage medium-size and small factories"; to define the tasks of all classes and social groups (workers, peasants, students); and in fact to manifest his endorsement of the vice-chairman's ideas.[52] From this moment, Lin was in reality the number two of the regime, Mao's "closest comrade in arms," and was given the green light for his campaign of ideological unification.

Basically, Mao was repeating in this letter his familiar theories on the need to break down barriers between classes by diversifying the occupations of all workers and getting them to take a

[51] See "The May 16 Circular," *Peking Review*, No. 21 (May 19, 1967).
[52] See "The Whole Country Should Become a Great School of Mao Tse-tung's Thought," *Peking Review*, No. 32 (August 5, 1966).

more active part in cultural life. But there were some new features: "The length of schooling must be reduced, and there must be a revolution in teaching; the domination of bourgeois intellectuals in our educational institutions must cease." Also, he no longer mentioned the Party at all. Here was a document written in the spirit of "the masses must liberate themselves," and nothing—good or bad—was said of the role that the Party might play in this great undertaking. Even if it left the way open for later clarifications, it was a tremendous omission.

Lin Piao interpreted it in his own style. Since the traditional instrument had been contaminated from within, the masses must be given the weapon of Chairman Mao's thought without reliance on intermediaries. This was the prelude to the unleashing of a cult such as China had never known. On May 18, at an enlarged Politburo meeting (and this time in Mao's absence), Lin made a speech on the value and content of Mao's thought. And he went at it in no halfhearted manner, to judge by the extracts that later appeared on Red Guard posters: "Chairman Mao has a much greater practical experience than Marx, Engels, and Lenin, who did not personally lead a proletarian revolution for a long time. Lenin was not in command for such a long time as Mao. . . . Comrade Mao is the greatest Marxist-Leninist of our era. He has continued to safeguard and develop Marxism-Leninism in a manner marked by genius, creative and consistent."

But in the same speech, when he joined in branding the former Group of Five for its ineffectiveness, Lin accused it of having deliberately opposed Mao's directives and of having perpetrated, by virtue of this, a real coup d'état. This dramatic charge was without precedent. The circulation, even unauthorized, of a document not approved by the Central Committee could not endanger the Chinese regime, and, to say the least, it is difficult to see this as a plot. It seems that the terms in which Lin attacked the "usurpers" caused a great deal of surprise, in view of the customary—though scarcely gentle—language that had been required in criticisms of far more dangerous deviators. If we are to credit a letter written by Mao to his wife, dated July 8, 1966, and brought to the attention of Party cadres in 1972, the Chairman himself was shocked by the excessive praise of his genius and by Lin's theory of the February coup d'état. But he agreed to the circulation of Lin's speech, explaining to his wife that he could not oppose it, although "for the first time in my life, I am stating my agreement with others against my own inclination."

The die was cast. The whole of the Left, as Mao himself has recognized, began to speak in the same terms as Lin Piao and in fact to dissociate Mao's thought, as a guide for the masses, from the organization of a Party that was no longer capable of giving them leadership. Exactly a week after Lin's speech, a group of young teachers in Peking University put up, on the wall of the office of the president, Lu P'ing, the first *ta tzu pao*—a poster in large characters, which are a sign of anger. Mao did not learn of this until a few days later; he then gave instructions that this unusual document should be broadcast on the radio and presented as a remarkable Marxist-Leninist text. This was done on June 1, 1966, the D-day of the Cultural Revolution.

Postscript
Tachai: A Different System for Work and the Distribution of Its Fruits

Every day, thousands of peasants from all parts of China come to Tachai to visit the model brigade that Chairman Mao has put forward as an example since 1964. After long journeys in trucks over the mountainous roads of the northwest, they unfurl their red flags as though for a festival, but they do not waste a minute of their brief stay. By the time they leave at nightfall, they will have dutifully toured the terraced fields, carved out on the slopes of the seven mountains of Taiheng by the heroic workers of the brigade. During their meals, generally taken in the open air, propaganda teams will have given them political and technical lectures so that, back in their communes, they can explain all about the Tachai methods and their ideological content. This continuous invasion goes on without noise or confusion. Each studious and disciplined group follows its program and tries hard not to interrupt or even distract the members of the brigade at work on the terraces or in the pigsties. As you watch this smooth-running process, you understand how 11 million Red Guards could have come to Peking in 1966 and spent weeks "exchanging experiences" without disorganizing the life and the work of its inhabitants.

Since the Cultural Revolution, the Tachai methods have been extended to the whole district. Visits are more numerous and sometimes longer; it takes time to see everything. I spent five days at Tachai and was "received," as one says here, by Madame Sung Li-ying, the number two of the brigade, by the ex-soldier Wang, and by two younger men. My interpreter, Tao, and I shared all their meals, went into their houses, and met their friends, while they talked about their lives and their worries. To round off this intimate contact with the peasant world of the northwest, Ch'en Yung-kuei himself explained to me the political history of his brigade.

The fame of this peasant leader has not yet spread beyond the frontiers of China, which almost comes as a surprise. His speeches rate more space in the national press than those of some members of the Politburo, and his portrait is found in every village, accompanied by Mao's famous directive urging: "Take inspiration from Tachai." Everyone in China knows the smiling face, with a white band over the forehead, of this peasant from the northwest. In his own region he is surrounded by a miniature but real personality cult; people speak of him in every connection and are always ready to tell of how—the son of a poor peasant, suffering under the old regime[53]—he became in every way the model of a revolutionary Communist. In the museum at Hsiyang, the capital of the district, all this is abundantly illustrated with photographs, graphs, and statistics. One can hardly tell which is more famous, Tachai or Ch'en Yung-kuei. Since the Cultural Revolution, the moving spirit of the model brigade has become a member of the Central Committee of the CCP and vice-chairman of the Revolutionary Committee of Shansi Province, but his glory is

[53] Coming from one of the poorest families in the village, Ch'en worked from the age of eight for a landowner who had driven his father to suicide by putting him out of his farm because he was too old. During the famines of earlier years, Ch'en's father had sold his wife and daughter, who never returned to the village.

linked above all to the work he has done in his village and his commune.[54] When one meets him, one is not disappointed. This self-taught man—he learned to read and write only in 1960, at the age of forty-six—is a born storyteller. A political storyteller, of course; his intelligence grasps intuitively, beyond the facts, the underlying processes that give meaning to them. This peasant with his lined and smiling face, whose "right ideas" obviously come from unbroken firsthand experience, showed me more clearly than anyone else the concrete day-to-day reality of social relationships in the countryside.

However, my visit began with a slight disappointment. After traveling all night—seven hours by train and two in a light truck—I found my first sight of Tachai at dawn far from inspiring. The famous village looked like a small working-class housing project weirdly transported to the mountains. The 438 inhabitants occupy half a dozen massive stone buildings, two stories high, enclosed by an avenue lined with weeping willows. True, the mountain forms the background to these curious buildings and the beauty of the landscape redeems them in broad daylight. But in the half-light this gray scene struck me as very ugly. Madame Sung, a frail woman of thirty-eight, was also not at her best at this unusual hour, but she saw that I was not carried away by delight. "Before 1963," she told me, "we lived in caves, but they were wrecked by the torrential rains. We built these homes ourselves, from our own resources." She praised their comfort and promised to show me everything after a bit of rest; the tour was to begin at eleven o'clock.

The brigade's 133 acres were spread out, sometimes quite far from the village, among the surrounding mountains. The nearest of these was called the Tiger's Head (the tiger is a much-loved animal in China) and part of the brigade was working there at the time. Everything had been made by hand; there has never been any question of bulldozers or tractors at Tachai. But the brigade consists of only 155 workers, half of whom are women. Madame Sung told me, moreover, that the climate is exceptionally hard. The winters are very cold (eight degrees below zero Fahrenheit),

[54] Ch'en is also chairman of the district's Revolutionary Committee, which gives him an effective influence on the development of the commune and of his brigade.

the summers are torrid, and at the end of July the sky pours out in a single week all the rain that did not fall during the preceding months. Sometimes the terraces can hardly stand up to the battering, and after the disaster of 1963 they had to be almost entirely rebuilt and strengthened. A large reservoir and a complete irrigation system were also created to safeguard the brigade against both drought and floods. All this was impressive, but I had seen terraces on my previous trip in the neighboring province of Shensi, and I could not see in what way those of Tachai were superior.

We had lunch at noon, and Madame Sung drew lessons from each dish. For instance, many peasants had doubted the possibility of fishponds, but fish was now a regular part of the family menu. People were eating plenty of pork, and this was owing to the "battle for the collective pigsty" led by Ch'en Yung-kuei during the 1960's. The vegetables grown on the brigade fields were also more varied, better, and less costly than those of the former individual gardens. Between these dietary lectures, illustrated by examples from the kitchen, Madame Sung recalled the days when most of the people, at the mercy of natural disasters under the yoke of the old society, lived like beggars and could not even imagine that one day they would have enough to eat. She herself had been sold by her family as a child wife at the age of thirteen, for a hundred pounds of grain.[55]

A different kind of question arose when we visited the neighboring villages. Wuchiaping is a stone's throw from Tachai, and Ch'en Yung-kuei's methods are now being adopted there. Homes like those of Tachai were being built, and the two latest harvests (1969 and 1970) had been almost as good as those of the model brigade. But the backwardness of earlier years seemed to be tremendous and could be seen in the appearance of the villagers. Li Hsi-chen, Ch'en's counterpart in the Wuchiaping brigade, was not sparing of self-criticism. The faults of his people, he said, were even graver than Madame Sung had let me know. They had cut themselves off from Tachai through selfishness; thinking that their land was better, they had refused to share its

---

[55] The buyer, Chia Chin-tsai, was himself a very poor peasant. She is happy with him and they have five children.

produce with the Tachai people. Besides, they had distrusted Ch'en and his tendency to deliver the maximum amount of grain to the state. They were willing to deliver only the fixed quota—7 to 10 percent of the harvest—to keep up their own stocks and sell some of the crop on the free market. But, by thinking of nothing but their own interests, they produced the poorest harvests in the commune—in 1964, for instance, only a third of Tachai's yield per acre and half of the norm fixed for the region.

The village, still a mixture—old houses standing beside the new buildings under construction—illustrated this account. The collective pigsty had not yet been organized and piglets were wandering all over the place. Family food jars were half empty; everything seemed to be less tidy and prosperous than at Tachai. Now, these two villages belonged to the same commune, with twenty-four brigades and eleven thousand people; in theory, it was supposed to see that "the pacemakers help the backward" and prevent differences in the standard of living. If the contrast with Tachai was so glaring in 1971, four years after the conversion of Wuchiaping, what must the position have been in 1964? How could the commune, the district, and the state have blandly allowed such a gulf to exist between the two little communities?

Li Hsi-chen took all the blame upon himself and his comrades. The state had helped them after the 1963 floods and reduced taxes in 1964. But the evil was within the brigade, for each large family continued to behave as a clan.

Elsewhere in the district the story was much the same. The example of Tachai had not been imitated in time because of the "Old Four"—old culture, old habits, old ideas, old traditions. These were manifested in various ways—clan links here, poor participation in commune undertakings there, and elsewhere internal struggles to score work points or enlarge private plots of land—but the results were similar: bad harvests, few people joining in work on the land, a stagnant standard of living, financial difficulties, and fresh social distinctions through the relative enrichment of a minority of tricksters or speculators. "Our petty-bourgeois egotism was leading us straight to ruin," said Wang Kua-chu, Party secretary in the Hu Chuang brigade, thirty miles from Tachai. "The Cultural Revolution and Ch'en Yung-kuei's rise to power in the district had to come before we could

mobilize the poor peasants and break the deadlock," he concluded gravely. It was only after this salutary shock that the
brigades ceased to "put work points in the command post," made
a fresh start on major projects, built flood walls along the rivers,
laid out communal fields to select seed crops, and, in short,
resumed the projects of the Great Leap Forward, "which Liu
Shao-ch'i had obliged us to shut down." Not a doubt of it—there
was the guilty man, the arch-traitor who had covertly encouraged
the "Old Four" and sought the downfall of Ch'en Yung-kuei
himself.

Ch'en joined us at the end of our visit, having left me time to
see everything and prepare my questions. Thanks to Madame
Sung, he had a general idea of my impressions and knew that I
was interested in social aspects rather than agricultural techniques. This suited him, for what he most wanted to explain was
how Tachai had "put politics in command." He started a long way
back with his conviction, born after the revolution, that in such a
poverty-stricken region simply sharing out the land, or even
forming cooperatives, could not really change the situation but
would only redistribute poverty. Hence his determination to bring
about more radical changes and his search for political solutions.
Although he attributed all this to the thought of Chairman Mao,
Ch'en was well aware that he was an outstanding leader of men
and that, because of the principle of delegated management, he
had always had enough elbowroom for his personal initiative and
for "the practical search for good solutions." True, his power was
limited to the brigade—or to what was left of it after the secession
of Wuchiaping[56]—but of this power he made the greatest possible
use, and with very definite aims.

"A collectivist brigade is not just the result of adding up a
certain number of peasant households and of common ownership
of their land. It is viable only if the method of work and the
method of sharing the fruits of work are also transformed. The
rightists claimed, when the cooperatives were created in the
1950's, that such changes were feasible only with the mechaniza-

[56] With its 83 families and 438 inhabitants, Tachai is one of the smallest brigades
in China. The neighboring brigade of Wuchiaping has 270 families and 1,100
people, still well below the national average. Tachai's size is, in fact, more like that
of a work team, the basic unit within each brigade.

tion of agriculture. Chairman Mao's line, on the other hand, shows that first we must put our trust in the people to produce and share our goods in a more and more socialist manner, before bringing in tractors and such equipment." In this way Ch'en firmly stated the origin of the conflict between the two lines.

He skated fairly quickly over the first period of the communes and the excessive hopes of the Great Leap Forward. To explain the "good line" he had to contrast it with the "bad," and at that time perhaps the distinction was not sharp enough. We went on to the next period, that of the "difficult years" and the "international revisionist counteroffensive against China." The rightist "monsters," he said, then showed themselves in their true colors and urged, "with a great fuss," a retreat in the social sphere to achieve an advance in production. They decreed that norms should be fixed on a family basis, private plots of land enlarged, and the free market encouraged. The highest leader who took the capitalist road—as Ch'en, no doubt from force of habit, called Liu—said, "We must not be afraid, for a time, to give free rein to capitalism." The other leader who took the same road, Teng Hsiao-p'ing, proclaimed, "No matter whether a cat is black or white, it is a good cat if it catches rats." [57]

However, these counsels were probably not so imperative, since at Tachai Ch'en took no notice of them. He stuck to the proletarian line, which had taught for a long time that not all methods are permissible under socialism. The inadequate production of the preceding years, he said, was not in the least due to an excess of collectivism, but to the partial and contradictory nature of that collectivism. "What held back the socialist momentum of our brigade was the system of payment based on work points, and the inadequate understanding between the cadres and the rank and file. That's where you can understand the importance of the watchword: 'Put politics in command,'" he announced with satisfaction.

The old system (in reality it still prevails in China and can be described as "old" only at Tachai) functioned like this: each job

[57] These quotations from Liu and Teng, circulated "with a great fuss" throughout China during the Cultural Revolution, cannot be found in any of their speeches during the period of their alleged guilt. It is thus impossible to find out when and to whom these leaders uttered such "absurdities."

carried a certain number of points, and the jobs requiring the greatest skill—or physical strength—were the best paid. At first sight, this is in complete conformity with the socialist principle of "to each according to his work." But in fact the work is related to the market value of its outcome. The strongest, the best-trained, and the cleverest chalked up many points, while others, especially women, earned little although they carried out their tasks very conscientiously. Since their work was thus devalued, they ended up by leaving the fields to devote themselves to domestic, or in any case nonagricultural, work. "Very often," Ch'en said, "we no longer had the manpower for jobs that were badly paid but indispensable."

The word "we" brought him to the second aspect of this sensitive problem. "We" meant the five permanent cadres of the brigade, who allocated the work and reckoned up its value. As delegated managers, they had a duty to bring on their comrades and guide them technically and politically. To do this, they naturally required a broad consensus, and if confidence in them declined, everything went from bad to worse. Now, the logic of the old system led inexorably to a deterioration in the relationships between the cadres and the members of the brigade. "As you have seen," Ch'en continued, "the fields of Tachai are very spread out. We were on the move from morning to night to get the workers there and to check on their work; but, first of all, we couldn't be everywhere at once and, secondly, we ourselves made no contribution to production. People blamed us for every unfair fixing of points and murmured all over the place that 'the cadres have an easy life—they stroll about on the mountains and get paid for it.' The newly rich—those who had chalked up the most points—often managed to block our proposals for collective investments by playing on the 'old ideas' of certain members of the brigade; their aim was always to raise the value of the points they had already accumulated without caring about the future or the common interest. To tell you the truth, only this minority benefited from the efforts of the brigade."

But fortunately Ch'en recovered himself in time, well before his credibility with the "poor peasants and lower strata of medium-poor peasants" was exhausted. With their help, he succeeded in introducing a new method of payment based on political yardsticks: that is, taking account of each worker's collectivist attitude of dedication, his honesty, and the quality of his work. "We cadres started to work like everyone else on building new terraces and we said, 'Reckon up your points yourselves; after all, you're together all day in the fields and you can see who is making a real effort and who is fulfilling his norm by a trick or because he's as strong as a bull. The best thing is for everyone to suggest for himself how many points he thinks he has earned, and for the rest of you to give your opinion.' This is how we established the system of 'personal declarations and public accounting' that is still in force. At first the meetings were frequent and pretty stormy. It wasn't that people cheated—no, most of them were too timid. But everybody was interested and everybody came to the fields; mothers and youngsters cheerfully started working three hundred days a year. Now, when you can rely on the power of the community like that, you're sure to get good harvests. And when the amount to be shared out is big, it's easier to agree on what each person deserves and to make your own estimate. At present we hold our public accounting sessions once or twice a year. It saves time, and it's fairer to make judgments over a long period. At the end of each period, we choose a 'model man' and we fix the scale of points by this yardstick. But the variation in earnings has to be limited. It's now between a maximum of eleven points and a minimum of five for a day worker."

It was not to be thought, however, that everything went smoothly, without hitches and without conflicts between the two lines. First, in 1963, there was the flooding disaster. The terraces were broken, the village was practically destroyed, and all the progress of earlier years was endangered. No harder trial for the little community could have been imagined; its neighbors, who had not taken up its methods, almost made fun of it. Yet in theory the whole district was at the mercy of state aid and all the brigades were in the same plight. In practice, this was not how things worked out. "The state offered us help four times," Ch'en declared proudly, "and four times we refused it. We went back to work and the families almost unanimously gave up their private plots (only two families voted against) so as to devote themselves better to restoring the terraces and building the stone dwellings. We did have a little grain in store, which enabled us to look

ahead, but the main factor was political; we were convinced that
our efforts were equitably valued, and that it was fairer and more
useful to put in extra hours in the brigade than to seek a solution
through cultivating little private plots. Of course, Comrade Sung
and I and the other cadres had the confidence of the brigade, but
the decisions of 1963 were taken without any pressure from us. So,
from 1964 onward, we succeeded in getting a maize crop that was
twice the estimate for our region and a little above the estimate
for the rich Yangtze region."

So, to judge from Ch'en's tone, it was victory all along the line.
But his expression suddenly darkened and the smile vanished from
his eyes. It was at the moment of triumph that the achievement
was suddenly menaced by the defenders of the "bad line," by the
"bourgeois general staff of Liu Shao-ch'i." "Our report on the
1964 harvest reached Peking," Ch'en said, weighing his words, "in
September of that year. It showed that each family in the brigade,
on the average, would sell to the state 1,500 kilograms of grain
crops, more than estimated. We explained, moreover, that this
result could have been obtained only through a collective effort,
because we did not fix the norms on a family basis. In Peking,
certain of these bourgeois gentlemen were at once filled with
panic. It was the period of 'socialist education' and the campaign
of the 'four cleanups.' The Party center was sending out work
teams to check on accounts, stocks, the use made of public
property, and the allocation of work points in brigades. It would
have been good sense to send these teams to backward communes. But no, if you can imagine it, it was we at Tachai who
were first on the list and who were sent the biggest and toughest
work team. As soon as they got here, these controllers announced
that I was suspended from my duties as secretary of the Party cell
and the Tachai administration. They also pushed out Comrade
Sung and her husband, though he was chairman of the Association
of Poor Peasants in our village, and decreed that they were going
to run everything themselves until the end of the checkup. The
brigade was thunderstruck."

My host still smarted from the insult. "Suspended," he repeated
two or three times, "for having applied political standards at
Tachai and given the national community twice as much grain as
the forecast. Well, at this critical time in the struggle between the

two lines, I went to Peking. I was personally received by
Chairman Mao, who had read our report and understood us better
than anyone. He asked me questions about our work and gave me
important instructions for the future. It was the greatest encouragement, the most powerful support, the most profound
help . . ." Words failed him for conveying the effect of such an
event. I could quite understand his emotion, but it seemed to me
that this time—and at the critical point—he was rather slurring
over the complexities of the "struggle between two lines." In fact,
it was not the unjustly persecuted innovator whom Mao was
receiving, but the Shansi Province member of the third National
People's Congress, which had just unanimously elected Liu
Shao-ch'i as Chairman of the Republic. Purely by chance, in 1965,
I had seen a documentary film of this session in a village cinema
near Nanking,[58] and it was in this film that Ch'en was presented
for the first time as the "model peasant." He was shown, if I
remember rightly, voting for Liu, and definitely in Liu's company
during a break in the session. The Party vice-chairman seemed to
be congratulating him as warmly as Chairman Mao, and he too
said, "In agriculture, we must learn from Tachai."

This was a delicate subject and I framed my objection with
extreme prudence and many circumlocutions, but Ch'en grasped
the point at once and was far less put out than I expected. "Yes,
indeed," he said, "I was a deputy from Shansi at the Congress in
December 1964, and the work team had finished its pointless
checkup,[59] so that I had once again become secretary of the
Tachai Party cell. As for my having voted for Liu, there's no
problem about that. At that time nobody imagined that he was a
'Chinese Khrushchev' and was 'taking the capitalist road.' That
fellow knew how to hide his game," Ch'en explained, very pleased
to enlighten me, "or else he wouldn't have kept his job for
twenty-four hours in a country entirely devoted to Chairman Mao.

[58] Marc Riboud and I saw this film at the "October" commune, near Nanking;
we were particularly surprised to find the village cinema crammed, though
apparently the working day was not yet over. I also remember being rather
intrigued by the wave of cheering that greeted each appearance of Ch'en
Yung-kuei, who was then quite unknown to me.

[59] In fact, the work team spent forty-two days at Tachai, from mid-October to
the end of November 1964.

At the time, I didn't even imagine that he had anything to do with the behavior of the work team at Tachai. But the Cultural Revolution taught us a lot, and the whole thing became clear with hindsight."

Suddenly he began to paint the work teams in rather different colors. He recognized, for instance, that a checkup on the management of brigades was necessary, that China "is a single treasury," and that the center had to intervene in the affairs of basic units "to help the backward ones and to prevent abuses." Besides, when they arrived in the communes, the work teams presented themselves as liberators of the rank and file and claimed that they were going to listen to everyone who had suffered from the bad management of the preceding period. In practice, however, their methods were not good and "did not help the masses at all." The tone of this new explanation was calmer; my host criticized without vilifying and even sometimes called the members of the teams "comrades." Still, it was clear that he did not take these comrades to his heart and found it hard to forgive their mistakes.

These teams were made up of a certain number of provincial leaders, their assistants, and some "little cadres." In the Tachai commune (to which the Tachai brigade belongs) there were seventy of these individuals altogether, or three to each brigade on the average, but it might have been different elsewhere. Once on the spot, these "comrades" suspended the administration—as at Tachai—and invited the "governed" to bring their complaints on political or accounting irregularities. "At Tachai," Ch'en went on calmly, "they didn't get very much, even from the formerly well-off families—we have twelve—who are less integrated with the brigade. We had no problems about the allocation of points and no tensions between the masses and the cadres. But just imagine what this method led to in the other brigades, where all sorts of quarrels had always been going on.

"When a cadre has to fix the points according to a hundred and thirty different norms, how can he help slipping into arbitrary decisions? Even if he's honest, he can't please everybody. Is it fair to put all the blame on the cadres, relying on statements from grumblers? After all, who were these accusers but former landlords and well-off families? Despite its 'Left' appearance, the method of the work teams was typically rightist; instead of liberating the poor, it eased the path of the bad elements. I could take an example from any of the four hundred and fifteen brigades in our district—the story was always the same. And then, is it right to turn up in a brigade and order straightway, 'Your managers are all suspended and suspect'? Here, in November 1964, heavy snow had fallen and, as they were expecting one of their provincial officials, they asked the brigade to clear the road. Nobody agreed; the people said that they wouldn't take orders from just anybody. 'We'll do it if Ch'en Yung-kuei tells us, otherwise it's out of the question.' So the head of the team came to see me to get me to bring along the brigade. I looked at him with an air of surprise: 'I've been suspended till the end of the checkup, I have no authority, how can I bring the brigade?'" Ch'en couldn't stop laughing about this episode. "But," he assured me nevertheless, "all this was not funny; it was very confusing and incomprehensible. Just think, these men in the work teams were often veterans of the war with Japan, they had known all about the problems of the countryside, they had been able to follow the mass line in the past. And now all of a sudden they were behaving like strangers, mixing with the masses as badly as oil does with water."

Ch'en now came to his actions during the Cultural Revolution. "Between February and April 1967, having taken power in the district, we too formed rank-and-file teams that went into all the communes to carry out investigations and spread the directives of Chairman Mao. We helped the cadres to understand their mistakes and accept the criticisms of the masses, so that their ideology could be changed and they could make a good fresh start in a revolutionary spirit. We also examined the problems of each brigade to understand their difficulties better and give them some help, not to punish this or that person. We started 'flying teams,' which helped the backward places; we put fields under cultivation even on waste land, to produce selected crops as a common effort, thus encouraging the understanding of the masses. This hard work was not in vain; in the Hsiyang district the 1967 harvest was 40 percent up on 1966. As you've seen for yourself, most of the brigades are now catching up with Tachai. People even wonder why it took them all this time to give up the old methods and work in a more collectivist, more rational way. But the reason is quite simple, as I've already told you. First we had to strike down the handful of leaders who took the capitalist road and unmask Liu Shao-ch'i. Without that, nothing was possible."

Madame Sung added the final touch to this lesson. "During the Cultural Revolution," she said, "we made the members of the work team come back to Tachai for 'struggle and self-criticism sessions.' They made us a handsome apology and fully admitted their connivance with Liu's general staff. As they seemed to be sincere, we didn't inflict any reproaches on them. We simply asked them to build a few terraces—just a spot of manual work to learn that it's harder to build terraces than to measure them." Madame Sung laughed heartily, but Ch'en did not; he even looked at her rather sternly. In fact, this Tachai attitude was not exemplary, having regard to the known directives of the leaders of the Cultural Revolution, who had categorically advised against "struggle and self-criticism sessions" aimed at those responsible for the "four cleanups" campaign. Indeed, it can well be imagined how spontaneous the "admissions" were.

Before coming to my questions, Ch'en mentioned a few personal problems. Here again, he sought to bring out a general contradiction from his own example. He admitted frankly that the many honors showered upon him were becoming a weight on his shoulders. He was afraid lest the numerous duties he had been obliged to take on should divert him from his work on the spot. As a member of the Central Committee, vice-chairman of the Provincial Revolutionary Committee, assigned to speak for Tachai in the provinces, in Peking, and even abroad—he had already been to Albania—he was afraid of becoming like one of those cadres in the work teams who, after giving good service to the people, had got out of touch. "I have decided to work with my brigade in the fields for at least two hundred days a year, and I must carry out this aim at any cost. I often say to myself, 'You were born in a family of workers and you must not forget how to work with your hands, or you'll forget your class origin.' The study of the works of Chairman Mao also takes a lot of time and must not be neglected. How can one manage to be equal to all these tasks, to revolutionize one's mind all the time and advance with the brigade?"

Tao, the interpreter, reminded me that we had to catch the Peking train at two o'clock in the morning and that, allowing for the road journey to the station, we had only forty minutes left. I hastened to put a few questions. How was it, I asked, that after so many struggles to spread the Tachai system, the method of payment—at least in all the communes I had visited near the big cities and in Kiangsi Province—was exactly the same as before the Cultural Revolution (which was obviously not to say that it was the same as the Soviet system)?

Before the Cultural Revolution, Ch'en replied, the system of work points had been regarded as fundamentally right, and as necessary during a very long period of socialist construction. "Now it is recognized as being nothing of the sort, because it leads to dangerous social polarizations within brigades and indeed slows down their productive enthusiasm. So the Party is seriously fighting for the adoption of our system of personal declarations and public accounting, and this is important. We receive at Tachai over a million and a half peasants every year, and they see for themselves how things work here. But our methods can be practiced only when they are well understood. They cannot be imposed from above. Some communes have opted by majority vote for the Tachai methods, but the Party has nevertheless decided that they should wait a while and make sure of broader support among the masses. Like it or not, the 'Old Four' are still very powerful in our countryside; you can't fight them by decrees. You must have persuasion and tangible results; you must spread the thought of Chairman Mao everywhere and teach people to fight selfishness and struggle against revisionism."

The engine of the truck was already ticking over, but Ch'en still wanted to hear about the position of peasants in my country. He apologized for not having asked me before and was worried about giving the impression that the world revolution was not close to his heart. I reassured him and got out some random remarks about the differences in landownership. To give him an example, I said that at home a peasant with twelve acres would be regarded as poor. "Is the land so bad? Or is there too much of it?" He would have liked to know more, for my remarks had disturbed him a little. "A poor peasant with twelve acres? After the revolution you'll have more problems than us with the 'Old Four.'"

But already his figure was vanishing in the darkness. The truck hurried along the empty road to make up for lost time; in China the trains are slow but are always punctual. Madame Sung said no more until she was sure that we would be in time. Then she reiterated her admiration for Ch'en Yung-kuei: "When you follow a good man, you become better; when you follow a wizard, you only learn magic dances." Was it an old Chinese proverb, or a final comment on the struggle between the two lines in the countryside?

CHAPTER THREE

In Quest of a
Commune of China

An Exemplary Anniversary

"This is the manifesto of the Peking commune of the 1960's," Mao said of the first wall poster of Peking University; and he went on to announce that China would soon witness the birth of "a wholly new form of state structure." [1] The poster, put up by seven young teachers in the philosophy faculty, did not, however, seem to have this ambition. Drafted by a young woman, Nieh Yüan-tzu—who was to become a national celebrity for a time—it dealt with problems already discussed in the press and was based chiefly on extracts from the "Circular of May 16," [2] which had not yet been

[1] The editorial in *Red Flag*, No. 3 (1967), which reports these words does not say to whom they were spoken but gives their date as June 1, 1966. See "On the Proletarian Revolutionaries' Struggle to Seize Power," *Peking Review*, No. 6 (February 3, 1967).

[2] This circular, like many other internal documents of the CCP in the past, inspired a whole series of editorials, commentaries, and speeches, in which phrases from the document were placed in quotation marks but their origin was not indicated. Later, when the circular was officially published in May 1967, it was simple to place these quotations—already well known—in their original context. We have therefore no grounds for saying that Miss Nieh, before drawing up her poster, had read the May 16 circular, which was reserved for Party leaders of a rank higher than hers. But she certainly must have made a close study of articles that had appeared the preceding week in *People's Daily* and other papers.

published. The boldness of Miss Nieh and her six colleagues consisted solely in the fact that they addressed themselves directly to their rank-and-file comrades, ignoring any kind of hierarchy, and thus started a new form of uncontrolled expression. It was no small innovation in a socialist country like China; even in the Hundred Flowers period, nothing had been published without the permission of the competent authorities. For Mao to encourage this "cry of wrath" against "reactionary academic authorities" and to hail it as a model of Marxism-Leninism was to sanctify this kind of direct protest and invite everyone to do likewise. A violation of the rules was thus raised by the highest authority in the country to the status of an exemplary sign of revolutionary spirit. The nationwide publicity given to Nieh Yüan-tzu's *ta tzu pao* (wall poster) was itself a historic event. This being so, in what sense did Mao see the episode as foreshadowing a Commune of China and the imminent coming of a new form of state in the whole country? He was led to this position by the questions posed in the fundamental debate of that spring of 1966, in which the reference to the Paris Commune played an essential part.[3]

Then, in the spring of 1966, *Red Flag* printed a resounding article on the ninety-fifth anniversary of the Commune. It was signed by Cheng Chih-su, a name absent from any Chinese *Who's Who*, and perhaps a collective pseudonym for Ch'en Po-ta and his four close comrades who were soon to form the Central Group for the Cultural Revolution. Among the "great lessons of the Paris Commune," this article stressed the "need for the proletariat, after taking power, to prevent its state organisms from being transformed from servants of society into masters." It may well be that the Communards, in their seventy-two days of power, were not keenly concerned about the dangers of such a long-term "revisionist" transformation, but the specter of "restoration" was an acute anxiety in the China of the 1960's. *Red Flag* added: "We have been racking our brains for years to find a remedy to the danger of a split between the proletarian state and the masses,

---

[3] Professor John Bryan Starr of the University of California at Berkeley has collected some interesting factual material on this subject in his essay "The Paris Commune through Chinese Eyes," *China Quarterly*, No. 49 (1972). I do not, however, share his conclusions.

while the answer to this problem has existed since 1871 and we need only adapt it to our conditions."

What was it? "The Commune's source of strength," declared the article, "lay in the enthusiasm and revolutionary initiative of the masses." Thanks to their neighborhood organizations, they had been able to control the executive right from the period of the Government of National Defense and, after the proclamation of the Commune, to neutralize the "mistaken" schemes of the followers of Proudhon and of Blanqui. No evil leader—no earlier-day Khrushchev—had been able to usurp power and sidetrack the Commune from its path, for three reasons: (1) "In the Commune, the proletariat was the master. . . . Its whole policy arose from proposals made by the masses, reflecting their interests. The leaders were elected by the workers and submitted to their control; they could, by law, be recalled and dismissed by the masses." (2) "The Commune was a working body, legislative and administrative at the same time. Its committees promulgated laws; the members charged with implementing them were responsible to these committees and to the people." (3) "The Commune set out to abolish that class property which makes the wealth of the few out of the labor of the many. In the words of Marx, it sought to transform the means of production, land, and capital, which are essentially the means of enslavement and of the exploitation of labor, into simple instruments of free and collective work."

Admittedly the Commune "could not have been a complete and mature dictatorship of the proletariat" because it was neither guided by Marxist theory nor directed by a proletarian Party. But it was an instrument that "allowed the exploited to take their destinies into their own hands to liberate themselves." Most of the major decrees of the Commune "were based on proposals from the masses, in particular to end the system of high salaries for officials, to cancel arrears of rent, to institute nonreligious education, and to abolish nightwork in bakeries." Finally, the article paraphrased Engels's words: "Do you want to know what the dictatorship of the proletariat is like? Look at the Paris Commune" with "Do you want to know what a degenerate dictatorship of the proletariat is like? Look at the USSR under the domination of the revisionist clique." The contrast was clear.

Moreover, in a China that (it was said) had met with an attempt at "restoration" a month earlier, in February 1966, this exposition of the lessons of the Commune amounted to putting forward an immediate program. The men in power in 1966 were certainly not a collection of bourgeois, heirs of the 1871 Government of National Defense, or Proudhonists or Blanquists, but neither were they capable of eliminating the "rotten elements" that had spread in their midst. On this point, Mao's warnings, from his essay "Where Do Correct Ideas Come From?" to his twenty-three-point resolution of January 1965, had not been without effect. In the essay on the Commune, amounting to about fifteen thousand words, there was only one reference to the Party of the proletariat—laudatory indeed, but merely pointing out that the Party was needed to ensure a "complete and mature dictatorship of the proletariat." This was as much as to say that it would be built—or rebuilt—in the course of events, in the movement unleashed by "the people's centers of revolutionary action."

The crux of the matter was whether these centers really existed, for no firm conclusions could be drawn from the experience of the Associations of Poor and Medium-Poor Peasants during the "four cleanups" campaign. The salvos fired by critics of the cultural machine had echoed more resoundingly, but only in fairly limited circles of Party members and intellectuals. As he said himself, Mao did not believe that the working-class masses had read these controversial articles, and this is why he showed his enthusiasm for the *ta tzu pao* of May 25; these posters in big characters, with their explosive content, would be far more accessible and effective than ordinary newspapers. Once people had the courage to express themselves thus, everything became possible, up to and including that "new form of state structure" inspired by the Commune. His private statement of June 1 clearly showed this hope.

The Students' Second Rebellion

Now, after the "Circular of May 16" and Lin's speech on the "February plot," the situation in China was strange, to say the least. Extracts from these documents filled the press and showed clearly that the Cultural Revolution would be neither an aca-

demic debate nor a Hundred Flowers campaign. Polemical
attacks threatened certain top leaders who had already been
badly mistaken in that regard and might have been guilty of acts
that were to be condemned, even of revisionist "crimes."
However, the leading group had not been reshuffled; it still
contained these "guilty men," as though to provoke doubts about
its integrity. In defiance of all precedent, news about confrontations at the top level was divulged while the debate was still
proceeding. The uproar in the universities, duly revealed by the
spreading of Nieh Yüan-tzu's poster, added still more to the
unusual atmosphere. Celebrations of the first Chinese thermo-
nuclear test, which had taken place on May 9, and of the treaty of
friendship with Albania were not enough to convince anyone that
things were normal.

On June 3, 1966, Liu Shao-ch'i decided to end the suspense. He
dismissed the mayor of Peking, P'eng Chen, reorganized the
Secretariat of the CCP, and removed the president of Peking
University and his deputy from their posts, as well as the chief
editors of the capital's newspapers.[4] He announced that Party
work teams would be sent into the main universities and teaching
centers to replace inadequate Party committees and help the
students to form their committees for the Cultural Revolution. It
was a big "sweep of the broom," to show at long last that "stains"
on the image of the Party would be energetically and definitely
wiped away. Headlines at once hailed "a new victory for the
thought of Mao Tse-tung" and crowds, "delirious with enthusiasm," demonstrated their joy to the sound of gongs and cymbals in
all the great cities.

"The leadership of the former Party committee in Peking . . .
has committed criminal antisocialist and anti-Party acts, degener-
ating into a bridgehead for the restoration of capitalism. Fortunately for the people, the Central Committee and Chairman Mao

[4] P'eng Chen was replaced as secretary of the Party in Peking by Li Hsüeh-feng,
formerly first secretary of the Party's North China Bureau. The post of deputy was
allotted to Wu Teh, first secretary of the Party committee in Kirin Province. On
the other hand, Madame Fan Chin lost her job as chief editor of Peking Daily and
Peking Evening, as well as that of deputy mayor of Peking. I met her and visited
these papers in 1965; see China: The Other Communism (New York: Hill and
Wang, 1967).

have taken the wise decision to extinguish this time bomb resolutely," wrote the commanders and soldiers of the army units stationed in Shanghai in their message of congratulations.[5] The revisionists had been identified and dismissed in time, because of the vigilance of the Party itself, and the worst dangers of the preceding months had been averted. In a calmer climate, the work teams would henceforth be able to direct the intellectuals and students in the ideological battle and help them to be truly filled by Mao's thoughts. There appeared to be no opposition to the dispatch of these groups; it was hailed in the press, including army papers, as a sign of the vitality of the Party and a proof of its determination to make a success of the Great Proletarian Cultural Revolution.

The Party was behaving according to its logic and its customs. Had it not taken these steps, it would not have been itself. But did they fit the circumstances? In the event, the actions of the work teams in the universities were to show, even more clearly than at the time of the "four cleanups," the Party's inability to allow "the people's centers of revolutionary action" to develop outside its control.

Each team was composed of about a hundred tried leaders and was well briefed on the line it was to pursue. In particular, when moving into a given university, it knew that the rank and file had the right to organize and speak up directly through posters, since Chairman Mao had given his approval. So the task was to create in the educational sphere the equivalent of Associations of Poor and Medium-Poor Peasants in the communes. And, just as in the countryside, the rank and file had to be allowed to check on the record of the cadres of the earlier period; its criticisms and suggestions had to be listened to, its needs taken into account. After that, education would be reformed, purged, and rendered healthy. The importance attached to this undertaking was such that the Party appointed to its work teams not only cadres of the highest rank but also the most popular "rebels," such as Miss Nieh Yüan-tzu of Peking University. Liu Shao-ch'i's wife, Wang Kuang-mei, too, joined a particularly large group that stepped in

[5] See "Nationwide Support for C.P.C. Central Committee Decision," *Peking Review*, No. 25 (June 17, 1966).

at Tsinghua, the great polytechnic university of Peking, personally directed by the minister of higher education, Chiang Nan-hsiang.

So these Party emissaries who took over "power" everywhere on June 9 lacked neither qualifications nor good intentions. Later it was to be said that they were the worst of revisionists, bent on setting up a "white terror." [6] Nevertheless, they carried the works of Mao and not those of Khrushchev in their struggle against everything more or less akin to revisionism. They set their faces in the first place against members of their own Party who were unequal to their tasks. Knowing from the start that many of these cadres owed their posts to the dismissed leaders of the former Party Committee of Peking, they were bound to suspect the whole lot and began by carefully investigating each individual case. They therefore decided that the cadres should stay shut up in their rooms to write self-criticisms, or at least to explain in writing whatever they knew about the "black gang" that had just been thrown out. Only those who could prove their good faith and satisfactory political level would be able to emerge. The method was traditional, but this time it was applied on the grand scale.

As for the students, they were called to meetings designed to set up their "preparatory provisional committee for the Cultural Revolution" and their "provisional Red Guard headquarters." They were then asked to go back to their classrooms to study the works of Chairman Mao and draw up posters in large characters, for which all the necessary equipment was supplied. Moreover, the work team announced a series of "struggle meetings" against the guilty cadres, whose misdeeds it would itself establish in advance. This, too, was a well-tried method—first the Party would judge its own members, and then the rank and file would know who should be criticized, and why.

In paternalist rather than authoritarian style, the members of the work teams joined in manual work and shared, as the phrase went, "the joys and sorrows of the rank and file." Wang Kuang-mei spent hours in the cafeteria peeling potatoes and waiting on the students—"a treacherous attempt at corruption,"

[6] In April 1967, *Red Flag* (No. 5) published a long "inquiry into how the work team at Tsinghua followed the reactionary bourgeois line in relation to cadres in June–July 1966," from which I have taken certain facts.

it was to be said later. So the Party's best traditions were respected, and for the first two weeks everything seemed to be going well. Leaders on the central and Peking levels willingly spent their afternoons at Tsinghua reading the students' posters, which they found most interesting. But on June 22 a dramatic event wrecked this good atmosphere: some students from the chemistry faculty, headed by an unknown young man called K'uai Ta-fu, put up a blasphemous poster on the notice board. "What is this farce, Comrade Yeh Lin [chairman of the work team]? Why must we stay in our classrooms and stew in our own juice when the hour of the great revolution has struck? You ask us to study when our aim is action"—and so forth.

At once Yeh Lin asked the student provisional committee to defend the work team in a debate with the dissidents. And on June 23, 1966, young K'uai—a lad of nineteen, of irreproachable social origin, the son of poor peasants—had to face the official leadership of the new student movement in a gathering arranged in advance against him. Presiding over the meeting was Liu T'ao, daughter of Liu Shao-ch'i and co-chairman of the provisional committee with the daughter of Vice-Premier Ho Lung. Reports of the meeting are inconsistent; some say that K'uai's verve succeeded in winning over his hearers, others that he simply showed himself to be an unreasonable and arrogant "extremist" (already!). In any case, from this day forward he appeared destined to become a national figure and his fame, indeed, was soon to eclipse even that of Nieh Yüan-tzu. Of course, this future leader of the Chingkangshan Regiment of Tsinghua—the most celebrated student group—did not become a rebel solely because of his impetuous character, but it would also be untrue to say that he was manipulated by "leftists" in the higher Party leadership. His rebellion proves above all that the rank and file, at least in the universities, gave a radical meaning to the explosive writings on the Commune and on its own role in the Cultural Revolution. This is why some students felt the traditional paternalism of the Party to be a brand of repression, soon labeled "white terror," and discerned in it a deliberate wish to "protect a handful of high officeholders while striking at many others."

In the debate on June 23, K'uai Ta-fu pointed out that all the small-fry cadres were shut up in their rooms, but the president of

Tsinghua was still a minister and—like his deputy, who at that time was leading a work team at a people's commune—did not even deign to enter into discussion with the students. It was a relevant point, and it was directly inspired by the warnings against the danger of usurpation of power from above and the lessons of the Paris Commune (the abolition of privileges for high officials, the prohibition of holding more than one post and drawing more than one salary, etc.). However, K'uai's insolence naturally touched off a series of reflexes on the part of the work team. If the students could not put this young provocateur in his place, the Party would do so. A charge sheet against him was drawn up with the help of his teachers, and a campaign against his "counterrevolutionary" tendencies was systematically organized. This merely inflated the incident and put weapons in the hands of those who had started it; on the Tsinghua campus, nothing was talked about from June 24 to July 15 but the "battle against K'uai Ta-fu." K'uai enjoyed himself by working up indignation with a vindictive new poster; he accused the work team of deliberately sidetracking the mass struggle toward a false objective. "I am only a nineteen-year-old student, with no Party card and no executive responsibilities, but according to you the whole purpose of the Cultural Revolution is to fight me and my ideas."

Following Nieh's poster at the end of May, K'uai's rebellion in June and July marked a new stage in the "struggle between two lines" with regard to the Cultural Revolution. In fact, Tsinghua's lead was followed in other universities, where resistance to Party direction spread. The first independent groups of Red Guards were born in this way, not with the help of experienced leaders but against them. Another typical feature was quickly observed: this attempt to organize students from above was a great factor in dividing them. It was this atomization of the student body which later caused great concern. In effect, when the work teams were deprived of their powers on Mao's demand at the end of July, these powers could be transferred only to the existing provisional committees of the Cultural Revolution. The latter wanted to throw off the tutelage of the old leaders and headed in their turn toward "intransigence," by suddenly taking charge in their own manner of the control of the imprisoned cadres. But, to avoid reversing their previous stand, they refused to come to terms with

rebels like K'uai Ta-fu. A section of the rank and file disapproved
of this behavior and even rejected the legitimacy of the provisional committees; this section formed its own groups, however
tiny they might be. At the beginning of August, even before the
Central Committee took its "sixteen-point decision" on the
Cultural Revolution, dozens of committees and Red Guard
detachments in the various universities and high schools of the
capital were bitterly contesting the title of "best defender of the
thought of Chairman Mao." The period of "broad democracy"
opened to the tune of broad division.

Mao's *Ta Tzu Pao*

Mao returned to Peking on July 17 after achieving, the day before,
a swimming feat in the Yangtze, at Wuhan, which electrified all
China. According to the official account, "he swam for sixty-five
minutes, covering almost fifteen kilometers in the direction of the
current, and showed no sign of fatigue." [7] Certainly, urgent
though the problem of the "heirs of the revolution" may be, that
of the succession to Mao was not on the agenda while the
Chairman was so full of vigor. Mao's performance was a kind of
manifesto, for certain passages in the "Circular of May 16,"
alluding to "individuals of the Khrushchev type who are waiting
for their opportunity," probably gave rise to anxiety.

Yet, to judge by his letter to Chiang Ch'ing on July 8 and his
first remarks after his return to the capital, Mao was not feeling
very optimistic. He pointed out to his wife that the Left could not
win everything at a blow and urged her toward prudence and
reflection. To his Peking comrades he said that he was disappointed by the calmness of the city. He quickly realized, however,
that this apparent calm hid the outlines of battles yet to come.
The masses were really moving in an independent way and

[7] "Chairman Mao Swims in the Yangtze," *Peking Review*, No. 31 (July 29, 1966),
gave a detailed and vivid account of Mao's exploit in the Yangtze. As we know,
Western swimming experts were somewhat intrigued by the Chairman's speed,
but it seems that there was a strong wind in the right direction on that particular
day. It may be added that July 16 has become a "swimming day"; every year,
thousands of soldiers and civilian volunteers cover the same distance as Mao in the
Yangtze.

demanding a radical break with the past. At the central conference at the end of July, he showed himself to be full of fire and
reaffirmed with even greater force than in June: "We are seeing
the birth of the Commune of China of the 1960's, and its
significance will exceed that of the Paris Commune itself." [8]
Clearly the rebellion of K'uai Ta-fu meant more to him than the
poster of May 25. He summoned the Central Committee to a
plenary session and, on the day it met, addressed a letter to the
Red Guards.

"I give you my warm support," he wrote. "Your revolutionary
actions are a sign of anger and condemnation toward the
exploiting classes, the revisionists and their henchmen. . . . In
supporting you, we also ask you to take care to unite yourselves
and all those who can be united. As for those who have made
serious mistakes, after these have been pointed out to them, they
must be given work and provided with a way out that will allow
them to reform and to become entirely new men. Marx said that
the proletariat must liberate not only itself but all mankind; the
proletariat cannot ultimately achieve its own liberation until it
frees all mankind. I urge you, comrades, to pay heed to this
doctrine." [9]

Thus Mao gave his own advice—and in a tone that was
certainly not authoritarian—before awaiting the verdict of the
Central Committee on the Red Guards. Four days later, to show
still more clearly that his ideas were not automatically those of the
Party, he put up his personal *ta tzu pao* on the door of the Central
Committee. Its heading, "Open Fire on Headquarters," was a
program in itself.[10] In a few sentences, Mao stated coherently

[8] See *Current Background*, Hong Kong, No. 891 (October 8, 1969).

[9] Long quotations from this letter were to be found in Lin Piao's report to the
Ninth Congress of the CCP, and also in Yao Wen-yuan's speech in Albania. See
Yao Wen-yuan, "Chinese Red Guards Will Unite and Fight Side by Side with
Albanian Youth Forever," *Peking Review*, No. 29 (July 14, 1967).

[10] Mao's poster of August 5, 1966, refers especially to the actions of the work
teams and links them to past deviations. Here is the complete text: "How masterly
was the writing of the first Marxist-Leninist *ta tzu pao* in the country, and also the
commentary in *People's Daily*! All our comrades should read them again. Yet, for
more than fifty days, some leading comrades, from the Central Committee to local
cases, have been acting in a diametrically opposed way. Taking up the reactionary
position of the bourgeoisie, they have exercised a bourgeois dictatorship and

what he had indicated during the preceding months: deviations in the Party do not occur by chance; the Party alone cannot achieve immunity from revisionist or other infections. On the basis of these two new documents, the August 1966 session of the Central Committee worked out its "sixteen-point decision."

Probably some leaders had their doubts about the great revolutionary anger of the Red Guards or about the capacity of the young people to unite "all those who can be united." Little is known of Mao's speech at this meeting. The few quotations that we possess seem to indicate that he discussed the risk of the appearance of organized factions in the CCP, even of revolutionary parties outside it: "We criticized the Kuomintang for its autocratic theory of a single monolithic party; to have no parties outside the Party is in fact autocracy; to have no factions within the Party is a mere optical illusion." [11]

The sixteen-point decision was adopted by a show of hands, or without a vote. In any case, in the later phases of the Cultural Revolution no one was accused of voting against it, and it can well be imagined that the Red Guards would not have forgiven anyone for being in opposition at such a moment and on such an issue. It is nonetheless true that certain leaders went into a political semi-eclipse. Liu Shao-ch'i slipped from second to eighth place in the hierarchy and others rapidly vanished from the scene.[12] Others again, having been dismissed after the events of February 1966, did not attend the meeting.

Nothing bears out the fantasies current in the West about the "hammer blow" struck by Mao at this session, or about the

strangled the movement of the revolutionary proletariat. They have confused truth with falsehood, black with white, and attacked revolutionaries holding opinions divergent from their own by white terror. They felt highly satisfied with behaving like this, arousing the arrogance of the bourgeoisie and sapping the morale of the proletariat. What treason! Viewed in connection with the rightist deviation of 1962 and mistaken tendencies, 'Left' in appearance but Right in reality, all this must lead us to serious reflections."

[11] See Jerome Ch'en, *Mao Papers: Anthology and Bibliography* (New York: Oxford University Press, 1970).

[12] Including Po I-po, vice-premier responsible for industrial development; Ho Chang-kung, formerly minister for heavy industry and in 1966 deputy minister for geology; Wang Feng, Party secretary of Kansu Province; Li Fan-wu, Party secretary of Heilungkiang Province.

"compromise decisions" that emerged from it. However, the sixteen-point decision was the outcome of ample discussions, entirely in Mao's style, which began even before the July central conference and lasted at least two weeks. The final resolution reflects Mao's concern both for the "mass centers of revolutionary action"—and hence for the destruction of the old system—and also for the continuity of the regime. Hence its insistence on the legitimacy of "groups, committees, and conferences of the Cultural Revolution, [which] should not be temporary organizations but permanent mass organizations, required to function for a long time." Hence too the stress on the "nonantagonistic" character of contradictions between the rank and file and the cadres, 95 percent of whom are good or perfectly open to reclamation. So it was a matter of "contradictions among the people" that had to be openly vented, without fears or reservations, in order to isolate the tiny minority of enemies and allow society to make a qualitative leap in its mode of organization and its level of political understanding.

Thus the main points of the resolution concerned the method rather than the content of this essential confrontation. First of all, Party leaders and members were urged to adopt a new and bold attitude to the "new revolutionary order of the masses," which had often taken them by surprise. They were to accept and even invite criticism, and respect the views of the minority. In no case were they to stick labels such as "anti-Party" or "counterrevolutionary" onto voices of protest from the masses ("Even in the case of real rightist elements," stated point 7, "the problem should be settled on its merits in the final phase of the movement"). Then, the masses were advised to organize groups and committees everywhere—not only in educational establishments—and to adopt throughout a system of internal democracy like that of the Paris Commune. But they were reminded at the same time that they should "make the revolution and help production," and handle with kid gloves those scientists and technicians who were contributing to the development of the nation and were not opposed to socialism, even if their ideological outlook was not revolutionary and could be changed only gradually. Everyone, finally, was asked to act rationally and to avoid violence.

Certainly, the members of the Central Committee did not

believe for a moment that broad democracy could be practiced harmoniously and without clashes. The final statement from the meeting, completing the sixteen-point decision, laid down that "disorders should not be feared" and that "restrictions that tie the hands of the masses should not be imposed." [13] But it also made a timely reference to Mao's "ten points" of May 20, 1963, concerning the "four cleanups," in which the Chairman had said clearly that mass organizations should not take the place of the existing administration or dismiss all the cadres who had made mistakes. Only in isolated cases, when the guilty men had made themselves truly hated by the masses, should the latter demand their dismissal. Moreover, the sixteen-point decision laid down that even this "right-wing handful," once deprived of the power to do harm, should be "given a way out so that it can return to the correct path."

In fact, in this first period of the reshaping of institutions, the model of the Paris Commune was the key idea set before the people, so that they should organize their "centers of revolution-ary action," begin to "follow national affairs," and "exchange experiences." All those who tried to put the brakes on this movement must obviously be fought; for this reason, the direction of the Cultural Revolution could be entrusted only to that wing of the Party which put the greatest trust in the masses, and not to the old machine. But changes of personnel—fairly limited, moreover—were to be made only at the top, while the rest of the administration went on functioning and had to adapt itself to circumstances step by step. Except for education, which was sent on holiday from June 1966, all other sectors were called upon to pursue their productive efforts and ensure the continuity of social life.

On August 18, 1966, the T'ien An Men Square saw the first of eight colossal meetings that allowed Mao to "receive," within three months, eleven million Red Guards, who came to Peking in successive waves to exchange experiences. The first rally provided an opportunity to let the nation know of changes at the top that

[13] See "Communiqué of the Eleventh Plenary Session of the Eighth Central Committee of the Communist Party of China," *Peking Review*, No. 34 (August 19, 1966).

had been made during the Central Committee meeting but not announced in any of its resolutions. Lin Piao was now officially Mao's deputy; he was presented as "the Chairman's closest comrade in arms" and the determined champion of the "revolutionary Left." Next came Chou En-lai, who was from now on to symbolize "continuity" and the practical needs of the revolution. Though a veteran Communist and (like Liu Shao-ch'i) a vice-chairman of the Party, he was not involved in the abuses of the headquarters; he had, in effect, been immersed in state administration and had even criticized the Party machine more than once. But Chou was, in a sense, squeezed between Lin and the Central Group for the Cultural Revolution, entrusted with the ideological direction of the struggle. This group, headed by Ch'en Po-ta, was composed partly of leaders who, in one way or another, had already been concerned with ideology and propaganda (for instance, T'ao Chu,[14] K'ang Sheng, and Wang Jen-chung), and partly of young people who had not yet held any national responsibilities (Chang Ch'un-ch'iao and Yao Wen-yuan from Shanghai, Wang Li, Kuan Feng, and Ch'i Pen-yü of *Red Flag*). The first vice-chairman of the group was Mao's wife, Chiang Ch'ing.

But Liu Shao-ch'i, Teng Hsiao-p'ing, and the other leaders who were under challenge were all there on the platform of honor, as though to remind these millions of Red Guards that the purpose of the Cultural Revolution was not to get rid of anyone but to make a radical transformation of society "by a path that has never been explored" and to conquer "heights that have never been reached." [15] Such was the position, at all events, at the end of the summer of 1966.

First Priority: The Seizure of Power

Less than four months later, the order of priorities of the Cultural Revolution had been reversed. It was no longer a matter of creating and consolidating mass organizations in order to shape a

[14] T'ao Chu, vice-premier and Party secretary for the Central-South China Bureau, took charge of Party propaganda and was for a time number four in the hierarchy.

[15] See the communiqué cited in note 13.

new state structure; on the contrary, the first necessity was to strike down the "usurpers" who were resisting and causing discord. Only by this means, it was now said, could the mass movement be consolidated, unified, and associated with a new power system. The new line was explained as flowing directly from the former one and likewise illustrated by references to the Paris Commune. Indeed, it reached its peak in February 1967 with the proclamation of the Shanghai Commune. But, while the sixteen-point decision of August 1966 is quite unequivocal, the decision about the "seizure of power by proletarian revolutionaries" lends itself to two meanings. It could be regarded as a new stage, more or less foreseen, or as a dash for victory enforced by difficulties that had not been seriously envisaged or analyzed in good time. It is therefore important to examine the two hypotheses concerning the "second line" and to compare the official explanations given at the time with the actual course of events.

The official version as given at the end of 1966 (it has now changed) can be summed up thus: the upholders of the "bourgeois line" in the Party represented only a tiny minority of cadres and members, but were cleverly able to exploit the "sectionalism, clique spirit, and ultra-democratism" and other "bourgeois and petty-bourgeois tendencies" that existed among the masses. Claiming to represent the Party and to embody its historic virtues, these rightists, instead of "making a self-criticism before the masses," intensified rivalries between groups and threatened to settle accounts with those whom they arbitrarily labeled as "counterrevolutionaries" or "adversaries of Chairman Mao." Thus they paid mere lip service to the sixteen-point decision, played a double game, and wrecked the working of the broad democracy. Since the latter was utterly indispensable to the progress of the interests of the proletariat and the cause of socialism in China, the "saboteurs" had to be overthrown and had nobody to blame but themselves.[16]

Besides, the first experiments in broad democracy had already shown that the existing state structure was inadequate to the

[16] See the January 1, 1967, editorial from *Red Flag* and *People's Daily*, "Carry the Great Proletarian Cultural Revolution Through to the End," *Peking Review*, No. 1 (January 1, 1967).

needs of society. "The struggle for the seizure of power by proletarian revolutionaries must be waged according to the Marxist principle: we must smash the old state machine . . . and must never be content with taking over power and following old rules and routines." [17] The first thing to do was to create provisional organisms to wield power, by means of discussions and exchanges of opinion, bringing in leaders of mass revolutionary organizations, revolutionary cadres from the Party and from local administration, and representatives of local army units (these were mentioned from the end of January 1967). These provisional organisms should create a united leadership and place the existing administrative team—remodeled if necessary—under its orders. Thanks to all this, "after a transition period, the wisdom of the broad masses will be given free play and a wholly new form of state power will be created that will correspond better to the socialist economic basis." [18]

Finally, to show that this second stage had been envisaged from the outset, it was stressed that "the emergence of the bourgeois line during the Cultural Revolution was not fortuitous" and was in fact predictable. Likewise, on the theoretical level, it had been realized all along that "to create the new, one must destroy the old" and that this was the only way to "inaugurate a new era in the history of the revolution and of the dictatorship of the proletariat . . . to enrich the lessons of the Paris Commune, of the soviets, and of Marxism-Leninism." [19] No wonder that this decision to take a new step forward was then presented as a great victory for the Cultural Revolution.

All this may sound convincing, but everything points to the conclusion that it was rather a question of keeping ahead of events. To begin with, the evocation of wicked plots by a "tiny minority" of conspirators can be interpreted in varied and contradictory ways, if indeed it is not inspired by mere witch hunting. The "great division" could not be explained simply by the tricks of a few highly placed swindlers—still less, in that it continued and even grew worse after these men had been

---

[17] See the *Red Flag* editorial "On the Proletarian Revolutionaries' Struggle to Seize Power," *Peking Review*, No. 6 (February 3, 1967).

[18] Ibid.

[19] Ibid.

overthrown. Besides, "sectionalism" and the other "petty-bour-geois tendencies" in the mass organizations did not arise only from ideas left over from the old society; their roots and their material basis grew from postrevolutionary society itself, so that it was obviously difficult to eliminate them by simple calls for reason and unity. But, more than this, the course of events tells its own story.

We have seen that the student organizations, divided virtually from their birth, had a marked tendency to split rather than to unite. When Mao addressed his letter of August 1 "to the Red Guards," they were far from being a homogeneous body. At first sight, this did not seem to matter too much; it could be hoped that the rival groups were ranged within one political spectrum, and their competition might even be fruitful by helping to spread the flame throughout society. The unification of the Red Guards could even be regarded as premature and disadvantageous—for in-stance, likely to deprive the movement of its genuine and diversified driving power. It was only in February 1967 that an attempt was made to create a "Conference of Red Guards in Higher Education" in Peking, and this turned out to be ephem-eral.

In October 1966 the Party center held an enlarged working conference (lasting for eighteen days!) to draw the first lessons from the Cultural Revolution. Complaints were made to Mao of the excesses caused by rival student groups outbidding one another, but he laid the blame chiefly on Party leaders who were afraid of these young people and did not know how to discuss with them. To Comrade Wu Hsiu-ch'uan—who described how his four sons and their friends, belonging to four rival groups, had turned his house into a battlefield—Mao replied philosophically: contacts with small groups have their advantages, they help one to be well informed and stay close to the masses; should one speak only to meetings of half a million people? But apparently he asked that one group should not be set against another—that would not help the situation.

His great worry arose rather from the fact that many cadres in central, regional, and provincial Party offices could not manage to understand the Cultural Revolution. "Some of them will never understand," he said, "and a minority will even be actively opposed; nevertheless, I hope that the greater part of them will understand in the end." But, despite everything, he remained optimistic because "this wave, still so new, compels all minds to react and to work in a new way." He admitted at the same time, however, that, for lack of time or energy, he too was not ready with answers to all these new problems. Everyone had to face the test, and he told his comrades, "I am as anxious as you that you should succeed in it."

It was at this conference that Liu Shao-ch'i made his self-criticism, first in connection with the "four cleanups" campaign, but especially for having sent the work teams into the universities in June. It was his last appearance among his comrades from the center, who were obviously resentful because he had led them into these difficulties. Politically he was finished; he admitted that he had been left behind by events, unable to influence them or take part in them. Mao contented himself with asking that Liu and Teng Hsiao-p'ing not be made responsible for all that had gone wrong: "The center as a whole has made mistakes." Decidedly, the danger to the Cultural Revolution came neither from the splits among the Red Guards, nor from the discredited "high officials" of the old general staff, but from the force of inertia in the Party machine and its difficulty in grasping the need to submit its power to control from below. This reluctance, in some ways "normal," arose both from the structure of the machine and from fear of being utterly overwhelmed by a storm of criticisms, far more radical and hostile than the early resolutions had foreseen.

In 1971 almost all the cadres I met began their accounts with: "At first I did not understand the Cultural Revolution." University officials confessed to me their perplexity when faced with the aggressiveness of unknown youngsters who suddenly claimed to be better Communists than their professors were and accused them of having fostered "the bourgeois order in education" for the past seventeen years. Cadres in industry told me that they had thought that the Cultural Revolution concerned only "the political superstructure" and not their sphere, which was already socialist. As a postscript to this chapter, I give some typical stories told by these Party members who, while apparently repentant, nevertheless continue to put the blame mainly on the "high officials"—now named—who led them into error or "aroused their dark side."

These accounts, however, show that their "bad tendencies" derived less from the Machiavellian advice of national or local "monsters" than from their objective situation, from the posts they held and their need to ensure the continuity of management. It was in vain that they read and reread decisions explaining the need to discard old methods and to listen to and invite rank-and-file criticisms; they could not accept that such criticisms should strike, through them, at the Party and hence at Chairman Mao, or that they should be hindered from governing, from consulting among themselves and acting in the collective and coordinated way to which they were accustomed. The ambiguity of their conduct is illustrated, above all, by the affair of the "black files." It aroused passionate feelings in the fall of 1966 and made no small contribution to intensifying the conflicts between the officials and the rebels. In a country where the Communist Party has held sole power for seventeen years, it inevitably has a monopoly of essential information on national affairs and even on individuals. Thoroughly organized and ubiquitous, it scarcely needs any specialized apparatus to build up files on people in whom it takes an interest for one reason or another; its members and their friends are always ready to supply the desired information. The rank and file knew perfectly well that this was a continuous system, and that the period of criticism could be followed by one of settling accounts with critics who had gone too far. Experience with the work teams in the spring of 1966 confirmed this knowledge. As soon as rebels like K'uai Ta-fu pitched their criticisms too strongly, the Party made haste to unearth a host of facts (generally trivial) about them and fastened the label of counterrevolutionary on them. True, the Central Committee session removed this stigma; but the files built up at Tsinghua by the work team had not disappeared and could be used one day—after another session and another decision— against those who had received a political black mark. Many students, however rebellious they felt, chose not to follow K'uai Ta-fu, the reprieved counterrevolutionary. It was wiser to be careful.

That was only one example; many others were less notorious but equally significant. How, indeed, could the Party officials be prevented from exchanging information on these young people who swarmed around the country to exchange their experiences? When a group of Red Guards from Peking arrived in Shanghai or some other city, was it not normal for the local authorities to ask their counterparts in the capital for facts about these "envoys of the Cultural Revolution"? And they were also interested in the behavior of these "envoys" in their home towns: what contacts did they have, what slogans did they put forward? Bit by bit, the machine gathered a great deal of material—"just in case." Sometimes, one gathers, it consisted merely of notes supplied by teachers or Party members on the social background or the scholastic record of these newcomers on the Chinese political scene.

The existence of these "black files" cast a heavy shadow on the progress of the debate among the rank and file, even when no immediate use was made of them. This helps explain why the Cultural Revolution spread slowly in industry; a worker, if labeled as a counterrevolutionary, had far more to lose than K'uai Ta-fu. The Central Committee's call "Dare to speak up" could win a response only if it were accompanied by concrete guarantees, of which the first had to be "no files on those who speak." The leaders of the Cultural Revolution decided on October 5, 1966, to give this guarantee, and urged all Party organizations to destroy, in the presence of those concerned, the "black files" built up since May 16, the date on which the Cultural Revolution was officially born.[20] In theory, this directive applied just to the educational sector, the only one in which anything much had happened, but it was assumed that it would be understood in the factories and in the whole country too. Moreover, those who had built up the "black files" were called upon to recognize their error publicly, and thus to show that there would be no question in the future of employing this "arbitrary" system, "calculated to repress the mass movement."

---

[20] It should be noted that this directive was signed by the Military Affairs Commission of the Party and endorsed by the Central Committee, which sent it to all provincial, city, and local Party offices. See *Documents of the Great Proletarian Cultural Revolution* (Hong Kong: Union Research Institute, 1968), pp. 89–91.

It need scarcely be said that, among officials, very few volunteered to make such a self-criticism. Those who possessed "mistaken" files preferred to destroy them behind closed doors, leaving no traces of the blunder, rather than to face their victims and lash their own backs in public. Other university officials claimed that they had only old files on students and teachers, legitimately built up before May 16. Ironically, the directive of October 5 led the machine men to get together, still more closely than in the preceding weeks, to decide which files should be handed over to those concerned and which should be regarded as state secrets, strictly classified, in accordance with earlier instructions.

The result was a violent conflict between the most militant Red Guards, who were convinced that they were particularly menaced by the "black files," and the majority of the cadres, both in the universities and in city or provincial Party committees. The rebels would allow no concealment. They demanded the right to check for themselves in Party archives whether there were any files on them. The cadres at once charged them with violating the rules on state secrecy and attacking the Party of Chairman Mao. In the universities, where the Party organizations were already greatly weakened, the Red Guards found it easy to move from threats to actions; they broke the seals of the archives and virtually occupied the administrative buildings. At Tsinghua, K'uai Ta-fu's Ching-kangshan Regiment took over without much opposition and won the support of certain more cautious groups. But the city and provincial committees were not to be dealt with so easily. They mobilized their own Red Guards or groups of workers against "those who violate the sixteen-point decision, engage in violence, and do not respect state secrecy." Here and there violent clashes occurred; but, even in places where only verbal abuse was exchanged, the mutual hostility soon became extreme. Many Party committees decided to move their archives to army buildings for the sake of security, but this heightened the suspicions and even led to Red Guard attacks on the barracks.[21]

[21] In a circular dated January 14, 1967, the Central Committee, as was to be expected, strictly forbade attacks on barracks. But at the same time it forbade Party officials to transfer files and other "black material" opposed to the mass

On November 16 a new four-point directive from the Central Committee sought to clarify the situation by laying down guiding principles. The "black files" should be destroyed, but only struggle by persuasion was permissible, not by force. No material on the students should be "hidden, transferred, copied, or regarded as private," but there should be discussion on the subject with "responsible comrades" who had made mistakes. It should be borne in mind that the question was merely one of a contradiction within the people and it was necessary to understand their way of thinking, allow them to correct their faults and continue their work, and not keep on harassing them by limiting their freedom of action. Two days later, an "important note" from the Peking Party Committee, approved by central authority, added in peremptory style that no organization or rank-and-file group had the right to arrest people or to set up its own prisons and courts; such actions were against the law and would be severely punished.[22]

But at the time when these instructions reached those to whom they were addressed—to be greeted as a victory by both sides—the most radical wing of the students, which called itself the Third Headquarters of Red Guards of the Capital, already had powerful "liaison posts" in Shanghai and most of the big cities. It went over to the attack on two other fronts: information and the working-class sphere. The prestige of its adversaries in the machine was so much weakened by the affair of the "black files" that masses of students and young workers enlisted without fear in the rebel ranks. The rebels therefore demanded "equality" in the publicity media and thus, in a sense, touched on a weak point of the power holders. Why should they hold a monopoly of the printed press, while the rank and file had to content itself with posters and wall newspapers? "In a broad democracy everyone should have the same opportunities to express his opinion," the rebels in Shanghai declared in eloquent posters; and they demanded that their own newspaper should be distributed to subscribers of *Liberation Daily*, the organ of the Party committee in the city.

---

movement, and gave peremptory instructions to those who had done so to get the material back and destroy it.

[22] See *Documents of the Great Proletarian Cultural Revolution.*

The latter categorically refused. Had it not been defending for years, as best it could, the line of Chairman Mao? Why should it suddenly have to share its position with uncontrolled intruders? Overtly it relied on technical difficulties in distributing two papers together—their weight would exceed the postal allowance. It was a bad excuse, for at that time nobody in China cared about technical rules. The radicals therefore besieged the office of *Liberation Daily* and prevented it from appearing; either both papers would come out, or none. The Party committee cried scandal and organized a protest meeting against those who were trying to stifle the Communist voice, but the Red Guards did not lift their siege and they held repeated demonstrations against "usurpers" who thought that they were the only Communists. This trial of strength had its symbolic aspect. The first "seizure of power by proletarian revolutionaries" occurred, in December 1966, in the *Wen Hui Pao* newspaper in Shanghai, which in November 1965 had published Yao Wen-yuan's attack on Wu Han and thus had the reputation of being most forcefully loyal to Mao's instructions.

In these circumstances, who was correctly interpreting the sixteen-point decision? Who was the best Maoist? And why had the debate, under the centralized auspices of Mao's thought, led straight to two diametrically opposed and antagonistic interpretations of the "proletarian line"? We can begin to find an answer by studying certain aspects of the method and progress of this debate.

"In the Great Proletarian Cultural Revolution, the masses can only liberate themselves, and no one can act in their place in any way." Point four of the sixteen-point decision is categorical and beyond argument. Yet some doubts may arise about the concept of "the masses," which is not strictly definitive and does not clearly indicate, as with the earlier example of the Associations of Poor and Medium-poor Peasants, how and of whom the new organizations were to be made up. To trust the masses means, in these conditions, to intervene in their affairs as little as possible, and in any case not to claim to direct them, the unifying factor being supplied by the thought of Mao Tse-tung. For the rest, "one learns to swim by swimming"; the masses themselves would find the right way to organize and unite. But can one learn by exchanging incomplete and biased truths? Can one follow national affairs by interpreting the little that one knows by a light filtered through barred windows?

Circumstances decreed that the first mass organizations were born among university and high school students, a social category that was already educated, able to express itself easily in writing, and with time to exchange experiences. Hence we have a rich collection of the documents put out by this section of the masses, in which we can note certain essential characteristics of its internal discussions. Verbal testimony gathered later, in 1971, only confirms an inevitable observation: the first and severest handicap of the Red Guards, from the outset of events, was the weakness of their knowledge about the past and the present.

It is striking, in fact, that when the Red Guards talked about the educational sphere, which they knew from experience, they were neither "extremist" nor too badly divided. From July 1966 onward, they analyzed the defects of the existing educational system and put forward original and effective remedies.[23] They attacked the length of education ("a child who starts school at the age of seven will be twenty-five or twenty-six when he gets his degree in higher education"); the method of transmitting knowledge ("it honors book learning, scorns practical work, cuts the students off from the workers and peasants, and isolates them from the great revolutionary movements of society"); and the organization of campus life ("students live in huge buildings eating polished rice and fine flour and are totally separated from young workers and peasants"). Finally they rejected selection by examinations, which gave all power to the professor (a system "as antidemocratic as it could be"). The Red Guards demanded above all that young people should be freed from this "slavery" and allowed to learn in the school of society; universities should give simple training courses lasting two or three years and be open to workers who had shown in practice their ability to innovate and to advance "the class struggle, the struggle for production, and scientific experiment." They demanded that, "in teaching methods, the stress should be on personal study and discussion;

[23] See "Students Propose New Educational System in Arts Faculties," *Peking Review*, No. 30 (July 22, 1966).

teachers should give adequate help, practice a democratic teaching method, follow the mass line, and firmly renounce methods of book cramming."

This sketch of a new program for higher education was certainly inspired by Mao's attacks on the old system[24] and influenced by the political debates of the 1960's. Be this as it may, the fact is that these student rebels knew what they were talking about, were never short of arguments, and were dealing relevantly with real problems. They were in revolt against a system that threatened to turn them into "revisionists," into a class distinct from the masses, and that moreover did not correspond to the technical needs of the country ("if the study time were halved," they wrote, "a professor could teach twice as many students"). In short, they stood on territory in which they were strong and capable. Since the need for educational reform had been recognized by the authorities themselves, the dialogue promised to be fruitful and unifying in the light of Mao's teachings, and likely to change the superstructure of society in a proletarian direction.

Better still, so long as the criticism of the students was aimed at cadres and professors who were too authoritarian, or simply too formalistic, it remained "nonantagonistic." Except for a minority of truly conservative directors or teachers, who refused to change their ways, almost everyone in the universities accepted—if against the grain—the need to admit mistakes and consider a different teaching method. Some professors, accused of having driven students to suicide by persecuting them during exams, were taken to task with a violence that perhaps seemed excessive and loaded with the infamy of being "bourgeois reactionaries" or "despots," but these were isolated cases. On the whole, the debate on the new university, guaranteeing the rights of students and giving them a place in administration, seemed to be proceeding under good auguries and could indeed have been a valuable example of the new relationships between "centers of revolutionary action" and the responsible executive.

---

[24] I have already quoted Mao's statement to the Nepalese students, which was quite rough on the Chinese educational system. But many other quotations from the Chairman (not always with exact references) were directed against ex cathedra teaching and exams designed as traps for students. We can be sure that these sallies did not fall on deaf ears in the Chinese universities of the 1960's.

These possibilities were to some extent wrecked by the work teams, whose intervention brought about an explosive political polarization on campus. But, apart from this, there was from the start a certain ambiguity about aims. For the students, to concern themselves solely with university reform was to be confined to an academic debate and, in a sense, to enjoy the privilege of problems of a professional kind. Yet what was at stake was the class struggle on the level of society as a whole, the "mortal struggle" between the proletariat on one side and the bourgeoisie and revisionism on the other. The task was to "unmask a handful of high officials who have taken the capitalist road" and keep China from changing color. Now this dangerous "handful" was not to be found on the campus, where, at most, only its agents or accomplices might be discerned. Could one fail to launch a merciless attack on suspects of secondary rank? Where else could one turn, to reveal what had been hidden in the preceding years behind the false unity of the CCP?

Even the Red Guards of the Preparatory Provisional Committee at Tsinghua, formed with the help of the work team, quickly showed this kind of curiosity. In June 1966 they posted up a "ten-point order to the cadres," calling on them to make complete confessions and "denounce those who pulled the strings from behind the scenes." When power at Tsinghua and other universities passed into the hands of more radical groups, these demands were made more forcefully—especially as, meanwhile, Mao himself had invited the rebels to "follow national affairs closely." Deeper questions were asked, and the chief aim was to find out who had created a bourgeois educational system in China and who was masterminding the white terror. The only way to unmask, one after another, the "great despots" who had infiltrated the Party was to subject the cadres to increasingly harsh questioning. But it was also the best way to turn the debate into an "antagonistic" trial of strength, and to change a discussion "within the people" into a dialogue of the deaf.

In reality, a college president or a dean, a Party secretary or a Communist leader on the campus might well confess to having made mistakes in the context of the old educational system, but it was hard for him to admit that he had "always taken the Soviet Union as his master" and that he had deliberately tried to restore

capitalism in China. When this was demanded, the least he could
do was to fight back against his accusers. Nor was it easy to see
how he could denounce those of his superiors who had allegedly
upheld the bourgeois line in the Central Committee in past years.
He could not drop names at random; besides, he knew very well
that divisions in the Party had never contrasted "good guys" who
were loyal to the proletariat with "bad guys" who planned to
restore capitalism. The demands of the Red Guards, influenced by
rumors of plots in high places and based on vague and unsubtle
knowledge, were unlikely to lead to a fruitful discussion, and in
most cases the men who were challenged evaded their difficulties
by taking refuge in "state secrecy." But this in turn fed the
suspicions; finally, in 1967, some Red Guards exclaimed, "What's
so terrible about these state secrets that can't be touched?" And
they went so far as to loot the archives of various ministries.

To show that there was nothing so terrible in the archives, the
Party would have had to reveal what it had hidden from public
opinion for seventeen years and give full publicity to the new
top-level debates. It did neither of these things. We are still
entirely in the dark about the past conduct of the leaders, and
reports of the interminable conferences of 1966—capsuled, to say
the least—boil down to quotations that are often double-edged.
Under these conditions, how could the Red Guards distinguish
between a "badly cured" ex-revisionist and a "100 percent good"
revolutionary cadre? Moreover, if they were to sally forth from
the isolation of the campus and extend their activities to the rest
of society, what solutions could they put forward when they knew
so little of the problems? So their zeal had to be spent in giving
new names to streets and squares, shutting "luxury" restaurants,
and searching the homes of former rich men or profiteers. The
press applauded these exploits (although the T'ien An Men
Square, or Square of Heavenly Peace, was to be known only
briefly as East Is Red Square) and thus encouraged this concentration on the superficial. It even published triumphant lists of the
booty brought to light by the young revolutionaries—hidden gold
coins and other treasures. However, a halt soon had to be called to
this way of bringing about the rule of the proletariat; by raiding
the good neighborhoods, the Red Guards were attacking not only
national capitalists and investors but also "distinguished revolu-

tionaries" well up in the hierarchy or noted intellectuals (who, on principle, were not supposed to be bothered). But by the time that searches were forbidden, in November, the young rebels no longer listened to orders and acted according to their own standards of what is done or not done in a revolution.

The second method of the Red Guards consisted of reinterpreting the speeches of their teachers, and of more highly placed leaders, in the light of the new line on "the unified leadership of society by the thought of Mao Tse-tung." In fact, this enabled them to denounce anyone they chose. Anyone who had laid insufficient stress on the radical aspects of that "thought" in the past, anyone who had dared to speak of order, of discipline, or of the need to carry out orders from above at any cost, was now automatically depicted as a "despot" who had deliberately ignored Mao's teachings on the "right to rebel." [25] Still worse trouble awaited those who had ventured to play down, even by implication, the importance of studying the Chairman's works, and had thus shown their hostility to Mao and their desire to fight against the dictatorship of the proletariat. So, in their "struggle" against Chiang Nan-hsiang, minister of higher education and president of their university, the Tsinghua students brought up against him some speeches he had made in 1965 to young Chinese who were leaving to study abroad (especially in France). The unlucky minister had indeed advised them not to boast of their superiority gained by knowledge of Mao's thought, and not to assume that they were "more Red" simply because they had studied his works. "Such a study," he had added, "helps you to become Red but is not enough to make every student a Red"—after all, John Foster Dulles was said to have studied Mao's works and had not thereby turned Red. "To study the Chairman's works is essential but not sufficient to become a revolutionary."

These few sentences, torn from their context, were then condensed to make a stronger impression; and posters gradually appeared on every campus in China denouncing the "crimes of

[25] In a speech made in 1939, on the occasion of Stalin's birthday, Mao declared that if the vast wealth of Marxism had to be summed up in a sentence, it would be: "It is right to rebel." Naturally this quotation was much in fashion from the start of the Cultural Revolution.

In Quest of a Commune of China

Chiang Nan-hsiang," who was accused of nothing less than having said that "Mao's thought gives us no superiority and is not enough to make us true Reds." Right away, the treachery of the former minister appeared to be flagrant, and there was no question of letting him explain anything. Humiliated, wearing a dunce's cap, dragged about from place to place, ordered to confess his revisionism, the ex-minister humbly bowed his head before the "wrath of the masses," but he did not open his mouth and confessed to nothing. Had he been allowed to speak, he could have shown without much trouble that Mao himself had always advised the Chinese to be modest, abroad as well as at home, and not to exaggerate the worship of his thought. Of course, if the minister and president had been in closer contact with the students in the past, if the latter had come to know him otherwise than through occasional speeches, the showdown between their political attitudes would have taken a different form. The fact is that the traditional system whereby veterans of the Long March generation each held several positions, watching over every sphere of society from their seats in the Central Committee, took its revenge on most of them. The case of Chiang is illustrative of this, but not unique.

From the end of July to the end of November 1966, the young people had full facilities to exchange their experiences. Living in schools and colleges where work had been suspended, traveling free, getting two or three meals a day, they spread all over China and established liaison posts that were soon as numerous and variegated as the groups in Peking. But what sort of information could they exchange when, altogether, they knew so little? Certainly they could turn the hoses on their former professors or "oppressive" cadres who had got new jobs, which enabled them to make difficulties for local authorities who protected these "oppressors" and ignored charges made against them. This was fairly easy, for the authorities were not equipped to intimidate them or frame them, as they could in the case of their "own" Red Guards. But these duels only increased the antagonism between the rebels and the established machine; they assisted neither the enlightenment of the former nor the explanations of the latter.

What emerged from these confrontations? First, that the absence of reliable knowledge is always a source of discord;

people who know too little and have a biased view of the facts necessarily become very intransigent and defiant and cannot come to terms with others who defend other truths that are equally biased and incomplete. Loyalty to the same doctrine is not necessarily a unifying factor, for a given premise can induce each side to take its own stand. In this great debate, the cadres—especially those in higher positions—had the advantage of knowing the record from the inside, but they had great difficulty in getting themselves believed; and their critics, who had very firm ideas about the past, clung to their own "truths." In such conditions, how was it possible to unite and overcome the contradictions?

From this lack of communication, the trend toward distrust of all cadres was born almost automatically. And since there had to be unity nevertheless, in conformity with the Chairman's directive, the most radical Red Guards—such as K'uai Ta-fu's group— ended up by uniting only with "victimized cadres," who had been deprived of all responsibilities long before the Cultural Revolution. But this method, designed to avoid any compromise with those who held (or "usurped") power, was by no means reliable. The rival groups soon discovered that the victims had been dismissed for being "rightists" or for administrative failings, and not for making a determined defense of the line of Chairman Mao. The "moderates," who did not object to alliances with the cadres who had the jobs, also had some nasty surprises. In the period of the "seizure of power," in the winter of 1966–7, revelations to the discredit of these officials came thick and fast and the Red Guards who had united with them, much bewildered, finished up in disarray. In short, there was no solid ground on which to resolve the contradictions between the students and the cadres; all along, unifying elements proved to be fragile and events worked in favor of disunity.

Mao was surely right when, at the October conference, he reproached his comrades for their inability to talk with the Red Guards. After all, experienced Communists should know how to answer questions, however aggressive or irritating, in order to raise the level of debate and dispel misunderstandings. But it must be admitted that it is easier to make this observation from a distance and with hindsight. Reports from this period show clearly that a tactful manner and a friendly dialogue did not always pay

off for the cadres; if received with too much attention, the young
envoys of the Cultural Revolution scented the trap of corruption
and often turned still more strongly against these "incorrigible
despots." What they feared like the plague was to be the
playthings of manipulators; there was no lack of official warnings
advising them to beware of "bullets coated with sugar" and of
those who would try to set one group against another. Split from
the start, the student movement was decidedly tricky to handle,
whether from inside or outside. Ultimate unity, in these circumstances, depended above all on the entry into the lists of the
workers, who were urged to establish their dominance over the
rival groups and thus pave the way to the "great union."
However, when the Cultural Revolution moved into the world of
industry, the fragmentation of society grew even worse, and its
causes, this time, were more difficult to conjure away.

Shanghai

"The factories and the countryside cannot take holidays like the
educational institutions and hold up production to make the
revolution. Student revolutionaries must respect the great mass of
workers and peasants, trust them, and be convinced that they are
perfectly capable of guiding the revolution to its goal." These
sensible words were spoken by Chou En-lai on September 15,
1966, to a million revolutionary students and teachers who had
come to Peking from various parts of the country. And he
reminded them—no doubt he felt it necessary—of the "very great
importance" of industrial and agricultural production, on which
depended not only the life of the population but also "aid to the
Vietnamese people" and "to the revolutionary struggle of all
oppressed peoples and nations in the whole world." [26]

A week earlier, in a resounding editorial, *People's Daily* had
given a detailed account of the techniques of the Cultural
Revolution in factories, mines, and communes. It explained that
any "intervention by third parties who fail to understand the
situation [in these institutions] can easily affect the normal

[26] See "Comrade Chou En-lai's Speech," *Peking Review*, No. 39 (September 23,
1966).

development of production" and that students should not get involved in the internal debates of workers and peasants.[27] The fact that the initiators of the Cultural Revolution had insisted from the early months on this clear division of responsibilities indicates that certain Red Guard "interventions" in factories and communes had been unfortunate, or badly received, and that the Central Group had very clear ideas about how the workers and peasants should act. Indeed, in the ensuing two months, directives concerning the industrial sector (though disseminated only through internal channels) were to come thick and fast, and they soon outnumbered those aimed at the countryside.

These documents were written in a much calmer tone than those addressed to the students, and displayed great confidence in the ability of the workers to organize themselves, factory by factory, without too many problems. Preambles about the historic role of the working class and its high level of proletarian consciousness were not merely formal; Peking's faith in it was firm. At the same time, it was recognized clearly, although implicitly, that the existing organizations in industry (trade unions and other committees) were not truly representative. So the first directives urged the workers to create committees for the Cultural Revolution, freely elected, and to build "double power" in every factory.[28]

It was explained that the members of these organizations should not be taken away from production, and that they should accept the principle of "broad democracy among the masses." In other words, the idea was to create genuine factory committees, fully representative of varying opinions in the rank and file, but united and capable of settling all internal differences "by democratic means." They would receive the necessary funds to organize their meetings and elections, but, in line with the working-class tradition of sound management and economy, they would do their

[27] "Make the Revolution and Assist Production," editorial in *People's Daily*, September 7, 1966.

[28] The most detailed document on double power is the "twelve-point directive of the Central Group for the Cultural Revolution on the revolution in factories and mines," dated November 17. It was published in the *Red Guard Journal* of the Peking Aeronautical Institute on December 23. See *Documents of the Great Proletarian Cultural Revolution*, p. 116.

best to limit their expenses. Besides, all these activities should take place after the eight-hour working day and should last not more than four hours a day, so as to leave each worker with his necessary rest time. Once in operation, these organizations could send delegates to nearby factories in the same district to exchange experiences (also after working hours). The directives did not suggest that these contacts should give rise to wider working-class conferences, but they did not rule them out.

But the key to the scheme was "double power" and the two levels on which it would work. In effect, alongside the working-class organization in each factory, there would be a "directing group responsible for production," which would continue to watch over the volume, diversity, and quality of output. This group, it was noted, "should also take part in the Cultural Revolution, but it should concentrate the weight of its efforts on the direction of production." [29] Of course, the people with responsibility in this sphere (mainly cadres and technicians) were required to account for their management to the workers and take all steps to meet their political or economic demands. In every sense, both groups were to enlist under the unified leadership of the thought of Chairman Mao and would thus have no antagonistic contradictions to resolve. Better still, this debate or confrontation would raise their level of understanding and "their spiritual force would rapidly be transformed into a great material force." [30] Not without a purpose, the key documents emanating from Mao on the Great Leap Forward, dating from 1958, had been distributed since the end of 1965 to all the leading organizations in industry. And the August 1966 resolution reaffirmed: "The Cultural Revolution is a powerful driving force in the development of the social productive powers of our country." So everyone was well aware of the path to be followed in changing the management system; and, at the beginning, the initiators of the Cultural Revolution seemed highly optimistic about its course in this sphere. The Party work teams—which, covered in opprobrium, had been withdrawn from the universities at the end of July—stayed in the factories, where they were made up of a small number of leaders, and no one appeared to object to them.

[29] See *People's Daily* editorial of September 7.
[30] Lin Piao, letter of March 11, 1966.

However, despite this careful, gradual, and harmonious start, it was precisely in the factories that the Cultural Revolution was to arouse, from November onward, such sharp conflicts that they brought about a change of policy in the whole country and a hasty turn to the phase of the seizure of power. In every industrial center—Shanghai, Tientsin, the northeast, and Peking—the system of double power suddenly broke down in the winter of 1966–7 and production, "vital for the population," was in danger of being paralyzed (or actually was, for short periods). What happened in industry during these four months culminating in the "January revolution" in Shanghai?

At the root of the official version today, there is a scarcely veiled charge against the students—that they introduced "the virus of factionalism in the industries"—as well as, naturally, a denunciation of a "handful of leaders" who took advantage of this to "set a section of the masses against another section." This charge is not entirely baseless, even though the student presence in the factories was marginal throughout this time. Society cannot be put into sealed compartments, especially in a revolutionary period, and the way in which one sector settles its conflicts inevitably influences others. The trial of strength between the Red Guards and the Party machine was bound to have repercussions in the factories and aggravate the contrasts. Besides, experience soon showed that problems could not be solved within the framework of a single factory. No management group ever had the resources to meet the demands of the workers; lacking precise instructions at the crucial time, it was condemned to swing between attempts at close-fisted resistance and ruinous generosity. Events in Shanghai are particularly instructive in this respect.

At the beginning of November 1966, the authority of the Party committee in the great city had already been seriously shaken by the affair of the "black files" when a certain number of workers' organizations—those who made the greatest demands—decided to set up their own "Headquarters of the Revolutionary Revolt of Shanghai Workers." A meeting was organized in Culture Square, which is relatively small, and the mayor, Ts'ao Ti-ch'iu, who was also one of the Party secretaries, was called on to meet three demands: (1) to recognize the Headquarters as a legal organization under the dictatorship of the proletariat; (2) to give an account of his administration to its inaugural meeting; (3) to furnish it with the necessary funds to spread its propaganda and give it a position in all the factories. Ts'ao ignored these demands; indeed, no directive from the Central Group required him to yield in such a situation. He sent agents to Culture Square and made sure that he got hourly telephoned reports of the course of the demonstration. The meeting, which began at two in the afternoon—that is, during working hours—attracted over forty thousand people, mainly young workers and students, and lasted until nine in the evening. Then a rumor spread through the crowd: the mayor was ready to receive delegates from the Headquarters, but not at the Party office. Everyone then marched to the supposed place of this encounter, an administrative building in a remote neighborhood. But the mayor was not there either. The waiting went on until dawn; Ts'ao's arrival was alternately announced and denied; and in the end no representative of the Party committee appeared to make an explanation.[31]

In the small hours, about two or three thousand militants decided that the mayor had set a trap for them and that there could be no dealings of any kind with him. They decided to go straight to Peking to appeal to the Central Group for the Cultural Revolution, or even to Chairman Mao himself, and they split up into three groups. One of these commandeered two or three coaches of the Shanghai–Peking train; another (a little later) forced the railroad workers to provide a special train; and the third, relying on good luck, started on its "expedition to the north" by way of Suchow, apparently intending to go on from there on foot. Mayor Ts'ao, for his part, consulted the Central Group, which strongly urged him to stop this expedition; the business should be settled on the spot with the help of the Party East China Bureau and in particular of Comrades Ch'en P'ei-hsien and Wei Wen-po, who had the reputation of being trusted

[31] In addition to eyewitness accounts that I secured on the spot in 1971, I take some of this information from "What Really Did Happen in China," by Gerald Tannenbaum (a collection of articles published in *Eastern Horizon*, Hong Kong, and later as a pamphlet by Angus & Robertson, Sydney, Australia). Tannenbaum is an American who lived in China from the end of World War II until the summer of 1971.

by Mao.[32] Ch'en at once undertook to head off the "expedition to
the north." The workers' coaches were detached from the train at
Nanking; the second group was stopped at Anting, a suburban
station on the outskirts of Shanghai; and those who had gone to
Suchow were ordered to halt their march and wait.

The travelers were defiant. They stayed in their trains and
refused to return to their factories. The most anti-Ts'ao Red
Guards came to their rescue and collected food "for the rebels"
from the population. Who was wrong and who was right? Who
was violating the directives and who was following them correctly? Confusion was heightened by various rumors that were not
confirmed by the press: the Party bureau and Mayor Ts'ao had
received a telegram from Ch'en Po-ta ordering them to stop
Shanghai workers from going to the capital; on the contrary, the
Central Group was backing the workers and had even announced
that one of its aides, Chang Ch'un-ch'iao, would come to satisfy
the demands of the Headquarters.

Chang, who had for years been director of the Shanghai Party
Committee's propaganda department, did indeed take the responsibility of going to Anting and endorsing the demands of the
vanguard of the Headquarters. In a public statement on November 14, he explained that the Central Group regarded the
Headquarters as a completely legitimate and revolutionary body
and that the incident was over. But he forgot the expedition
encamped at Suchow, which had meanwhile set up the "Second
Army Corps of Shanghai Workers." Their leader, Keng Chin-
chang, a down-to-earth Communist worker, demanded the recognition of his organization and put forward five demands, more or
less modeled on those of the Headquarters. Neither Ch'en
P'ei-hsien nor Ts'ao Ti-ch'iu could bring himself to swallow the
pill, and they flatly refused to go to Suchow. Chang, the
openhanded representative of the Central Group, declared (according to Red Guard posters): "If you won't sign, I will." Only
then did Mayor Ts'ao go with him to the temporary center of the
Second Corps (also called the "Suchow Brigade") and add his
signature to that of Chang. From that day, Shanghai had two big

---

[32] To judge from his letter to his wife, then being circulated, Mao had advised
her in July 1966 to meet with and listen to these two leaders.

organizations which, though they grew out of the same "rebellion," were nevertheless entirely independent, if not rivals.

Less than a week later, two new Headquarters appeared on the scene, proclaiming their intention to defend the dictatorship of the proletariat in Shanghai and, of course, demanding official recognition and funds to make propaganda. One, the "Red Power Defense Army," gained acceptance so quickly that it was at once suspected of being on the best of terms with the Party authorities. The other, founded by Ch'en Hung-k'ang, a non-Party worker from the No. 15 radio factory, was called the "Third Headquarters" and claimed to be linked with the Red Guards who used the same name and who were known for their radicalism. The official press ignored all these developments and confined itself to praise in general terms for the class spirit of the workers and their great devotion to "making the revolution and assisting production." But what was not said in the official papers was revealed and dramatized by the posters and news sheets of the rank and file. When the Party committee made public an instruction to factories not to punish workers who had been absentees, the rebel posters declared that all members of the expedition had been roughed up by the Shanghai Security Bureau and fifteen leaders of the Headquarters had been secretly condemned to death or to long terms of imprisonment. Of course, the sentences were not to be implemented until after the end of these events, and a high official was alleged to have said, "We shall settle accounts with these mutineers after the autumn harvest" (a reference to the uprising led by Mao in 1927).

The official press gave warnings against "those who invent rumors to spread discord," but in truth the discord was there without any rumors. Each recognized Headquarters claimed hundreds of thousands of members and demanded a corresponding amount of funds and propaganda facilities. The claims were quite impossible to check and seem unlikely. The Suchow Brigade, formed on November 14 with barely 500 workers, was said to have 520,000 members by the twenty-first. The Red Power Defense Army stoutly declared that it had 800,000 working-class members, without counting its student allies from the "Scarlet Guards," a group claiming to be more "Red" than the Red Guards. More modestly, the Shanghai Workers' Headquarters claimed only 400,000 members but reckoned on massive support from the most hardened Red Guards. Competitive recruiting swept through all the factories, and men who were most committed to this battle had practically no time to spare for their work.

However, on December 9 the Central Group calmly repeated its "rules" concerning the Cultural Revolution in industry and scarcely modified its earlier forecasts.[33] It insisted that the eight-hour working day must be maintained "firmly" at any cost, and the quantity and quality of production must be guaranteed. But it gave up worrying about hours of rest; if the workers wanted to hold discussions all night, after their work, that was up to them. Point 7 recommended that as many problems as possible should be resolved "by consultation" within each plant, but recognized that in exceptional cases "the workers may appeal to higher organs and, if it is really necessary, send representatives to the capital." But "there must be no departure of large delegations from factories or mines." Further on, the directive recalled that the constitution of the People's Republic of China recognized the right of workers to form their organizations, which was a tacit recognition of all the Headquarters. Finally, the workers were called on to remain faithful to their "class characteristic of simplicity": "Do not create bureaucratic structures, do not ask for costly equipment, do not become officeholders detached from production, for all this risks alienating you from the masses." The closing sentence again urged each rank-and-file unit not to interfere in the affairs of other units. Thus, in essentials, the line was unchanged and the few detailed amendments did not weaken an orientation based on double power in every factory.

Yet one can scarcely say that the "Rules of December 9" were interpreted with much discrimination in the plants. To begin with, the situation was hard: big organizations were in existence and their members or sympathizers were making competing demands in order to come out on top. Then, once the principle of appealing to higher authority, including that of Peking, was established, the men responsible for management "adopted a wrong strategy and

---

[33] See "Ten Regulations of the CCP Central Committee concerning Grasping Revolution and Promoting Production," in *Documents of the Great Proletarian Cultural Revolution*, p. 133.

passed the contradictions on to a higher level." [34] To posters
demanding equal wages or protesting against the bonus system,
the production groups replied more or less in this style: "Go and
ask the high-ups about that." But which high-ups? The only
competent authorities, the Municipal Party Committee and its
East China Bureau, were harassed by the Red Guards and had no
real authority. To the great fury of Mayor Ts'ao, the rebels of
Futan University had succeeded on December 10 in "striking
down" Yang Hsi-kuang, Party secretary at their institution, who,
like the mayor, also held a position as secretary in the Party
committee of the city. This "despot," now unmasked, accused his
superiors, who had deliberately protected him while aware of his
failings and his revisionist tendencies. At the end of the anti-Yang
meeting at Hengkew (the Shanghai stadium), the fates of Ts'ao
and of Ch'en P'ei-hsien, his "protector" in the East China Bureau,
appeared to be sealed. Even hitherto "moderate" movements,
such as the Red Power Defense Army, hastened to disengage
themselves very clearly from the "guilty men" and went so far as
to demand immediate self-criticisms. It need hardly be said that
on this level, in Shanghai, no problems could be solved any longer.
To whom could one turn in such circumstances, except to the
Central Committee and to the Central Group for the Cultural
Revolution in Peking?

In Shanghai, at the end of December, the powder barrel blew
up. We need not search for reasons in one or another isolated incident; no such incident could have caused this explosion in a less
tense situation. But we may note the particularly aggressive demonstration by apprentices, accompanied by a sit-in at the heart of
the city—the Revolutionary Committee of the Revolt of Shanghai
Apprentices was indeed to advance a list of demands that were
notably extensive and difficult to meet in short order. We can also
cite the return to the city of workers who had been sent to the
countryside in preceding years, now demanding work near their
homes, and the invasion of the better neighborhoods by squatters
who occupied the apartments of capitalists and even state-owned
buildings. But the real problem arose from the "surrender"
of most of the lower-echelon power holders in industry.

[34] See the *Red Flag* article "Proletarian Revolutionaries, Unite," *Peking Review*,
No. 4 (January 20, 1967).

Double power in the factories was collapsing because "groups responsible for production," who held the purse strings in each unit, were suddenly giving up their prerogatives. Their answer to the delegates of workers' committees was: "You want funds to go to Peking? You want retroactive pay raises? Well, here are the accounts of the plant—go to the bank, draw out the money, and distribute it as you please." There was no longer any need to control the management; it was simply vanishing. Later, Mayor Ts'ao and Party Secretary Ch'en were to be blamed; there was even talk of a plot devised under orders from Liu Shao-ch'i and the "revisionist" fat cats. But at the time what was necessary was to improvise urgent steps to stop the massive exodus of workers to Peking and the paralysis of the economy. This was far from easy. None of the Headquarters enjoyed enough authority to take command, and it was impossible to get these rival organizations to unite.

On January 5, 1967, *Wen Hui Pao*, the one newspaper in the hands of the rebels, published a "message to the whole population of Shanghai" signed by eleven organizations, of which only one, the Shanghai Workers' Headquarters, was strictly working-class. The others were student groups and most of them were strangers to the city—Red Guards from Peking, Harbin, and Sian. It was an urgent appeal to the "class brothers" to return to work and obey the directive to "make the revolution and assist production": "We, as partisans of revolutionary revolt, warmly greet your return to make the revolution together and ensure the success of production together." It was addressed primarily to the members of the Red Power Defense Army, who comprised most of those who had quit work and in whose ranks were many cadres belonging to the groups responsible for production.

Next day, in the half-paralyzed city, over a million workers attended a mammoth meeting. The former leaders, Ch'en P'ei-hsien, Ts'ao Ti-ch'iu, and also Wei Wen-po (another big man in the East China Bureau), were attacked and derided, while leaders of the Headquarters called on the working class to struggle against the "evil wind of economism" and not to be corrupted by those who were handing out money belonging to collective resources. Mayor Ts'ao was relieved of his duties, and the others were placed under the surveillance of the masses and summoned to make written confessions. Meanwhile, working-class teams undertook to get the economy going again. Chang Ch'un-ch'iao, this time accompanied by another member of the Central Group who came originally from Shanghai, Yao Wen-yuan, hurried back there to help the "great alliance of proletarian revolutionaries."

In fact, despite the dramatic message of January 5 and the relative success of the meeting next day, Shanghai was still without any organized authority and productive work was being resumed in a very patchy way. True, there was no thought of a general strike and no sector was completely paralyzed (the furnaces of the steelworks were never put out and electricity cuts seldom lasted long), but nothing was working properly. Factories were inadequately staffed; showdowns between rival groups became more frequent; many cadres were dragged about the streets, often in trucks packed with workers, with placards of shame on their chests and dunces' caps on their heads. Shanghai's "January revolution" certainly deserved its name, but it was a revolution that seemed remarkably devoid of leadership.

On January 11, owing to the mediation of the envoys from Peking, thirty-two organizations agreed on a ten-point "Urgent Notice":

1. Everyone should "make the revolution and assist production."
2. All those who had gone to Peking or were going off to exchange experiences elsewhere in the country should at once return to Shanghai.
3. All travel permits given out by managements of factories were null and void; moreover, these managements must repay, if necessary by installments, the considerable funds allocated for these journeys.
4. Plant funds were frozen so that the state economy should no longer suffer.
5. All salary and welfare questions would be settled in the final phase of the movement, except for special cases, which would be referred to central authority.
6. Students who had gone to work in the factories should lose the special wages they had been granted by the former managements.

7. All public buildings and apartments belonging to national capitalists should be cleared within a week, and those who had occupied them by force should go home.
8. All those who disturbed social order, assaulted people, or looted and stole property must at once surrender their booty.
9. All revolutionary organizations were called upon to implement the above points.
10. The Municipal Party Committee and the Ministry of Public Security were to apply these provisions.[35]

This time, the "Urgent Notice" was signed by a large number of genuine Shanghai organizations, including the Suchow Brigade and the Apprentices' Committee. Moreover, the whole Chinese press reprinted the document and, on Chairman Mao's recommendation, it was raised to the status of an example, like the first *ta tzu pao* of Peking University the previous year. According to the newspapers, the Shanghai events gave a decisive answer to three basic questions posed by the Cultural Revolution in industry: "Why did the revolutionary Left not liberate itself after the arrival of the work teams in the factories? Why did the struggles between factions among the masses spread so widely and even lead to bloodshed? Why had there been, quite recently, a major reactionary bourgeois counteroffensive and a development of counterrevolutionary economism?" The answer was that all this had come about only because "a handful of representatives of the bourgeoisie still held power, including financial power." So "the struggle of the revolutionary masses to take their own future into their hands can take many forms, but it consists ultimately in the need to win power. *With power the masses have everything; without it they have nothing.* . . . More than a century ago, in the *Communist Manifesto*, Marx and Engels coined the famous slogan: 'Workers of the world, unite!'—thus sounding the war drum for the first struggle of the proletariat to conquer power. . . . Today, in the new situation in our country, hundreds of millions of revolutionaries respond once more to the great appeal

[35] The complete text of this document may be found in "32 Shanghai Revolutionary Rebel Organizations Issue 'Urgent Notice,'" *Peking Review*, No. 4 (January 20, 1967).

of Chairman Mao: 'Proletarian revolutionaries, unite broadly to take power from the leaders who are following the capitalist road.' . . . We, the great masses of workers, peasants, and soldiers, and no one else, are the undisputed masters of the new world!" [36]

The "Urgent Notice," the many posters, and the intensive press campaign, endorsed by Mao, had an electrifying effect in Shanghai. Productive work was largely resumed in this city of over ten million people and clashes between groups ceased (or at least greatly diminished), although no centralizing authority was really functioning yet. The Municipal Party Committee and the Ministry of Public Security, charged in point 10 with applying the provisions of the Notice, were in fact no more than shells devoid of content and no longer had the necessary means to act. The city police itself was divided into factions corresponding to the various Headquarters and acting on their own account. According to trustworthy witnesses, a few army patrols sometimes went through the city, but *no one* ever saw the soldiers intervene in any way, in the factories or in public places, against any Red Guard or rebel group.[37] So the balance was precarious; all organizations agreed on the need to form a Shanghai Commune and were negotiating on the methods, but apparently none of them had very clear ideas on the best way to put into practice the slogan that was already appearing on the walls: "All power to the Commune!" When this was finally proclaimed, on February 5, 1967, its representative quality was loudly disputed and the factional clashes were resumed in great style. But meanwhile other events taking place outside Shanghai were to bring about a change of policy on the part of the central authorities and condemn even the formula of a commune based on the direct and uncontrolled power of the masses.

T'an Chen-lin: The Party Held at Bay

"Do you still need the leadership of the Party? Do you want to destroy all the old cadres? I speak here in the name of all the

---

[36] See the editorial in *People's Daily* of January 22, 1967: "Proletarian Revolutionaries, Unite Broadly to Take Power from Leaders Who Take the Capitalist Road!"

[37] Certain Western myths inspire the belief that the Shanghai People's Commune was put down in the same way as the Polish workers' strike at Gdansk in 1970, but in reality there was no police action in Shanghai.

veterans of the revolution, and I had rather be jailed or beheaded than be a silent witness of the humiliation of so many of our old comrades." T'an Chen-lin, who spoke thus at an enlarged meeting of the CCP Politburo in January 1967, was in no risk of being challenged when he described himself as "one of the oldest comrades of Chairman Mao, who has been in a better position than anyone else to assimilate Mao's thought." In 1927, in fact, he had been at Mao's side in the famous autumn harvest uprising in Hunan, and had been the first to follow him to the Red base of Chingkangshan. In the Maoist hierarchy of the period, he ranked directly after Mao and Chu Teh, the co-founder of the new strategy of revolutionary war. But, in this month of January 1967, T'an was not raising his voice solely because of his distinguished past; since the eclipse of Liu Shao-ch'i and Teng Hsiao-p'ing (preceded by the elimination of P'eng Chen), he had the great honor of being in effect secretary-general of the CCP.[38] Together with the Central Group for the Cultural Revolution, responsible for ideological leadership, the Party Secretariat was now the only functioning organism. To say "Appeal to the Central Committee" was understood to mean "Telephone or write to the Secretariat," for the Central Committee as such no longer met and most of its working departments were no longer functioning. So it was to T'an Chen-lin and the two other members of the Secretariat, Li Hsien-nien and Li Fu-ch'un, that Party leaders in Shanghai and

[38] In the Secretariat elected at the Eighth Congress in 1956 (and confirmed at the second session in 1958) T'an held fourth place after Teng Hsiao-p'ing, P'eng Chen, and Wang Chia-hsiang. But the last-named, one of the survivors of the group of "twenty-eight Bolsheviks," had not been seen in public since 1963, and there is every reason to believe that he was dismissed after the tenth session of the Central Committee in September 1962. P'eng Chen, as we have seen, was officially relieved of his duties on June 3, 1966. Teng Hsiao-p'ing had finally made his self-criticism at the same time as Liu, in October 1966, but was already in disgrace. Two other members of the Secretariat, Lu Ting-yi and Lo Jui-ch'ing, had been dismissed in the spring of 1966. If we add that K'ang Sheng, another secretary, had moved to the Central Group and that Li Hsüeh-feng, who had replaced P'eng Chen in the Party leadership in Peking, was in trouble in the summer because of the affair of the work teams (which he had also favored), we see clearly that T'an Chen-lin, Li Fu-ch'un, and Li Hsien-nien were the only secretaries actually holding their posts. The priority given on every occasion to T'an shows definitely that he was *primus inter pares* in this trio and could be regarded as secretary-general, although this title was soon to be finally abolished.

other provincial cities addressed their cries of distress throughout this period. But they were given neither comfort nor practical advice. The Secretariat was overwhelmed and powerless; it can be understood that T'an, utterly exasperated, wanted to know what could be meant by the leading role of the Party when it was a target of the revolution.

T'an did not put his questions to Mao—who did not attend the meeting—or to Lin Piao or Chou En-lai, but to T'ao Chu, number four in the hierarchy since August 1966, who was in the best position to influence events. Paradoxically, the protagonists in what was to be the first great trial of strength at the top level were old friends from the 1930's. Both were reputed to be long-standing champions of the "very radical line" and they even had a specialty—agriculture—in common. There was every reason for them to work happily together, and we can be sure that, at the time of the reshuffle of August 1966, T'an Chen-lin's voice helped T'ao Chu to attain this senior rank. But five months of the Cultural Revolution had made them into irreconcilable foes, and their conflict could only end in the fall of one or the other—in the event, of both. But just who was T'ao Chu and what responsibility did he have in the collapse of the Party machine?

Though a native of Hunan like Mao, and a fellow pupil and friend of Lin Piao in Canton in 1925, T'ao Chu was not the mere regional leader of Central-South China depicted by some foreign commentators. From his participation in the short-lived Canton Commune of 1927 to his flattering promotion forty years later, he had been involved in most of the significant events. Consecutively or simultaneously, he had been a guerrilla comrade of T'an Chen-lin in the later 1920's, a hero of the Long March, chief of the general staff of Lin Piao's army at the time of the taking of Peking in 1949, initiator of land reform in the south, a staff member of *Red Flag* during the Great Leap Forward, Chou En-lai's aide in the Chinese delegation to the Twenty-second Congress of the CPSU in 1961, political commissar of the army, secretary of the Party's Central-South China Bureau, and the author of many books, several of which were translated into foreign languages.[39] As a leader of national stature, therefore, T'ao

---

[39] For T'ao Chu's life, see Donald W. Klein and Anne B. Clark, *Biographical*

Chu had made his mark during the debates of the 1960's by his "radical" position on the reform of traditional opera (started by K'o Ch'ing-shih in Shanghai) and we may be sure that he was wholly committed to the Left line of the Cultural Revolution. Known for his organizational talents, he became deputy to Ch'en Po-ta in the Central Group and was at the same time given responsibility for the key sector of propaganda, which earned him his rank in the hierarchy (oddly enough, the number-four position has never been a lucky one).

On taking up his duties, T'ao Chu spoke to a meeting of ten thousand people in Peking on July 30, 1966, and, "brandishing his fist," said that he was essentially a proletarian revolutionary. "When you no longer trust me, you can strike me down," he declared.[40] He is also credited with this dictum: "Except for Chairman Mao and Vice-Chairman Lin Piao, no leader should be immune from criticism; I myself put my trust only in Chairman Mao and his closest comrade in arms." It was T'ao, finally, who wrote the explosive editorial in *People's Daily* of August 23, 1966, which stated: "The Central Committee of the Party is the Central Committee; the Party organization of a region or a unit is the Party organization of that region or unit. If any Party organization goes against the true leadership of the Central Committee and the thought of Mao Tse-tung, why should it not be criticized? Why should one not be opposed to it? Why should its critics be labeled as 'anti-Party'?" [41] In short, as later accusations charged, T'ao Chu did all he could to "spread distrust of all leaders and all Communists" and was thus the chief protagonist of the pernicious ultra-Left line.

But he was also "the lock that had to be broken in order to attack Liu Shao-ch'i and Teng Hsiao-p'ing, the real leaders of the bourgeois general staff." Refusing to point them out as targets, T'ao Chu seems to have distributed throughout China films of Mao's eight meetings with the Red Guards on T'ien An Men

---

Dictionary of Chinese Communism (Cambridge, Mass.: Harvard University Press, 1971), p. 808.

[40] See Yao Wen-yuan's article aimed against T'ao Chu, "Comments on T'ao Chu's Two Books," *Peking Review*, No. 38 (September 15, 1967).

[41] See editorial in *People's Daily* of August 23, 1966: "Workers, Peasants, and Soldiers Must Resolutely Support the Revolutionary Students."

Square, deliberately showing that Liu and Teng were still on the platform of honor. Thus, he "gave a false impression" of Mao's relationship with Liu and Teng in order to "deceive the masses and serve his revisionist masters." [42]

The slogan that was soon to appear on the posters—"Down with Liu, Teng, and T'ao!"—was, of course, an example of the classical technique of conflation. T'ao Chu had little to do with Liu and Teng, except that he had contributed to their downfall on the eve of the Cultural Revolution. Nevertheless, the problem raised by T'an in January 1967 was relevant, and his complaints against his old friend T'ao were not baseless. To stimulate the Cultural Revolution, T'ao's centralized propaganda had done as much as possible to set the rank and file against the leaders but nothing, or very little, to help the latter and create the right atmosphere for a dialogue. The limitation—"a handful of bourgeois usurpers"—certainly deceived nobody. The hand was big enough to contain all the top brass, and the formula was used everywhere and exploited everywhere. While, in Peking, the Politburo was calling on people to examine their consciences, in Shanghai the rebels were dragging thousands of Communist cadres through the streets to disorderly self-criticism sessions. That, according to T'an, was the outcome of six months of T'ao's "management" of propaganda.

The Party secretary got his ammunition especially from the humiliation inflicted in Shanghai on Ch'en P'ei-hsien and in Nanking on Chiang Wei-ching. Indeed, in view of their record, these two leaders from East China could not be regarded as lukewarm or bureaucratic Communists. If they were suddenly accused of "revisionism" or "anti-Maoism," then "all the old cadres will sooner or later meet the same fate." [43] Is this what you

---

[42] On this affair of "film technique," see the attack on Hsiao Wang-tung, minister of culture, in *New China Notebooks*, No. 244, p. 21. Hsiao was accused of "being responsible, on the orders of [T'ao], for distributing films of Chairman Mao's meetings with the Red Guards" that made the presence of the "Chinese Khrushchev" rather too obvious.

[43] In an attack on T'an, published by *Wen Hui Pao* of Shanghai on June 1, 1968, under the eloquent heading "Unmask T'an Chen-lin, the Black General of Evil Winds for Reversal of Verdicts," it was claimed that he had demanded the rehabilitation not only of Ch'en and Chiang but also of Wang Ming, who had long

want? T'an asked his comrades. No, apparently it was not what they wanted. But this was not all; as old T'an was also vice-premier and minister of agriculture, he was quickly able to make a preliminary review of the Cultural Revolution in the countryside. Attacks on the work teams in the universities and factories had echoed in the communes, where similar groups had been at work during the time of the "four cleanups." As a result, in communes or brigades, all those who had been dismissed for inefficiency or corruption were now trying to take their revenge and founding committees "to reverse authoritarian verdicts." They were supported, moreover, by Red Guards coming in from outside who knew nothing about the situation and were only seeking to "struggle against the existing leaders." T'an warned, "If you want a harvest next year, the time has come to stop this settling of accounts." This point, too, found the Politburo far from indifferent. "I agree with control from below and with the principle of broad democracy, but not with this 'seizure of power' which we have seen in Shanghai and even in the farming communes," he said, and he swore to fight "to the end, at any risk" against this form taken by the Cultural Revolution.

T'an's remarks can fairly easily be pieced together, thanks to the articles and posters which appeared some months later to denounce his challenge to the "mass line" and the "opposing trend of February 1967." It is much harder to learn about the answers made by T'ao Chu, for he was dismissed practically overnight and labeled as a member of the "general staff of the bourgeoisie," thus joining Liu and Teng Hsiao-p'ing. What could he urge in his defense? That it was not his fault if the antagonism between governors and governed proved to be more explosive than had been foreseen? That no reasonable propaganda could have stopped the masses from expressing the complaints that they

been a refugee in the USSR. Of course, this charge was designed to show that the "guilty man" had always been a rightest and to insinuate that he too might have been in cahoots with the Russians. But the writer in *Wen Hui Pao* felt the need to strengthen his case by answering an article which had appeared in *Pravda* on March 29, 1967, "applauding and encouraging" T'an. On checking up, I found that the *Pravda* article merely copied Western and Japanese agency news items on T'an's position against the overthrow of old revolutionary cadres. Wang Ming never came into it at all.

had stored up against the men in power at every level, and that good advice was not enough to bring the managers into a dialogue on equal terms with subordinates who had turned into uncontrollable critics? Last but not least, was it because of extremist propaganda that tried Communists like Ch'en P'ei-hsien were unable to influence the masses, after a lifetime of talking about their close links with these very masses?

But, if we can only guess at T'ao Chu's defense, we have plenty of information—often indirect, it is true—about this January debate as a result of which the Central Group lost three of its foremost members.[44] It shows that T'an won the unreserved backing of three other members of the Politburo who, like him, were vice-premiers. Li Hsien-nien, minister of finance, Li Fu-ch'un, minister of the State Planning Commission, and Ch'en Yi, titular foreign minister, were as shocked as he was by the turn of events and did not conceal their determination to do all they could to oppose the extremist trend.

Ch'en Yi, the renowned and outspoken marshal,[45] even spoke

[44] T'ao Chu was officially head of the Central Committee's Propaganda Department and at the same time an adviser to the Central Group for the Cultural Revolution. His two aides in propaganda, Wang Jen-chung and Liu Chih-chien, were also principal aides to the Central Group. In January 1967, all three were relieved of their duties, but no indication was given as to who had replaced them. There is every reason to think that the Central Group was simply reduced from eighteen to fifteen members. The Propaganda Department likewise remained without anyone at its head. Through the first eight months of 1967, it was provisionally directed by Wang Li, a member of the Central Group.

[45] Like T'an Chen-lin, Ch'en Yi had been among the first to join Mao in his base at Chingkangshan in 1927. In 1934, at the time of the Long March, these two leaders were entrusted with a suicidal mission: to stay in Kiangsi and draw on themselves the weight of the Kuomintang troops in order to gain time for the March. Having gloriously carried out this task and saved some of their men, Ch'en Yi and T'an were among the creators of the New Fourth Army, which was active in the southeast behind the Japanese lines. In January 1941 this army was the victim of a surprise attack in southern Anhwei by Kuomintang forces, and its commander, Yeh T'ing, was taken prisoner. To settle this incident, which caused a great stir, the CCP sent Liu Shao-ch'i to Anhwei and he made contact in the first place with T'an. This link between T'an and the "Chinese Khrushchev" was duly pointed out in articles in Wen Hui Pao and elsewhere and used against the unfortunate T'an. But we can be sure that the same charge could equally have been made against Ch'en Yi, who was in the same place and involved in the same events in 1941.

scornfully of the "little generals of the Red Guards" and advised them to do a tour of duty in Vietnam, in order to learn about revolutionary war before giving lessons to others. Chou En-lai probably supported the four vice-premiers, but we have no reliable information on that subject.

In a Politburo reduced to about ten titular members, the moderate line was thus assured of a majority. But it seems that—for their own reasons—the two spokesmen of the "Left," Ch'en Po-ta and K'ang Sheng, supported T'an against their comrade in the Central Group, T'ao Chu. As upholders, if not initiators, of the line of "seizure of power" by the rank and file, Ch'en Po-ta and K'ang Sheng were afraid of being pushed aside once more and advised "attacking on a narrower front." In other words, they agreed in a general way to defending the vulnerable cadres but urged, at the same time, that precise targets be designated—such as Liu and Teng, and some local leaders who were beyond redemption—on whom the wrath of the masses could be concentrated. Thus, the positive unifying factor, the thought of Mao, would be reinforced by another link—a joint attack by all the groups on the individuals who embodied the "dark side" of China.

Finally, a third delicate decision, accepted by Lin Piao himself, involved the dispatch to all sensitive areas of work teams from the army (obviously, they were not to bear this discredited name, but were to be called "army propaganda teams for the thought of Mao Tse-tung"). Thanks to the links between Communists in the army and civilian cadres, thanks to their prestige and ability to gain a hearing among the masses, they would be particularly equipped to "calm the situation by reasoning" and to mediate between rival mass groups and Party organizations. In short, the army teams were to succeed where the old cadres had failed; they would be able to recognize the truly Left rank-and-file committees, hold discussions with them to guide them toward unifying action, and—with them—dominate the whole movement. The pinpointing of targets, desired by Ch'en Po-ta and K'ang Sheng, would ease the task of these new envoys of the central leadership of the Cultural Revolution. In the order of the day from the Military Affairs Commission of the Party, dated January 23, 1967, on "the resolute help of the People's Liberation Army to the left-wing mass revolutionaries," we find for the first time an attack on Liu and Teng by name. Point 5 of this order (destined to reach all ranks by internal channels) announced clearly: "The nation must be instructed in a thorough manner in the struggle between the proletarian line represented by Chairman Mao and the bourgeois reactionary line represented by Liu Shao-ch'i and Teng Hsiao-p'ing." [46]

The most spectacular result was the creation, in the northeastern province of Heilungkiang, of the first Provincial Revolutionary Committee, based on a "triple alliance." This union, cited as an example to all proletarian revolutionaries, took place on January 30, 1967. The leading figures were P'an Fu-sheng, first secretary of the Party in the province, Wang Chia-tao, military commander of Heilungkiang Province, and delegates from the "Harbin Red Rebels' United Headquarters." An official account described the operation thus:

> On January 12 the rebels took over the newspapers, the radio stations, and the provincial and municipal Public Security departments, all in a single day. Their voices have since been heard through all channels. Then they imprisoned the leaders of the counterrevolutionary organizations in Harbin [the "Red Flag Army" and the so-called Rong Fu Jun] so that these organizations were speedily broken up. At the same time, a mass meeting, wisely given great publicity, was organized to condemn the leaders of the "Red Defense Detachment" and the "August 8 Regiment" as monarchists [that is, manipulated by the authorities]. . . . On January 30, Comrade P'an Fu-sheng and Commander Wang Chia-tao went of their own accord to the Red Rebels' United Headquarters to study the methods of taking power. The members of the Headquarters took the initiative in inviting Comrade P'an and Commander Wang to be chairman and vice-chairman of the Revolutionary Committee of Heilungkiang and completed the drafting of the first proclamation. . . . At the inaugural meeting, next day, over 100,000 revolutionary rebels expressed their proletarian and militant approval and shouted with enthusiasm: "We are not only able to destroy the old world, we are equally able to build a new world!" [47]

[46] *Documents of the Great Proletarian Cultural Revolution*, p. 196.

[47] See "Basic Experience of the Heilungkiang Red Rebels in the Struggle to Seize Power," *Peking Review*, No. 8 (February 17, 1967).

The Commune Loses Its Name

The Shanghai People's Commune was finally proclaimed on February 5, 1967. According to *Wen Hui Pao*, the main newspaper, a million workers came to the inaugural meeting. They formed a great procession "to celebrate warmly the greatest day in the history of proletarian and revolutionary Shanghai." [48] The paper did not name the speakers, but reported their speeches in lyrical terms:

> Their giant voices announced to all China and to the whole world that the Municipal Party Committee and the City Council of Shanghai had been destroyed and that a new organ of power had been established, in keeping with the doctrines of Chairman Mao and the principles of the dictatorship of the proletariat. . . . The Shanghai People's Commune is governed jointly by the workers [of the Shanghai Workers' Revolutionary Rebel Headquarters], the peasants [of the Committee of Rebel Revolutionary Peasants], and the soldiers [local units of the army]. . . . It has destroyed the dictatorship of the old state, dominated by counterrevolutionary revisionists. Its organizational principle is democratic centralism as defined by Chairman Mao. Its aim is to safeguard the broadest democracy for the proletariat and exercise the harshest dictatorship against its enemies. Its directing members are elected by the revolutionary masses according to the principles of the Paris Commune. . . . For the present, it is directed by a provisional committee formed by consultations between mass organizations, commanders of army units stationed in Shanghai, and revolutionary cadres loyal to the proletarian line of Chairman Mao. . . . Comrade Chang Ch'un-ch'iao, deputy leader of the Central Group for the Cultural Revolution, and Comrade Yao Wen-yuan, a member of the Central Group, were present at the meeting and spoke. Comrade Chang announced that he would take part in the work of the provisional committee, in accordance with the suggestion of the Central Group and with the agreement of all the founding organizations.

One might have expected this great piece of news to be broadcast on a grand scale—Shanghai was twenty times more important than Harbin—but no such thing happened. The report

[48] Editorial in *Wen Hui Pao* of February 6, 1967, reproduced in *The Great Power Struggle in China* (Hong Kong: Asia Research Center, 1969), p. 90.

of the February 5 meeting was not published in any other Chinese paper, and in 1971 I was unable to obtain a copy of it. No one denied that it had appeared in *Wen Hui Pao*, but I was told that the issue was completely sold out. Photographic or film records were equally beyond reach. However, people who had joined in the great procession spoke about it frankly and often with much eloquence, but only when they were asked. The Commune lives chiefly in the memories of individuals—its anniversary is not officially celebrated—and the uninformed foreigner will be told only about the birth of the Shanghai Revolutionary Committee, duly presided over by Chang Ch'un-ch'iao, on February 24, 1967. A member of this committee, still in office, said to me laconically: "Shanghai People's Commune was not a satisfactory name." Did everything turn, then, on the choice of a name?

In reality, many things happened during the nineteen days between the proclamation of the Commune and the creation of the Revolutionary Committee which was to replace it. When Chang Ch'un-ch'iao and Yao Wen-yuan returned to Peking to report on their efforts, they were not the only ones to give a version of events to the central authorities. The leaders of the Headquarters, whose organizations had inexplicably not been included in the provisional committee of the Commune, also made their way to the capital. Keng Chin-chang, the energetic leader of the Suchow Brigade, who had endorsed the "Urgent Notice" but not the proclamation of the Commune, sent tele-grams to his followers to tell them that he had been received first by Chou En-lai and then by Ch'en Po-ta, and that both had recognized the revolutionary credentials of his organization and its right to be represented in the new committee. Keng's supporters publicized, by means of posters, the remarks report-edly made by the two leaders, to the effect that the situation in Shanghai was not developing correctly because one large rebel organization alone had assumed all responsibilities, instead of joining with others in a genuine proletarian union.

Critics of Chang Ch'un-ch'iao also found arguments in the absence of national publicity for the Commune; this was taken to show that Chairman Mao was displeased, and divisive rumors spread as merrily as ever, with each group in effect resuming its freedom of action. Above all, no rebel Headquarters had really succeeded in consolidating itself; the original rank-and-file groups did not fully concede authority to these general staffs and tended to regroup in an independent way. The Red Power Defense Army, formerly the most moderate, was practically broken apart and its detachments were now drifting toward the "Lianse" (or "Fourth Liaison Headquarters"), which came forward as the most extremist organization, solidly rooted in the factories, and the least interested in top-level compromises. The rebels of the first period—the would-be marchers to Peking—were confused by this ugly and mysterious dispute which set their original groups, the Workers' Revolutionary Rebel Headquarters and the Suchow Brigade, at loggerheads, with the leaders denouncing one another in posters. The prolonged absence of Keng Chin-chang did not strengthen his personal position, and his enemies made good use of it to accuse him of all possible sins—he was ambitious and hypocritical, he had requisitioned a luxury apartment, and (shame on him!) he had spent a night "in the same room as his secretary." And, almost daily, each Headquarters sent its "special squads" to carry out a punitive raid on another one, while charges flew back and forth of "violating the principle of struggle by reasoning and not by force." The situation was once again in utter confusion.

However, when he got back to Shanghai on February 24, Chang Ch'un-ch'iao was able to play a trump: he had been twice received by Mao himself. At another vast meeting, he was heard with the respect and attention due to one who brought word from the Chairman. Chang's speech was relayed directly to cinemas and factories by means of closed-circuit television, and thus reached an unprecedented audience. Despite this, he announced that his speech, designed to transmit the directives of Chairman Mao, had a private and almost confidential character. Indeed, the text was published only in a specialized collection of "reference materials on the Cultural Revolution." [49] Yet, in a city which had been living for two months in the uncertainty of provisional arrangements, if not of an institutional void, this was the decisive historic moment.

"Were we right to proclaim the Commune and, after its

---

[49] Long extracts from this collection were reproduced in the "Survey of the China Mainland Press," by the U.S. Consulate-General in Hong Kong, No. 4147.

creation, do we still need a Communist Party?" These were not exactly the relevant questions in Shanghai, but Chang Ch'un-ch'iao posed them at the outset of his speech with the one aim of giving the answers supplied by the Chairman. On the first point, Mao's reaction was Delphic: the principle of the Commune should not be challenged, but he wondered whether the process leading to its foundation had been correctly taken from stage to stage. Then, even if a true people's commune, modeled on the Paris Commune, was possible in Shanghai, this was probably not the case in the other cities of China. It would be dangerous, and premature to say the least, to try to impose on all China a solution which in present circumstances was valid only for the most advanced working-class center. So it was necessary to be cautious and help those who were less advanced to make a success of their own processes of revolutionary renewal. Mao neither approved of the Commune nor condemned it; he spoke in conditional terms.

To the second question—"Do we still need the Party?"—his answer was, by contrast, clear: "I believe that we need it because we need a hard core, a bronze matrix, to strengthen us on the road we still have to travel. You can call it what you please, Communist Party or Socialist Party, but we must have a Party. This must not be forgotten."

Then Chang revealed on his own account that Mao was worried about the fate of many of the cadres. The tendency of certain rebels to "overthrow all those in responsible positions" seemed to him regrettable for two reasons. Leaders who were honest and devoted to the people must not be thrown into the same bag as profiteers, who, by feathering their nests, had cut themselves off from the masses. A line must be drawn distinguishing the former from the latter, and even those who had made mistakes should not be cornered and allowed no escape. Second, it must not be forgotten that Shanghai was a complex industrial metropolis; it could not be suitably run by young students and workers who lacked the qualifications to exploit its potentialities harmoniously. Young people, especially workers, had many virtues and should be trusted, but they needed essential allies—comrades from the army, the secular arm of the revolution, who knew how to neutralize counterrevolutionaries; and experienced cadres, who, knowing the techniques of management, could contribute effectively to the sound functioning of the productive system. Finally, Mao seems to have alluded to the international consequences of lightheartedly proclaiming a Paris Commune in China, which might bring about a coalition of all the nation's enemies. But we should be cautious about this part of the directive because, unlike the earlier sections, it has reached us in a number of versions and some of them are very dubious. He appears to have said in effect that a commune should be a real commune; a self-styled commune that failed to live up to its principles would ultimately undermine the enthusiasm of the people of Shanghai and do harm to China's general position.[50]

In any case, from this day on, all plans to set up communes in other cities were abandoned. There was no further mention of the Peking Commune, which, according to posters, had been set up in February under the leadership of Hsieh Fu-chih,[51] nor of the Taiyuan Commune, in Shansi Province, which appears nevertheless to have been set up on February 4, around the same time as that of Shanghai.[52]

In short, the phase of the "seizure of power" changed its form—or its content—at the end of February, and the model of the Paris Commune was no longer to be spoken of by the proletarian Left. The page was turned, and a new period began with an appeal from the Central Group on "four things that should not be done": "We ask the revolutionary masses and the soldiers to say nothing, to do nothing, not to call meetings, and not to put up posters against the creation of the great revolutionary proletarian alliance." Priority was given to the unification of the movement, which was to press forward, certainly, but without

[50] This version, rather loosely formulated but quite plausible, is found in the U.S. Consulate-General's "Survey."

[51] An Agence France-Presse report on February 13 said that Peking had been redecorated for the proclamation of its commune and that, according to Red Guard posters, the chairman was to be Hsieh Fu-chih, vice-premier and minister of public security, who had been since February 1966 one of the most active figures in the Cultural Revolution in the capital. Hsieh was in fact to become the top man in Peking, but only from April 20, 1967, and as chairman of the Municipal Revolutionary Committee, not as head of the Commune.

[52] The creation of the Taiyuan Commune was reported in a dispatch published in *New China Notebooks* of February 4, 1967. But it was not mentioned in the *Peking Review* or in any other official publications.

chaos and without divisions. It was not yet a retreat, at least officially, but even this mere tactical readjustment was to prove hard to implement. After the abandonment of the Shanghai People's Commune and the neutralization of the first extremist wave, China was to encounter the opposite wave, that of restoration, before the great explosion—decisive in a sense—of the "hot summer" of 1967.

Postscript
The Tribulations of the Worker Ku
in Shanghai

The great Diesel engine plant in Shanghai certainly deserves the title of "pilot enterprise" which it has held since 1958. Founded in 1947 by a capitalist with American backing, it started out with the pompous name of Agricultural Machine Works of China, but its production was then small and it seemed unlikely to count for much on a national scale. It employed only 340 workers and its range of production was extremely limited. Only after being nationalized in 1949 did it become a real show window of socialist efficiency and an example of the ability of the workers to develop an undertaking and diversify production by relying on their own resources. The plant re-equipped itself by making on its own premises most of the machine tools—over five hundred different types—which it needed to manufacture Diesel engines of various sorts, mostly intended for irrigation pumps. Its hour of glory came during the Great Leap Forward. It was, indeed, one of the first Chinese plants to abolish the Soviet-type rules based on individual competition for productivity and economic incentives. Thus the plant was able to meet the increased demand arising from this period of large-scale hydraulic public works and to develop in a remarkable fashion. In 1965, at the time of my first visit, it had more than 6,000 workers, who owned a complete neighborhood, built by themselves, possessing modern dwellings, clubs, schools at every level, and even cinemas and theaters.

I had in any case intended to see it again in 1971, but my curiosity was much increased when, at a meeting in Peking, an official of the New China News Agency mentioned an incident, cunningly staged by extremists, which had apparently occurred in May 1967 in this Shanghai factory. No news of this incident had leaked out abroad, but my informant regarded it as highly significant. It showed, according to him, that the ultra-Left had provoked real mutinies in 1967, not out of sectarianism but with the deliberate intention of seizing power. As I was just leaving for the southeast, he advised me to seek information on the battlefield itself. It was a valuable suggestion, and it gave me a chance to have a long discussion with a group of workers at the Diesel plant and to hear a particularly eloquent veteran employee relive the Cultural Revolution as it happened in Shanghai in 1966 and 1967.

However, my second visit began with a slight disappointment. The official from the Revolutionary Committee of the plant, Comrade Sun, was mainly interested in showing me the progress achieved in production thanks to the "repudiation of the bourgeois line of Liu Shao-ch'i." In each workshop, I heard a long explanation of how the mass movement had been consolidated by many technical innovations in manufacture, by improvements to the engines, and by economic use of raw materials. Nothing was said about the incident of May 1967, the ultra-Left, or any episode of violence. I already knew from experience that, in China after the Cultural Revolution, people are more willing to talk about the "group warfare" in the universities than about confrontations in the factories. So at this point I was giving up hope of learning anything from Comrade Sun about the left-wing mutiny of the Diesel workers.

But while we were lunching in a spruced-up corner of the dining hall, thinking that I had nothing to lose, I regretted in a friendly way this reticence concerning a historic incident which nevertheless had been brought to my attention in Peking. Comrade Sun at once bombarded me with questions. Who had talked to me about this affair? How? Why? He did not manage a smile until he was certain of the purity of my sources and my intentions. Then, also wishing to show me that ultra-leftism was

not purely a by-product of sectarianism, he suggested gathering
some participants in the battle of four years ago so that they could
tell me everything. While we made our way to the meeting hall
near the plant gate, giving up the rest of our tour, messengers
went to find these witnesses in various workshops. Sun was in a
good mood again and assured me that he had sent for workers—
men and women, young and old—who would be able to answer
all my questions because, having belonged to different groups,
they had found themselves in opposing camps during the "incident of May 20."

The room was soon filled by workers, some facing me around
the long green table, some farther away as if they intended only to
listen, and some standing near the door as if contemplating a
getaway. No one was prepared for this occasion. The subject must
certainly have been discussed fully and over a long period in the
plant, but it was clearly one that is handled differently "in the
family" and in front of strangers. After a short introduction, Sun
called on a veteran worker named Ku. This tall, robust man of
about fifty, in impeccable blue working clothes, was one of the
340 workers who had been in the plant under capitalism. I was
told, "Everyone respects him because of his integrity, his class-
consciousness, and his contribution to the political and productive
development of the enterprise." He rose slowly during this
introduction, which he listened to with evident satisfaction.
Calmly finishing his green tea, he gave me a shrewd and
sympathetic look. He began with a joke—an unusual thing—and
admitted cheerfully that he had followed the most varied groups,
moderate or extremist, and switched from wing to wing in the
course of events before regaining a correct political balance. All
this was said with a smile and by no means in the style of a
self-criticism, but rather, perhaps, to claim the right to make
mistakes and find one's own way.

To begin with, in the summer and fall of 1966, Ku had
supported the managerial team of the plant and defended the
director, Chu Wang-ping, against the first rebels of the group,
who were called "Revolt of the Red East." He explained that this
initial attitude was to have a major influence on his later
evolution. The people who wrote the first posters, he said, were
young workers who had never known real capitalism, and they

exaggerated their grievances against the management. Instead of making concrete proposals, they accused Chu and his team in a wholesale way of having "restored capitalism 100 percent" in order to "oppress the working class."

"We veteran workers," Ku continued, "formed our own group called 'Look More to the Present,' and we answered the youngsters by pointing out the socialist victories which had given them the right to work, to education, to security, and to dignity. Since we had known the days of poverty and humiliation, we naturally defended a present which we owe to Chairman Mao and the Communist Party."

However, Ku stated that he was not a Party member, nor were most of his companions in the "Look More to the Present" group. But the foreign friend must bear in mind the influence of the Party on the whole working class if he wanted to understand its conduct. Comrade Sun nodded approvingly and everyone present, young and old, seemed to agree.

"Were all the rebels young?" I asked in order to get a more precise picture.

"Only at the beginning," Ku replied promptly. "Later, the question of age ceased to matter. Anyway, we were not against the youngsters. Our mistake was really to trust in the good will of Chu Wang-ping and people like him to carry through the Cultural Revolution with us and improve things by discussion. As I see it, these men identified themselves with the Party, and they knew how to exploit our feelings of gratitude and loyalty toward Chairman Mao for their own twisted purposes. They were very cunning and they stopped at nothing to lull our proletarian vigilance. Do you know whom they got elected as chairman of the Workers' Committee for the Cultural Revolution in our factory? One of the 'Revolt of the Red East' group, who had written the first *ta tzu pao* which denounced them! Well, for a long time they had been using this strategy of sugar-coated bullets with us, the veteran workers; they let us believe that they couldn't manage without us and tied our hands by economic incentives. They were out-and-out revisionists, as sly as Khrushchev himself!"

"But, according to the notes I made in 1965, wage differentials were already very slight here."

"Yes, in theory, but the revisionists had many ways of favoring those whom they found useful for bringing in the corrupting system of economic incentives. Their policy of bonuses, for instance, enabled them to increase the differences between each of the eight categories of wage earners."

"But I was told that these bonuses were collective, given to a workshop and not to individual workers."

"That's accurate; you were told the truth. But the share in the bonus, within each workshop, wasn't the same for all the workers. For the lower categories it was no more than 15 or 20 percent, but for the foremen, technicians, and workers in higher categories it could go up to 45 or 50 percent of the basic wage. When the bonus was very high, some people could double their wages while the lower-paid got nothing but the crumbs."

"He knows what he's talking about," Comrade Sun put in cheerfully, "because he's one of those who got a good share."

Ku laughed, like everyone else, and seemed to be flattered rather than annoyed by this remark; but he made a gesture indicating that he wanted to go on without these minor details being brought in.

"All this time, Chu Wang-ping and his fellows were saying that our first duty was to increase production and we mustn't leave the factory. Discuss everything, they told us, but after work; every Diesel engine that comes out of the assembly shop is another weapon for the proletariat in its struggle against the bourgeoisie. And to make engines we had no need of Red Guards, whether they came from Shanghai or Peking. They claimed that this was what the Party asked of us, and they managed to tie us up in knots with this double talk. When some rebels who had decided to go to Peking were stopped at Anting, Chu asked me and some other older workers to go and convince them to return to the factory. As you know, Anting is right nearby. You get there in twenty minutes by cycle and we know the district well, because there's a car plant there which belongs to the same group as us. But on that day—it was in November—the weather was awful; it was raining in torrents and, besides, all this was happening during working hours. Chu told us to go all the same, suddenly forgetting his speeches about the priority of production. The Anting station was black with people, talking all the time, day and night, rain or no rain. We found some of our fellows, caged up in damp wagons, cold and tired, but determined to go on to the end. They talked to us without anger or bitterness, fraternally in fact, and asked us to support them in the name of working-class solidarity. I suddenly felt shaken by their tone and their determination. But on the other hand I kept saying to myself that there was no need to go to Peking to settle our affairs, since Chu and the management group were ready to discuss everything in the plant itself. In short, I began to hesitate, but I was still tied up in knots."

"Was your group linked with the Red Power Defense Army? Did it support the Shanghai Party Committee?"

"Linked—that's one way of putting it. We didn't go out of the factory much, but someone may have sent a telegram or two to support the Red Power Defense Army. I can't say positively. But basically we had much more respect for the Party committee, in the city and in the factory, that's for sure. But don't imagine that, because of that, we were against the Cultural Revolution. We'd listened carefully to the sixteen-point decision and we thought it was 100 percent right. We'd also read the editorials in honor of the Red Guards and we were not altogether opposed to them. But everything was complicated because we trusted our old leaders and we wanted to resolve our problems by working with them."

"In practice, did you settle anything in this period? Did you change the bonus system, for instance, or the rules for apprentices?"

"Yes and no. In practice there were no more bonuses because the factory was slowed down. As for the apprentices, we didn't all agree. These apprentices are being trained to work in other factories, not to stay here, so they get food and clothes instead of proper wages. Some say that's wrong, but some say it's a matter for national authority. Anyway we didn't see much of the apprentices—they never missed a meeting or a demonstration in town. The student-probationers worked harder—or at least they stayed in the factory—so we agreed to give them full wages. But this was one of Chu Wang-ping's sugar-coated bullets. The basic question was power, not these economic arrangements. We had to stop the revisionists from taking command and get reliable chiefs, completely loyal to Chairman Mao and the proletarian line. That was the vital question we felt passionately about."

Comrade Sun obviously felt that Ku was going on too long, and

asked him to tell us how "the renegade Chu Wang-ping" had
tried to corrupt him. Ku thanked him for this interruption, and
went into the episode in a lively style.

"At the end of December, Chu called me into his office and
said: 'The production group is proposing to raise wages. You, as a
star worker, deserve a lot more than the 124 yuan you're getting.
The people's state is exploiting you; it's not right. We're offering
you 200 yuan a month, backdated to the first of June, the date of
the first rebel *ta tzu pao* in China.' Then he did some addition on a
bit of paper and gave me about 500 yuan, without even asking me
for a receipt or anything. 'The Workers' Provisional Committee
agrees,' he said, 'it's all aboveboard, don't look at me like that.' I
took the money, like those who went in before me and after me,
but I never spent a penny of it; this time I felt that something was
badly wrong. I put the money aside and waited. On the eleventh
of January, when the 'Urgent Notice' to the people of Shanghai
explained that this handout of state funds was a counterrevolutionary plot, I was among the first to give back Chu's 500 yuan
and denounce his economism and his crimes. And then I
straightway joined the real rebels."

But this was not the end of Ku's political troubles. In fact, grave
events followed the overthrow of the old Shanghai Party Committee and its "acolytes" in the Diesel factory. Revelations on the real
character of these "revisionist traitors" filled Ku with bitterness.
"I couldn't manage to understand," he said seriously, "how all
these men had succeeded in infiltrating the Party of Chairman
Mao and abusing our trust with impunity and for such a long time.
I remembered with disgust their pledges of loyalty to Communism, to the Chairman, and to the working class, their tricks and
their promises, and frankly I was torn by doubts and indeed by
bitterness. I didn't want to admit that I shared the blame and that
I ought to have shown more discernment since the start of the
Cultural Revolution, or even before. No, I said to myself that they
had wickedly deceived me by exploiting my gratitude and loyalty
to the Party. In these circumstances, how could I avoid being
fooled again by another lot of fine speakers boasting of their
Communism? Here, nobody agreed with anybody else. The whole
neighborhood was covered with posters; you could have spent
your entire life reading them. Well, we had to choose new leaders

and decide our attitude toward the Revolutionary Committee which had just been set up. With the experience I'd had, I was a bit inclined to reserve my approval. I knew some of the rebels who had taken power in the factory and I knew that they were good workers. But hadn't I been fooled already by similar oaths of loyalty to Chairman Mao? To tell you the truth, I'd grown very distrustful, and so I was more open to the arguments of the extremists, of those anarchists whose slogan was 'Down with all leaders and all who want to be leaders!' Besides, in their posters, these people were spreading all kinds of lies about the Communists in the factory, accusing them wholesale of being 'black lieutenants of the rotten dynasty of Liu Shao-ch'i.' In short, they took all Communists, including the original rebels, as targets. Besides, I didn't know that among them there were a good many former Communists and other dangerous elements who were trying to settle old quarrels with the Party. They were always flattering to us veteran workers and pretended to listen to our advice. Actually they listened only to themselves. As soon as you agreed with them, they shouted: 'Who are you to give orders to us? Do you think you're a boss or something?' "

So Ku broke with the extremists of the Lianse, who had a majority in the factory and were supported by most of his friends. He told all this in a firm voice, without a trace of self-accusation, and seemed scarcely troubled by his dramatic story. After some digressions about the cunning tricks of the "anarchists," he came to the famous "incident of May 20." On that day, the extremists, taking advantage of a technical dispute with the other groups and the army propaganda team, took over the factory. Having occupied the offices, they drove out the unarmed soldiers with steel ingots and "spread anarchist terror in all the workshops." All the faces in the room took on grave expressions, and silence weighed on them heavily. It seemed that the incident still plunged everyone into stupefaction—how could such a scandal have occurred in a pilot factory, so often held up as an example to the nation? Comrade Sun alone remained calm; he intervened, almost gaily, to cite crushing evidence against the ultra-Leftists of the Lianse. He clearly wanted to establish that this mutiny was planned in advance, and pointed out that they had prepared their ammunition long beforehand and had teamed up with the worst kind of class enemies. On the actual facts, Sun had little to add; he said, indeed, that he had not been on the spot. Ku used this interruption to sit down, drink another cup of tea, and make some final reflections.

"You may ask me how I could reconcile my loyalty to Chairman Mao with my support for an extremist group that didn't hesitate to attack unselfish soldiers whom the Chairman himself had sent to help us. Personally I took no part in the violence of May 20—everyone here knows that—but that doesn't lessen the seriousness of my responsibility. To begin with, I saw only the formal side of the incident and not its deeper political content, although this arose from the very intentions of those who provoked it. What exactly happened on May 20? In fact, the Lianse claimed that power in the factory had been usurped in January by a group that wasn't really on the Left. It was also against the formation of a united committee drawing together representatives of this group and of the revolutionary cadres. The army team condemned this attitude, but at the same time recognized the Lianse as a legitimate mass revolutionary organization. Really, though there were so many little groups and detachments, the rank and file were divided into two camps— those who thought that the seizure of power in January was right and those who agreed with the Lianse that it was illegitimate. So on May 20 the Lianse, who had a majority in the factory, decided to take power in turn, to make use of funds and propaganda facilities, and to go into the city in the factory trucks to make contact with other workers. The army team stood firmly against all these actions and blocked the factory gate. The Lianse leaders at once claimed that the team was exceeding its powers and violating Chairman Mao's directives on the right of the masses to liberate themselves. So there was an argument, this led to insults, and you know the rest. We were all moved by the courage of those soldiers, who really didn't fight back blow for blow and had to retreat, carrying their wounded, even some dead from what I've heard. But we also thought that the army team wasn't backed by its superiors, and even that it had been disavowed. Only later did we understand that the soldiers had refrained from asking for reinforcements with the sole aim of avoiding worse bloodshed, so as not to throw oil on the fire of our fratricidal battle."

Ku's tone became less confident—perhaps from weariness—when he came to his definite conversion to the correct line and his break with the extremists. He described the anxious atmosphere that pervaded the factory after May 20 and the hesitations of many older workers, who began, as he did, to draw away from the Lianse. This could well be explained by uncertainty as to the outcome of this trial of strength, but also by the concern of these veterans for the "common asset" that their factory represented.

"I told you that I've been working here for twenty-three years, since the birth of the factory under the old regime. We veteran workers have seen it grow and we've given all our energies, all our lives, to developing it and making it work better and better. Now, most of these Lianse agitators had their mouths full of slogans, but they did nothing to organize production. Every trifle had to be discussed till the cows came home, but still everybody did as he pleased. There was no longer any question of safety procedures, or any kind of procedure, to tell you the truth. Some people never came to work at all, or wandered about the workshops as if they were at one long festival. When we told them that Diesel engines wouldn't get made all by themselves and that the country needed them, they made fun of us. One of them said to me, 'Old Ku, you'll never free yourself from your slave mentality, you don't understand a thing about democracy or socialism.' Another shouted in the workshop: 'Leisure belongs to socialism as much as work; there's no harm in resting and talking during working hours.' We explained to them that their attitude was wrong, that it went against the working-class tradition of work well done, and besides that, that we were going to get into trouble if the production of the factory went down or stopped. But they wouldn't listen to reason. Being in a majority, they kept calling for a vote on trifles, but after most of the workers had turned away from them they stopped accepting the results of votes and said: 'The minority can be right, that's in the sixteen-point decision.' In short, deaf to all argument, they always claimed to be the cream of the revolutionaries. Besides, they really thought they could do as they pleased. I'm not even talking about the language they used—you never heard such a variety of insults. But when it came to blows, they didn't play around either. They didn't want any bosses, but that didn't stop them from having well-organized shock teams which struck out right and left when anybody spoke out of turn. Believe me, when Comrade Sun talks about anarchist terror, he's not exaggerating."

Comrade Sun took this up to give some examples of the ill treatment inflicted on junior cadres. He even told the story of an assistant kitchen chief who, because of this title, had been labeled a "despot" and accordingly ill treated. Bursts of laughter suddenly spread and lightened the atmosphere. We were getting to the end of the story, which was a bit more cheerful but none the less dramatic. Between May and July 1967, the Lianse gained ground in Shanghai and the Diesel plant was not altogether isolated. Despite the incident of May 20, the leaders of the Municipal Revolutionary Committee came to the factory to seek an acceptable unifying solution. They made inquiries, they went from workshop to workshop to calm people down, and, according to Ku, there were hopes that everything would end up in a friendly way "as between comrades." But in August the divisions again grew more acute, leading to violence all over the place and particularly in the machine-tool workshop.

"It became clear," said Ku, "that the Lianse was out to provoke a huge fratricidal battle, and relied on the breakup of the Municipal Revolutionary Committee. We also had the feeling that it was following a concerted plan and somebody was pulling the strings behind the scenes. At that time, many of these activists simply quit the factory and tried to get us to join their teams to intervene elsewhere. When I refused, they insulted me and charged that I was afraid of losing my job, and even that I was a worker-bureaucrat at heart. But a few weeks later, in September, we heard of the new directive of Chairman Mao, according to which 'there is no fundamental conflict of interests within the working class.' So I had been right in refusing to treat comrades as one treats enemies. Indeed, after this directive from the Chairman, the vast majority of the workers here and elsewhere took a stand against the irreconcilables who, having nothing further to hope for, were still rejecting any compromise solution."

The solution, quickly described, was nevertheless imposed from outside. In the fall of 1967, the administration buildings were "liberated" from the extremists. But when and how? Was this a surprise action organized by the Shanghai Revolutionary Committee? Why was this second battle neither given an exact date nor described as an "incident"? [53] Ku said enough to suggest these questions, but he at once assured me that, at the time of the reoccupation of the administration buildings, there were only a few dozen fanatics holding out against any reconciliation. "They had taken up the slogan: 'Live or die like Lianse men!' Nobody set a trap for them, you can believe me. Besides, among these diehards there were few workers from here. Those who had left the factory in July and then recognized their mistake were all forgiven; they went back to their jobs. Others, like myself, had never been bothered, beyond a bit of discussion about our attitude. I explained myself then just as I've done today, and my comrades elected me to the Revolutionary Committee of my workshop. Later, we found out that these diehards—those who wouldn't listen to reason—were simply provocateurs and counter-revolutionaries. That was why they didn't trust the promises of their comrades when they were guaranteed an escape route." Ku's voice now became sad and he quickly sat down, leaving the eloquent Comrade Sun to sum up the political lessons of this remarkable story.

It was getting late and the room was slowly emptying, the more so when the next witness—an engineer named Pao, who had also broken with the Lianse—proved to have no narrative talent. His statement was filled with quotations from Mao and political clichés and then got bogged down in a technical problem. He was followed by a twenty-three-year-old woman worker by the name of Fu, who gave a good-humored account of life in the girls' dormitory at that time. Sun laughed heartily, but looked discreetly at his watch. He suggested that we should listen to one more witness, the veteran worker Kao, and then give the foreign friend a chance to rest. Kao described his studies in the works of Chairman Mao, which had helped him to think dialectically, and made no reference to the incident of May 20. But as he accompanied me to the car, Sun assured me that I now knew as much as he did about the whole affair and the "crimes of the

[53] Later, during a dinner with members of the Shanghai Revolutionary Committee, I learned that the Diesel engine factory had been "liberated" from the extremists on September 4, 1967, by workers from nearby factories.

anarchists." His final words were: "Extremist ideas are alien to the Chinese working class; they were brought into our factory by certain students who knew nothing about the revolution or about production. I hope you will explain that in your country."

CHAPTER FOUR

The "Hot Summer" of the Cultural Revolution

The February Counteroffensive

On April 10, 1967, Tsinghua University opened its gates to 200,000 workers who came to see the repudiation—and humiliation—of the "monsters" of the old bourgeois general staff. Neither Liu Shao-ch'i nor Teng Hsiao-p'ing figured in this spectacle; the central role was given to Wang Kuang-mei, Liu's wife. She was placed on a platform, made of four chairs, so that everyone could admire her symbolic costume. Accused of having a weakness for jewelry and "bourgeois" clothes, the wife of the Chairman of the Republic wore a necklace of gilded Ping-Pong balls, high-heeled shoes, an old robe of the classical style, and a coolie hat of the colonial era. On her right stood Yeh Lin, former head of the work team, Chiang Nan-hsiang, minister of higher education and president of Tsinghua, and Liang T'ien-feng, another work-team leader and formerly minister of forestry. On her left, three other "guilty men"—Lu Ting-yi, P'eng Chen, and Po I-po—wore placards on their chests denouncing their complicity in the "black gang." The purpose of the rally against the old leaders was "to revile them on the political, ideological, and theoretical level, and strike them down completely so that they could never reappear in the leadership of the Party or again attempt the usurpation of power." [1]

Four years later, at this very place, it was explained to me that these slogans were contrary to Chairman Mao's directives and that K'uai Ta-fu had stage-managed the affair on his own account to increase his popularity. Thanks to hidden accomplices in the propaganda media, he had been able to secure extraordinary publicity for the Tsinghua meeting; it was filmed, broadcast, photographed, and described in Red Guard posters and newspapers all over the country, but not in the official press. In all the pictures, I was told, K'uai and his staff of the Chingkangshan Regiment of Tsinghua could be seen in prominent positions.

But what caused this fear of seeing the dismissed leaders reappear in the leadership of the Party? In that April of 1967, the motivators of the Cultural Revolution were again talking about a plot, hatched in the preceding two months by the very men who in January had seemed to be laid low and reduced to total impotence. The Machiavellian T'an Chen-lin, it was said, had regrouped his shattered forces and launched a sinister "February counteroffensive," aimed at nothing less than strangling the Cultural Revolution and rehabilitating all the "overthrown despots." So, this time, steps must be taken to put an end forever to such attempts at "restoration." "Whether great or small," wrote *People's Daily*, "all the Party leaders who took the capitalist road are as wicked as snakes. They do their best to seem harmless and beg for pity, like snakes numbed by cold weather. But, once revived by warmth, they bite. If we relax our vigilance and fail to criticize and repudiate them vigorously, they will plan a comeback in force and plunge the working people into a bloodbath." [2]

Despite the gravity of these charges, the national press has never given a full account of the February counteroffensive, which is still hidden behind a veil of embarrassment. Accusations against T'an were published in 1968 in *Wen Hui Pao* of Shanghai and the Red Guard papers, but neither in *People's Daily* nor in

---

[1] These phrases occurred often in the *People's Daily* at that period—see *New China Notebooks*, Nos. 180–200—and presumably inspired the organizers of the Tsinghua rally.

[2] *Peking Review*, 1967.

Red Flag.[3] Today, the reasons for this embarrassed silence are better known.

The fact is that events during the winter of 1966–7 had shown that any policy of rebuilding the structure from above, even with great flexibility and the best intentions, would lead to "false seizures of power" and to the repression of the most radical groups. This logic, not easy to observe at the time, led to the violently anti-institutional reaction of the spring of 1967, and then to the "hot summer" which was to bring the most destructive moments of the whole Cultural Revolution. The experience of these months showed, in a sense, that the Cultural Revolution was doomed to swing between two extremes—utter destruction or restoration—without being able to find a unifying middle path.

First, however, the essential facts. At the end of January 1967, the Central Group for the Cultural Revolution decided to repeat in every province the transfer of power which had been made in Heilungkiang, based on the "triple alliance" of revolutionary cadres, army commanders, and the rank-and-file groups which were furthest to the Left. To make this scheme a success, the central government worked in three ways: (1) it asked the great mass of the cadres to "judge for themselves whether it was right to seize power in their own institutions, and who were the leaders who had taken the capitalist road and must be ejected from power";[4] (2) it pressed for the reunification of rebel and Red Guard organizations in each locality, and stressed the constructive self-criticisms of "selfish and anarchical" groups which had been too intransigent;[5] (3) it gave army commanders a free hand to

---

[3] Jean Daubier, who was in Peking in 1967, writes in his book *A History of the Chinese Cultural Revolution* (New York: Vintage, 1974), p. 147: "This is one of the most important but also one of the least known phases of the Cultural Revolution. At a time when the wall posters provided an impressive amount of information about events as they occurred, the precise steps leading up to the countercurrent remained cloaked in mystery. Contrary to what had happened earlier, controversies within the top echelons of the Party leadership for the most part remained secret."

[4] See the *Red Flag* editorial "Cadres Must Be Treated Correctly," *Peking Review*, No. 10 (March 3, 1967).

[5] The national press published, for example, the self-criticism of the Lu Hsün Armed Corps, a Shanghai Red Guard Organization, and a critical analysis of the Third Headquarters of the Peking Red Guards.

mediate between candidates for the new organs of power and to select or support those who were most genuinely on the Left.

On February 3, the Central Group urged all the young people to break off their "Long Marches" to historic spots and return to their schools or factories. Next day, another directive announced that educational institutions would reopen on March 1 and specified that all teachers, whether "good" or "criticized," should have their jobs back. Also, on February 4, it was decided to call a halt to "exchanges of experience" in all national defense industries. On February 12 came a warning that "the masses have no right to burn anyone's Party card, and Party discipline is exclusively the concern of the Party itself." Five days later, another directive hit at nation-wide rebel organizations, in particular those of demobilized soldiers and of apprentices, which were to be dissolved at once.

On the other hand, on February 20, the first Congress of Peking Red Guards was organized. Miss Nieh Yüan-tzu, author of the first *ta tzu pao*, was chairman, and the leading positions were entrusted with much fanfare to "notorious rebels," for the four vice-chairmen—K'uai Ta-fu of Tsinghua, Wang Ta-p'ing of the Institute of Geology, T'an Hou-lan of the Further Education College, and Han Ai-chin of the Aeronautical Institute—had all been victims of the work teams. National leaders turned out in large numbers to bless this team of leftists, and the speakers did not neglect to denounce the old Party leadership for applying the infamous label "counterrevolutionary" to these admirable leaders of the student movement (it had not been applied to Miss Nieh, of course; but she, after all, was a teacher and not a student). Two months later, when the Peking Municipal Revolutionary Committee was finally set up, Nieh Yüan-tzu was among the five vice-chairmen, while the four students named above were members of its executive group.[6] So the Left was presented as the chief beneficiary of the structural changes now taking place.

Moreover, in the provincial or municipal Revolutionary Committees that were given widespread publicity, representatives of the masses obtained most of the positions. At Shanghai, for

[6] The committee was reorganized in December 1967, but the five Red Guards on its executive staff were not removed.

instance, out of twenty-five members of the new executive, eleven came from the rank and file and had a leftist reputation, eight were revolutionary cadres (including Chang Ch'un-ch'iao and Yao Wen-yuan), and six were from the army. Out of 237 committee members in Shansi Province, 110 represented mass organizations, 59 the cadres, and 68 the army. Most of these members did not belong to the executive group and were required to devote part of their time to manual work; they were neither to give nor to receive gifts; their names were not to appear in the press; and they had to submit to a "small rectification campaign" before representatives of popular organizations every two months. No one could really say that the old administrative style was being restored.

Yet the striking feature of this period of "centralization" or "unification" was its extremely slow progress. Despite good arrangements and a hail of directives, the "triple alliance" committees were created with great difficulty, or collapsed as soon as they were set up.[7] This, indeed, was the basis for the indictment of T'an Chen-lin and similar "snakes." When the clamp that gripped them was somewhat loosened, they allegedly took the opportunity to organize the Party cadres and wangle "false seizures of power." Instead of playing the game loyally, they tried to hoist the old machine into the saddle again and stirred up a spirit of revenge. Thus, T'an was accused of deliberately lying to Chou En-lai by declaring, contrary to the truth, that the Red Guard organizations in the Agricultural University and the Institute for Agricultural Science—"East Is Red" and "Red Flag"—were ultra-rightist, "black," and anti-Party.[8] Thus deceived, the premier was induced to receive leaders of the "Liaison Center of Red Rebels," T'an's protégés, which allowed this conservative force to make political capital. Encouraged by this

[7] In fact, apart from those of Peking and Shanghai, only four Revolutionary Committees got on their feet in China's twenty-seven provinces or autonomous regions.

[8] A detailed description of the "false seizure of power" in the Ministry of Agriculture and of other "crimes" of T'an Chen-lin was given by the Canton paper *Chung-ta Hung-ch'i* on April 4, 1968, and by *Wen Hui Pao* on June 1, 1968. Naturally, these events were described from April 1967 onward in the papers and posters of the Red Guards.

success, "little T'ans" in the provinces copied the maneuver, and a wave of repression hit the best local militants.

This account of the misdeeds of T'an and his "snakes" is doubtless rather farfetched. The Party machine was too battered by the blows it had taken in the "January storm" to reorganize itself so quickly and seek a trial of strength with the rebels. In Shanghai at least, I could find no victims of this "white terror" that came from the February counteroffensive. On the contrary, all eyewitnesses told me of the extraordinary distrust accorded during this period to the cadres, who had lost all their prestige. The strategy of the Party center, consisting of "narrowing the target" and concentrating the fire on Liu Shao-ch'i and certain other dismissed leaders, proved to be neither useful nor capable of promoting unity; but, whether the Party center wanted it or not, the mud had stuck to all Communists. In spite of appeals from above, the masses were still divided by this attitude toward the cadres. Under these conditions, it was futile to rely on a harmonious reconciliation effected under the auspices of the "good" cadres.

It can well be imagined, indeed, that when they had to choose among a patchwork of rival organizations, these cadres tended to prefer those who had criticized them least. Thus they involuntarily paved the way for the next explosion, and it soon came. But we must also remember that in February 1967 they no longer stood alone in face of the uncontrollable mass movement; there was now an arbiter—the army—which had the power to tilt the balance in favor of one side or the other. The real story of the February counteroffensive was therefore that of the mistakes made during these months by well-intentioned army men, who were utterly loyal but incapable of identifying the Left among the countless groups that were all claiming to represent Chairman Mao's thought. Many army men recognized this openly, but were not eager for self-criticism on the matter. They admit that, up to September 1967, their efforts at mediation were seldom crowned with success, and in particular were seldom favorable to the Left. What they do not say is that the authority of the army seriously declined and that at the crucial time, in the "hot summer" of 1967, sections of the masses almost turned against them. It is quite clear that the Cultural Revolution had created certain problems within the army itself.

The Contempt of the Military

When he launched his slogan "Open Fire on Headquarters," Mao was by no means urging the army to train its batteries on Party offices. He had thanked Lin Piao on May 7, 1966, for his excellent work in the military sphere, and congratulated him on having maintained and developed the political traditions of the People's Liberation Army, but he still thought, according to his utterances of January 1967, that the army should not intervene in the Cultural Revolution. It was soon observed that this nonintervention had its limits. In the first place, the "mass sources of revolutionary action" needed concrete help which the army could not refuse; then, the army itself, in certain sectors, faced problems which were not very different from those of civilians (in its schools, for instance, and in its artistic units and academies). In autumn 1966 the Peking garrison had to be called upon to help in receiving the eleven million Red Guards who were streaming into the capital to "exchange experiences" and threatening to disorganize the production system and the distribution of food supplies. Then, when the movement reached the educational and cultural sectors of the army, it proved necessary to create in November the "Cultural Revolution Group of the Military Affairs Commission of the Central Committee." [9]

The chairman of the Cultural Revolution Group was Hsü Hsiang-ch'ien, one of the ten marshals (though he had lost this title with the abolition of ranks). A veteran of the Long March and the war against Japan, he had seldom appeared in public since 1960, apparently for reasons of health. While he was a man of some prestige and a member of the Central Committee, Hsü was nevertheless one of the three marshals who had never belonged to the Politburo of the Party.[10] Thus, so far as is known, he had never

[9] Apparently, at the time of its inception in November 1966, this "all-army group" was headed by Liu Chih-chien. But by January 1967, when the Cultural Revolution Group received some degree of publicity, he was no longer in command.

[10] The other two were Yeh Chien-ying and Nieh Jung-chen. The former succeeded Lin Piao in 1971 and is now apparently the top man in the army.

been involved in civilian conflicts, and perhaps this is just why he was chosen. Chiang Ch'ing was attached to him as his leading adviser, while other civilians—notably Kuan Feng, formerly of *People's Daily*—were given full status in this special group.

Nothing in this was surprising. Though they had been trained in the "best school" and had never abused their power, the soldiers were, above all, Communists closely linked to Party policy, and in the past they had been through as many deviations as the civilians. In March 1966, on the very eve of the Cultural Revolution, Lo Jui-ch'ing—chief of the army general staff and also one of the Party secretaries—had been dismissed and indicted along with other members of the "black gang." [11]

The group responsible for the Cultural Revolution in the army was concerned, in the first phase, to see that the movement in the army schools and other institutions did not get out of hand, so that no harm would be done to the army's excellent image. It attacked this task with energy. Practically no reports leaked abroad of "seizures of power" in the schools, artistic units, hospitals, and even factories and farms belonging to the army; but documents show that all these institutions had wall posters, discussions, and criticisms of the Party committees.[12] A more delicate problem— and more difficult to keep secret—arose from the battle between the Red Guards and the Party machine over "black files." Soldiers were involved in defending them and even came under attack. They showed admirable restraint during the first attacks on their barracks, but we can believe that the experience did not increase their sympathy with their assailants from the ultra-Left.

This was understood in high places in Peking—so much so that the decision on army intervention, taken on January 23 and

[11] Lo Jui-ch'ing, formerly minister of security and then chief of the general staff, was subjected to a special procedure in March 1966 and tried to commit suicide. During the "hot" month of August 1967, much was said about his "mistaken ideas," but these recriminations never revealed exactly what was the disagreement between him and the majority on the Central Committee's Military Affairs Commission, which ordered his dismissal. It seems to me very unlikely—if not totally unrealistic—that he demanded Chinese military intervention in Vietnam and was dismissed for this reason. But the other theory suggested in the West, that he supported the alliance with the USSR, is equally hard to prove.

[12] See *Documents of the Great Proletarian Cultural Revolution* (Hong Kong: Union Research Institute, 1968).

countersigned by Mao on January 28, 1967, stressed the need to sponge over these incidents and "resolutely support the Left." [13] These directives, while detailed with regard to the conduct of operations, were very vague about the definition of Left and Right. It was stated in general terms that groups who wanted to preserve the old order were conservative, and hence on the Right, while those who rebelled against oppression were true revolutionaries and hence on the Left. But in January 1967, after the first "seizures of power," such definitions—broad enough in the earlier period—seemed to lose all real meaning. Not a single group asserted that nothing in China should be changed. The differences were far more subtle, and the moderates, who protested mainly against methods of violence, could rely in this respect on categorical quotations from Chairman Mao. Besides, after the "January storm," the principal conflict was between rebels who were content with their victory and others who disputed it, either because they wanted to go further or simply because they demanded a share of power. Who, then, was "more to the Left"? In Shanghai, for instance, was it right to support the newly created Revolutionary Committee or those who thought that it was not representative enough? In provinces where such organs of power had not yet been set up, things were still more confused; each group considered itself most fitted to be the core of the Revolutionary Committee that had to be formed. No one frankly urged a return to the obviously outdated old order; no one could be called conservative. And if all the groups were on the Left, how could a choice be made?

On top of these complications, already considerable, there was the necessity to maintain order and vigilance toward the class enemy. Files compiled by the Party on people suspected of being in "black categories" could no longer be used after the "affair of the black files." It was now out of the question to make use of this material, even secretly. The duty of an army team, if it got hold of any files, was to destroy them, preferably in the presence of those concerned. In December 1966, a month before the army intervention, Ch'en Po-ta and Chiang Ch'ing, in a series of speeches spread by means of posters throughout China, strongly attacked

[13] Ibid., p. 211.

the ministries of Public Security and Justice (especially the Bureau of the State Prosecutor) and called them "typical organs of the dictatorship of the bourgeoisie." [14] The records of these Ministries were put under seals or partially destroyed. Every mass organization was called upon to make its own check of its membership and prevent representatives of the "black categories" from slipping into its ranks. They had little success in this, to judge by the mutual accusations about the social background or political quality of their leaders and members. Needless to say, the army men could not trust the "black material" provided by the rank and file. They had to make their own inquiries in short order to gauge the value of the denunciations exchanged by the groups. Meanwhile, they had to guarantee the safety of ordinary citizens and stop the groups from "judging" and imprisoning their opponents, making punitive raids on one another, or breaking the law in any way. It was a heavy task. To sum up, the envoys of the army had to remedy most of the failings and contradictions of a mass movement which, for a variety of social, historical, and political reasons, could not manage to unite or to discipline itself.

Evidence from various sources shows that the army teams did, at all events, succeed admirably in their practical work in the sphere of production. Each team, composed of several dozen cadres (sometimes more), installed itself in a factory to live with the workers and get production going again. In the northeast, where the situation was most critical, the intervention of these teams brought about a speedy resumption of production (even in 1971 there were more soldiers in the factories of this region than in Shanghai or Peking). Army assistance to agriculture seems to have been still more effective. However, this massive involvement of soldiers in the labor front was bound to influence their political attitude during the delicate period of the winter of 1966–7. The army teams were especially appreciative of groups which seldom left the factories and thus helped them to do their job. We can assume, on the other hand, that soldiers with the task of keeping order had mixed feelings about the "most radical rebels" who

[14] These speeches were made on December 18 and 26 at Red Guard meetings in Peking. Summaries, taken from posters, appeared in the Tokyo newspaper *Yomiuri Shimbun*. The author of these articles gave me notes on the subject in Tokyo.

continued to bother them. As a result, local and provincial army commanders came down on the side of the "moderates," whereas their mission was to support the "radicals."

Did these "mistakes" arise from connivance with certain Party cadres who were old comrades and friends? In the summer of 1967 this sensitive question was naturally raised by some "fanatical" critics of the army, but their charges were scarcely supported by evidence. In reality, the February counteroffensive was the by-product of a political choice by the Party center, not the outcome of a plot between army commanders and civilian cadres. In the decision to stabilize and unify the movement, taken at the end of January, there was a perfectly reasonable desire to achieve the speedy creation of new organs of power, based on moderate elements, and silence the extremists who were impossible to deal with. If the policy was to win back the majority of criticized leaders and cadres, to merge the rank-and-file groups, and to get production started up again, then none of the "seizures of power" carried out under the auspices of "T'an Chen-lin's snakes" and the army could be regarded as "false." They were so described in mid-March because the majority of the Central Group saw that stabilization was going too far. And the hullabaloo which followed showed that the Central Group had a strong conviction that this great mass movement was rich in further possibilities, if it was held in check less and above all if it was not repressed. It was proclaimed from this time on that a divided movement was better than a new "stifling" conformity imposed from above. Moreover, the less the movement was interfered with, the sooner it would manage to organize itself and unite. If this was really the position, then the conduct of the army had indeed been mistaken. Lin Piao said so clearly in a speech made in private on March 20 (or 30), which was passed on only in the army, but of which we possess some extracts. The vice-chairman took his stand above the battle. He was no longer the spokesman of the army or of any particular group, and his distinctive position had a formal sanction, since the status of arbiter could be conferred only by Mao himself. So there was no ambiguity; when Lin criticized army commanders, he was by no means criticizing himself. He rebuked them, in particular, for their inability to "distinguish between Left and Right groups" and the haste with which they had applied mistaken labels to some perfectly revolutionary organizations. But Lin obviously ruled out any idea that this "misconduct" was due to scheming. If some officers had gone too far, it was because of the bad influence of the "leaders who took the capitalist road" and not because of their own repressive tendencies. Besides, in most cases, they had believed their actions to be legitimately defensive, and it was through inexperience that they had resorted to force where persuasion might have sufficed. They were nevertheless blamed, and wall posters highlighted the "Anhwei Province incident," in which troops opened fire on "a legitimate revolutionary group disputing the false seizure of power in the Party committee of the province." [15]

On April 1, in a solemn announcement and in the context of the Anhwei incident, the Central Committee reiterated that no one had the right to describe the masses as counterrevolutionary, or to dissolve their organizations, or to arrest their leaders and militants without inquiry. In addition, no one should be labeled counterrevolutionary simply for having criticized local army officers or even for having invaded their premises. "Many students," it was explained by way of example, "moved into the Chungnanhai compound [where Mao and most of the leaders live], into military establishments, and even the Ministry of Defense, but they were not required by the Central Committee or the Military Affairs Commission to make a self-criticism, write confessions, or anything of the kind. The difficulty was always resolved by explanations and they returned to their homes of their own accord."

Five days later, a ten-point order from the Military Affairs Commission, endorsed by Mao himself,[16] laid down in a still more categorical fashion: (1) that the army must do a purely political job and was strictly forbidden to open fire; (2) that it was forbidden to make arrests, especially on a large scale—when dealing with genuinely counterrevolutionary elements, evidence must be conclusive and the arrests must first be approved by the Central Group; (3) that mass organizations which had made

[15] The resolution on the subject of this incident, dated March 27, 1967, did not clarify just when it had happened. See *Documents of the Great Proletarian Cultural Revolution.*

[16] It carried the notation: "Comrade Lin Piao: This document is very good. Mao Tse-tung." See *Documents of the Great Proletarian Cultural Revolution,* p. 409.

mistakes must be helped and not labeled as counterrevolutionary; (4) that no punitive measures must be taken against groups—Left, Center, or Right—which had moved into army premises; (5) that no organization should be obliged to make a self-criticism, or to make its members write confessions, and that no enforced self-criticism would be accepted; (6) that all army men who had committed the above actions should at once make reparation and take steps to compensate the victims.

On April 9, the military's Cultural Revolution Group was remodeled. Its chairman, Hsü Hsiang-ch'ien, was replaced by Hsiao Hua, director of the army's General Political Department, a young veteran with a strong leftist reputation.[17] Many local commanders were summoned to Peking for a spell of re-education, and many military regions were restaffed from top to bottom. It was a large-scale rectification operation undertaken in the heat of the battle. But, despite the uncertainties of the situation, it went ahead without mishap, in an orderly and disciplined way. Officers who were great in years and prestige criticized themselves without haggling. True, no attempt was made to humiliate them and their treatment was quite unlike what some civilians had endured. Those who were kept in active service had to obey the new political requirements—this too they did without flinching—but benefited from the extenuating circumstances attached to the army as a whole, which was not to be put in the dock.[18]

A new appeal, "Support to the Army and Love from the People," summed up this period. It told the masses that they must trust the army, and urged the army to "sustain the people resolutely and energetically in its revolutionary actions." An editorial in Red Flag explained: "If the revolutionary masses have revealed failings and made mistakes in the course of the

[17] Hsiao Hua had joined the Red Army in the Chingkangshan mountains at the age of fourteen. This made him ten years younger than most of the veterans of the Long March, but he nevertheless had earned that distinction.

[18] Even Red Guard posters, which did not spare veterans such as Chu Teh, generally made a distinction between retired officers (such as the former commander-in-chief himself) and those on the active list who were not to be accused. In view of this, the attacks on Chu Teh were truly unworthy, for they were made against a man of over ninety who had retired from political life—though still a titular member of the Politburo—and was one of the most distinguished leaders of the Chinese Communist movement.

movement, army officers, full of warm feelings, should help them to overcome and correct these shortcomings. All criticism coming from the masses should be given a friendly welcome. No one is guilty for having spoken up, and those who listen must profit from it. If mass criticisms are a little too harsh, this does not matter much. By integrating itself further with the masses and hearing their criticisms with greater modesty, our army will gain a more correct knowledge of the world and will transform it." [19]

The sentence "No one is guilty for having spoken up . . ." was in quotation marks, and is said to have been taken from Lin Piao's speech of March 20. But the speech was never published or even reproduced in Red Guard posters; this is perhaps why we know so little about the errors of the army during the February counter-offensive. And the army kept to itself its own analysis of this period.

Fire on Liu Shao-ch'i

At the end of March, army officers were not the only ones to make self-criticisms. At a new meeting of the Central Committee, the discussion was "very hot" and more than one leader beat his own back for mistakes made in recent months. The country learned of this through posters or in the official press, which means that the reports were, to say the least, biased. It emerged that the Central Committee had decided to terminate the Party Secretariat and to concentrate all executive powers in the hands of the Central Group for the Cultural Revolution. But according to other accounts, some leaders of the Central Group—including Ch'en Po-ta and Chiang Ch'ing—had also criticized themselves or at least admitted to making mistakes in the direction of the movement. Unfortunately, these reports are unreliable and difficult to verify, so we can only guess at the content and meaning of these decisions. The one thing we do know is that the Central Group admitted to having made poor use of the powerful means of propaganda put at its disposal. It promised to "improve the quality of writings on the struggle between the two lines," and for

[19] See the *Red Flag* editorial "Warmly Respond to the Call to Support the Army and Cherish the People," *Peking Review*, No. 19 (May 5, 1967).

this purpose it set up a special "brain trust" of about thirty (perhaps about fifty) writers specializing in philosophy, history, and economics. Their task—"to make studies of high quality, forceful and well documented, which would stand the test of time and strike irremediable blows at the enemy"—was in line with the aim of "narrowing the target" and unifying the movement by highlighting "the contrast between the two lines." Liu Shao-ch'i's name was still not mentioned, and no decision was made about the fate of the Chairman of the Republic. But there is no doubt that the initiators of the new campaign were setting out to make him a symbol of evil to help the masses to "repudiate his absurd theories," or at least to show what had to be spurned. It was also necessary to show that no "counteroffensive" would be able to rehabilitate this man and his dismissed accomplices. This would calm the atmosphere and encourage the cadres to grasp, at long last, the meaning of the Cultural Revolution.

This seemed to be confirmed by the series of "forceful and well documented" essays that resulted. The note was struck by the first, "Patriotism or National Betrayal?" signed by Ch'i Pen-yü, a member of the Central Group.[20] He began by recalling the affair of the film *Inside Story of the Ch'ing Court*, shown in Peking in 1950; it was displeasing to Mao, but not to "the highest leader who, while still in the Party, followed the capitalist road." Ch'i Pen-yü then devoted about ten thousand words to proving that this "poison plant" of the cinema was supremely unpatriotic, because it defended the reformists at the Ch'ing court and denigrated the rebels (the Boxers). The author followed a deliberate though complicated plan, setting up little by little an analogy between the ideas of Emperor Kuang Hsü and those of Liu Shao-ch'i. An admirer of the Japanese modernizers, the Emperor undertook in 1898 a series of reforms on the model of the Meiji, and claimed that his policy would make China into a prosperous and powerful nation within thirty years. Wishing to promote capitalist development, he was inclined to make concessions to the foreigners, thus "letting the imperialist wolf into the Chinese fold." According to Ch'i, the "highest leader who . . . followed the capitalist road" had contemplated a similar scheme

[20] Printed in *Peking Review*, No. 15 (April 7, 1967).

in 1949; he had even said precisely that China would need thirty years to modernize its economy and had "taken small steps in every sphere in favor of the development of capitalism." [21]

It was added for good measure that, during the war with Japan, Liu had developed a "philosophy of survival" and instructed comrades who were imprisoned by the Kuomintang to sign "anti-Communist statements" in order to gain their release. The indictment, derived from a historical film, ended with eight questions in which the accused was called on to explain by what right he considered himself a "revolutionary veteran," when in reality he was only "a fake revolutionary, a counterrevolutionary, and a Khrushchev on our doorstep." [22]

Was it really helpful to raise the ghosts of the Emperors and Empresses of the Ch'ing court to strike this blow at the "Chinese Khrushchev"? Was it not indeed dangerous, in these emotional days, to recall the xenophobic slogans of the Boxers against the "foreign devils," even if the Boxer Rebellion had been wholly justified in its context? Ch'i Pen-yü was in fact accused some months later of having been among the instigators of the Red Guard attack on the British Embassy in August 1967. The evidence for his role in this event ("a stain on China's world image") was as flimsy as his own evidence against Liu. But, even if he could not be called a true xenophobe, he had nevertheless played gratuitously with fire in making the Boxers the lauded ancestors of the Chinese revolutionary movement, for the sole purpose of showing that a "high leader" had defended an unpatriotic film. Really, the game was not worth the candle. [23]

[21] Ch'i Pen-yü quoted many remarks attributed to Liu on the benefits of capitalist development, but they are obviously torn from their context and virtually falsified.

[22] As a result of this question, Liu was regularly called the "Chinese Khrushchev."

[23] Several trustworthy informants told me in 1971 that the ultra-Left had decided to drive all foreigners, even friendly ones, out of China, and that in places where it was very powerful foreign residents had quite a hard time during certain periods. But I was also told that certain alleged leaders of this ultra-Left—primarily Wang Li and Ch'i Pen-yü—protected and favored an organization set up by foreigners in Peking, the "Bethune-Yenan circle," and had even given important positions, such as the direction of the radio, to the leaders of this group. The leading figure in it, the American journalist Sydney Rittenberg, was arrested at the

But this meeting of the Central Committee at the end of March also produced a series of documents on the building of socialism, entitled "Capitalist Road or Socialist Road," and here the problem was far more complex. The authors of these essays seemed to have a full grasp of the Soviet debate of the 1920's; they knew what to say about such "absurdities" as "technique in command," "priority to large-scale industry," "the piecework principle and massive dependence on economic incentives," "the theory of the neutrality and objectivity of science," "the selection of cadres by skill in production rather than political understanding," and so forth. The material which they had ransacked was quite enough to show their knowledge of the history of the Soviet development model. But their aim was not to explain "the tragedy of capitalist restoration in the USSR" [24] or to criticize dogmas of the past. On the contrary, they aimed to give ideological coherence to the mass movement by placing it in the tradition of the historic struggle of Communism, and attributing all the "absurd theories" to revisionists of various epochs, from Bernstein to Liu Shao-ch'i.

This was a confusing mixture of serious reflections on a basic theme with disingenuous personal attacks, which would not survive the most elementary historical examination. No author who wanted to contribute to the theory of the working-class movement would have made such glaring factual errors, for fear of giving weapons to his opponents. But this was a one-sided political operation, not a debate on different ideas about the building of socialism. We are assured that these documents greatly assisted the Chinese masses to grasp "the difference between the capitalist road and the socialist road," and to launch once more, from 1968 on, "the general line of the Great Leap Forward."

---

end of 1967 at about the same time as his "protector," Wang Li. Several other "extremists" of the Rittenberg group were also arrested and did not reappear until five years later, early in 1973—completely rehabilitated. At a banquet to mark International Women's Day, on March 8, 1973, Chou En-lai spoke to foreign residents of Peking about these events and made apologies to those who had suffered from such a manifestation of xenophobia. Present at the banquet were I. Epstein, M. Shapiro, D. Crook, and their wives, all former members of the "Bethune-Yenan circle." By contrast, there is no information about Rittenberg, who seems to have been accused of spying.

[24] This was the title of one of the essays, which appeared in May 1967, and also a phrase sanctified in the Chinese press at this period.

Can one say, however, that this way of "deepening" the issues represented a unifying element in 1967? Did it really help the rank and file to "understand the true nature of Liu Shao-ch'i" and to unmask the "snakes" who allegedly wanted to rehabilitate him? The events of the spring of 1967, and still more of the "hot summer," show that it did nothing of the kind. The method, which consisted of attributing to Liu ideas which he had never upheld, particularly on economic development, must be seen as harmful on two counts. It cannot have convinced those who knew the record well, or who could simply remember the former leader's speeches; and it encouraged everyone else to confer on him a diabolical personality, since he had contrived to hold his position while maintaining these criminal "absurdities." So the cadres were still more in the dark about the real purpose, while the rebels aimed primarily to "strike down the demon and his lieutenants."

Something else, equally confusing, was bound to be noticed. The leaders of the Central Group seemed determined to make a bugbear of a leader who was still alive, but he had merely been reduced to silence and they had doubtless decided from the outset not to hand him over to the vengeance of the masses. Thus, the Tsinghua students laid a trap for Liu in order to "listen to him," but they were obliged to release him at once—on Mao's personal orders, it is said.[25] The Chairman had good reason to believe that the confrontation would be far from impartial. So Liu went on living at Chungnanhai, as a close neighbor of Mao, and apparently there was no question of bringing any proceedings against him for his countless crimes. But if these principles were to be maintained, what was the point of stirring up so much excitement by stoking passions against the "arch-traitor"? Was it any wonder that people who read attacks on Liu should want to grill this enemy, and ultimately distrust those who forbade them to do so?

[25] It was in December 1966 that a group of students lured Liu to Tsinghua by telling him that his daughter was wounded. Their captive was freed less than an hour later; clearly, the order must have come from a very high level to be obeyed so promptly.

The Red Guards' Offensive

When the movement started up again after the February counteroffensive, the spotlight was once more on what is now called sarcastically "politics in the Red Guard style." According to the version given today, the splits and rivalries among the student groups allowed the ultra-Left, in this second phase of the Cultural Revolution, to foment a certain number of "plots," thus revealing its dangerous and negative character. The movement of the young people, which had acquired, despite its mistakes, a certain prestige in 1966, thus became merely a toy in the hands of ambitious leaders and notably of hidden protectors in very high positions. And the degeneration of the Red Guards played a central role in the worsening of the situation. This deserves a closer look.

From the end of November 1966, the Central Group decided on the temporary suspension of "exchanges of experiences" by young people and asked them to stop coming in large numbers to the capital. (Generally speaking, these exchanges did not begin again until the "hot spring days." [26] Similarly, the army was asked to concern itself with giving the Red Guards military training and thus influencing their development. From the end of December, new slogans urged the students to integrate themselves with the working class, and it was implied that their organizations could merge with those of the "revolutionary rebels." Then, in the beginning of 1967, another appeal advised the students, still on vacation, to go to the farm communes and help to prepare for the sowing. Finally, as we have seen, an effort was made at the time of the February reorganization to reunite the Red Guards on a territorial basis in unifying "congresses" of each city or province.

But these measures proved to be powerless to discipline the movement of the young people. Oddly enough, they did not even succeed in reducing its numbers. Free travel was stopped in November, but the students nevertheless kept on moving around the country and strengthening their "liaison posts," ever more numerous and well organized. A certain number of students did

[26] All the directives stressed the temporary nature of the suspension and justified it by climatic reasons.

indeed go to work in the factories or communes, or enlisted in the army, but it seems that just as many young workers and peasants found shelter in university dormitories, which were still controlled by Red Guards. It is even said today that recruiting agents were busy everywhere, in factories and communes, looking for muscular young people to join their forces. They are also said to have offered asylum on the campus to certain dubious elements, to idlers who had left their work, and to youngsters who had been forbidden to live in the capital or in other cities, who were thus able to return there. Neglecting to check on the background or quality of their members, they concentrated on increasing their "intervention troops," attracting "peripheral elements" who did the Red Guards no good. Hence, from the spring of 1967, students were in a minority in the university groups (though of course no one has any valid statistics) and the Headquarters, while still composed only of students, were as averse to all unification suggestions as at the outset.

Consequently, the Red Guard Congress of Institutions of Higher Education in Peking, solemnly inaugurated in February, was never able to give birth to a real united leadership group. It took scarcely a month for the leaders to split into two irreconcilable factions—the "sky faction," so called simply because its first meeting was held in the Aeronautical Institute, and the "earth faction," set up in the Institute of Geology. A similar situation prevailed in the provinces, with the additional complication that envoys from the Peking Red Guards were very much in favor and were often invited to join in top-level discussions. The Central Group certainly did not encourage these splits among the students, but it accepted them as a fact of life and declined to arbitrate on their internal differences. This new line was made explicit in a *Red Flag* editorial in May.[27] But, in thus abandoning any fresh attempt at mediation, were not the leaders of the Cultural Revolution encouraging extremist competition between groups? Were they not themselves paving the way to that murderous group warfare which, according to the account now given, was to prevent any stabilization and forestall a reasonable

[27] See the *Red Flag* commentary "Grasp the Principal Contradiction, Hold to the General Orientation of Struggle," *Peking Review*, No. 22 (May 26, 1967).

solution for almost a year? Last but not least, did this attitude of "nonintervention" represent the view of the whole Central Group, or was it temporarily imposed by a majority which, on this point, had ulterior political motives?

We must raise these questions before taking up the thread of events because each successive Chinese version has given us a fresh explanation about the responsibility of those who "pulled the strings behind the scenes." Thus, all the events of this "hot" spring and summer were to be re-evaluated four years later to serve in the indictment of Ch'en Po-ta and in the Lin Piao affair. In these circumstances, it seems best to make a careful use of all the information we have, without overlooking the question marks set against the trials of strength that were to occur so suddenly beginning in May 1967.

Faithfully imitating the Central Group in this respect, the Red Guards gave no reports in their mass-circulation papers of the debates that were held internally or in their "liaison posts." But their decisions were at once made known by the general diffusion of slogans through posters, and sometimes took shape in spectacular commando actions which seemed to be completely coordinated. Thus, at the end of April, the whole of China saw a crop of posters attacking Chou En-lai, at the very moment when raids on the secret archives of certain ministries were beginning in Peking. This well-organized campaign led to violent skirmishes all over.[28]

[28] According to an official statement, reported in posters in Peking, 133 violent battles or incidents took place in China in April and the first ten days of May, and claimed 63,000 victims. This figure, necessarily approximate, seems to have been given on May 14 by Hsieh Fu-chih, chairman of the Peking Revolutionary Committee, in a speech whose text was not made known abroad. On isolated acts of violence, especially in the capital, numerous eyewitness accounts can be checked and confirm one another. A friend who was then working in China, and who is a convinced supporter of the Cultural Revolution, told me that he saw with his own eyes Red Guard commandos who, in broad daylight and in the center of the city, suddenly jumped out of a truck and beat to death, with truncheons, one or more "enemies" who were taken by surprise. Other witnesses, who cannot be suspected of hostility to the Red Guards, also told me of illegal arrests, searches, and even looting, perpetrated by the commandos of rival factions. Army patrols sometimes saved the victims of these attacks and provided bodyguards for people who felt themselves to be especially threatened, but these measures could only limit the harm to a slight extent.

It was planned at a national meeting called by the "sky faction" at the Aeronautical Institute, bringing together representatives of about twenty leftist groups from the major provinces and even some "rebel" workers from Peking, Shanghai, and Shenyang (including the famous Lianse and a "violent" group of workers from the railway-engine plant in the capital). In theory, however, this was merely a liaison consultation.

At this meeting, it seems, Wu Ch'uan-p'in, a student leader from Canton—and a future member of the Revolutionary Committee of Kwangtung Province—explained that the Cultural Revolution was blocked because China had not two but three headquarters. The third was directed by Chou En-lai and acted as "a filter and a brake" toward the mass movement. "It is not correct," said Wu, "for the head of the government to decide whether the rebels should take power or not in a ministry. Chou En-lai is the head of the government; he must answer for the crimes committed by the 'Red capitalists' like all other high leaders, and not give us orders on how to treat them. He is the protector of T'an Chen-lin, Ch'en Yi, Li Fu-ch'un, and Li Hsien-nien, and the real instigator of the February counteroffensive. His headquarters must be denounced and destroyed." [29]

This incitement is enough to explain a spate of personal attacks on Chou—posters described him as "half dog and half sheep," "an expert in trickery," and so forth—and some violent "rebellions" in ministries, which had hitherto been more or less spared. The Central Group at once took firm action to stop the campaign against Chou and prevent a search for material designed to strike down the premier. The leaders seem to have known how to get this result; they telephoned direct to the leaders of the relevant student groups. According to some exceptionally chatty posters, Ch'en Po-ta called up K'uai Ta-fu to make him promise that there would be no more posters aimed at Chou En-lai. Members of the

[29] All information on the "factional meetings" at the Aeronautical Institute in 1967 and 1968 comes from the indictments drawn up against Wu Ch'uan-p'in in 1969 and against K'uai Ta-fu in 1971. The former is said to have admitted his errors from July 31, 1968, at a meeting of the Kwangtung Revolutionary Committee—he was a member of its executive—but the "campaign of repudiation of his anarchist ideas" took place only from 1969. K'uai was far more reluctant to plead guilty, as we shall see later.

Central Group certainly made similar approaches to other Red Guard leaders.

But intervention from above was less easy with regard to "rank-and-file criticism in the ministries." There was no directive that could be invoked to forbid it. Some ministries, starting with the Ministry of Higher Education, had been "overthrown" in the first phase of the Cultural Revolution, so it was not obvious why others should be taboo. The only ruling had come from Chou En-lai himself; since November 1966, he had been demanding immunity for certain institutions which were an embodiment of China in foreign eyes—including *People's Daily*—for reasons of national prestige and to avoid injuring "relations among the peoples." But a repetition of this advice was scarcely timely. It would only harm Chou and have little chance of halting the mass offensive against ministries compromised by the February counteroffensive.

Besides, a convergence of circumstances brought it about that the ministry most under attack was precisely the Ministry of Foreign Affairs. There were reasons other than a "premeditated plot" by the Red Guards. The Cultural Revolution had stirred up a radical mood among young Chinese overseas and given a terrible fright to the ruling classes of Asian countries, especially those with big Chinese communities. In neutralist Burma and Cambodia, in Hong Kong, and in anti-Communist Indonesia, anti-Chinese measures were taken and claimed their victims. The Chinese Embassy in Jakarta was sacked, despite the heroism of its staff, who "bravely resisted this Fascist onslaught." When the chargé d'affaires, Yao Teng-shan, and the consul-general, Hsu Yen, returned to Peking on April 30, they were greeted as heroes and escorted in triumph by seven thousand people, led by Chou En-lai and Ch'en Po-ta. Next day, at the May Day festivities, they were personally received by Chairman Mao and Vice-Chairman Lin Piao. They took advantage of this popularity to give press conferences at which they naturally denounced the Indonesian regime, but also laid a share of the blame for the victory of "Suharto Fascism" on the former leaders of the CCP. They recalled the visit to Indonesia in 1963 made by the "highest Party leader who . . . followed the capitalist road," and claimed that he had "deliberately gloried in his shabby surrender" to disarm and

"wipe out the revolutionary movement of the Indonesian masses."
On this occasion in Indonesia, Liu was alleged to have behaved
like Khrushchev in the United States in 1959.[30]

More elaborate studies soon attacked the entire foreign policy
of Liu. Its essence was said to be "three surrenders and one
annihilation"—surrender to imperialists, to revisionists, and to
reactionaries; and annihilation of revolutionary movements
abroad. But of course the "highest leader" had not been able to
carry through this vast scheme all by himself. On his trip to
Indonesia in 1963, he had been accompanied by Ch'en Yi and by
a whole group of officials from the Ministry of Foreign Affairs, all
of whom were still in their jobs. The wrath of the Red Guards
against this "nest of treason" was thus fed by "justified"
suspicions, and these were increased by news of repression in
Hong Kong—where a big strike broke out in May—and of
incidents, described as "100 percent Fascist," in Burma. Who had
been in cahoots in the past with these counterrevolutionary
monsters? The Red Guards of the Foreign Languages Institute,
which was attached to the Ministry of Foreign Affairs, swiftly set
up a "liaison post of revolutionary rebels" and resolved to
completely unmask "the traitors hidden in this bourgeois institution." To do this, they had need of documents, and in May they
made two raids on the Ministry of Foreign Affairs archives. They
brought away loads of classified files—it is said that these filled
whole trucks—in the hope of finding crushing evidence, obviously
against Liu, but also against Chou En-lai and Ch'en Yi, who had
always controlled this sphere of the government.[31]

A leader of the Central Group (perhaps Ch'en Po-ta or Chiang
Ch'ing) at once contacted the rebel liaison post and demanded the
restoration of the archives because they contained "state secrets."

---

[30] To add weight to his charges, Yao Teng-shan had the Red Guards shown the
film made during Liu's visit to Indonesia. This was a masterstroke, for, as may well
be imagined, this film was mainly devoted to banquets, official festivities, and
scenes of "fraternization" between Liu and the Indonesian leaders, among them
"the Fascist Suharto," who had then held high positions in the Sukarno regime.

[31] The two raids took place on May 13 and 29, 1967. In the first, the invaders
merely occupied the archive building and tried to look for the "interesting" files.
Thrown out of the "fortress" by army patrols who were summoned to the rescue,
they prepared a second raid, and this time they hastened to carry off all the
material they could get hold of.

A young extremist is said to have answered: "But what is so terrible in these secrets that the people may not see them?" This was quoted to me in 1971 to show that "this was not a question of youthful sectarianism or of innocent curiosity." Foreign agents, it was alleged, were seeking to get hold of information belonging to the Chinese state. The logic was far from clear to me. But it appears from various accounts that the Central Group avoided getting into an all-out battle to defend Ch'en Yi. This historic figure, hero of the Kiangsi era and the war of liberation, marshal and vice-premier, had never been afraid since the start of the Cultural Revolution to defy the Red Guards; indeed, he had defeated them several times in debates on the thought of Chairman Mao. But as a close friend of T'an Chen-lin, more or less compromised in the February counteroffensive, he had by now been obliged to make a whole series of self-criticisms.[32] In May 1967 his position was clearly weak, and the Central Group called on the rebels to return the stolen files not to the Ministry of Foreign Affairs but to the Peking garrison. Only there, it declared, would they be safe. This was also a hint that they should be placed on neutral ground and that only the army was worthy of confidence and firmly on the side of the mass movement. Because of this, the army emerged as China's one sheet anchor, and it was no wonder that the question of its integrity—which was raised at the end of July—plunged the leadership into deep dismay.

But even before the ordeal of the "hot summer" began, two

[32] From the start of the Cultural Revolution, Ch'en Yi took up a defiant attitude toward the Red Guards of institutions attached to his ministry and sent work teams to hold them in check. In his quips, which became famous when collected by the Red Guards who were criticizing him in 1967, he made fun of these youngsters who were ready to criticize anyone except themselves. He flatly refused to subject his ministry to foreign-language students and advised them to "go and fight the enemy in Vietnam, not in my office." But at the time of the "January storm" this position became untenable, and on January 17, Ch'en Yi made a self-criticism and agreed to the creation, on the following day, of a "liaison post of revolutionary rebels of the Ministry of Foreign Affairs." The next month, during the February counteroffensive, he seems to have organized the unification of the Red Guards in such a way that the liaison post was dissolved. This compromised him beyond all limits, and even Chou En-lai, his friend since they had studied in France in 1921, declared, "Ch'en Yi must be criticized." At the end of April, Chou promised to take personal charge of the Ministry of Foreign Affairs and preside over the "sessions of criticism of Ch'en Yi."

events complicated the situation still further. On May 16, 1967, the official press reprinted the famous "Circular of May 16," which had launched the Cultural Revolution a year before. Almost at once, the streets of Peking filled with well-drilled young militants wearing the armband of the "May 16 Armed Corps." They spread extremist slogans attacking "all leaders," declaring that in the circular Chairman Mao had spoken of "individuals of the Khrushchev type" in the plural, and that consequently mass criticism should not focus on a single "high leader who . . . followed the capitalist road." But if the troops of this Armed Corps were in the open, their generals were in the shadows. What new "secret society" was pulling the strings to cause disorder? The principal student leaders, from K'uai Ta-fu to Nieh Yüan-tzu, declared that they were not involved, and the members of the Central Group could not be suspected of such a misdeed. Yet there must be someone directing this strange Armed Corps.

"Attack with Words, But Defend Yourselves with Weapons"

Another decisive event took place at Wuhan on July 16. Two national leaders, Hsieh Fu-chih and Wang Li, were making a fact-finding tour of the provinces, and at Wuhan they were to encounter especially tricky problems. Everything was still in suspense in this great industrial city, and the regional military commander, Ch'en Tsai-tao, was trying to form a stable Revolutionary Committee by relying on a mass organization called the "Million Heroes," which seemed to him to be furthest to the Left. But his efforts were meeting strong resistance from several working-class and student groups which claimed to be victims of violent repression and accused the Million Heroes of conservatism. They charged that this organization was merely the creation of the old Party committee and had in its ranks a large number of suspect cadres and former profiteers. The battle between these two rival blocs, raging since the beginning of July, had brought about a partial halt of productive activity, and especially of the communications network, which was vital for the entire country.[33]

[33] The Japanese paper *Mainichi Shimbun* stated on July 24, on the basis of Red Guard posters, that between April 29 and July 3 about 2,400 Wuhan factories had

The dramatic character of the situation in August 1967 was made clear in all the accounts that I heard in 1971, but details are still missing on the events in Wuhan. For this town, as there were no foreign eyewitnesses, Red Guard posters are our only source of information. Even documents of the Party center concerning Wuhan—which are private in any case—are scanty and far fewer than those, for example, about the "January storm" in Shanghai or about certain violent episodes in Peking. For the people who talked to me in 1971, the guilty man was by that time Wang Li, not the obstinate commander Ch'en Tsai-tao. Admittedly, it could not have been foreseen that Ch'en would reappear at the People's Palace within a year, on the very occasion of the anniversary of the army, without any explanation and as if nothing had happened. During my stay, he was still "a war lord who had succeeded in making his way into the ranks of the Party." [38] But more stress was laid on the fact that his "bad action" had "given a pretext to unscrupulous plotters of the ultra-Left to launch a long-prepared offensive against the army and the Central Group, the two pillars on which China is sustained, to spread chaos and seize power." [39] Nothing more was said in Peking about Hsieh Fu-chih, but Wang Li was flatly described as "the black general of the noxious May 16 group." [40]

One of my confidential informants (of high rank) also assured me that "the masses had understood what they ought to think on the subject of Wang Li, well before the Wuhan affair," and that the campaign against him had begun at least six months before his fall in the autumn of 1967. I was able to confirm in Shanghai and in the northeast that there had indeed been many posters against

[38] The American writer William Hinton, who visited China at the same time as I did, took up without any reservations this version which makes Ch'en Tsai-tao into a kind of war lord in the old Chinese tradition. But, just when his book was being published in July 1972, Ch'en was taking part in the army celebrations. Doubtless, in his next book, Mr. Hinton will explain to us how a typical war lord could become chief of the Wuhan Military District in Mao's China and reappear, after a short eclipse, as one of the great commanders of the People's Liberation Army.

[39] See my article "The 'Fanatics' of May 16," in *Nouvel Observateur*, July 19, 1971.

[40] Hsieh died early in 1973, but he had been absent from the political scene since 1970, his eclipse having coincided with that of Ch'en Po-ta. Evidently, he had kept his rank as a member of the Politburo of the CCP.

The two national leaders inquired into the situation for four days. Then, on the afternoon of July 19, they summoned Ch'en and informed him of their conclusions. These were far from gratifying to this senior army commander, a veteran Communist, and once the right-hand man of Marshal Hsü Hsiang-ch'ien. He was summarily required to make a self-criticism, to "restore the dignity" of the organizations which he had judged to be counterrevolutionary, and to disavow the one which he had supported as revolutionary. According to certain accounts, Ch'en listened impassively to these demands and answered, "Bring me a signed instruction from Chairman Mao and I will do everything you ask." Meanwhile, he shrugged his shoulders and said, "You can cope with the masses of Wuhan on your own." Another commander, Niu Hai-lung, at the head of Military Unit 8201 (formerly the 29th Division of the Security Forces), went further and said that he was ready to risk his life to defend the Million Heroes. With this, the army men walked out of the Tung Hu Hotel, leaving the two central leaders to cope as best they could.

But there was no time to think things over. The group under challenge—the Million Heroes—duly informed of this stormy scene, mounted an attack on the hotel. Soldiers of Unit 8201, mobilized by the fearless Commander Niu—or perhaps acting on their own initiative—joined in this attack, which was launched at one o'clock in the morning of July 20. The bodyguards of the two leaders were soon neutralized,[34] and it is even reported that Hsieh's personal secretary was knifed to death. The treatment of the leaders varied; Hsieh Fu-chih was in uniform (he had been a lieutenant-general before the abolition of ranks), whereas Wang

suspended production or reduced it by half, and that about half a million workers had been involved in 120 armed clashes which had led to 700 deaths. According to the same source, the clashes increased during the first half of July and rail traffic over the bridge across the Yangtze was halted for several days. At that time the Wuhan bridge was the only one to cross this river, which divides China in two (the Nanking bridge had not yet been completed). So, even if the figures given by the Red Guards must be treated with caution—they are in any case much exaggerated—there can be no doubt that the group warfare in Wuhan created an outstandingly serious problem for China.

[34] It may be noted that these were students (or "muscular" recruits) from the Peking Aeronautical Institute, and belonged to the faction which had a Left reputation.

Li was only a civilian "plotter." Hsieh was therefore placed under house arrest in the hotel—he managed to escape a few hours later and took refuge with the rebels of the Hydroelectric Institute—but Wang Li was taken to the headquarters of Unit 8201 and, it appears, savagely beaten up.[35] The news of the kidnapping reached Peking only on the afternoon of July 20. Mao and Lin Piao were away from the capital, but the temporary chief of the general staff, Yang Ch'eng-wu, and Premier Chou En-lai reacted at once with the greatest of energy.

Yang sent an ultimatum to General Ch'en and warned him that an airborne division of the River Navy, belonging to the 15th Army and stationed in Hupeh Province, would intervene at once. Chou En-lai took off for Wuhan himself so that he could personally bring back his colleagues in the national leadership. The same day, he returned to Peking to organize a triumphal welcome for the victims of the "mutiny." The latter arrived next day, bringing in their plane the unfortunate Ch'en and several other dismissed commanders. All the leaders who were present in the capital awaited them at the airport, and a cheering crowd escorted Hsieh Fu-chih and Wang Li into the city. At an improvised meeting, Chiang Ch'ing addressed the Red Guards and "revolutionary rebels" and drew this lesson from the incident: "You must attack with words, but defend yourselves with weapons." It was an invitation to the Left to arm itself and, in case of need, to resist "treacherous" army commanders such as Ch'en Tsai-tao.

Meetings on the same theme went on almost without a break for three days, in factories and in universities, to culminate on July 25 in a monster rally on T'ien An Men Square, which drew over a million people. The next day, the Party center replied to a

[35] The Red Guard posters in Peking gave much space to detailed descriptions of the torments suffered by Wang Li, to show the guilt of his captors. But, when examined, they add up to a version that strains belief. Wang Li was said to have had a broken arm, a half-fractured leg, an injured eye, and multiple bruises, but this did not prevent him from escaping on foot, across the fields, less than twelve hours after these tortures. Moreover, despite his wounds, he did not take a day's rest before speaking at meetings and press conferences as soon as he got back to Peking. For a man in his fifties, even in exceptionally good shape, these performances and this power of recovery appear somewhat miraculous.

telegram of loyalty from the Wuhan Military Distr apparently played down the significance of the incident extent; it regretted that "some cadres, including Comr Ch'en Tsai-tao, made mistakes," but declared that they c rejoin the ranks of the revolutionaries and be forgive masses.[36]

But, forty-eight hours later, a dramatic note was st more. All the central authorities addressed a lette revolutionary masses, commanders, and fighters of V which they denounced the "handful of leaders foll capitalist road" who had caused this grave incident. equally indignant about "a handful of bad leaders of Heroes organization," and declared that they had been in the ocean of anger" of hundreds of millions of w soldiers. The "Wuhan affair," the letter concluded, example of class struggle, a most profound lesson in between two lines, between the proletariat and th sie." [37]

From this, one gets the impression that the Ce reacted very sternly on the spur of the moment, th somewhat on what interpretation to place on the V but was finally swayed by the radical trend. This w the appearance of an editorial in *Red Flag*, markin birthday of the People's Liberation Army on Aug stated plainly: "The campaign of criticism is aimed a top leaders within the Party *and the army* who h capitalist road" (italics added). This article, a "blasp the army, was widely broadcast to the soldiers by t as if to encourage them to rebel against their officer Guards, who now knew that they could put no trus of the dictatorship of the proletariat," made ever themselves. They raided army depots and barr attacked trains carrying war matériel to Vietnam. really did seem to be on the brink of civil war, and have happened in this chaos, wherein rival group Wang Li himself put it—"a crowd of headless dr

[36] See *Documents of the Great Proletarian Cultural Revolu* [37] *Documents of the Great Proletarian Cultural Revolution,*

Wang (and apparently also against Hsieh) in these regions. Everything suggests that there had been as many in Wuhan at the time. But in these circumstances, I asked, why did the Premier risk his life to free this suspect leader? "Because we wanted him alive," my informant said without blinking an eyelid, "to learn about his accomplices from him." If so, the Wuhan affair is evidently not so simple as we thought at first. But can we take these belated revelations at face value?

What is clear, anyway, is that the vagaries of the internal struggle within the Central Group were echoed in the poster campaigns. Though the members of the Central Group were in theory beyond attack, having been chosen by Mao, in practice each of them had his detractors and his defenders in the rank and file, who did not hesitate to express their views in posters. As these campaigns were fueled by fragmentary "information" on the stand taken by this or that leader in the various discussions, detractors often turned into defenders, and vice versa, according to the period and the facts that could be gleaned.

The attitude of the rank and file toward Hsieh Fu-chih is a good example of this phenomenon. At the outset of the Cultural Revolution, he was minister of public security, which did not make him very congenial to the Left, who spared neither his ministry—violently attacked in December 1966—nor his personality as an old *apparatchik*. But, from January 1967 on, the Red Guards in Peking—and their counterparts in the provinces—became convinced that "old Hsieh" was on their side and really wanted to take the revolution through to the end. Hsieh therefore forged close links with the chief student leaders, won their friendship, and assured himself of their support during the difficult period when the Revolutionary Committee of Peking, of which he was to be chairman, was being set up. Nor was it by chance that in this very phase of the swing to the Left, in April 1967, he was made vice-chairman of the Cultural Revolution Directorate of the army. But it was also in the nature of things that the opposing faction should begin to put up posters denouncing his "dubious" record and his bad interpretation of Mao's thought.

In a sense, the case of Wang Li was similar. This future "extremist" had belonged to the commission which, working with P'eng Chen's Group of Five, had drawn up the "revisionist" report on the Cultural Revolution. True, he had also taken part in the study on the Paris Commune and signed several documents in that vein, but he was nevertheless regarded as rather a maverick —the more so since he had inherited T'ao Chu's post at the head of the Propaganda Department, thanks (it was said) to the support of T'an Chen-lin. But in the spring of 1967, the Left suppressed its doubts, while he became the real bugbear of the moderates.

In the light of this limited but reliable information, the Wuhan affair appears in fresh colors. Ch'en Tsai-tao was not defying Central Group leaders as such. When he replied to Hsieh and Wang, "Bring me a signed instruction from Chairman Mao," he was thinking that these two men spoke for a minority in the Central Group and were not authorized to give orders in the name of the "great helmsman." In July 1967, in Wuhan as in all the industrial towns, a strong leftist wave was reviving the slogans about a "Commune of China," and Ch'en may well have thought it his duty to put on the brakes by relying on a more moderate group. In any case, his defiance certainly cannot be interpreted as a resurgence of the war-lord spirit, but rather in this sense: "I am in command here and I know what I ought to do." [41] It derived, above all, from a false estimate of the balance of strength in the Central Group, based on personal feelings about the Group's deeper intentions. When Chou En-lai told him that Hsieh and

[41] Many Western Sinologists have stressed the importance of regionalism in the Cultural Revolution. They point out rightly that China did not become a centralized state until after 1949 and that the new regime could not wipe out the differences between various provinces and autonomous regions in so short a time. Noting also that the power of the Party center was much weakened during the Cultural Revolution, they attach a primary significance to what they call attempts by the regions to free themselves from the tutelage of Peking. But they cite very little evidence, and none exists to show that the army was torn by regional rivalries. In fact, the commands of various military districts were changed many times during these events—as Western sources themselves state—without meeting obstacles or provoking rebellions of the war-lord type. The only known case of disobedience by a commander was that of Ch'en at Wuhan, but in my view it has really nothing to do with regionalism. This, indeed, is recognized by the CIA's analyst of the Cultural Revolution (whose bias against Maoism may well be imagined), Philip Bridgeham, in essays published in China Quarterly, No. 41 (January–March 1970). On events in Wuhan, see also Thomas W. Robinson, "The Wuhan Incident: Local Strife and Provincial Rebellion during the Cultural Revolution," in China Quarterly, No. 47 (July–September 1971).

The two national leaders inquired into the situation for four days. Then, on the afternoon of July 19, they summoned Ch'en and informed him of their conclusions. These were far from gratifying to this senior army commander, a veteran Communist, and once the right-hand man of Marshal Hsü Hsiang-ch'ien. He was summarily required to make a self-criticism, to "restore the dignity" of the organizations which he had judged to be counterrevolutionary, and to disavow the one which he had supported as revolutionary. According to certain accounts, Ch'en listened impassively to these demands and answered, "Bring me a signed instruction from Chairman Mao and I will do everything you ask." Meanwhile, he shrugged his shoulders and said, "You can cope with the masses of Wuhan on your own." Another commander, Niu Hai-lung, at the head of Military Unit 8201 (formerly the 29th Division of the Security Forces), went further and said that he was ready to risk his life to defend the Million Heroes. With this, the army men walked out of the Tung Hu Hotel, leaving the two central leaders to cope as best they could.

But there was no time to think things over. The group under challenge—the Million Heroes—duly informed of this stormy scene, mounted an attack on the hotel. Soldiers of Unit 8201, mobilized by the fearless Commander Niu—or perhaps acting on their own initiative—joined in this attack, which was launched at one o'clock in the morning of July 20. The bodyguards of the two leaders were soon neutralized,[34] and it is even reported that Hsieh's personal secretary was knifed to death. The treatment of the leaders varied; Hsieh Fu-chih was in uniform (he had been a lieutenant-general before the abolition of ranks), whereas Wang

---

suspended production or reduced it by half, and that about half a million workers had been involved in 120 armed clashes which had led to 700 deaths. According to the same source, the clashes increased during the first half of July and rail traffic over the bridge across the Yangtze was halted for several days. At that time the Wuhan bridge was the only one to cross this river, which divides China in two (the Nanking bridge had not yet been completed). So, even if the figures given by the Red Guards must be treated with caution—they are in any case much exaggerated—there can be no doubt that the group warfare in Wuhan created an outstandingly serious problem for China.

[34] It may be noted that these were students (or "muscular" recruits) from the Peking Aeronautical Institute, and belonged to the faction which had a Left reputation.

Li was only a civilian "plotter." Hsieh was therefore placed under house arrest in the hotel—he managed to escape a few hours later and took refuge with the rebels of the Hydroelectric Institute—but Wang Li was taken to the headquarters of Unit 8201 and, it appears, savagely beaten up.[35] The news of the kidnapping reached Peking only on the afternoon of July 20. Mao and Lin Piao were away from the capital, but the temporary chief of the general staff, Yang Ch'eng-wu, and Premier Chou En-lai reacted at once with the greatest of energy.

Yang sent an ultimatum to General Ch'en and warned him that an airborne division of the River Navy, belonging to the 15th Army and stationed in Hupeh Province, would intervene at once. Chou En-lai took off for Wuhan himself so that he could personally bring back his colleagues in the national leadership. The same day, he returned to Peking to organize a triumphal welcome for the victims of the "mutiny." The latter arrived next day, bringing in their plane the unfortunate Ch'en and several other dismissed commanders. All the leaders who were present in the capital awaited them at the airport, and a cheering crowd escorted Hsieh Fu-chih and Wang Li into the city. At an improvised meeting, Chiang Ch'ing addressed the Red Guards and "revolutionary rebels" and drew this lesson from the incident: "You must attack with words, but defend yourselves with weapons." It was an invitation to the Left to arm itself and, in case of need, to resist "treacherous" army commanders such as Ch'en Tsai-tao.

Meetings on the same theme went on almost without a break for three days, in factories and in universities, to culminate on July 25 in a monster rally on T'ien An Men Square, which drew over a million people. The next day, the Party center replied to a

---

[35] The Red Guard posters in Peking gave much space to detailed descriptions of the torments suffered by Wang Li, to show the guilt of his captors. But, when examined, they add up to a version that strains belief. Wang Li was said to have had a broken arm, a half-fractured leg, an injured eye, and multiple bruises, but this did not prevent him from escaping on foot, across the fields, less than twelve hours after these tortures. Moreover, despite his wounds, he did not take a day's rest before speaking at meetings and press conferences as soon as he got back to Peking. For a man in his fifties, even in exceptionally good shape, these performances and this power of recovery appear somewhat miraculous.

telegram of loyalty from the Wuhan Military District and apparently played down the significance of the incident to some extent; it regretted that "some cadres, including Comrade [*sic*] Ch'en Tsai-tao, made mistakes," but declared that they could still rejoin the ranks of the revolutionaries and be forgiven by the masses.[36]

But, forty-eight hours later, a dramatic note was struck once more. All the central authorities addressed a letter to the revolutionary masses, commanders, and fighters of Wuhan, in which they denounced the "handful of leaders following the capitalist road" who had caused this grave incident. They were equally indignant about "a handful of bad leaders of the Million Heroes organization," and declared that they had been "drowned in the ocean of anger" of hundreds of millions of workers and soldiers. The "Wuhan affair," the letter concluded, "is a living example of class struggle, a most profound lesson in the struggle between two lines, between the proletariat and the bourgeoisie." [37]

From this, one gets the impression that the Central Group reacted very sternly on the spur of the moment, then hesitated somewhat on what interpretation to place on the Wuhan affair, but was finally swayed by the radical trend. This would explain the appearance of an editorial in *Red Flag*, marking the fortieth birthday of the People's Liberation Army on August 1, which stated plainly: "The campaign of criticism is aimed at a handful of top leaders within the Party *and the army* who have taken the capitalist road" (italics added). This article, a "blasphemy" against the army, was widely broadcast to the soldiers by the army radio, as if to encourage them to rebel against their officers. And the Red Guards, who now knew that they could put no trust in this "pillar of the dictatorship of the proletariat," made every effort to arm themselves. They raided army depots and barracks and even attacked trains carrying war matériel to Vietnam. This time China really did seem to be on the brink of civil war, and anything could have happened in this chaos, wherein rival groups resembled—as Wang Li himself put it—"a crowd of headless dragons."

[36] See *Documents of the Great Proletarian Cultural Revolution*, p. 478.
[37] *Documents of the Great Proletarian Cultural Revolution*, p. 484.

The dramatic character of the situation in August 1967 was made clear in all the accounts that I heard in 1971, but details are still missing on the events in Wuhan. For this town, as there were no foreign eyewitnesses, Red Guard posters are our only source of information. Even documents of the Party center concerning Wuhan—which are private in any case—are scanty and far fewer than those, for example, about the "January storm" in Shanghai or about certain violent episodes in Peking. For the people who talked to me in 1971, the guilty man was by that time Wang Li, not the obstinate commander Ch'en Tsai-tao. Admittedly, it could not have been foreseen that Ch'en would reappear at the People's Palace within a year, on the very occasion of the anniversary of the army, without any explanation and as if nothing had happened. During my stay, he was still "a war lord who had succeeded in making his way into the ranks of the Party." [38] But more stress was laid on the fact that his "bad action" had "given a pretext to unscrupulous plotters of the ultra-Left to launch a long-prepared offensive against the army and the Central Group, the two pillars on which China is sustained, to spread chaos and seize power." [39] Nothing more was said in Peking about Hsieh Fu-chih, but Wang Li was flatly described as "the black general of the noxious May 16 group." [40]

One of my confidential informants (of high rank) also assured me that "the masses had understood what they ought to think on the subject of Wang Li, well before the Wuhan affair," and that the campaign against him had begun at least six months before his fall in the autumn of 1967. I was able to confirm in Shanghai and in the northeast that there had indeed been many posters against

[38] The American writer William Hinton, who visited China at the same time as I did, took up without any reservations this version which makes Ch'en Tsai-tao into a kind of war lord in the old Chinese tradition. But, just when his book was being published in July 1972, Ch'en was taking part in the army celebrations. Doubtless, in his next book, Mr. Hinton will explain to us how a typical war lord could become chief of the Wuhan Military District in Mao's China and reappear, after a short eclipse, as one of the great commanders of the People's Liberation Army.

[39] See my article "The 'Fanatics' of May 16," in Nouvel Observateur, July 19, 1971.

[40] Hsieh died early in 1973, but he had been absent from the political scene since 1970, his eclipse having coincided with that of Ch'en Po-ta. Evidently, he had kept his rank as a member of the Politburo of the CCP.

Wang (and apparently also against Hsieh) in these regions. Everything suggests that there had been as many in Wuhan at the time. But in these circumstances, I asked, why did the Premier risk his life to free this suspect leader? "Because we wanted him alive," my informant said without blinking an eyelid, "to learn about his accomplices from him." If so, the Wuhan affair is evidently not so simple as we thought at first. But can we take these belated revelations at face value?

What is clear, anyway, is that the vagaries of the internal struggle within the Central Group were echoed in the poster campaigns. Though the members of the Central Group were in theory beyond attack, having been chosen by Mao, in practice each of them had his detractors and his defenders in the rank and file, who did not hesitate to express their views in posters. As these campaigns were fueled by fragmentary "information" on the stand taken by this or that leader in the various discussions, detractors often turned into defenders, and vice versa, according to the period and the facts that could be gleaned.

The attitude of the rank and file toward Hsieh Fu-chih is a good example of this phenomenon. At the outset of the Cultural Revolution, he was minister of public security, which did not make him very congenial to the Left, who spared neither his ministry—violently attacked in December 1966—nor his personality as an old *apparatchik*. But, from January 1967 on, the Red Guards in Peking—and their counterparts in the provinces—became convinced that "old Hsieh" was on their side and really wanted to take the revolution through to the end. Hsieh therefore forged close links with the chief student leaders, won their friendship, and assured himself of their support during the difficult period when the Revolutionary Committee of Peking, of which he was to be chairman, was being set up. Nor was it by chance that in this very phase of the swing to the Left, in April 1967, he was made vice-chairman of the Cultural Revolution Directorate of the army. But it was also in the nature of things that the opposing faction should begin to put up posters denouncing his "dubious" record and his bad interpretation of Mao's thought.

In a sense, the case of Wang Li was similar. This future "extremist" had belonged to the commission which, working with P'eng Chen's Group of Five, had drawn up the "revisionist"

report on the Cultural Revolution. True, he had also taken part in the study on the Paris Commune and signed several documents in that vein, but he was nevertheless regarded as rather a maverick —the more so since he had inherited T'ao Chu's post at the head of the Propaganda Department, thanks (it was said) to the support of T'an Chen-lin. But in the spring of 1967, the Left suppressed its doubts, while he became the real bugbear of the moderates.

In the light of this limited but reliable information, the Wuhan affair appears in fresh colors. Ch'en Tsai-tao was not defying Central Group leaders as such. When he replied to Hsieh and Wang, "Bring me a signed instruction from Chairman Mao," he was thinking that these two men spoke for a minority in the Central Group and were not authorized to give orders in the name of the "great helmsman." In July 1967, in Wuhan as in all the industrial towns, a strong leftist wave was reviving the slogans about a "Commune of China," and Ch'en may well have thought it his duty to put on the brakes by relying on a more moderate group. In any case, his defiance certainly cannot be interpreted as a resurgence of the war-lord spirit, but rather in this sense: "I am in command here and I know what I ought to do." [41] It derived, above all, from a false estimate of the balance of strength in the Central Group, based on personal feelings about the Group's deeper intentions. When Chou En-lai told him that Hsieh and

[41] Many Western Sinologists have stressed the importance of regionalism in the Cultural Revolution. They point out rightly that China did not become a centralized state until after 1949 and that the new regime could not wipe out the differences between various provinces and autonomous regions in so short a time. Noting also that the power of the Party center was much weakened during the Cultural Revolution, they attach a primary significance to what they call attempts by the regions to free themselves from the tutelage of Peking. But they cite very little evidence, and none exists to show that the army was torn by regional rivalries. In fact, the commands of various military districts were changed many times during these events—as Western sources themselves state—without meeting obstacles or provoking rebellions of the war-lord type. The only known case of disobedience by a commander was that of Ch'en at Wuhan, but in my view it has really nothing to do with regionalism. This, indeed, is recognized by the CIA's analyst of the Cultural Revolution (whose bias against Maoism may well be imagined), Philip Bridgeham, in essays published in *China Quarterly*, No. 41 (January–March 1970). On events in Wuhan, see also Thomas W. Robinson, "The Wuhan Incident: Local Strife and Provincial Rebellion during the Cultural Revolution," in *China Quarterly*, No. 47 (July–September 1971).

Wang had spoken in the name of the whole Group and not of a faction, Ch'en surrendered without fuss.

This being so, his mistake surely brought grist to the mill of the Left in the leadership, and obliged it to react in united style. For, if the Party center could turn a blind eye to anonymous poster attacks on its members, it could not allow a public defiance of its authority by a man in an official position. It was impossible, above all, to permit a regional army commander to choose whom he would deal with in Peking, unless its collective power to intervene politically were to be reduced to zero. Whatever his own opinions about Wang Li, Chou En-lai went to Wuhan not to "bring him back alive" but to stay politically alive himself. Had he allowed Ch'en to create this precedent, he could not have prevented similar incidents from occurring elsewhere and wrecking his prestige.

As for the Left, which showed on this occasion the full extent of solidarity between the civilian and military old guard, it naturally looked for solid guarantees against the repetition of such incidents. In fact, when Chiang Ch'ing made her inflammatory speech to the Red Guards on July 22, she was doubtless afraid that Ch'en's attitude might be infectious—she did not even know exactly how things would turn out at Wuhan—and her slogan of "defend yourselves with weapons" was no doubt launched to prepare for the worst.

All this seems to follow quite logically without any need to scent a plot. If the situation was deteriorating so fast in August 1967, it was not because conspirators had published a treacherous editorial or started a campaign of "deliberate distrust" of "Chairman Mao's soldiers." It was because the Left, now uppermost in the Central Group and the Cultural Revolution Directorate in the army, proved in this crucial month its inability to discipline and direct this "crowd of headless dragons" which, voicing the contradictory needs of society, turned to violence—as if driven mad—through its failure to overcome its divisions.

The August of the Ultra-Left

August in Peking began with a kind of continuous street fair, occupying T'ien An Men Square and the adjoining avenues, with the theme of "Grill Liu Shao-ch'i!" For a whole week, day and night, hundreds of thousands of demonstrators camped in the heart of the capital, in front of the gate of Chungnanhai, demanding that the "highest leader who . . . followed the capitalist road" should be handed over to them. This cry united all groups and factions in a short-lived reconciliation; they merely jostled one another to hold the strategic position which would enable them to be the first to grab hold of Liu if he emerged from the sanctuary. The crowd was patient and never dreamed of storming Chungnanhai (which could scarcely have resisted a mass assault) and the most battle-tested groups made no attempt to send their commandos to kidnap the "highest leader." Calm—if one may use the word—prevailed, and the group leaders were content to lead their followers in chanting slogans against Liu and quotations from Mao. The Chairman, like Vice-Chairman Lin Piao, had been away on a tour of inspection in the provinces since early July; at the time of the siege of Chungnanhai, he was in Wuhan. The other leaders, primarily Chou En-lai, found it hard to get used to the serenade of slogans which resounded under their windows without a break. Through Ch'i Pen-yü, a member of the Cultural Revolution Directorate, they negotiated with the noisiest groups and secured a truce of five hours a night, enabling them to sleep from one to six o'clock in the morning.

It does not seem that Ch'i or Wang Li promised to hand Liu over; but their periodic appearances in T'ien An Men Square were interpreted by the Red Guards as an encouragement. Indeed, if the demonstration had had no hope of gaining its ends, they would surely have made this known and taken advantage of their popularity to persuade it to disperse. Wang, Ch'i, and Kuan Feng doubtless thought that this united and continuous meeting had an educational value, that it enabled the masses to exchange experiences and to deepen their understanding of the "struggle between two lines." Despite the sweltering heat, the demonstrators remained cheerful and, while they waited, they had plenty of time to discuss the great events of the hour. There was much talk of the lessons to be drawn from the Wuhan affair and also of the news from Burma, where Ne Win, the "Burmese Chiang Kai-shek," was continuing his repression of the revolutionaries. Whatever the subject, they always managed to pin a crushing responsibility on Liu Shao-ch'i, which renewed their energies to demand a decisive showdown with the "traitor."

Although a stack of evidence points to the responsibility of the Peking students for the violence in the northeast and at Nanking —where armed conflict soon began—the main charge later made against them was that they had hatched a more surprising plot: giving up hope that Liu would be delivered to them, they were waiting for Chou En-lai to appear so that they could seize him.[42] A Central Committee meeting, called in Mao's absence, would then have made Wang Li (or, according to a later version, Ch'en Po-ta) head of the government. None of this happened, for at one in the morning of August 5 it was announced by Hsieh Fu-chih— not by Chou—that Liu was to be criticized but that there would be no "grilling" him. Hsieh must have been very persuasive—or must have brought instructions from Mao himself—for he immediately secured the dispersal of this frighteningly insistent crowd.

On August 7 the battle of Peking was renewed by Wang Li, who made a major speech about everything from foreign policy to the question of the army. On the latter subject he seems to have been very moderate, since he attacked no commanders on active service and concentrated his fire on Ho Lung and Hsü Hsiang-ch'ien, two former marshals who had already vanished from the political scene. Similarly, he made public some extracts from the resolution of the 1959 meeting of the Central Committee at Lushan, which had dismissed P'eng Teh-huai, and from many articles attacking Lo Jui-ch'ing, who had been dismissed in 1966. All this was intended to bear out his theory that there had been a "handful of revisionists" in the army, and especially to indicate targets which had already been destroyed and to "narrow the front of attack."

This technique—of attributing all possible misdeeds to a symbol

[42] Several foreign eyewitnesses have described the prolonged August demonstration, but none of them refers to the existence or even the possibility of this plot against Chou. Jean Esmein, in *The Chinese Cultural Revolution* (New York: Anchor, 1973), stresses the role of Ch'i Pen-yü; Jean Daubier, in *A History of the Chinese Cultural Revolution*, says that on August 5 Liu made a self-criticism which was relayed by loudspeaker to T'ien An Men Square, though I have found no evidence of this. Neither writer mentions Chou in connection with the whole episode.

of guilt in order to highlight the "difference between the two lines" and rally the "vast majority of the masses"—had already been used against Liu. But experience had shown that it had the paradoxical result of spreading suspicion to almost everyone. The attack on P'eng Teh-huai and Lo Jui-ch'ing was contrary to the slogan of "Support the Army," even if the accused were "dead tigers" and had not been identified with the army for a long time. If commanders of such distinction—and no one in China could forget the historic role of P'eng Teh-huai—had at one time plotted against Chairman Mao, how could one be sure that their equals, still on the active list, were not concocting similar plots? And then, why the delay of eight years in publishing the resolution condemning P'eng, when the army had been, since his dismissal, in the clean hands of Lin Piao? Besides, if the masses were being urged to settle accounts eight years old with a powerless retired marshal, was this not a way of diverting them from burning questions?

In Peking, this curious campaign led to no direct conflicts between mass groups and soldiers—though such conflicts were spreading in the provinces—because leftist activity was concentrated on the Ministry of Foreign Affairs. It was in this field that Wang Li, Kuan Feng, and Ch'i Pen-yü made the mistakes that caused their downfall.

At the beginning of August, the Propaganda Department, directed by Wang Li, suddenly circulated Lin Piao's essay (published in September 1965) "Long Live the Victory of the People's War." Adorned by commentaries to stress its universal significance, it was presented as a great program of foreign policy designed to "strike down American imperialism and its lackeys" by giving active aid to the peoples of Asia, Africa, and Latin America. It was a renewal of the theory of the encirclement of the cities (the developed nations) by the countryside (the Third World), patterning world revolution on the model of the Chinese revolution.[43] The victories of the Vietnamese in their war of

[43] Lin Piao's essay was reproduced in *Peking Review*, No. 32 (August 4, 1967). It should be noted that in a speech on November 6, 1967, on the occasion of the fiftieth anniversary of the Bolshevik Revolution, Lin Piao himself returned to the central theme of his essay by saying, "To rely on the masses, to create revolutionary support bases in the countryside, to encircle the cities from the

resistance against the United States, and the appearance of armed struggles in India, Indonesia, and Burma, were cited to show the relevance and effectiveness of this strategy. But, in his speech of August 7, Wang Li made the new assertion that the men responsible for China's foreign policy had not yet done anything to put this international line into practice; indeed, under the orders of their protector "behind the scenes"—obviously Liu, but perhaps Chou En-lai—they had tried to quench the flames of the people's war abroad. This was a clear incitement to a "seizure of power" at the Ministry of Foreign Affairs.

The liaison post went into action at once. But it did not seek to replace experienced leaders by a bunch of foreign-language students. It had a candidate of greater prestige, even if his fame was quite fresh: Yao Teng-shan, "Chairman Mao's Red fighter on the diplomatic front." The operation was carried through with flying colors and without any noteworthy conflict, and Yao, beginning on August 8, began to bombard Chinese embassies abroad with cables which he signed as minister. The content of these dispatches has never been revealed and it is very hard to say just what was the "Red Guard diplomacy," as it is now called. But we know of some examples of Yao's activity. On August 10, the Mongolian ambassador was summoned to receive a "very forceful protest" against the conduct of a Mongolian diplomat who had "trodden underfoot and insulted, in his car parked outside the Friendship Store, a portrait of Chairman Mao, the Red sunshine in the hearts of the Chinese people." On August 11, the Burmese chargé d'affaires received a "very forceful note against the military provocations of the reactionary Ne Win government, which had made a serious violation of Chinese air space in Yunnan Province." Finally, on August 20, D. C. Hopson, the British chargé d'affaires, was summoned to be informed of a "most imperative and forceful protest to the government of the United Kingdom against the persecution of the Chinese patriotic press by the British authorities in Hong Kong."

This "imperative" note amounted, indeed, to an ultimatum; it called on the British government to release the nineteen Chinese

---

countryside—these are the historic tasks which the oppressed nations and peoples of the world must carry through to success in our epoch in order to win power."

journalists arrested in Hong Kong "within forty-eight hours, failing which Britain must bear responsibility for all the ensuing consequences." [44] This gesture—so my informants in Peking declared to me in 1971—was foolish; you do not send an ultimatum unless you are determined to carry it through. Yao had neither the power nor, probably, the will to send troops to Hong Kong. So, in order not to lose face, when the forty-eight hours had passed, he called on his "friends and protectors in the May 16 group" to do something against the British at any cost. The extreme Left promptly organized a mass demonstration at the British Chancery in Peking, and sent in some "specialized commandos" who firebombed the offices and beat up Hopson. In 1971, my hosts said categorically that "this action was premeditated and designed to stain China's reputation in the world." An outburst of justifiable anger, they explained, must be distinguished from an act of barbaric violence, calmly carried out by an incendiary squad which arrived with trucks loaded with cans of gasoline.

The burning of the British offices on August 22 was the straw that broke the camel's back. Mao was back in Peking, and he intervened indignantly against Yao Teng-shan. He had not the faintest intention of endorsing the "seizure of power" at the Ministry of Foreign Affairs and, according to Red Guard posters, he asked dryly, "If Ch'en Yi is not minister, who is?" And he is said to have added, "Ch'en Yi made fewer mistakes in forty years than his critics have made in forty days." [45] Then he had a long talk with Chou En-lai, who described how, as a "prisoner" of the Red Guards from the Foreign Languages Institute, he had been subjected to their interrogation in the course of forty-eight testing hours. Chou, we can guess, said something like: "If I am not Premier, who is?" Was it Wang Li or Ch'i Pen-yü or Kuan Feng,

[44] See "Most Vehement Protest Against Persecution of Patriotic Press by Hong Kong British Authorities," *Peking Review*, No. 35 (August 25, 1967). Note that the protest was published on August 25—that is, after the expiration of the ultimatum given to the British. This seems to show that it was not intended as a real ultimatum, but as a way of shouting louder.

[45] These remarks by Mao were revealed in Red Guard posters, but only in November 1967, well after the climax of the crisis and the disappearance of Yao Teng-shan.

who were speaking everywhere as if they headed the government? But, before taking any decisions, Mao waited for Lin Piao and Ch'en Po-ta to return to Peking. We can assume that he then called a Central Committee conference; none of the leaders appeared in public for several days at the end of August, and September began with a veritable hail of fresh resolutions and reshuffles at the top level.

Thus, the Cultural Revolution Directorate in the Army again changed its chairman; the "young veteran" Hsiao Hua, soon to be accused of belonging to the ultra-Left, was replaced by Wu Fa-hsien, commander of the air force. Chiang Ch'ing lost her post as adviser to this body but remained vice-chairman of the Central Group, now shorn of Wang Li, Kuan Feng, and several lesser leftists (Ch'i Pen-yü, put on probation, was to be dismissed some months later). Mao was still reflecting on the conclusions of his tour of the provinces, but on September 5, at a conference of delegates from rival factions in Anhwei Province, his wife revealed the outlines of the new orientation. No doubt this task was entrusted to her so that she could publicly retreat from her rash slogan of July 28: "Attack with words, but defend yourselves with weapons."

"Comrades," she began by announcing, "I am not in favor of armed struggle and you must not think that I approve of it, for this is absolutely not so. I firmly support Chairman Mao's call for a peaceful, not an armed, struggle. Certainly, if the class enemy attacks us, we cannot allow ourselves to be without an iron bar in our hands. But in the present situation we don't need any armed struggle. Such a struggle always claims victims among the people and injures their heritage. Why should we behave like wayward sons? The slogan 'Attack with words, but defend yourselves with weapons' must not be deprived of its class content and separated from the circumstances and conditions of the time. . . ." [46]

After this withdrawal, which had a tinge of self-criticism, Chiang Ch'ing read a Central Committee directive which ordered the groups to give back the arms they had seized in August and to cease all violent action, and authorized the army to defend itself against armed attacks. She added that, had she been a soldier, she

[46] *Documents of the Great Proletarian Cultural Revolution*, p. 595.

would never have let anyone take away her gun; the soldiers who had allowed themselves to be disarmed to avoid shooting at their class brothers had shown an extraordinary and truly admirable restraint. So they must not be attacked, even in words; on the contrary, the revolutionary masses must defend and protect their honor. The slogan launched on August 1: "Unmask the handful of high leaders in the army," was thus denounced as mistaken and harmful.

Then came a criticism of factions which refused to unite—very apposite, since the Anhwei delegates belonged to two irreconcilable factions—and an announcement that Revolutionary Committees would be quickly set up everywhere. Finally, Chiang Ch'ing made a strong attack on the May 16 Armed Corps—this was the first official mention of its existence—and held it up as a symbol of the political misdeeds of the ultra-Left. The forces of this organization were not numerous, she said, and consisted mainly of young people; but their chiefs, who were not seen in the open, were really bad people—even American and Soviet agents— "bourgeois filled with hate for all of us." These tricksters played on the political instability of the youth in order to set them against all the leaders of the Central Group and particularly against Premier Chou En-lai. Having recalled that Chou had been savagely attacked by the Right not long ago, she found it strange and significant that he should now be made the target of the ultra-Left. In reality, those who took up leftist positions were counterrevolutionaries; "seeking the same aims, they hope to succeed where the Right failed." Evidently the position was understood, and the hour had struck for the struggle against the leftist trend.

On September 7, two days later, another member of the Central Group, Yao Wen-yuan, added his voice in the columns of *People's Daily*. He took as his target two books by T'ao Chu, published in 1962 and 1964, and showed that their author, now a leftist, was then squarely on the Right. This was a rather dubious method of proving that the ultra-Left was merely an embodiment of the Right; after all, T'ao Chu could have followed his individual path, and there was no law that a rightist must remain so all his life. But it was clear that the case of T'ao Chu—"this renegade and lackey"—was the last thing that Yao Wen-yuan cared about.

What he wanted to put across was this: "Today there exists a handful of counterrevolutionaries who follow the same method. They use similar slogans, ultra-Left in appearance but ultra-Right in reality, to stimulate a harmful tendency toward 'distrust of everybody,' to open fire on the headquarters of the proletariat, to sow discord and fish in troubled waters. They seek, although vainly, to shake and split the proletarian headquarters led by Chairman Mao, in order to achieve their criminal goals which they dare not admit. Those who created and control the organization called 'May 16' are a counterrevolutionary clique of plotters of just this type. They must be completely unmasked." [47]

A few phrases, lost in this maze of metaphors, seemed nevertheless to be a preparation for a more fundamental shift. "There are no 'masses' in the abstract," Yao suddenly stated. "The masses, in a class society, are divided into classes. Nor is there any 'management' in the abstract; management, in a class society, invariably implies the resolution of relationships between classes; it involves the question of which class holds and wields power." These were elementary truths—for Marxists, of course—but had they been remembered a year earlier when the slogan was raised that "the masses must liberate themselves" and when the masses were urged to manage their own affairs? If the concept of the masses was abstract and its class content had to be carefully analyzed—as the Communist movement maintained—then it had to be admitted that the authors of the "sixteen-point decision" on the Cultural Revolution had not done this vital piece of homework in good time. Was this why the mass movement had ended up by taking a chaotic and anarchical form, giving aid and comfort to the divisive efforts of "plotters" on both flanks? Yao did not say so clearly, but doubtless this was to guard himself against the charge of "lacking confidence in the masses," which had cost the old leaders so dear. Nevertheless, he was discreetly paving the way for a new formula: "The working class must direct everything," which he was himself to launch in 1968 and which was gradually and inevitably to become: "The Party of the working-class must direct everything." This latter proposition is in favor today, just as

[47] See Yao Wen-yuan, "Comments on T'ao Chu's Two Books," *Peking Review*, No. 38 (September 15, 1967).

it was before the Cultural Revolution. But before it could be "dialectically" restored, without hurting too many feelings and without denying the fundamentals of the line on the complete autonomy of the masses, the turning point of the fall of 1967 had to be followed by long months charged with conflict.

Chairman Mao's Two Thousand Words

Chiang Ch'ing's speech and Yao Wen-yuan's article could not fully express the direction which the Central Group took at the end of the "hot summer" of 1967. They were decisive, certainly, with regard to the tendency of the groups to arm themselves at any cost by taking army weapons. The army was ordered to protect its arsenals and authorized to open fire on attackers, and this was enough to discourage such attempts. But the search for arms in August 1967 was only the consequence of a political situation; it was the result rather than the cause of what was called "the great division within the masses." If this endured, there was a risk of new and bloody struggles. In any case the groups who were already armed were in no hurry to restore the weapons to the soldiers—except for the matériel destined for Vietnam—and the army was not told to regain them by force. The truce between the rival factions was likely to be short-lived unless it was accompanied by a genuine political détente.

Now, this could not be achieved by denouncing the "plotters" of the "May 16" group. This group belonged specifically to Peking, and to put it in the dock meant nothing very precise to the vast majority of the people. More than anything else, apparently, this showed the scale of the divisions within the Central Group, and the identity of certain "plotters" could be guessed without much trouble. True, when Chiang Ch'ing and Yao Wen-yuan spoke of an attempt to weaken the proletarian headquarters from within, they did not mention the names of Wang Li or Kuan Feng, but it was scarcely difficult to make the link between their disappearance from the political scene and this unprecedented attack on a group which had hitherto been utterly ignored. With their dismissal—and that of Hsiao Hua—certain positions for which they had been the spokesmen were officially deprived of all legitimacy and were now defined as "ultra-Left."

But from this to recognize, as we must, the differences between their speeches and those of, for example, Chiang Ch'ing, Ch'en Po-ta, Hsieh Fu-chih, and even Yao Wen-yuan—this was a step which the uninitiated found difficult.

K'uai Ta-fu expressed this with some ingenuity in an editorial in his paper, the *Chingkangshan of Tsinghua University*, headed: "What Ultra-Left Policy?" This article was quoted against him in 1971; it was taken to prove his adherence to the "May 16" group and his deliberate intention to attack Chairman Mao by "rebelling" against Chiang Ch'ing's speech. But, to judge from the few extracts that are known, he neither attacked nor defended any leader; he simply declared that the very idea of the "ultra-Left" was abstract, indeed arbitrary. If this article proves anything, it is the confusion of the student leaders. Even those who took part in big-league politics, such as K'uai, could scarcely find their way among the wranglings at the top level. They were obliged to ask certain questions about the new orientation, for which they were likely to pay the price.

In theory, Mao himself gave the answers. On October 7, he issued through the Central Committee a report of his impressions from his long tour of the provinces. But this document, regarded as historic and even decisive with regard to later events, must at first glance have been fairly confusing, if only because of its form and presentation. It was preceded by a preamble in which the Central Committee urged everyone to study it carefully, while forbidding its publication in the newspapers "whatever their importance," and stating that it was only a draft record of an interview with Mao, who had not personally read it through. However, the text was not very long—about two thousand words—and reading it through could not have taken much time. Moreover, despite the ban on publication, it soon appeared in Red Guard posters, and the central press itself gave great prominence to certain extracts, beginning with this key quotation: "There is no basic conflict within the working class; under the dictatorship of the proletariat, in particular, there is no reason for the workers to divide into organizations belonging to two great antagonistic factions." [48] According to my informants in 1971 (especially those

---

[48] This quotation appeared in practically all Chinese publications after October 1967. The complete text on Mao's impressions from his tour of the provinces

in the army), it was this directive from the Chairman that at last made it possible to make a serious start on the process of unification at the mass level and to form Revolutionary Committees in the provinces and in industry.

But, while this call to unity was clear and imperative, the rest of the document created more problems. In general, Mao declared that he was content with the situation:

> There has never been [in China] such a broad and deep mass movement as this. In the factories and the countryside, in the schools and the army units, in the whole nation, everyone is talking about the Cultural Revolution and feeling involved in national affairs. Before, when families came together, they wasted a lot of time in small talk. Now, everything is different. As soon as they meet, they talk of great problems; fathers and sons, brothers and sisters, husbands and wives, even adolescents and grandmothers, all join in the discussion.

Alongside this gratifying fact, there was another, not so good: "We are too serious, too tense, we lack unity and liveliness." Mao did not give the impression of being greatly worried by the dramatic ordeals through which China had passed; his tone was serene, even somewhat detached. One might say that he was by no means surprised by what he had seen on his trip.

True, this conversation between the Chairman and someone who summarized it later gave only the most cursory indications of his feelings. It was not an analysis in depth, or even the outline of a balance sheet of the fifteen months of Cultural Revolution. Mao did not try to explain how a great division within the working class had exploded despite the absence of "basic conflict"; he merely remarked, as an aside, that the bad leaders of the earlier period and the "anarchist tendencies" in the rank and file both had something to do with it. It was the future that mattered to him, and he particularly criticized the tendency of each group to set itself up as the nucleus of the "great revolutionary alliance." "Wang Ming, Po Ku, and Lo Fu," he said, "also tried to establish themselves as the only leading group, but they failed. . . . These matters are not settled by people appointing themselves, for the leading network is formed only in the struggle and must be

---

appeared on October 19 in the Canton rebel paper *Spring Lightning*, and then in other Red Guard sheets.

recognized by the masses as a whole." [49] Then he advised each faction to criticize its own faults and inadequacies rather than the errors of its rivals. In his view, this would in practice be enough, because fundamentally "both of the two great factions subscribe to the revolutionary outlook."

On the tricky problem of the cadres—which involved the relations between governors and governed—Mao spoke at greater length, but he did not dramatize anything. He recognized that events had revealed a certain antagonism between the rank and file and those to whom it had entrusted its power. He saw three main reasons: (1) a section of the cadres had in effect "taken the capitalist road"; (2) many others had given themselves excessive salaries, taken on airs, and failed to consult the masses and to treat other people as equals; (3) through lack of democratic spirit, they had not allowed other people to speak. As soon as the masses had had the opportunity to express themselves, during the Cultural Revolution, everything they had on their minds burst out and the cadres found themselves in an awkward position. "But from now on," Mao concluded, "we must absorb all these lessons and resolve the problem correctly by improving the relations between the cadres and the masses." Stress must be put on the education of both, on the correction of mistakes and the winning back of those who had been in error, in the Yenan tradition. "What is so important about these mistakes?" he asked with a show of surprise. "Really, the one thing that matters and the one thing that is good is to correct mistakes."

The fact remained that this document provided no recipe for filling the institutional vacuum that had been created in China. Mao devoted only one sentence to the Party, and this merely recalled that it had emerged strengthened from the rectification campaign during the war against Japan. He made virtually no reference to the army; he simply paid a formal tribute to its commanders and soldiers as well as to the Red Guards and to the broad masses of workers, peasants, cadres, and revolutionary intellectuals. Nor was there anything about the ultra-Left, which

[49] We may note that Mao's only negative example involved the three leaders of the group of "Twenty-eight Bolsheviks" who had directed the Party before him. They had not set themselves up at all; they had been appointed by the Comintern.

at that time was the big headache for his lieutenants. As a whole, the document could have been written in the very first phase of the cultural reform, before the "January storm," the February counteroffensive, the Wuhan affair, and the "hot summer." But perhaps this was just the point—was this an indirect and discreet recommendation to go back to the original scenario, which had envisaged more flexibility and fewer excesses?

Surely Mao had brought back from his three-month tour of the provinces more than could be found in the two thousand words divulged on October 7. Besides, he detached himself somewhat from the interview (he had "not read it through"). But he nevertheless authorized the large-scale dissemination of this document, and we must rely on it to discover his thinking and his orientation in the fall of 1967. Now, the most striking feature is that the schemes for a huge remolding of institutions in China are put into cold storage. There is no longer any question of the pattern of the Paris Commune, or of "heights that have never been reached in the past"; no longer do we hear a note of enthusiasm and of confidence in the "mass sources of revolution-ary action." Of course, Mao urged neither a return to the old regime nor a rehabilitation of those who had flourished in it. The search for forms and methods of mobilizing the people was to continue, and the "mass line" was to be practiced more than ever. But this must be done without violence, without falling into utopian traps, and without trying to destroy everything before new plans were ready. Mao's directive implied: "I told you to 'open fire on headquarters,' not to destroy it; we need the people who have made mistakes, and anyway we can't solve our problems in a single Cultural Revolution." In a sentence ad-dressed to the Red Guards, he said rather mysteriously: "We are at the very moment when the little Red Guard generals"—this phrase was without quotation marks and probably was not ironical—"run a risk of making mistakes; they must learn from the experiences of those among them who have made errors in the past." Perhaps this was not a complete answer to the questions asked by student leaders about the notion of the ultra-Left, but at least it was a warning. At all events, this casual phrase did in a sense raise the curtain on a new period of the Cultural Revolution, in which the "little generals" were soon to be left behind by events. Later, it would be said that they had invited their own downfall by their "irresponsible" conduct in the summer of 1967, and that this would never have happened if, instead of listening to the treacherous counsels of "evil elements" disguised as "extremists," they had paid more attention to the wise advice of Chairman Mao and his headquarters.

One more fact about the "hot summer" is worth noting: Lin Piao virtually did not appear during the entire period. Nothing was heard from him at the time of the Wuhan affair, and this silence is odd, to say the least, even bearing in mind that he had a special position and was no longer directly connected with the army.[50] Nor did he say anything about the "seizure of power" in the Ministry of Foreign Affairs, and no major document bore his signature during the summer, not even the order of September 5 forbidding the seizure of army weapons.[51] Lin Piao reappeared on the scene only in November, to make a long speech on the anniversary of the Bolshevik Revolution. In it, he alluded to "the most recent directives of Chairman Mao" in order to urge the "young Red Guard fighters" to go triumphantly forward. "Unless the proletariat continues to advance on this path to reach a radical solution of the problem of taking and consolidating power, it will never be able to win the final victory; and, should it seize power, it will be in danger of losing it and falling once again, like the Soviet people, under the domination of a new privileged bourgeois stratum." [52] Truly, whatever the lack of precise explanations, the "little Red Guard generals" were getting plenty of advice in this autumn of 1967.

[50] However, Lin Piao was in Peking during the first ten days of August, and we know that on August 9 he made a speech to the Military Affairs Commission of the CCP. Not a word of it leaked out abroad.

[51] This detail may be significant, since the order of April 6 forbidding the army to open fire had been signed by Lin.

[52] It was in this speech that Lin spoke of the world strategy of "encircling the cities from the countryside." The full text is given in *Documents of the Great Proletarian Cultural Revolution.*

Postscript
The Reconciliation Between a Rebel
and a Cadre in Shenyang

"Our city was formerly called Mukden, which means 'New Prosperity.' It was from here that the Manchus set out in the seventeenth century to conquer China, and even when they ruled in Peking the Emperors came back twice a year to bow before the tombs of their ancestors." Sung Kuang, the deputy mayor of Shenyang, who thus introduced his city and the province of Liaoning to me in 1965, was by no means a "regional chauvinist." A native of Shanghai, he had been in Manchuria only since 1943 and simply because the Party had sent him. His remarks were not boastful; when he spoke of the wealth of the northeast and of the outstanding part it played in the war of liberation and in the industrialization of the new China, he relied on indisputable facts.

Sung Kuang's account stays in my memory as a lucid historical lesson. Since the 1920's, the northeast, and Liaoning Province in particular, had shown that its natural resources destined it to be the Ruhr of this part of Asia. Not surprisingly, it aroused the greed of Japan and, more discreetly, of the Soviet Union. Japan resorted to force in 1931 and set up the puppet state of Manchukuo; the Soviet Union, after dealing the final blow to Japanese militarism in 1945, calmly removed Manchuria's industrial equipment. Having little confidence that their Communist allies could win a civil war, the Russians decided to reap the maximum profit from their temporary occupation of this valuable region. However, less than three years later, it was in the northeast that the People's Liberation Army won its decisive battles against the Kuomintang in the "Liao-Shen" campaign, directed by Lin Piao. When the ten best Nationalist divisions, with their generals and officers, laid down their arms in the besieged city of Shenyang on November 2, 1948, the outcome of the war was in fact decided.

After the proclamation of the People's Republic, the flow of industrial equipment between the USSR and the northeast was resumed in the opposite direction. Soviet advisers recommended that the Chinese use the former Manchuria as a "locomotive" to pull their country out of underdevelopment. Up to 1960, heavy material poured in, especially to Liaoning Province, in which there arose the greatest engineering center in China, the famous Anshan complex—150,000 workers in fifty integrated plants. The opencast coal mines at Fushun increased production five times over, while Shenyang became one of the chief centers for the manufacture of heavy machinery (and no doubt of armaments). Then, almost overnight, in the summer of 1960, the Soviet advisers packed their bags and departed; the USSR refused thereafter to supply a single spare part for the machines that had been installed. Sung Kuang spoke of this at length, but without too much bitterness. "Left to ourselves, we beat all records to get out of the difficulty; we really learned to rely on our own resources."

Liaoning Province seems to have set a new record since those days—in the scale of armed clashes during the "hot summer" of 1967. Few reports leaked out abroad, for the northeast is "forbidden territory" because of its strategic position on the Soviet frontier. Besides, the protagonists were not proud of the 1967 battles and—for once—the Red Guard posters tended to minimize them. However, in 1971, when they talked about the misdeeds of the ultra-Left, my informants in Peking often alluded to the madness of the extremists who four years earlier had tried to start a new "Liao-Shen" campaign in the northeast in the hope of matching the historic exploits of the People's Liberation Army. Having thus aroused my curiosity, my hosts advised me to get information on the spot, since I was due to go there.

When I reached Shenyang in May 1971, forewarned by my experience at the Diesel plant in Shanghai, I did not expect my guides to raise these sensitive questions on their own. I mentioned at once the bits of information I had obtained in Peking. The press director for Liaoning Province, the smiling Comrade T'ung, a former war correspondent in Korea, lifted his arms to the heavens: "What do you think? Everywhere in China the masses were split into two big rival factions, but here we had three." And he held up three fingers to stress his words, while assuring me, as though it were a huge joke, that one extra faction "makes one hell of a difference." But, instead of enlarging on the subject, he invited me to a football match between northeast China and the People's

Republic of the Congo. It would be a good opportunity to relax and to meet interesting people.

The prevailing color of the reserved benches was indeed significant, for it was the grass green of the army. Were the civilian leaders of the Revolutionary Committees in the provinces less keen on sports than their military comrades? Or were they in a minority in these committees anyway? T'ung led me with firm steps toward the senior officials, while everyone watched me with the greatest curiosity.

Of course, the top officials held their curiosity in check, and although each of them spoke to me for a few minutes before the match, it was only to welcome me and ask me how many days I should be staying in the northeast. Even Ch'en Hsi-lien, chairman of the Liaoning Revolutionary Committee and head of the military district, honored me by taking an interest. He was a national personality, not only as a member of the Politburo, but above all because he had been much spoken of during the Cultural Revolution. I hadn't imagined him to be so corpulent; his appearance was casual, for he floated in his badly cut tunic and wore canvas shoes. A military aristocrat? A restorer of the old regime? The epithets thrown by the Red Guards in 1967 did not seem to fit this commander, whom one could not have picked out among his soldiers. Yet one sensed the gestation of a new hierarchical system from the respect with which Ch'en Hsi-lien was addressed by his subordinates, the careful allocation of places in the stand, and the length of time it was considered proper to hold the chairman's attention. Even my interpreter, Tao, attached enormous importance to the fact that Ch'en had "received us at such length." Speaking in the plural, he said: "We were greatly honored, and it is a good omen for your visit."

Indeed, as soon as we got back to the hotel—which was the center of Shenyang's social life—T'ung asked me to a dinner given for us by the Revolutionary Committees of Liaoning and Shenyang. We had no need to move; it would be held in the hotel. Thanks to the football match, I was now aware of the relative importance of each of the guests. However, the army men were in a minority among the twenty or so at the table, and the first speaker was very much a civilian. Comrade Pi Wen-t'ing was small, frail, and quite elderly; he began by saying that "no formalities and no chairman are needed among friends," but all the same he presided over the dinner by proposing toasts and by giving me a commentary on the origin and contents of each dish. All of a sudden, T'ung made it known that the "foreign friend" was especially interested in the history of the Cultural Revolution in the northeast.

Comrade Pi had been waiting for this; he really had very little interest in the cuisine and was delighted to turn to serious matters. He began in a rather curious way. Pointing to the man who faced him across the table, whose height and broad shoulders had already caught my attention, he said: "That young worker, Wang, was my worst enemy. He rebelled against me and people like me and gave us a very hard time. In a different society, we should have been lifelong enemies. But under the dictatorship of the proletariat things don't happen like that. We come from the same class, don't we? We're both guided by the thought of Chairman Mao, aren't we? Our battles, instead of dividing us, have drawn us together, have enabled us both to revolutionize our ideas and change our subjective view of the world in order to change the objective world. So here we are, both members of the Liaoning Revolutionary Committee and both receiving you, like old friends. There's nothing unusual about our reconciliation, but I think it will convey to you the whole meaning of the Cultural Revolution."

The sturdy Wang confirmed this with a nod, and added shyly that he had never underestimated the importance of revolutionary cadres in the building of socialism, even if he had not imagined at the time that he himself would become a cadre. The two army men, Yen Tsuan-yuan and Hu Shan-ch'u, who were at the head of the table—in the best places, as at the football match—took up the tale one after the other to expound the teachings of Chairman Mao on the role of the cadres in a historical perspective.

I ventured a few remarks on the difference between the correct methods of Mao and the very bad ones of Stalin, which ended in wiping out the best Communists in the Soviet Union. This caused consternation; the "foreign friend" was not supposed to make such comments and no one had an answer ready. The rebel Wang was the first to find his tongue: "With Comrade Stalin, as with any other cadre, one must take account of his entire record and not judge him by an isolated fact." I pointed out that the "isolated fact" of Stalinist repression had played an immense part in creating a certain type of society in the Soviet Union. Comrade Pi now replied rather sharply: "Chairman Mao has said that Comrade Stalin was a great Marxist-Leninist and resolutely defended the dictatorship of the proletariat after the death of Lenin." I took refuge in turn in the Chairman's authority: "To defend and consolidate the dictatorship of the proletariat, Chairman Mao says, a whole series of cultural revolutions is absolutely essential. Now, so far as I know, Stalin held power for thirty years without starting the smallest cultural revolution. Instead of trusting the working class, he relied on the political police. Is that the best way to strengthen the proletarian regime? And wasn't Khrushchev, who was one of his favorites, the product of his system?"

I expected this controversial link to produce anything but agreement. But Yen, a forceful army man, suddenly came out on my side. "You've got a point there—it was unforgivable that Stalin never made a cultural revolution. We shall soon have another one, in conformity with the teaching of Chairman Mao, which you have interpreted very well." Everyone brightened up, relieved to have got out of the difficulty. Comrade Pi proposed a toast to the second, "absolutely essential" Cultural Revolution. He frankly inspected my glass to make sure that I had drunk the last drop of *mao-tai* (rice wine, pretty strong stuff) and that I was pledging with this *kam-pai* my support for the future struggle. Leaving the subject of Stalin without regret, we went back to the Cultural Revolution.

Comrade Pi took up his story with the ritual phrase of rehabilitated cadres: "At first, I did not understand the sixteen-point decision." He was very hard on himself, but punctuated his self-criticism with bursts of laughter which were rather puzzling. When he poked fun at his old position as secretary-general of the Liaoning trade unions, was he thinking of this bureaucratic institution or of his way of running it? Anyway, his good humor was infectious, and everyone kept perfectly calm although he spoke of really monumental mistakes. But, Pi admitted, the fact was plain—he had "taken the capitalist road." He made no excuses; he knew Chairman Mao's directives by heart, and as an old Communist he should have understood and implemented them. But he did nothing of the kind, because his outlook had been basically bourgeois and not proletarian. Buried in his office, "bigger than the room where we are now," he took decisions on the basis of secondhand reports and was guilty of the "three divorces"—from the masses, from reality, and from practice. This made him the "docile instrument," if not the active accomplice, of the handful of leaders who took the capitalist road, notably the "evil" Ma Ming-fang, one of the secretaries of the Party's Northeast China Bureau and chief of the Central Committee's Finance and Trade Bureau. The latter nominated him to a work team which was concerned with three factories, and he went there to preach "social peace" in the name of production from morning to night. Laughter spread all round the table.

"This Ma Ming-fang was very cunning," Pi continued. "He said that he was very keen on the Cultural Revolution and he even organized a huge meeting on August 18 on the square in front of this hotel. But he said to us that this revolution concerned only the intellectuals and the students and not the industrial sphere, which, as it belonged to the people, was developing according to the proletarian line of Chairman Mao. According to him, in the factories we had only to fight for a better carrying out of the plan. I repeated this rubbish like a parrot. But one day Comrade Wang, whom you see here and who was leading a rebel group, suddenly accosted me. 'You, Pi Wen-t'ing, what do you know about the plan in our factory? You go from your factory to your home in a car, even avoiding the working-class neighborhoods.' This was absolutely true, but I at once accused Wang and his group of attacking the Party and stuck the 'counterrevolutionary' label on them." This time, Pi found nothing to laugh at.

Wang interrupted, not without sympathy, to reduce the incident to more modest proportions. In 1966, he did not know Pi personally and had not the least idea of how he went around. He had made a general attack on the majority of cadres in the leadership, who said that they were "in the service of the people" but preferred to look down on "their people" from a good distance. "I didn't invent the charge that they avoided the working-class neighborhoods and came to the factories only to show off. Everyone was saying it. Most of the cadres like Pi were a bit annoyed, but then they stopped going about by car; they learned to ride bicycles again, like other people." Pi cheerfully confirmed this.

From the rest of the story, I gathered that the Cultural Revolution up to the autumn of 1966 took the same course as in Shanghai and other industrial centers. But Pi pointed out a major difference. Whereas in Shanghai the "true rebels" took power in January 1967, Shenyang saw a "false seizure of power." The wicked Ma Ming-fang and a few "high priests"—such as Ku Chu-hsin, of the Party's Northeast China Bureau, and Yu Ping, secretary of the Party Provincial Committee—made a tactical self-criticism and disguised themselves as rebels to set up a "new administration." They thus launched their own faction, which entered the pseudo-revolutionary competition and misled the masses by pointing to false targets. Such was their audacity that, in February 1967, when the army propaganda teams intervened, they spread the rumor that the soldiers were backing the Right and not the Left, with the sole aim of undermining the prestige of the People's Liberation Army. Comrade Pi rather forgot his own peregrinations, and his voice trembled with indignation as he sketched this general picture.

The two officers took up the narrative, which concerned them directly. "We lacked experience in February 1967," said Yen Tsuan-yuan, "and we could not avoid all the traps that were set for us. We had to educate ourselves among the masses before our efforts could produce positive results." Hu Shan-ch'u was even more modest. "Until October 1967 we could do nothing to reconcile the mass groups. It was only after Chairman Mao declared that there was no basic reason for the great split in the working class that the workers became more receptive to our appeals for unity. The merit is entirely that of the Chairman and his exceptional links with the masses—it is not ours."

Pi returned to his own story. From the end of December 1966, the trade unions ceased to function and the work teams were withdrawn from the factories. Pi became one of the rank and file again, and went to work in a factory. He no longer wanted to be a cadre, but only to immerse himself in the working class and its mass organizations. But, in the first few months of 1967, the schemers from the general staff of Liu Shao-ch'i were busy inciting a section of the masses against men like Pi, "in the desperate hope of thus having their own crimes forgotten." In the factory where Pi worked, many workers refused to shake hands with him and went on insulting him in their posters. But it was precisely during this very unhappy period that his political understanding developed most. He understood both the ideological causes of his own errors and the true faces of the "great despots" whom he had long supported. Moreover, he found comrades in the factory who resolved to help him and were ready to accept him in their organizations. Thanks to them, he did not yield to apathy and returned to the battle with all his strength, alongside those who wanted to carry the Cultural Revolution through to the end.

Thus Pi Wen-t'ing came to the crucial situation which led to the outbursts of the summer of 1967. "As you were told in Peking, we had not two but three big rival factions. These were the Liao Ko Shan [Post of Proletarian Rebels of Liaoning], the Rebel Headquarters of August 31, and the Liao Lien [Rebel Committee for the Grand Alliance of Liaoning]. The rank and file of each faction was working class and revolutionary, but at the top level they were often infiltrated by bad elements—hardened petty bourgeois, sometimes even counterrevolutionaries and class enemies. As you see, I am objective; I don't rank any group above the others, although I was far from neutral at the time." The guests conceded this. I wanted to know whether this charming attitude also applied to the "wicked" Ma Ming-fang, but I framed my question without the shadow of a challenge. Pi considered it relevant and apologized for having forgotten to tell me that Ma and those like him were eliminated during the spring. "They were too obvious as accomplices of Liu—why, as members of his general staff. The masses unmasked them and then their tricks were in vain. But they had worthy successors, better camouflaged and harder to detect. These fellows called for distrust of everybody and spread crazy slogans, such as the 'Three Noes'—no recognition of preparatory committees, no support for attempts at unification, no participation in provisional organs of power. Why? you may ask. That's quite simple. If the masses took no part in the organs of power that were being set up, and refused even to recognize or support them, how could these structures function under the dictatorship of the proletariat? After a period of anarchy, the old props of the capitalist road would be back in power. That was what they were hoping for. In Chinese we call it 'sowing discord to fish in troubled waters.' "

At last we reached the "hot summer" of 1967. Pi adopted a didactic style, so that I could grasp the logic of the "conspiracy." Who was doing most to restore unity and assist production? The army comrades. Who was therefore the main obstacle to the black schemes of the troublemakers? The army comrades. Who, among the army comrades, worked best for unity? Comrade Ch'en Hsi-lien. The design of the "plot" was therefore transparent. The men who launched the so-called Liao-Shen campaign were in fact taking orders from the "May 16" group in Peking—though no one knew this at the time—and the latter, thanks to connections with certain elements at the Party center, knew all about the locations of barracks and arsenals. So, at the end of July, Pi explained, "they lit the fires of a real civil war at Fushun and Anshan, before concentrating their attack on the headquarters of the Liaoning Military District at Shenyang. Our soldiers did not fall into the trap set by these provocateurs, and refused to reply by opening fire. Some civilians were killed at Shenyang, but this was definitely not the army's fault; they were victims of armed struggle between the groups themselves. Some bad elements tried to exploit these 'martyrs' to turn the masses against the army, but they failed to turn truth into falsehood because they had not succeeded in compelling the army to use its weapons. But the army did even better; it refused to give solemn funerals to the very numerous victims from its own ranks, especially here in Shenyang, and thus avoided appearing to be a faction demanding vengeance for its own dead. For the army, the vital thing was to stop the violence, not that a dead soldier should be more honored than a student or a worker. And, believe me, this attitude impressed the masses and gradually turned them away from those who stirred up the armed battles."

Pi scrupulously followed his rule of not praising his own faction or putting the blame on any one group. But this attitude, necessitated by the "great reconciliation," sometimes made it hard for me to follow events. Did the groups secure weapons only to attack the army? Did they then fight among themselves? Just what was meant by "a real civil war"? By taking refuge in generalities, while also stressing the extreme gravity of what had happened, Pi involuntarily confirmed the impression that a sort of collective frenzy, expressed in a war of all against all, had taken hold of the main industrial region of China. But my queries were interpreted as a trick to get information that was not intended for foreign friends. Pi gave no details of the battles at Fushun and Anshan, and said no more about the attack on the army headquarters in Shenyang; he concentrated on the general revulsion which these extraordinary acts of violence—the most serious known in China throughout the Cultural Revolution—produced in the working class, even among the fanatics who had just been fighting one another. In addition to "the absurdity of a fratricidal struggle and the hopelessness of trying to impose by force solutions that could come only from a rational discussion," there was also the "insult to the army." Of course, the underlying theme did not vary: the guilty men were bourgeois disguised as revolutionaries, "a doomed class clinging desperately to its positions," heirs of the Kuomintang, and so on. In conclusion, the narrator assured me that the working class soon came to itself after the violence. "Mourning its dead, victims of this new treachery by the enemy, it firmly resolved to create the great union called for by Chairman Mao."

With this lyrical touch, Pi prepared to move on to the chapter of reconciliation; but he took a break, and I made use of it to turn to the two army men, Yen and Hu, in the hope of getting some concrete facts about the events in which they had apparently been cast as targets. Had they not saved the situation by their restraint at the critical moment? But in my hopes of flattering them into talking, I was forgetting the well-known modesty of Chairman Mao's soldiers. Yen replied that the political wisdom of the soldiers was entirely due to the very precise instructions given by the Chairman, by Vice-Chairman Lin Piao, and on the regional level by Commander Ch'en Hsi-lien. Knowing from the outset that the enemy would not be able to exploit the credulity of a section of the masses for long, he and his comrades were able to remain relatively calm. Also, he minimized somewhat the scale of the seizures of weapons carried out by the groups at the army's expense. As a rule, he said, they took arms from the police and not from the army. "For us, there was never any question of having to surrender, like the Kuomintang troops in 1948 after the defeat in the real Liao-Shen campaign. The bad elements who shouted slogans of that kind were mistaking their dreams for reality. As you've been told, their main exploit was storming the military district building in Shenyang. But it was a building like the one where we are now, not an arsenal. So that was a symbolic gesture, and even though it caused casualties it didn't have much significance."

The other officer intervened at once—not that he wished to contradict his comrade, but he nevertheless did not want the foreign friend to get the impression that these incidents were unimportant. "When passions are let loose, armed groups with mere rifles can do an enormous amount of harm, especially when they are acting blindly and attacking false targets chosen by unprincipled faceless men hidden in the shadows. At Fushun, as a matter of fact, they got hold of one or two tanks; it wasn't enough to start a Liao-Shen campaign, but it was quite enough to cause damage and inflict casualties. Inquiries into these events are not complete. Even today, we still don't know all that was planned behind the scenes. These men killed many excellent comrades and wounded a large number of workers, and we must unmask the very last of them because such actions could be perpetrated only by hardened and incurable counterrevolutionaries. But it's true, as Comrade Pi was saying, that their deeds evoked a general revulsion among the workers and a turn away from violence. A fool picks up a stone to drop it on his own foot."

In the autumn, Commander Ch'en Hsi-lien called together the leaders of the three factions. It was the rebel Wang who looked for Pi to take him to this meeting. But this first reconciliation effort led to no great success. According to Pi, everyone present was aware that the workers were sick of violence. Everyone had read Chairman Mao's statement stressing that there were no basic reasons for a split in the working class. Nevertheless, they were not yet capable of overcoming their disagreements. The discussion lasted for two days and two nights but led to no agreed statement. Each faction put forward a draft well salted with the quotations from Chairman Mao to which it wanted to give prominence. The other factions refused to accept it, though the differences in content were relatively slight. To accept a draft from one group was to admit its political dominance and to grant its authors a superior mastery of Chairman Mao's thought. Unable to overcome this difficulty, the participants agreed on only one point—to forbid recourse to violence. Each faction undertook to keep a watch on its troops and to be held responsible for outbreaks on their part. This amounted to only a truce, but it was to start an irreversible process.

In his account of the period of pacification which led to the formation of the Revolutionary Committees of Liaoning and Shenyang in mid-May 1968—eight months after the first reconciliation meeting—Pi stressed the resumption of the study of the works of Chairman Mao under the auspices of the army comrades. He gave figures of the number of books distributed and the hours of study devoted to them in each factory; he spoke of collective readings out loud and of certain methods, aimed at the absorption of the Chairman's thought, whose vaguely religious connotations aroused strange echoes for me. I stopped taking notes and asking questions, but he was not at all put off. Having proved that the reconciliation was mainly due to the study of Mao's works and that the credit belonged to the army, he nevertheless recalled the traumas left behind by the violence. He gave the impression that, in the autumn, the former opponents suddenly realized the futility of their fratricidal strife, and above all the scale of the damage it had done to all of them. This, Pi assured me, was why, if any group showed signs of "starting again," it was at once rebuked by the masses as a whole, and moreover incurred the risk of bearing the main blame for the inexplicable violence of the earlier period.

"For all that," he continued, "the problems had not disappeared, and it was not by chance that it took us many long months to create the new organs of power. But the desire to behave reasonably was so great that calls to violence no longer elicited a response from the masses and their authors were soon unmasked. Certainly, there were some crooks who kicked shins under the table and pretended that they were not to blame. They came to a bad end; sooner or later, we caught them in the act and punished them as they deserved. And who were these ultra-revolutionaries, these irreconcilables? Recent inquiries have shown that most of them were old anti-Communists who had faked their records or former rightists of the anti-Party clique of Kao Kang. That was the real face of these destroyers of revolutionary cadres, these hypocrites who pretended to stand for a complete renewal and wanted to get rid of all those who had held posts of responsibility in the past."

Pi was so bitter that I did not dream of asking questions about these "extremists." But I inquired about the methods of consultation which led to the formation of the present administration. The reply was calm and richly adorned with quotations from Chairman Mao about "simplified administration" and the "three in one" combination. This consists of bringing together, in the executive, people of three age groups (young, not so young, and veterans) belonging to three categories: former cadres, soldiers, and representatives of mass organizations. It was easy to produce the correct number of army men from among those who had been at work in factories or provisional administrative units. Nor was it hard to find representatives of the now reconciled three factions. The question of the former cadres was more delicate. Most of them had been put under the surveillance of the masses and were working at various places. It was necessary to choose those who had best re-educated themselves during this period, with a serious discussion of each case.

But was there not, all the same, a marked antagonism between the cadres and the rank and file? "No," said Pi, "the contradictions between the masses and the great majority of the cadres were not antagonistic. I spoke to you sincerely about my past errors to show you that, although cadres like me were in great need of being criticized, we were also ready to make amends and educate ourselves in the movement. If the troublemakers had not stirred up a section of the masses against us, the criticism from below would never have taken this aggressive form, which was contrary all along to Chairman Mao's instructions. Look around you—at this table you have old cadres like me, workers who belonged to the three rival factions, army comrades, and new cadres like Wang. Well, aren't we all friends?"

Wang was scribbling some notes. He was preparing to make a reply to Pi and, ill at ease with impromptu speeches, was making an outline in advance. He began by drawing an entirely complimentary portrait of Pi—a tried militant of working-class origin, an underground fighter in the war against Japan, a greatly valued Communist organizer who had returned to the northeast on the eve of the Great Leap Forward and done a great job of work. In his career, taken as a whole, his merits greatly outweighed his faults. Then Wang suddenly changed the subject.

"We have seen in China," he said, "a democracy without precedent in history. We ourselves couldn't have imagined it before the outbreak of the Cultural Revolution. Anyone could say and write what he chose, without any restriction, organize his comrades, put up his posters or theirs. Everyone was really discussing the great issues, from boys and girls to grandmothers, as Chairman Mao said. But nobody was experienced in such general discussions, and we were all bound to make mistakes. Comrade Pi has spoken of his, Comrades Yao and Hu of theirs, and now I must tell you about mine and those of my friends. Although we were rebels right from the beginning, although at first we knew how to resist the threats and pressures from the old leaders who had taken the capitalist road, still we have obviously made mistakes. Our error was to imagine that, because we had been right once, we could no longer go wrong. But this uncompromising overconfidence stopped other people from supporting us, and thus they came to form their own groups. As we had been the first, we thought we had a right to take the best positions and be the nucleus of the new power. In short, we put our own interests above the common interest; we showed a factional spirit, we became sectarian. Officially we were for unity, but the only unity that suited us was on our own terms. When the others suggested an alliance, we refused to join in and accused them of being conservative or ultra-Left. From this first error, our attitude toward the cadres followed." Wang turned over a page; we all listened attentively.

"We were well aware of point eight of the sixteen-point decision of August 1966 and we never intended to get rid of all the cadres. Besides, Chairman Mao had warned us against ultra-egalitarianism and ultra-democratism, and we quite understood that we must choose new leaders from among experienced comrades, find capable cadres, and work with technicians who had been won over to our cause. Those who said, 'We don't want any more leaders,' were mostly students, not workers. But when it came to choosing this cadre rather than that one, things got complicated and passions were aroused. If one group backed a cadre, the other group automatically rejected him and looked for material to discredit him and his protectors. This brought grist to the mill of a minority, linked to the students, who said, 'In theory the cadres are mostly good, but if you look at them one by one they're all bad and they should be distrusted.' Besides, we were not only talking about personalities; in each case, we brought in great principles. We had to decide on the ideological nature of old mistakes and draw the lessons. Yes, we put too much passion into these arguments, and those who wanted to push us to extremes and make us fight each other profited from it easily. If we'd known how to unite in good time and free ourselves from our egotism, things would surely have turned out quite differently. Next time, in the second Cultural Revolution, we won't make the same mistakes." With this pledge, followed by a final toast, we said goodnight, exhausted but optimistic.

Everyone escorted me to my room, at the great risk of waking up the Congolese football players who were the only guests in the enormous hotel. Shenyang had been peacefully asleep for several hours. In the profound silence, it was hard to imagine that on this very spot, under my window, people had held discussions day and night and also fought to the death. Perhaps the same thought occurred to the Chinese. Throughout my stay in the northeast, the theme of reconciliation was constantly repeated in every narrative, as though to convince me—or to convince the speaker—that it was for real and that it had put a final end to the inexplicable and bloody excesses of the summer of 1967.

CHAPTER FIVE

1968: A Difficult Stabilization

A Series of Crises

Autumn is the most beautiful season in China, and perhaps Mao had this in mind when he chose the first of October to proclaim the People's Republic. In Peking in 1967, its eighteenth birthday was celebrated in the joy of harmony regained. The festival, apparently, was dedicated to "the Red Guards who astonish the world," and the New China News Agency reported, "The crowd cheered the young fighters as they crossed T'ien An Men Square shouting their slogans: 'Smash the old world to pieces!' and 'Revolution is justified, we are right to rebel!' . . . Special attention was attracted by their immense placards with reproductions of the 1966, 'Circular of May 16' and of Chairman Mao's poster, written on August 5, 1966: 'Open fire on headquarters!' . . . As they went by, they all turned to the central platform with shouts of 'Hurrah for Chairman Mao! May he live long, very long!' " [1] On this day, the "little generals" of the youth went up on the platform of honor (if they were not there already), where they were warmly applauded by the national leaders who surrounded Mao and Lin Piao.

But in reality this was the applause accorded to actors who are

[1] See *New China Notebooks*, No. 265 (October 2, 1967).

making their final exit. As Mao had foreseen, the "little generals of the Red Guards" were to make grave mistakes during the "phase of broad unity," or "consolidation of the Cultural Revolution"— the preferred term today. Seven months after the October parade, when the platform was filled again for the fireworks display of May 1, 1968, Ch'en Po-ta ostentatiously refused to shake hands with the student leaders, thus publicly expressing his disapproval of "their group warfare which spreads confusion in society." [2] Three months later, in July, "Working-Class Mao Tse-tung Propaganda Teams" numbering several thousand men occupied all the campuses and, in conjunction with the "army teams," took charge of the university and high school sector. At the nineteenth anniversary parade on October 1, 1968, the gist of the message on the big placards was: "The working class will direct everything."

The crushing of the Red Guards was rapid, unexpected, and by no means painless. In March 1968 a new top-level crisis broke out in Peking—an altogether surprising crisis, since it put the finger on several army leaders who were notably close to Lin Piao, and on Miss Nieh Yüan-tzu, who had hitherto been regarded as the embodiment of the new revolutionary wave. At this point, Lin Piao himself had to step into the arena, whereas in previous crises he had held aloof from the infighting, at almost the same eminence as Mao. Then the early summer saw a second wave of violence, notably in Canton and Peking, which aroused fears of another "hot summer." It did not spread so widely as the first, but it nevertheless helped to seal the fate of the Red Guards, who were immediately reduced to silence. But to tell the truth, it is hard to say how widely it did spread, for the very reason that the young authors of posters—those priceless sources of information —could not express themselves as they had before.

In fact, the progress of the "consolidation" was measured by the drying up of the sources that might have chronicled its advance. Directly after the festival of October 1, 1967, the rebels and Red Guards were told to stop putting up posters in the city and to discuss them only within their places of work. Like so many

[2] The Red Guard poster which reported this incident attributed the following words to Ch'en Po'ta: "You have deceived Chairman Mao. You have gone too far. If you form a broad alliance, I will shake hands with you again."

other instructions, this was obeyed in a very patchy fashion, but posters accessible to everyone became rarer and more cautious. After the occupation of the universities by the working-class teams, they vanished for good; public places were meticulously cleaned up and the official press regained its former monopoly of information. The face of every Chinese city thus underwent a radical change, even if a few notice boards remained here and there, under strict control, as a souvenir of the period of "broad democracy." It was now useless to look to them for those tales of battle which, even if they dramatized events, had reported many facts and given many quotations from unpublished speeches and directives.

However, the official press did not immediately revert to its former grayness. Despite its ponderous style, which Mao had once described as unreadable, it was still obliged to mention facts which were too remarkable to be completely buried. The battle for the setting up of Revolutionary Committees in all the provinces went on until September 1968 and was directly followed by the struggle for the rebuilding of the Party. The newspapers inevitably commented on these events and even quoted more or less impromptu speeches by leaders. But, when the Ninth Congress of the CCP at last met—without advance notice—on April 1, 1969, the period of emotional and vivid editorials came to a decisive close. Discretion was carried so far that, after the opening of this historic assembly had been announced with much excitement, not one newspaper saw any necessity to write of its progress. On April 28, nearly a month after the opening session, the New China News Agency simply circulated Lin Piao's report to the Congress and was content to record that it had led to a great debate lasting fourteen days, in which Chairman Mao had personally taken part. There was no question of giving a list of the other speakers, or even of stating how often the Chairman had intervened. Films showed him making his speech (or speeches) so that no one could be unaware that he was in excellent health and in full possession of his powers, but nothing—not even a quotation—leaked out concerning his important new instructions. The Cultural Revolution and "broad democracy" were truly ended, or perfectly consolidated, if one prefers that phrase.

It might be imagined that the new leadership, constituted in private but with great formality, would make use of this period of silence to strengthen itself and to unite in directing the "great union of the masses" which had at last been brought about. As we know, things did not work out that way; and the news blackout merely helped to make the prolongations of the Cultural Revolution more sensational. Observers, no longer hoping to get any news from official papers filled with monotonous hymns of hate against Liu Shao-ch'i, turned their eyes to the platform at T'ien An Men, where the leaders showed themselves in public twice a year, on May 1 and October 1. On October 1, 1970, it was noted that Ch'en Po-ta was no longer one of the party. A year later, the whole parade was canceled at the last moment, and it was swiftly realized that this was to hide for a while the absence of a leader even more highly placed than Ch'en. This was not Mao, as was supposed; the great missing man was Lin Piao.

Can we trace a chain of cause and effect between the eclipse of the Red Guards, the dismissals of the "army Left" in March 1968, the return to silence, and the fall of Ch'en Po-ta and Lin Piao? The links are certainly not clear or direct, and the news famine that accompanied these events does not help in bringing them to light. Nevertheless, the outlines can and should be discerned. The record, even if it thins out after 1968, shows in my view that the die was not cast after the dramatic phase of the "seizure of power" at the end of 1966, or even after Mao's declaration in the fall of 1967 that priority should be given to reconciliation and to winning back the cadres. It was the phase of consolidation that caused terrible splits among the initiators of the Cultural Revolution. But it cannot be maintained that it brought old differences to light and divided the "true Maoists" from those who were "to the Left of Mao." The return to the orthodoxy of the previous period—which, let me repeat, has nothing to do with Soviet orthodoxy—posed dramatic problems for everyone, and if one thing emerges clearly from the record it is that alliances within the Central Group were ephemeral, being made and unmade with extreme frequency. These internal shifts reflected the puzzlement and hesitation of leaders in search of a new political balance, in a society which had shown its physical inability to "smash the old world to pieces" and to free itself from the shackles of a certain mode of production and management.

From the fall of 1967 the need to restore a great number of former hierarchical fixtures and to get productive activity moving again was accepted as inevitable. The most advanced elements in the mass movement, unwilling to bow to it, had to be sacrificed. It is revealing, indeed, that Lin Piao and Ch'en Po-ta energetically shouldered this task, and thought that they could safeguard the future by urging intensive study of doctrine instead of pitched battles. Did they believe that, by this method, they could create a continuous Cultural Revolution—peaceful, virtually self-managed, and capable of developing without violent pressures either from below or from above? In practice, this was scarcely feasible; when the driving force of the movement slackened, that of the directing core of the Party was strengthened in proportion. But here again, the question of how and to what extent the Party could be rebuilt deeply divided the leadership, even though none of its members, no doubt, desired a simple return to the system of exclusive Party control. Let us look, however, at the salient episodes of these years. Although they are not as well known as those of the preceding period, they are equally rich in lessons.

"Support the Left and Not the Factions"

Throughout the Cultural Revolution, each phase of stabilization began with an attempt to get the university students and high school pupils back to the classroom. Thus it was in February and March of 1967, after the "January storm," and again in October 1967, after the "hot summer." The Central Group's directive of October 14, 1967, was clear: the universities and schools must reopen without delay and all young people must return to their studies, at least for half the day. In the afternoons they could carry on the revolution by discussing, first and foremost, educational reform and suggesting new methods step by step. They were reminded that most of the teachers were good or relatively good, and new procedures of admission to institutions on various levels could be worked out with them quickly. Since the main principles of the forthcoming reform were well known, thanks to a whole series of old directives by Chairman Mao, there need be no major obstacles to a resumption of classes and a simultaneous pursuit of the revolution.

All this was easily said. But most of the teachers, whether "good" or merely "employable," were still paying for the misdeeds of the "reactionary academic authorities" by having to work in factories or communes and in general were not available on the spot. The same was true of the students, for many of them had gone to immerse themselves in the working class or joined the army, while the others—those who had enlisted in the Red Guard shock troops—certainly had not done so with the purpose of studying better. True, they could find no objection to devoting several hours a day to reading the works of Mao, but under whose direction? Surely the old "bourgeois" professors were not going to conduct these classes! Besides, these young people were nothing but a collection of groups, more or less merged into two or three large factions, which never agreed about the quality of teachers who should be used or about the new admission system for their institutions. The October 14 directive was bound to arouse their suspicions, because it took account of none of these realities and seemed to aim solely at locking the students up in their ghetto again.

But, if the authors of the directive were not guiltless of this purpose, they also had broader intentions. They were interpreting in terms of the educational sphere the slogan "Make the revolution and assist production," which had received fresh force from Mao's latest instructions. In fact, they were saying almost the same thing to the students, the workers, and even the soldiers, drawing a clear inspiration from this idea: the large factions that had been created among the masses should quietly review their mistakes while harnessing themselves to practical tasks, and bear in mind that, since they were all revolutionaries, they had no antagonistic conflicts to resolve. The mass organizations were "the Left," and from now on none of them had any need to prove that it was more Left than the others. That problem, which had caused so many battles, had been purely and simply removed by Mao's historic statement: "There is no basic conflict within the working class." In practical terms it meant more or less this: "Let's all get down to work in solidarity and brotherhood, and together we shall peacefully find the solutions that we need for our common benefit." The great debate was, so to speak, to be frozen—to be resumed later, in a unifying form, on questions that were better defined and more concrete.

Nothing illustrates this new line better than the watchword given to the army: "Support the Left and not the factions." Accompanying documents indicated that the soldiers had made many involuntary mistakes by trying at all costs to decide which faction deserved to be backed, and by applying a double standard to mass organizations. Some were forgiven anything, others were forgiven nothing; those regarded as leftist were allowed to do anything they pleased, while those regarded as rightist were suspect no matter what they did. There was no reason to persist in this harmful path. For the soldiers too, the best way to support the Left was to get down to practical work in the factories and communes, and to organize groups everywhere to study Chairman Mao's thought.

Lin Piao stressed this second point forcefully by repeating his famous warning that the 700 million Chinese would be 700 million grains of sand unless they acted under the unifying direction of Mao's thought. "Central and local authorities and mass revolutionary organizations must organize various stages of study, with the aim of making the whole country a great school of Mao Tse-tung's thought," he said, and put forward as a central theme for reflection: "Combat selfishness and repudiate revisionism." [3] This formula was not entirely new, but Lin believed that it had acquired special relevance since the early questings of the Cultural Revolution. One commentary read: "If we do not struggle against selfishness and make the revolution against ourselves, we shall be unable to carry through the criticism of revisionism, we shall allow ourselves to be ruined by the revisionist element within ourselves, and we shall certainly be in danger of slipping into the quagmire of revisionism." [4] Hence,

[3] See *New China Notebooks*, No. 270 (October 7, 1967), pp. 4–5.

[4] See editorial in *People's Daily* headed: "Combat Selfishness and Repudiate Revisionism, the Basic Principle of the Great Proletarian Cultural Revolution," circulated by the New China News Agency, October 6, 1967.

everyone, whether high or low, should make an individual or collective analysis of the mistakes that he had made because of his selfishness, and should accuse himself rather than his neighbor. If his neighbor did the same, it would be easy to reach understanding. To strengthen the campaign, badges with Mao's face on them were issued to all soldiers and made easily available to the entire population, and this self-criticism on the mass scale was backed by a further increase in the already fantastically numerous printings of the Chairman's works, especially the "Little Red Book."

Visitors to China at this time were naturally struck by this intense evangelical activity, which was oddly combined with a decided political lull; but it also coincided with a no less remarkable upsurge in production. In October 1967, Chou En-lai and K'ang Sheng took an important Albanian delegation to Wuhan, Tsinan, and other places which had been noted as hot spots in the summer. The storm had already passed. Though the Chinese government published no statistics, it stated at the end of the year that all plans for 1967 had been completed on time; this implies that the backlog had been made up in the later months. The year 1968 began in an atmosphere of productive optimism which strongly recalled the launching of the Great Leap Forward ten years earlier.

Since the display of *ta tzu pao*'s was now confined to the inside of factories, it is hard to establish how the explosions of passion had yielded so quickly to this calm. Most of the objective evidence—it can almost be tabulated—shows that struggles between factions had been replaced by happy competition at work, without too many setbacks. But the framework of industry, like that of society as a whole, was still amazingly vague and changeable. It is even difficult to grasp whom Lin Piao was addressing when he urged central and local authorities to organize stages of study. Mao is said to have demanded, after returning from his tour of the provinces, that Revolutionary Committees be set up everywhere by the end of 1967. This instruction, while quite plausible, was not published anywhere, and in any case it was not implemented. At the end of December there were only nine provincial Revolutionary Committees functioning in the twenty-nine provinces, and six of these could scarcely be regarded as truly established, having been set up during the dubious periods of the February counteroffensive or the "hot summer." This makeshift situation also prevailed at lower levels and in the various branches of industry. In short, everything was working, and even working very well, but nobody knew exactly who was steering the ship, or how.

Some foreign observers now claim that all levers of command were in the hands of the army. However, army commanders themselves did not confirm this when I spoke to them in 1971, and it is doubtful, moreover, whether the army had enough leadership and technical cadres to cope, all by itself, with the state administration and the whole of industry. Everyone says that the help of the army cadres was valuable, but this does not explain everything. A better explanation is that the Chinese industrial complex was sufficiently tuned up to run correctly in the unfavorable conditions of administrative upheaval. Official accounts now stress that "the Chinese workers were able to turn their spiritual force into a material force"; some Red Guards declare that they showed themselves capable of keeping the plants going without the help of cadres; others say that the workers, once they had regained their unity, knew how to make the most effective use of the civilian or army cadres placed at their disposal. One can choose among this range of answers, and add, not implausibly, that the workers had no choice but to hold on to their jobs and keep their wages flowing. This would doubtless encourage them to postpone all unsolved problems to a later date and concentrate on production. Yet the situation in industry remained precarious, for any new outbreak of struggles threatened to upset it again; and the leaders of the Central Group were understandably anxious that the universities should cease to be permanent sources of unrest.

Thus, the reasons for the changed attitude toward the student movement are clear. If it, too, had known how to apply itself to constructive tasks, there would have been no dramas and the Red Guards, like other people, would have been integrated with full honors in the "consolidated" structure of society. Speeches by Chou En-lai, Ch'en Po-ta, and Chiang Ch'ing—to mention only the leaders most concerned with the problem—had always testified to their good will toward the "youngsters" and their firm desire to "protect" them. But the student movement would not let itself be "frozen." We need not charge it with "petty-bourgeois" eagerness to smash everything, or with ideologically impure tendencies to conspire, when we recognize that the educational sector could not start functioning again of its own accord, in a vacuum, after the shocks of the preceding years. Here, everything had to be rebuilt and redefined, and nothing could be effectively undertaken so long as the great problems of society were still in the balance. Born to "smash the old world," the movement of the young people could not manage to withdraw into the "little academic world"; it could not content itself with discussions about teaching reforms or new procedures of university admission. Its emotions were constantly caught up by other battles, greater and still incomplete, whose every turning point stirred it into action.

The present account of the "errors of the Red Guards" makes little mention of a fairly long truce which prevailed in the universities from mid-October 1967 to mid-March 1968, or of the circumstances in which it was broken. The students did, however, try during these six months to set up united commissions of inquiry charged with analyzing the position of graduates, defining the type of technician most suited to the socialist mode of development, and examining many other concrete problems. It was a time of détente on the campus, or at least the fighting had stopped. But this did not mean that the students renounced their say on matters of general interest; and when we are told that they were obsessed by "plots," what is generally left unsaid is that the Central Group regularly explained the internal crises by which it was shaken in conspiratorial terms. Now, the conspiracy which was "revealed" in March 1968—the fifth in the series—was on such a scale that it was bound to evoke a call to arms among the students. The campus thus became the scene of a "hundred days' war" which was to be the last in the brief history of the Red Guards.

The History of a "Plot"

At the time when the leaders were carrying through their consolidation, they did not merely require the workers to work and the students to remain calm. They also had on their hands the formidable problem of the "overthrown cadres"—another situation that could not be frozen. China is not a country of statistics, as one has to keep repeating, and in order to know how many cadres were affected by the administrative reshuffle, we must extrapolate from the partial facts published in certain regions on the reduction in administrative and technical personnel.[5] Thus, the number of people to be reclassified comes to about 6,500,000, nearly 1 percent of the total population. To this we must add the "strongly criticized" teachers and the "little cadres" who were challenged in the rural sphere, so that it all adds up to a great many people. At the outset, the planners of the Cultural Revolution wanted merely to create a system of popular control, not to eliminate all these officeholders. But the "January storm" of 1967 presented them with a fait accompli; the cadres had been overthrown on a mass scale. It does not matter much how surprised or dismayed they were by the size of this phenomenon. In any case, at every phase of consolidation they had to issue appeals, repeated as often as their basic slogans, for "a correct treatment of the cadres."

For this, there were objective reasons which are illuminated by even approximate statistics. No branch of the economy could, at that time, profitably absorb all these former officials; simply to disperse them among the masses would have been a waste of manpower. Besides, the administrative experience of a great number of managers had always been considered indispensable to the smooth running of the economy. So the Central Group tried every time to persuade the cadres to make their self-criticism and render themselves acceptable again to their former subordinates, while urging the latter to appreciate their good faith and give them tasks appropriate to their professional level. But in practice this effort at persuasion never produced the expected results, and for this too there were objective reasons. By restoring former

[5] We also possess certain facts dating from before 1959, since China published statistics fairly regularly until that year. Thanks to this, the partial figures from 1968 on the numerical composition of the new administrative organs can be compared with 1958 figures concerning the old administration. My calculations are very rough and designed to be purely indicative; in particular, I have taken no account of the probable increase in the staffing of the old administration between 1958 and the outbreak of the Cultural Revolution in 1966.

officials to their posts, those who had overthrown them were tacitly held to blame and the mass movement was undermined; besides, the rehabilitated cadres very soon showed tendencies to take revenge on people who had "criticized" them too much. As a result, having pleaded in their favor, the Central Group was forced to reprimand them in order to stop them from behaving like "snakes," and this again impeded the process of reintegration.

In October 1967, in the second great attempt at consolidation, the Party center decided to act with more subtlety. It repeated its appeals for a "correct treatment of cadres"—adorned with suitable quotations from Mao[6]—but it also laid down a system of arbitration designed to favor a smoother formation of alliances between the masses and the former officials. Briefly, the system was to appoint outstanding people from the Left in each province or locality to decide the correct balance between different components of the "broad union," and to use their authority to convince, bit by bit, everyone concerned. These "mediators" were nearly always army veterans and thus benefited from the prestige (opportunely restored) of the army, "that pillar of the dictatorship of the proletariat"; moreover, the authority they received from the Party center was so definite that their position could not be challenged. To give an example: in its directive of November 12, 1967, "on the question of Canton," the Central Group stated unreservedly that Comrade Huang Yung-sheng, commander of the Canton Military Region, "enjoys our full confidence and will therefore take decisions in our name to encourage the formation of new institutions." In Peking, where the existing Revolutionary Committee was purged of its ultra-Left members, its chairman, Hsieh Fu-chih, was also given the job of forming committees in the neighborhoods and districts surrounding the capital. Of

[6] It may be noted, incidentally, that the quotations chosen in October 1967 were less laudatory of the cadres than those published in February. The keynote in the autumn is struck by this quotation: "Toward cadres who have made mistakes, we must use persuasion to help them to correct themselves." It is interesting in this connection to compare the *Red Flag* editorial "Cadres Must Be Treated Correctly" (*Peking Review*, No. 10, March 3, 1967) in February 1967 with one from *Liberation Daily*, the army paper, on October 4, 1967, headed: "Strengthen the Education of Cadres and Take as a Leading Principle: Combat Selfishness and Repudiate Revisionism" (reprinted in *New China Notebooks*, No. 268, October 5, 1967).

course, it was made clear that these "trusted men" would act through persuasion by regularly consulting the mass organizations, but this time at least everyone knew who was to take the initiative and who, in case of disputes, could impose an "authorized" arbitration on the spot. The new system seemed to bring speedy results, for nine Revolutionary Committees were set up in the first three months of 1968, as many as in the entire year of 1967.

Yet the road to success was tortuous, and these three months did not pass without the appearance of some negative features. On the one hand, popular participation in political discussions was clearly on the decline, and this was frankly deplored.[7] On the other hand, the disagreements that were no longer voiced by the rank and file were subtly accumulated at the top level, and led to splits and bitter rivalries greatly at odds with Chinese Communist traditions. Indeed, the crisis that suddenly broke out in March 1968 was certainly the most shocking and mysterious of all those which the leadership had endured since the start of the Cultural Revolution. It was not so much that the protagonists were from the army—after all, they were human too—as that it revealed a worsening in personal relationships and a recourse to methods of political conflict still more dubious than those of the past. The flurry of charges and smears that ensued was without precedent. There had never been so much talk of implausible plots and revenges as in this spring of 1968, and China still bears the scars of these events which could easily have come straight out of a cheap thriller.

In its simplest terms, the March affair can be outlined as follows. Yang Ch'eng-wu, acting chief of the army general staff, Yü Li-chin, political commissar of the air force, and Fu Ch'ung-pi, commander of the Peking garrison—all members of the Cultural Revolution Directorate in the army—joined together to get rid of a certain number of "mediators" in the provinces, whom they

[7] The editorial in the Shanghai *Wen Hui Pao* of February 6, 1968, deplored the attitude of some workers "who make baseless excuses to stop coming to meetings" or claim that "anyway no one says anything new." In November, even *People's Daily* mentioned this phenomenon, though more discreetly, since this paper was available all over the world. But in an article on November 24, it brought in a few sentences aimed at those who "think that they have better things to do than to criticize dead tigers."

suspected of being not really on the Left and of favoring the former cadres rather than militants who came from the masses. The three conspirators did not lack accomplices among men of their rank in the army and among old Party members, but they also sought to enlist young rebels, notably Miss Nieh Yüan-tzu. They aimed, it is said, to rehabilitate leaders who had been dismissed for ultra-Left tendencies, especially Ch'i Pen-yü, Wang Li, and Kuan Feng, known to be particularly linked with the student movement. Much later, it was to be "revealed" in Peking that they themselves were among the leaders of (inevitably) the "May 16" group, and nowadays it is added that their "hidden master" was none other than Lin Piao.

None of this was said in 1968, naturally. Rather, the surprise was to see Lin Piao plunging directly into this battle and bringing the whole affair into the public arena. If the aim had been to reveal its political content, this breaking of the old rules of discretion might have been regarded as healthy, but it must be said that neither Lin nor any other leader contributed anything plausible about the deeper reasons for the dissidence of the three army chiefs. Besides, the career of one of the accused, Yang Ch'eng-wu, was so closely linked with Lin's that he was bound to smear his own image by blackening Yang's. The "guilty man," whom Lin described as an unprincipled careerist, had in fact been political commissar in the famous Fourth Regiment, which Lin had commanded during the Long March; he had even distinguished himself at Lin's side during a glorious incident in that epic, the capture of the bridge over the Tatu River.[8] For three decades, they had been found together at every decisive moment, and it can safely be said that Yang owed his promotion to chief of the general staff, at the outset of the Cultural Revolution, to the trust which Lin had always shown him. The second plotter, Yü

[8] The capture of this bridge in May 1935 has been described by Edgar Snow (following eyewitness accounts gathered at Pao An and in Mao's circle) as "the most critical episode of the Long March" (see *Red Star Over China*). It may be added that Yang was not only one of the chief protagonists but also the historian of this epic; in China he was widely known as author of *Tales of the Long March*, a national bestseller for a whole decade. Finally, Yang is cited by Mao in his *Selected Works*, Vol. IV, for his outstanding contribution to the Liao-Shen campaign in 1948.

Li-chin, also a veteran of the Long March, had accompanied Mao on his tour of the provinces the summer of 1967, and one needs a certain amount of imagination to believe that he had "anti-Maoist tendencies," whether to the Right or to the ultra-Left. But what had these conspirators actually done?

The affair apparently began on March 8, when the commander of the Peking garrison, Fu Ch'ung-pi, had the building of the Central Group surrounded by several truckloads of troops. He is said to have planned to arrest certain leaders or to search their offices; the indictment is not very explicit, and in any case gives no indication of whether there were any casualties or damage. The same evening, during a Central Committee meeting, Chiang Ch'ing got a phone call from Nieh Yüan-tzu, who asked urgently to see her on a matter of great importance. They met at dawn in the presence of Ch'en Po-ta, and Miss Nieh's spontaneous confession enabled the leaders to understand the mysterious troop movement of the day before. She admitted that she had taken part in a conspiracy with Yang, Yü, and Fu; but, taking stock of her error, she had decided to reveal their plans and denounce them. Nevertheless, on the next day, Yang, the alleged brains of the plot, flatly denied that he had spoken to Miss Nieh or to other student leaders of any plot to "overthrow the Central Group" or to "rehabilitate the dismissed men of the ultra-Left." The file was then passed to Lin Piao himself, who took charge of the inquiry.

According to Red Guard posters, Lin had four long meetings with Mao before he reached his conclusions. After these summit talks, the official press was allowed to publish from March 30 onward a series of "recent directives from Chairman Mao," which are a landmark in the Cultural Revolution.[9] Naturally, Mao made

[9] The first of these directives appeared in a *People's Daily* editorial on March 30: "Revolutionary Committees Are Fine" (see *Peking Review*, No. 14, April 5, 1968), and runs as follows: "The basic experience of the Revolutionary Committees is summed up in three points: they are composed first of representatives of revolutionary cadres, second of army representatives, third of representatives of the revolutionary masses, thus incarnating the revolutionary triple alliance. These committees must apply a single direction, put an end to imposed administrative structures, have a reduced and improved personnel, a simplified administration, and constitute themselves in a manner that is revolutionary and linked to the masses."

no mention of Yang or the other "plotters"; in his usual way, he
avoided names and did not concern himself with individual cases.
His directives show in essence that he wanted to hear no more of a
revival of the movement from below. He put the cadres in first
place in the Revolutionary Committees, with the militants of the
Cultural Revolution ("representatives of the masses") holding only
third place, after the army men, who thus ranked second.
However, he desired an end to "imposed administrative structures," demanded a major reduction in officialdom, and thus
opened the door to novel methods of reclassifying the cadres. But
the third directive is especially significant, and deserves full
quotation:

> "In the conditions of socialism, the great Cultural Revolution is
> basically a great political revolution made by the proletariat against
> the bourgeoisie and all other exploiting classes; it is the continuation
> of the struggle which for many years has set the Chinese Communist
> Party and the broad popular masses, *under its leadership*, against the
> Kuomintang reactionaries; it is the continuation of the class struggle
> between the proletariat and the bourgeoisie" [10] (italics added).

So the Cultural Revolution was no longer an upheaval on which
no one had ever ventured before, impelled by pressure from
below thanks to "mass sources of revolutionary action." It was a
chapter in a familiar struggle that had obeyed inviolable rules for
many years and could be crowned with success only under the
leadership of the Party. This was in fact the first time since the
start of the Cultural Revolution that Mao had spoken of the Party,
and he did so to lay a striking emphasis on its indispensable
directing role. There had been no question of this in his private
instructions taken to Shanghai by Chang Ch'un-ch'iao in February
1967, for he had then merely pointed out that China still needed a
Communist or Socialist Party. The new feature of his March 1968
directive was not his declaration that the class struggle continues
under socialism—his favorite theme for a long time—but his
identification of this struggle "between the proletariat and the
bourgeoisie" with that between the CCP and the Kuomintang
reactionaries. In these circumstances, if Yang Ch'eng-wu and his

[10] See "Chairman Mao's Latest Directive," *Peking Review*, No. 16 (April 19,
1968).

friends were really seeking to revive the slogans about the Paris Commune and to stop a "consolidation" implemented from above, Mao was very clearly condemning them. This, we can be sure, is what he told Lin Piao to explain publicly and definitely to the army cadres and to the whole country.

However, Lin chose a remarkably clumsy way of carrying out this task. On March 25, he explained the "Yang Ch'eng-wu affair" to ten thousand army cadres who were studying in Peking by ascribing it to a Byzantine rivalry between two "historic" factions in the army. Yang, allegedly, had wanted to fill all the key jobs with his comrades in arms from the days of the war against Japan, and had particularly favored veterans of the Fourth Army which had operated in the Shansi-Chahar-Hopei region.[11] Thus, he had tried to get rid of several commanders entrusted with important political tasks and duly authorized by the Central Group, notably Huang Yung-Sheng in Canton, Hsieh Fu-chih in Peking, and Ch'en Hsi-lien in Shenyang. But his schemes failed; he was wrong, and he was in a minority. He was dismissed, not the other men; they were right, and they were in the majority. Painted in these colors, the affair boiled down to a mere reshuffle in the high command; there had been many others, including during the Cultural Revolution, and they had never been given such publicity. Moreover, the People's Liberation Army is not like other armies; it takes pride in its high political quality and boasts that its commanders have never strayed into cliquishness. When he suddenly revealed that this army had factions capable of such rivalries, Lin Piao appeared paradoxically to be demonstrating that the "unifying force of Mao Tse-tung's thought" was incapable of maintaining the cohesion of the most tested warriors—and this in his own circle. Finally, his account did not stand up on the simple factual level, because Yang's accomplices, Yü and Fu, were

[11] After the Long March, Yang's Fourth Regiment was an independent unit within the 115th Division, commanded by Lin Piao. In 1937, in the north of Shansi Province, Lin encircled and destroyed General Itagaki Seishoro's Fifth Japanese Division, achieving one of the great victories of the war. But after 1938 Yang directed guerrilla actions in the Shansi-Chahar-Hopei frontier region, under the command of Nieh Jung-chen. All the troops engaged in this fighting were called the Fourth Army (not to be confused with the New Fourth Army, operating in the south).

not Fourth Army veterans and had never fought the Japanese in the Shansi-Chahar-Hopei region.

Continuing his attack, Lin, in the second part of his speech, went so far as to reduce the conflict between Yang Ch'eng-wu and Wu Fa-hsien, chairman of the Cultural Revolution Directorate in the army, to a Sicilian family vendetta. Wu, Lin charged, had expelled from Peking an air force commander who had been having "an illicit love affair" with Yang's daughter, at the request of the airman's jealous wife. Instead of thanking Wu for thus saving his family honor, Yang had called him a counterrevolutionary and demanded a self-criticism from him. Obtaining no satisfaction, he had decided to take his revenge on Wu by placing his accomplice Yü Li-chin in the supreme command of the air force. To do this, he set spies to watch Wu and, for good measure, several other leaders, including Chou En-lai. Only at the end of his account did Lin sound a political note; he declared that Yang had lied when he denied being in contact with Miss Nieh, and that he was one of the "hidden masters" behind the groups which "wanted to bring down the heavens" and to throw society into confusion.[12]

Lin's meeting with the army cadres was not yet over when Peking was already covered with posters aimed against Yang, Yü, and Fu, and above all against a nameless "master behind the scenes," still more highly placed, who was giving the trio their orders. These *ta tzu pao* declared that the plotters were really gunning for Lin Piao himself, and that they would never have dared to harbor such ambitions without the backing of a very powerful "secret boss." The clouds thickened; distrust of everyone reigned as in the heyday of the "hot summer." The next day, a procession of 100,000 people marched through the streets of the capital shouting slogans of hatred against the enemies of the "proletarian headquarters." Finally, on March 27, at a giant meeting presided over by Ch'en Po-ta, Chou En-lai and Chiang Ch'ing made speeches about the "Yang, Yü, and Fu affair." Chou's speech marked an epoch in the history of the Cultural

[12] Long extracts from Lin's speech appeared in the Canton Red Guards' paper, *The East Is Red*, July 3, 1968. We may also note that Yang was replaced as chief of the general staff by Huang Yung-sheng, who—like Wu Fa-hsien—was to vanish from the scene at the same time as Lin in September 1971.

Revolution, but for a reason which had little to do with the affair itself. For the first time, one of the nation's major leaders officially and publicly accused Liu Shao-ch'i of having four times deserted the ranks of the CCP between 1922 and 1949, and of having four times entered the camp of the Kuomintang. "Some people," Chou said, "were only nominally members of the Communist Party, while in reality they were essentially members of the Kuomintang."[13]

Chou was surely aware that Mao's new directive, drawing a parallel between the Cultural Revolution and the fight against the Kuomintang, was to appear a few days later. As an experienced politician, knowledgeable in crowd psychology, he decided to interpret it in advance in the most literal sense; he announced that the enemy in 1968 was physically the same as before 1949, that—today as much as yesterday—the people to be destroyed were Kuomintang elements. It was also the most effective way to repair the Party's image at a stroke. From now on, the "high officials who . . . followed the capitalist road" were no longer deviators within a body that could be criticized and that was in permanent danger from the revisionist infection; they were simply Kuomintang members who had infiltrated the CCP. It was no longer a question of "making the revolution against oneself," or of being "a particle of revolutionary force and also a target of the revolution," but of fighting against enemy agents who had, and had always had, nothing in common with the Party. The Party therefore remained an unblemished force that could be trusted to lead the masses from victory to victory. In time, it would become clear that Chou's speech on March 27, 1968, was the prelude to his irresistible rise to the top of the hierarchy, and to the corresponding decline of Lin, even though this permutation took another three years to work itself out.

In the short run, by making this new escalation in the charges against Liu Shao-ch'i, Chou appeared to be guaranteeing the continuance of the Cultural Revolution. Suspected by the radical wing of leading the "third headquarters," and somewhat favorable to the restoration of the cadres, Chou promised that the "reversal

[13] The speeches of Chou and Madame Chiang at this meeting were published almost at once in Peking Red Guard papers and later, on April 4, in the *Red Flag* of the Sun Yat-sen University in Canton.

of verdicts" would not be allowed, and even piled up such accusations against certain former leaders that their rehabilitation became strictly impossible. He crammed T'an Chen-lin and Yang Ch'eng-wu, P'eng Chen and Wang Li, into the same bag by asserting that their tricks had always served the interests of the "great hidden master," Liu Shao-ch'i. In fact, he subtly out-pointed the Left on its own chosen ground: "You wanted to narrow the target and make Liu the symbol of the capitalist road? Well, I'm going one better—I make him the symbol of treason. You were afraid of a restoration and the return of the 'great despots'? I can prevent that better than you by renewing the authority of the Party and bringing back peace in a society that wants no more of your chaotic battles and your factional fights." Even if it was not spelled out, this was the meaning of Chou's speech, and it is highly likely that this tone perfectly interpreted the spirit of Mao's "recent directives" which were to begin coming out three days later.

The only question is whether these implications, which seem quite clear today in the light of the events of the ensuing three years, were understood in this way at the time of the "Yang, Yü, and Fu affair." After listening to Chou on March 27, the Peking crowd heard Chiang Ch'ing tell them in detail how the shady schemes of the army plotters had been foiled at the last moment thanks to the confession of Nieh Yüan-tzu—who was defended by the speaker—and they listened to her cops-and-robbers stories about the "double game" of the ultra-Left. Actually there was not much reassurance in this; adding up the Kuomintang members disclosed by Chou and the leftist traitors contributed by Madame Chiang, there were plenty of reasons to distrust anyone and everyone. After all, if Liu Shao-ch'i had deserted four times—which made him the record monster—and if Yang Ch'eng-wu, the friend of Lin Piao, was in cahoots with the traitor, in whom could one believe now? As the meeting dispersed, brawls soon broke out between the rival Red Guard groups and Miss Nieh herself was seriously wounded by her opponents.[14] The "hundred days' war" was to begin on the campus not much later.

[14] The news of Miss Nieh's mishap was reported by Agence France-Presse on March 29 and 31, which proves that it was very quickly known in Peking. Jean

The Hundred Days of K'uai Ta-fu

"Someone had to stop it. . . . If the masses of workers hadn't come to the campus, we would all have killed one another. . . . They just saved us, and not only in the political sense." In 1971, in each of China's five great universities, former Red Guards used almost identical language to tell me of their last battles in the spring and summer of 1968.[15] The veterans of this strange war were not very numerous on the campuses. These "survivors" were far from proud of it, and stressed the decay of their movement when warning new students against similar errors. Since there had been neither victors nor vanquished, the spokesmen were chosen from among former members of various groups; thus, they testified impartially to the aberrations of each camp. They gave similar explanations freely to foreign visitors, merely refraining as a rule from naming their "bad leaders" (who are not supposed to be known abroad) but making up for this by providing an impressive number of concrete details on the fratricidal struggle. Notably at Tsinghua, where the campus is vast (about two hundred acres) and the science students managed to make very sophisticated weapons—even including a rocket—it took me almost a whole day to gather on the spot the plentiful information about their martial exploits.

One fact was curious. In the factories, in 1971, a veil of shyness covered the incidents of violence, and people—very reluctant to talk about them—at once raised the level of the discussion. In the universities, on the other hand, I had to devise ways to get above simple battlefield narratives. Detailed though they were, these accounts left me dissatisfied. One had to agree—it was obvious that this ruthless group warfare could settle nothing in the educational sphere and still less in society as a whole. It was—as I kept hearing—cruel, fruitless, and inexcusable. But how had they

---

Daubier also refers to it in his *History of the Chinese Cultural Revolution* (New York: Vintage, 1974). However, the wound was certainly less serious than it was made out to be, for Miss Nieh made a reappearance—a short one, it is true—on the political scene in July 1968.

[15] In 1971, I visited five major Chinese universities: Peita (Peking University) and Tsinghua in Peking, Futan in Shanghai, Sun Yat-sen in Canton, and the Communist Labor University in Nanchang.

got into it? Pseudo-theoretical disquisitions on the petty-bourgeois tendencies of the students, as a particularly unstable social group, supplied no adequate explanation. These proved, at the most, that in a society without adequate channels for political debate, the most unstable group is bound to run amok, reflecting in its violence the general inability to solve problems by rational means. In this sense, the student battles of 1968 tended to show that it was necessary for someone to stop the attempt to endow Chinese society at short notice with an institutional structure based on proletarian "broad democracy." There was something symbolic in the fact that a movement so rich in hopes should have collapsed—at least with respect to the crucial problem of institutions—in the very places where it had begun.

Above all, when one listens to the accounts given in 1971 by the former Red Guards, one cannot help reflecting that one of the main stumbling blocks which their movement came up against time and again was the terrible shortage of information, from which it suffered. In 1968, after two years of questioning and struggling to get material on old debates in the Party, the student leaders were no further along than at the start. On the contrary—the mysteries of the top-level crises in the Cultural Revolution were added to those of the earlier period. Who gave them a truthful explanation, for instance, of the fall into disgrace of the very men who had come to visit them in 1966 wearing the halos of members of the "proletarian headquarters," personally chosen by Chairman Mao? Was it not ironical that the students had now to justify themselves for having listened to Ch'i Pen-yü, Wang Li, Yang Ch'eng-wu, and other dismissed leaders, when these men had spoken to them in the name of the Party center, even of Mao himself? One can understand their skepticism when one learns that their papers, which took up the initial themes of the Cultural Revolution, were abruptly condemned for ultra-leftism in 1968.[16] How were they to know whether the whole Central Group had

[16] Certain documents from the Red Guards of Changsha were violently criticized by K'ang Sheng, which earned them great publicity in the West as a program "to the Left of Mao." In reality, all these writings in Hunan (and by Red Guards in other provinces) copied the ideas of Mao and his team in the first phase of the Cultural Revolution. What they reveal is the divergence that had meanwhile occurred between the Peking leadership and the student movement.

changed its viewpoint, or whether they faced a small group among its members who would soon be stigmatized as "despots"? After all, at the dawn of events, national leaders who were then immune from attack had tried to forbid similar documents and had soon been forced to repent. Had not Chairman Mao said, "Those who try to repress the Chinese student movement have always come to a bad end"? At the time, this quotation had been plastered all over every Chinese campus.

The former Red Guards of Tsinghua repeated to me in 1971, "We were too arrogant; we did not know how to submit our petty-bourgeois outlook to proletarian ideology." I was to find this meeting most instructive of those I had in the universities. At Peking University, my questions about Miss Nieh Yüan-tzu were swiftly brushed aside by the vice-chairman of the Revolutionary Committee, Professor Chou P'ei-yüan, a man nationally known for his character and his distinction in science. "She's quite well, but she's no longer here; anyway she's not a student," he said to me laconically in perfect English before moving on to more "interest-ing" subjects.[17] By contrast, his opposite number at Tsinghua, Liu Ping, vice-secretary of the Tsinghua University Party Committee, jumped at my question about K'uai Ta-fu and, after satisfying himself as to the sources of the information I already had, at once asked some "veterans" to come and bear witness to the misdeeds of the former leader. "Since you have already been told about the 'May 16' group, these comrades will tell you about the part which their friend and onetime chief, K'uai Ta-fu, played in that plot," he declared in introducing the witnesses, Tsu and Lin, who had both belonged to the Chingkangshan Regiment but, they hastened to say, had withdrawn from the battle "in time."

Though he looked very young, Tsu Hung-liang was no longer a student and had indeed got on quite well. His new dignity as a member of the Tsinghua University Party Committee gave him plenty of confidence, and he soon showed the qualities which had doubtless earned him this promotion; he was a fanatic for

[17] Unlike Tsinghua, which is wide open to visitors, Peking University receives very few foreigners. Professor Chou did not neglect to point out to me that I was among the first to hear his account of the Cultural Revolution.

criticism and self-criticism. He sketched a subtle portrait of K'uai
Ta-fu to explain the extraordinary hold which that skillful leader
of men had over his followers. At the same time, to strengthen his
account, he analyzed the errors of the whole of the ultra-Left and,
step by step, thus made a kind of reconstruction of the political
background to the "hundred days' war." His revelations had their
own bias, needless to say, but they nevertheless included certain
detailed facts which gave a meaning to the generalizations I had
heard before. In a sporting spirit, Tsu volunteered the information
that K'uai "persisted in denying that he belonged to the 'May 16'
group," and that all the sessions of "struggle and repudiation"
mounted against him by the masses had not succeeded in making
him budge an inch on this subject. But Tsu refused to give any
credence to these denials; the accumulated evidence was conclusive and, he said, "K'uai's behavior made no sense unless he was a
'black general' of the group, which was a real secret society." For
Tsu, therefore—and for everyone present—one had to begin by
accepting the interpretation of the indictment, or else one would
understand nothing of the whole story. I raised no objections on
principle, for fear of depriving myself of this unique source of
information.[18]

Tsu began by saying that, after the defeat of the "Yang, Yü, and
Fu plot," the ultra-Left had played its best cards and was at bay.
So it was absolutely compelled to create a diversion in order to
gain time and regroup its forces. The only sphere in which it was
still powerful and capable of acting in a coordinated manner was
that of the universities. In fact, the "sky faction" of Peking had
regular contacts with most of the ultra-Left groups in the
provincial universities and had a kind of national "shadow
cabinet." K'uai Ta-fu and Han Ai-chin (of the Aeronautical
Institute) were leaders of equal standing; but K'uai, who was
much better known, could order storms or sunshine everywhere—
at least, so he thought. "We don't yet know," Tsu went on,
"whether K'uai's 'liaison post' held a secret meeting in April 1968,
as appears likely, but we do know its plan of action down to the

[18] The American writer William Hinton was received by the same team, and
indeed several times, so he has collected more abundant material. But I did not
know this at the time of my visit, and in any case I prefer to stick to my own notes.
For his account, see the special number of *Monthly Review*, July–August 1972.

last detail." It aimed to expel the minority political groups from the campus by force and confront the Central Group with the fait accompli of a unilateral "seizure of power" in all the big universities. Thus, it thought, the Central Group would be obliged either to accept this exclusively leftist stronghold or to launch a repressive action which would compromise it in the eyes of a section of the masses. K'uai had interpreted Mao's recent directive on the struggle between the Party and the Kuomintang in his own fashion by saying, "The Kuomintang of today are the Fours [a minority group at Tsinghua] and those like them. If they have protectors in high places, we shall be glad to see them intervene so that we can unmask them and fight them in the open at last." The great offensive was fixed for April 23.

Even at Tsinghua, the plan failed. The Fours learned of the regiment's preparations and did not let themselves be trapped. A second attack on April 29 was more successful; the best troops of the Fours were surrounded in the Science Building, in the heart of the territory controlled by K'uai. But the besieged fighters refused to lay down their arms; they too believed that their enemies were the Kuomintang, so they decided to resist to the end. The campus was suddenly transformed into an armed camp; no one could enter it, not even ambulances or firemen. The Fours attempted a number of diversionary actions to free their besieged comrades, but in vain, and these skirmishes unhappily cost ten deaths and several dozen wounded. K'uai, who in any case could count on three or four times as many troops as his opponents, took his time, planning to starve out the surrounded Fours while mustering for a final assault on May 30.[19]

"This date was not chosen for what you might call military reasons"—Tsu wagged his finger as a negative sign—"but to settle accounts politically with Premier Chou En-lai. A year earlier, precisely on May 30, K'uai had presented to Chou a list of candidates for the Tsinghua Revolutionary Committee composed solely of his supporters—they didn't even recognize the existence

[19] Estimates of the numerical strength of each side are rather vague and sometimes contradictory. It seems that, at Tsinghua, K'uai's regiment had between 600 and 900 student fighters and as many, or more, fighters recruited from outside (or volunteers who came along to fight). The Fours had perhaps 300 students in their ranks and an undetermined number of allies.

of the 'splitters' from the Fours—and of cadres who had been eliminated during the 1960's for various reasons. Chou rejected this factional list as incompatible with the spirit of the broad union among the masses, and indeed regarded it as dangerous because the suggested cadres were, to say the least, suspect. K'uai did not forgive him. So he decided to force Chou's hand on the anniversary of his original rejection. He said to me arrogantly, 'If he doesn't accept our candidates this time, the masses will see clearly that he is defying their will.' I asked him, 'Are you sure you're acting correctly? Have you reflected on Chairman Mao's warning that we Red Guards are in danger of making mistakes?' His reply was: 'Yes, I've reflected on it as much as you have, but I see no mistakes along our road,' and he laughed in my face. He thought he was well protected by his 'May 16' friends, you can be sure of that, for he wasn't the kind of wild man who goes lightheartedly into a showdown with a premier."

Having failed again on May 30, K'uai urged his comrades in the provinces to join the battle. The flames reached Canton in June,[20] then Kiangsi, and then Kwangsi, where his allies again began to seize weapons from Vietnam-bound convoys.[21] Then K'uai and Han Ai-chin called a national conference at their "liaison post" in the Aeronautical Institute—this information was reliable, Tsu declared—and started to work out plans for a "second seizure of power" by the Chinese proletariat. "They surpassed themselves this time," Tsu said, laughing. "They went so far as to lay down the structure of the organs of power in all the provinces and the way to rebuild the Communist Party. Do you know that K'uai has never been a member of the Party, or even of the Communist Youth League? Yet he thought he had a right to pronounce on the

[20] The Revolutionary Committee in Kwangtung Province, formed only on February 21, 1968, came up against violent opposition from the "Red Flag" group (although the leader of the group, Wu Ch'uan-p'in, was a member of its executive). The group warfare in Canton was waged on a considerable scale between May and July, and its results were visible as far away as Hong Kong; more than sixty bodies, mutilated and thrown into the Pearl River, were washed up on the territory of the British colony.

[21] On June 24 the Central Group published an "urgent appeal" demanding the cessation of violent conflicts in Shensi Province, and on July 3 a still more imperative order about the situation in Kwangsi, explicitly condemning attacks on convoys going to Vietnam.

makeup of the Central Committee and on its role in society. As though by chance, his proposals were made up of the same rubbish that had been peddled a year earlier by those who gave him his ideas, Ch'i Pen-yü—a great personal friend of K'uai—Wang Li, Kuan Feng, and other men of the Yang Ch'eng-wu type." (Had we met a few months later, Tsu would doubtless have added to this list the names of Ch'en Po-ta and Lin Piao, as is the current custom in China.)[22]

Tsu admitted that all this was not yet known in July 1968. But the country wanted no more violence, and the working class in particular had had enough of this nonsense; this was why the Central Group's decisions of July 3, condemning the armed struggles in Kwangsi, found a tremendous echo among the masses. While K'uai was keeping up the siege of the Science Building at Tsinghua and building castles in the sky about a seizure of power, the workers in at least sixty factories in Peking were already organizing their teams to step in and put an end to the group warfare in the universities. At ten in the morning of July 27, they showed up in large numbers, peacefully, at the gates of Tsinghua; they chanted, "Act by reason and not by force!" and held up giant placards bearing the order of July 3. The Chingkangshan Regiment's sentries, posted by K'uai at all the entrances, hurled insults at them, calling them "slaves of the bourgeois headquarters" and "vermin commanded by Yang Ch'eng-wu"; but in face of their numbers (almost 100,000) and their determination, the students were forced by degrees to retreat.

K'uai still did not admit that he was beaten. "They won't do to us what they did to the workers in the Shanghai Diesel plant," he is reported to have said to his staff. He gave orders to delay the occupation of the campus by all means possible, to gain time to

[22] It is obvious that putting all the dismissed leaders into a single conspiracy makes it utterly incredible. One cannot see, indeed, why the men who had a majority in all the directing bodies should have set up a "shadow cabinet" with the aim of replacing those who were in power. Among the inconsistencies, we may also note that if Lin Piao, Yang Ch'eng-wu, and K'uai Ta-fu had been part of the same team, the last-named would certainly have had no need to seek military information—as is charged—by devious and risky methods; he need only have applied to his accomplice, the vice-chairman, or to Yang, the army chief of staff. But it is pointless to worry about these details when the whole structure does not stand up.

alert Chairman Mao and Vice-Chairman Lin Piao. His commandos set up a number of deadly ambushes for the workers, but,
despite their superiority in numbers, the workers did not let
themselves be drawn into a battle (besides, Tsu added, they were
not armed). Meanwhile, K'uai slipped out by a secret route and
managed to send to Mao, to Lin Piao, to the Central Group, and
to the Military Affairs Commission of the Party an "urgent
message" in which he declared, "A hundred thousand workers,
manipulated by a sinister hand, have invaded Tsinghua University, wounding and capturing hundreds of fighters of the Chingkangshan Regiment. Our lives are in danger and we appeal for
your help, asking you to receive us at once." Only after his return
did K'uai make contact with the leaders of the workers' teams and
suddenly declare that he was ready to talk. In reality, his aim had
not changed. He had simply thought up a new stratagem, to get
all his troops out secretly and leave the occupiers an "empty
town," in imitation of the tactics of the Red Army during the war
against Japan.

So, while K'uai was meeting with the workers' leaders, his
messengers spread throughout the campus secret orders to
reassemble outside the Tsinghua enclosure. Smiling and relaxed,
he agreed to be reconciled with the Fours, to suspend all fighting,
to form the grand alliance, and so forth. Refusing nothing that was
demanded of him, he merely added every time that he could make
no decisions on his own for the regiment, and he would have to
consult the rank and file democratically before signing an
agreement. Moreover, to sabotage the task of the workers'
negotiators, he had their telephone lines cut and created many
technical obstacles. Thanks to his delaying tactics, the regiment's
troops were able to escape from Tsinghua at nightfall. Toward
two in the morning, K'uai also disappeared and took refuge with
his friend Han Ai-chin from the Aeronautical Institute.

At dawn on July 28, the two leaders of the "sky faction" were
summoned by Chairman Mao. Nieh Yüan-tzu, T'an Hou-lan, and
Wang Ta-p'ing also attended this morning meeting, which lasted
several hours. There were no other witnesses or stenographers.
Tsu had therefore to admit that he did not know exactly what
Mao said and could give me only an outline. Mao seems to have
given the "little generals" a very hard time, and declared straight

out that he had personally sent the Working-Class Mao Tse-tung
Propaganda Teams into the universities. It was henceforward
impossible to ascribe this decision to a "sinister hand." Mao then
explained that this was the only way to restore peace on the
campuses and help the students to resume their normal activities.
If they failed to come up to expectations or if the violence began
again, the alternatives were these: either to put the universities
under military control or simply to dissolve them.[23] Tsu was
convinced that "the Chairman said all this in the tone of an
ultimatum, with the greatest possible clarity and severity." But
the impenitent K'uai Ta-fu insisted on giving a biased and
ambiguous report, even claiming that Mao had offered him
encouragement. True, he agreed to lead his followers back to
Tsinghua and enter negotiations with a view to forming the great
alliance. But he blandly repeated that he had been received by
the Chairman because of his "urgent message," and he even put
up a *ta tzu pao* with these words of Mao placed in quotation
marks (though no quotation from the interview was meant to be
published): "A hundred thousand workers are invading Tsinghua.
Your Chingkangshan Regiment is distressed by this. I am distressed too."

Tsu attached enormous importance to this "flagrant falsifica-
tion." He was positive that Chairman Mao could not have been
distressed by the occupation of Tsinghua, since he had ordered it
himself and he was soon afterward to send a famous gift of
mangoes to the Working-Class Mao Tse-tung Propaganda
Teams.[24] By attributing to Mao an utterly invented quotation,
K'uai, an irreproachable rebel in 1966, showed in Tsu's opinion
that "he had degenerated meanwhile into a mere bourgeois

[23] See also William Hinton, *Hundred Day War: The Cultural Revolution at
Tsinghua University* (New York: Monthly Review Press, 1972), p. 213. This
account states that Mao presented the Red Guard leaders with four possible
alternatives: (1) placing the campus under military control, (2) continuing the
fighting until one side won, (3) dividing the school into two parts, (4) dissolving the
whole school.

[24] On August 4, the foreign minister of Pakistan brought Mao several dozen
mangoes as a gift. Mao, in turn, sent them to Tsinghua and this gesture was given
great publicity. These mangoes have been preserved—it is not for nothing that
Tsinghua is a scientific university—and are exhibited in a special room, which I
declined to visit.

politician." [25] However, Tsu had scarcely conquered his indignation when he came to facts which were, to say the least, unexpected. Incredible though it may seem, when the Tsinghua University Chingkangshan Big Alliance Committee was finally formed on August 16 under the guidance of the workers and the army team, it elected as chairman K'uai Ta-fu, that discredited "bourgeois politician," who on July 27 had ordered his troops to fire on the workers dispatched by Chairman Mao. Here, I pointed out to my informant that something in his account did not add up. If everyone from the supreme leaders to the most humble student in Tsinghua understood what view should be taken of the arrogant fellow who had lit the flames of the "hundred days' war," then why had they enthroned him as a leader of the unified university, a position which he had sought in vain in May 1967 and which he had tried to seize by force? Personages of greater experience, especially Party committee Vice-secretary Liu Ping, rushed to Tsu's rescue and minimized the importance of this position; it was entrusted to K'uai only provisionally, and it was not a chairmanship in the true sense of the term but only the leadership of a functional group, under strict control, created with the sole aim of calming people down and bringing all the reluctant fighters back to the campus. Despite these explanations, this climax to the story was far from clear.

Today, in fact, K'uai is no longer chairman or even a member of the Revolutionary Committee of his university, nor does he belong to the executive of the Revolutionary Committee of Peking (the public has never been informed of his expulsion or of the procedure employed). According to Tsu, he was ruined by his taste for conspiracies. Not content with having received a leading position at Tsinghua, he wanted to prolong the life of his own organization, his personal regiment. As he could not do this openly, he called a secret meeting of his staff at the Summer Palace, on the outskirts of Peking, and to be free from all control they held their discussions in the middle of the lake during a boating expedition. Apparently, he had not given up his "crazy"

[25] From this time on, no student leader was a member of the Peking Revolutionary Committee (of which Miss Nieh was vice-chairman), but the press never mentioned that they had been dropped or replaced.

hopes of reviving the flames of violent conflict at Tsinghua and throughout China. "The inquiry into this matter is not finished," Tsu said. "He refuses to say who were his highly placed accomplices, to admit his faults and to draw the lessons."

The story of K'uai Ta-fu ends at this point.[26] With regard to Tsinghua (and other universities) we possess some dates which are worthy of comment. The Tsinghua Revolutionary Committee was definitively set up only on January 25, 1969, and included a mere seven students among twenty-seven members. The Party committee was reconstituted in January 1970, and 95 percent of its members were cadres from the former Party organization. The university did not begin to admit new students until June 15, 1970, and classes were resumed—experimentally at that—only in the fall. At the time of my visit, on May 21, 1971, there were 2,800 students (as against 12,000 before the Cultural Revolution) and 7,000 faculty and salaried staff (the same number as in the past). These facts clearly indicate that the July 1968 operation did not yield the results desired by Mao and that it was ultimately necessary to dissolve the old Tsinghua and start recruiting students, two years later, to rebuild the university from scratch. In theory, the current method of admission does not rule out the return of former members of the student groups who left, at the end of 1968, to go into productive work (mainly in the countryside). Units of labor can suggest them as candidates if they distinguish themselves by their political behavior and their attitude toward work. But this is a different question—I shall return to it in the postscript to this chapter—which is not directly related to the history of the Cultural Revolution. Here we must simply note that, in this final phase, after the failure of attempts to "consolidate" the student movement, the leaders took the deci-

[26] William Hinton had the privilege of listening to a tape recording of a "struggle session against K'uai" which took place on March 25, 1971. It emerges that K'uai, confronted with a screaming crowd of detractors who promised him a light sentence if he admitted his crimes, chose not to cooperate with his accusers. The American writer speculates at length on the reasons for this attitude and considers all the most farfetched explanations, with one exception—that K'uai refused to plead guilty because he was innocent, and had never belonged to the "May 16" group or any other conspiracy. See *Monthly Review*, July–August 1972, and *Hundred Day War*, pp. 276–87.

sion to send the students away from the cities. But they were not the only ones to say goodbye to urban life in the second half of 1968.

The May 7 Schools for the Cadres

"The experience acquired by the May 7 school for the cadres at Liuho, Heilungkiang Province, with regard to the dispatch of cadres to basic work, is very good. . . . We already have the experience of the simplification of administrative structures; add to this the dispatch of cadres to basic work, and we shall understand in a relatively complete manner what is meant by the method of revolutionization of organs [of power] and of cadres. Just recently, Chairman Mao has stressed: 'When the masses of cadres go to work in basic production, they will all have an excellent chance to relearn. Except for elderly, feeble, sick, or invalid persons, all cadres should follow this path. Likewise, cadres who have remained in their jobs should go by turns and in groups to basic work.' " [27]

It was from this editorial note in *People's Daily* of October 5, 1968, that China learned of the birth of the "May 7 schools for cadres." In the extremely vivid report which followed the announcement, the Party paper described the transformation of several hundred cadres from Heilungkiang who were the guinea pigs in this experiment. On May 7, 1968, the anniversary of Mao's famous letter to Lin Piao, they began the reclamation of five hundred acres of land at Liuho, in Kingan District, and in the ensuing five months "they together developed agriculture, forestry, stock raising, subsidiary occupations, and fish breeding, and also built small workshops by relying on their own resources." But even more than this productive achievement, it is the "rapid change in their ideology" that is cited as an example by *People's Daily*. It wrote:

> During the great Cultural Revolution, certain cadres were criticized; they were then filled with bitterness and no longer wanted any responsibility, preferring to take a "couldn't care less" attitude and even seeking a pleasant corner to spend carefree days in the spirit of:

[27] See "Liuho 'May 7' Cadre School Provides New Experience in Revolutionizing Organizations," *Peking Review*, No. 41 (October 11, 1968).

"When the sun rises I rise too, and when the sun sets I go home." But once at the May 7 school, thanks to the sharp class struggle waged there and the life of intensive work, the "couldn't care less" men changed. Rising before the sun and going to bed after dark, they were transformed in the deepest part of their being. . . . Some cadres, desk-bound for a long time, no longer even noted the course of the seasons; they always had low morale and empty spirits. Arriving in the countryside, they breathed the fresh air and lost their apathy. They say: "Since we have been at the May 7 school, many changes have been at work in us; but what impresses us most is that, from being cadres, we have become simple workers, and from being officials, men of the people. Whatever your rank as an administrator, once you take up the sickle or the hoe, you lose a good half of your bureaucratic arrogance."

Peasants from neighboring communes helped the cadres to reclaim the land, to sow, and to build their school, but it remained a distinct and independent unit. It was not an ordinary farm, but a real school "following the example of the Anti-Japanese Military and Political Academy, founded by Chairman Mao at Yenan in 1936." [28] At Mao's demand, the pupils at the May 7 school gave priority to political education, "linked theory to practice," and were obliged in principle to supply all their own needs, as their elders had done in the 1940's in the glorious era of the people's war. True, as China was no longer at war, they had the benefit of facilities which would then have been unavailable. They could buy on credit, for instance, and return periodically to their homes in the towns. They also received visits from their families and sometimes had them stay. In time, when their life was well organized, they would follow a less rigorous routine to make a just balance between manual work and study, between political work among the masses and scientific experiment, between toil and leisure.

After the publication of the note of October 1968, the exodus of cadres to May 7 schools took on impressive proportions. In Kwangtung Province, for example, more than 100,000 cadres left in the last three months of 1968. Other regions, in healthy emulation, could do no less, and it is estimated that over three

[28] See "What Kind of a School Is the 'May 7' Cadre School?" *Peking Review*, No. 45 (November 8, 1968).

million "desk-bound" and "couldn't care less" people rediscovered themselves among the fields early in the new year. Among them were cadres of "irreproachable" quality, and the departures, based on volunteering, were carried out with fanfare amid cheering crowds. At all events, these departures did help to resolve one of the bitter problems of earlier years—the integration of cadres with the masses. The Chinese countryside thus absorbed, all at once, the most intransigent Red Guards and their bureaucratic opponents.[29] There was no lack of virgin land in a country in which only 10 percent of the area is cultivated, and the protagonists in the struggle found themselves removed far from the theater of operations, sometimes each on his own farm, sometimes all together as with the "May 7 Chingkangshan Army," or in certain parts of Hunan and Kiangsi. From now on, the cities were truly calm. However, the cadres were offered a "way to return" similar to that provided for the Red Guards (the new procedure for admission to the universities and to factories, which were short of young technicians). Beginning in 1969, new rules were drawn up to ensure their ultimate reabsorption by the administration, which was now to be rather less "simplified." All the same, *People's Daily* made clear in an editorial on August 18, 1969, that the schools were not temporary—"they represent a permanent system of the transformation and the raising of the level of political consciousness of the cadres." In effect, Chinese officials would always go there in rotation for a number of weeks or months; thus, they were a stable institution in the service of the Party.

Among my hosts, guides, and interpreters in 1971, a good many had been through May 7 schools. Some had wives or relatives who came to see them every two weeks, others were waiting their turn to put in a spell of several months. The schools that I visited, near Peking and Shanghai, did not strike me as greatly different from fairly prosperous communes; the work was neither more nor less

[29] The "Hsia Fang," or "Down to the Countryside," movement had been employed previously, not only as a strategy for restoring order in the cities, but also as part of Mao's continuing endeavor to wipe out the "three disparities": between intellectuals and manual workers, between peasants and industrial workers, and between urban centers and rural sectors. See Stanley Karnow, *Mao and China: From Revolution to Revolution* (New York: Viking, 1972), pp. 446–7.

difficult. But I could easily believe one of my guides (from Shanghai, in fact) when he told me in a good-humored way that he had found this period on the land quite an ordeal—planting rice with three fingers, in particular, was something he would never forget. Still, he admitted that his stay in the experimental rice fields was preferable to the mass-criticism sessions of earlier years. As for the study of Chairman Mao's thought, it is virtually the same in the May 7 schools—neither more intensive nor different in method—as in the governmental or cultural institutions in the cities.

However, according to some recent Chinese indiscretions, there is an important political story behind these schools which are now familiar and well integrated into the system. In 1968, Lin Piao opposed their creation because it amounted in his view to "sending the cadres on vacation." [30] We can imagine how the cadres appreciated this description. Fine vacations, in which one had to build one's own dwelling or reclaim the land in order to eat! Though brief and undated, this quotation from Lin does not seem to have been invented simply to discredit him. As the recipient of the letter of May 7, 1966, he was well placed to point out that its intentions were only partially implemented in the schools that bore its name. Even if they were not on vacation, the cadres remained among themselves and their schools were distinctive enclaves. Was this the best way to integrate them with the workers and peasants? Tempered by work and study, rather than by "progressive fusion" with the workers, they would return sooner or later to their "desk-bound" life and resume their distinctive existence as officials. In his 1966 letter, Mao had not said by any means that the aim of the Cultural Revolution was to re-educate the cadres in this way. If he had recalled the traditions of Yenan, it was to relate them to the model of the Paris Commune, to attack the barriers that separate alienated men in specialized tasks, and to develop in everyone a many-sided quality. In his perspective of that time, the cadre should work part-time in a factory or a commune, while the worker should also be involved in administration and the peasant in industry;

[30] The news of this accusation against Lin Piao was published by Bernardo Valli in *Corriere della Sera*, Milan, June 28, 1973.

intellectuals should participate in manual work and manual workers in intellectual tasks. There was no question then of simply urging officials to take agricultural "cures," in the hope that this work and a Spartan life would make them lose their "bureaucratic arrogance." Cadres in China had been doing that already—in a different form—and Mao's letter did not seek to improve this system, but to create a new one: bureaucrats should do all that they could to immerse themselves in the world of other social groups, and vice versa.

Two years later, when Mao told the cadres in his new directive that basic work would give them "an excellent chance to relearn," he was above all offering them a lifeline after a storm which they had mostly not understood too well and which, more often than not, had left them filled with bitterness. The contrast with 1966 is glaring, but it can astonish no one who is aware of the events that led up to it. When hard facts had revealed the dimensions of the hostility of a large part of the masses toward the cadres, it became hopeless to expect a speedy fusion of these two elements, still less a harmonious cooperation in taking the strides envisaged in the letter of May 7, 1966. All that could be done was to look for the silver lining and institute a harsher system of productive work for officials, which might give them a better image in the eyes of their "subjects." This also commended itself to Mao because the May 7 schools fitted perfectly into his new plan for a reformed administration, certainly less ambitious than the "Commune of China" but not lacking in originality. Since the fall of 1967, the sequence of his instructions had shown that he wanted to rebuild the unity of society under the auspices of the Party and restore the rule of "centralized leadership and delegated management," while avoiding for the future the excessive growth of the Party machine and considerably limiting its role in the country. It was stated and repeated that "no one is in the May 7 schools as a punishment"; it was the cadres who asked to go there to "relearn" proletarian behavior. This may be true, and is at all events plausible if one bears in mind the political conditioning that prevails in China. It does not alter the fact that the schools are primarily an instrument in the hands of the Party, which is responsible both for its internal ideological atmosphere and for the relationships between its members and the masses. And it seems clear that Mao gave it this instrument at the very moment when he was seriously undertaking (as we shall see) the rebuilding of the Party. Besides, by adopting this solution he was doubtless hoping to achieve several aims:

1. in the short run, to end the struggles of the groups against the cadres;
2. to make a lasting reduction in the administrative structure and keep a great many officials working in agriculture, even if by rotation;
3. to give the new Party leaders a new weapon in their battle against the partly inevitable bureaucratization of officials on various levels;
4. to give a pledge to the masses that the cadres would never become a "new aristocracy," because they would be periodically guided, in their places of seclusion, to regain the best Communist traditions of Yenan.

Yet, in practice, the May 7 schools also had certain drawbacks, which their opponents doubtless pointed out in 1968. Once the Party was rebuilt, it would in fact be deciding—albeit tactfully—who was to go to them and for how long. Now, the Party is not an abstract entity, and to say that "it" decides is a figure of speech; the leaders on various levels would be doing so in its name. And, in the light of experience, fears naturally arose that the first nominees for re-education would be the cadres who had given them trouble by criticizing their management, rather than apathetic and docile "deskworms." Besides, the 1968 decision had already shown that the Party was choosing to shelter the cadres from the criticism of the masses and to look after their political level itself—a bad omen for the right of the masses to take a hand in these matters later. Last but not least, the schools were emphatically presented as a kind of "reserve" on which the Party could draw for re-educated cadres, which firmly ruled out other avenues to responsible positions, while in any case the principle of "simplified administration" meant that there were considerably fewer jobs. To add another drawback which may seem to be a detail: all the pupils in the May 7 schools kept their official salaries, which were sometimes very high and greatly exceeded the incomes of peasants on neighboring communes. This could be justified by the fact that their families stayed in the towns, where life was much more expensive, and would have been in difficulty without the money. But the exemplary aspect of the collectivist life of the cadres, in the eyes of the peasant masses, may well have been somewhat tarnished by this large difference in earnings.

The leaks about Lin Piao's opposition to this policy are too vague for us to say that he advanced the above objections. But if these "indiscretions" contain a part of the truth—as seems plausible—it follows that in 1968 his analysis of the situation as a whole differed markedly from Mao's. For Mao, sending the Red Guards and the cadres "with bad attitudes" to the countryside represented, from all the evidence, a radical means of putting an end to the upheavals of the Cultural Revolution and consolidating what could be preserved from that experiment. Lin Piao, on the other hand, seems to have been dubious about the end of the revolution and an overly hasty return to Party traditions; he was apparently less worried about the excessive unrest in the cities and the harsh treatment inflicted on the cadres. He was not ready to accept the idea that it was necessary to revert to the kind of administration of "before the Cultural Revolution," even in improved form. The alternative was to persevere in the effort to "unify society under the leadership of Chairman Mao's thought," and to press on at all costs with the transformation of China into a doctrinal "school," open to everyone and granting no privileges to any social group. If he was indeed trying to urge this policy—and there is strong evidence for the assumption—he must necessarily have been quite averse to plans for the complete reconstruction of the Party, which was the backbone of the regime as it existed before "broad democracy." This would go far to explain his conduct in the period that led to his fall.

A Reformed, Rectified, and Revitalized Party?

The collapse of the Party organizations in the first phase of the Cultural Revolution had not been foreseen, and in reality it was not in the interests of anyone, even of the so-called ultra-Left. Everyone had an interest in the survival of this structure in one

form or another, in the very heart of the movement, so that it
could be used at the first opportunity to serve this or that scheme
of reshaping society. This is quite clear from official speeches in
the period of the "seizure of power," which were already stressing
the new role of a renewed, rejuvenated, and transformed
Communist Party. So, when the Party began to fall apart, it was
no wonder that the leaders were profoundly baffled; you can
transform only something that is still working, not a body that is
completely dislocated and absolutely crumbling. At the time of
the consolidation of the end of 1967—that is, after the elimination
of the ultra-Left—the Central Group recognized that it no longer
had even the means to call the Party militants together, and was
therefore unable to summon the Ninth Congress, which had been
promised and duly scheduled since August 1966.[31] So it decided to
fall back on a procedure which was, to say the least, not
customary: to take a huge opinion poll among the committees and
organizations (which the Party no longer controlled) on the
question "What do you expect from the future Congress, and how
should it be called?"

This nine-point questionnaire has never been published, and
must be reconstituted from the answers which were summarized
on November 17, 1967, in a long official document (for internal
use only). The Central Group then sent the results to all civilian
and military committees in the country for additional study,
emphasizing in its prefatory note that the questionnaire had been
"discussed with great enthusiasm in the factories, schools, villages,
and army units." This gives us an idea of the scale of this inquiry,
whose results were necessarily approximate—as with all opinion
polls—but nevertheless provide invaluable pointers.

The answers strikingly reflect the atmosphere of Maoist fervor
that then reigned in China. Priority was given to this problem:
How could the "thought of Mao Tse-tung," its continuity as a
guideline, be safeguarded in all the Party's actions? Nevertheless,
the suggestions and aspirations expressed by the rank and file in
this regard did not arise simply from the personality cult. They
reveal, in particular, a scarcely veiled criticism of the old methods

---

[31] See *Documents of the Great Proletarian Cultural Revolution* (Hong Kong:
Union Research Institute, 1968), p. 615.

of the Party whereby it arrogated to itself the Chairman's ideas, a demand for greater access to sources, and an insistence on firm guarantees against the perpetuation of former errors. We read in the document: "Some comrades very sincerely hope that Volumes V and VI of Chairman Mao's works will be published before the Ninth Congress meets." Other comrades ask for the early publication of a collection of Mao's instructions given during the Cultural Revolution, and of "a historical summary of the struggle between the two lines within the CCP." Others also suggest the speedy production of a well-documented work "on the theory of social contradictions under socialism, on classes and the class struggle, on proletarian revolutions and the dictatorship of the proletariat," covering "the original developments which Chairman Mao has added to Marxism-Leninism on all these subjects." Seen from outside, it seems that the comrades were asking for documents which they already had in plentiful supply, but the reality was more complex.

In point of fact, the four volumes of Chairman Mao's *Selected Works* which had appeared covered the period from 1926 to 1949 and stopped short at the founding of the People's Republic. Many of his speeches and directives since the revolution had obviously been circulated in the country, and it would be untrue to claim that the Party had hoarded them all for its own advantage. Nevertheless, they had never been collected in readily available volumes or arranged in any way. Likewise, his explanations about the period of the Great Leap Forward and the controversy with the USSR about "social contradictions under socialism" were scattered in the most varied publications, some were unpublished and known only through Red Guard papers, and the ordinary man in China often found it as hard to get hold of them as did the foreign researcher. This situation was distinctly peculiar and may well express a certain indifference on the part of the leaders toward the circulation of writings which were vital to the rank and file.

But was it only indifference? To judge by the answers to the questionnaire, the militants vaguely scented something more. On this point in the inquiry, they made no precise criticisms of the old leaders or of the Party as an institution, but they insisted overwhelmingly on the need to write into the resolutions of the

Ninth Congress and the future Party statutes "that Vice-Chairman Lin Piao is the closest comrade in arms and the designated successor of Chairman Mao." The stress laid on this demand, and the fact that it was directly linked to questions about "the leading role of Chairman Mao's thought" and about free access to ideas, are fairly eloquent. The guarantor of this entire policy, in the eyes of the rank and file, was none other than Lin Piao, and the feeling was that this should be clearly stated and made irrevocable by being written definitely into the statutes. Apparently this was a way of saying that the future of Maoism could not be entrusted without precautions to the future Party leadership, and that its continuity should be ensured—at least for a time, one assumes—by making Lin Piao irremovable.

Unanimous on the role of the vice-chairman, the responses were contradictory on a number of other points. Some proposed as the watchword of the coming Congress: "*Revitalize* the Party organization," other militants who found themselves "criticized" preferred "*Reform* the Party organization." Others rejected both of these slogans in favor of "*Rectify* the Party organization." Despite appearances, this was not simply a scholastic debate or a sterile disagreement over terminology. "Revitalize" conveys a certain optimism about the state of the Party which is not in all ways expressed by "reform," and "rectify" is clearly another interpretation that returns directly to the problem of realities and specific means of dealing with them. "Certain comrades suggest," the summary statement continues, "that rectification should begin during the period prior to the convocation of the Congress; others are of the mind that it would be better undertaken after the meeting, on the basis of a new program and new Party statutes." Opinions were no less divided on the question of who should be responsible for the drafting of the new Party statutes. For some, the task should rightly fall to the Party center, which should then submit its documents for discussion by a "vast number of committees and organizations of the masses"; others appeared to prefer an inverse procedure, which would surely delay the convocation of the Congress.

But who was to take part in the Congress, given that the Party organizations were not functioning and therefore could not select delegates? That obstacle did not seem insuperable to some of those questioned, who appositely recalled that in 1921, at the First Congress of the CCP, there had also been no normally elected delegates. The analogy between these two situations could not be pushed too far, for even if the Party was starting from scratch, it was hard to admit that it must proceed by the methods used at its birth—a meeting of twelve founding fathers chosen by themselves. "Some comrades" (the formula occurs repeatedly in the document) therefore proposed the summoning of an assembly of ten thousand people, "who would fill all the seats in the Great Hall of the People" in Peking. We know from other speeches made at this period—by Hsieh Fu-chih on October 26, 1967, for instance—that this scheme had the advantage of a certain credibility. China has twenty-nine provinces, autonomous regions, or cities with special status, and the Revolutionary Committees in each of these major administrative units average between two and three hundred members, often more. Adding them together, one gets enough people to "fill all the seats"; but such a gathering would be far more like a Congress of Soviets than a Party Congress. So the majority of those questioned inclined rather to a solution "which combines the principles of from the top downward, from the base upward, from outside to the inside, and ample consultation with everyone." Translated, this means the nomination from above of a certain number of delegates (chosen from people known to the Party center); the election from below of army representatives (in the army, the Party organizations were still functioning); the cooption from outside of activists in the Cultural Revolution, recommended by Revolutionary Committees in their provinces or localities; and, of course, much consultation with the rank and file to eliminate candidates who were found to be unacceptable.

Having scrupulously set out the disagreements that existed among the rank and file over practical problems—but obviously related to basic differences—the document identified the issues on which there was unanimity of opinion. The respondents to the questionnaire firmly believed that Liu Shao-ch'i, Teng Hsiao-p'ing, T'ao Chu, P'eng Teh-huai, Ho Lung, P'eng Chen, Lo Jui-ch'ing, Lu Ting-yi, Yang Shang-k'un, and Wang Ming should not take part in the Congress, and thought that it should discuss their expulsion from the Party. They found it still less proper that any of these men should be elected to the Central Committee or invited to join the Politburo: "We don't want them there, even to give a negative example." This phrase, placed in quotation marks, was described as a great cry from the heart. But it was immediately followed by this surprising qualification: "The comrades said clearly that the question of 'those who teach by a negative example' should be dealt with by Chairman Mao and that they would firmly obey his decision, whatever it might be."

This appeal and the ensuing declaration of absolute loyalty to Mao implied a subtle criticism of his method of bringing back the old cadres, which seems to reveal the mood of the rank and file, or at least of the authors of the report on the inquiry. It was not by chance that they brought in the name of Wang Ming, who had long ago taken refuge in the USSR and obviously had no chance of being at the Congress in any capacity. To say that "Wang Ming should never be in the Central Committee" was to hint that there had not been much advantage in keeping him there in the past. It was not necessary to be especially initiated into old Party secrets to know that, at the Seventh Congress, Mao had insisted on keeping this old leader of the "twenty-eight Bolsheviks" in the Central Committee. It was also Mao who had coined the expression "teaching by a negative example" in order to make his decision palatable and convince his comrades of the need to keep fallen leaders in their midst. In this fashion he had won back a number of former deviators (especially among his predecessors, starting with Li Li-san), but he had failed with Wang Ming, who had taken the first opportunity to rejoin the Soviet fold. So at the end of 1967, with the publication of the inquiry and in the context of the "rectification" of the Party, his comrades were reminding him of this experience and begging him in the name of the masses not to give the men who had now fallen (list supplied) the second chance of which Wang Ming had made such bad use. It may seem extraordinary that such an appeal should be necessary. For over a year, Liu and "those like him" had been dragged in the mud and accused of such crimes that it was hard to imagine—at least for outsiders—that Mao could blandly get them elected to a "rectified" Central Committee or Politburo. However, so long as he had said nothing about it himself and had made no promises, his comrades and the whole country felt that there was room for doubt.

Mao's decision—regarding Liu, at least—came in October 1968, almost a year after the inquiry, and at the time of the departure of the Red Guards and unsatisfactory cadres to the countryside. The Central Committee, then holding its twelfth enlarged plenary session, passed an irrevocable sentence on the former vice-chairman of the CCP. It expelled Liu from the Party and deprived him of all his positions, including that of President of the Republic (although this was constitutionally within the sphere of the National People's Assembly—the Parliament—and not of the Central Committee). A special resolution also declared that it had been established by inquiries in depth that Liu, while in captivity, had betrayed the Party five times—in 1922, 1927, 1929, 1935, and 1936. In other words, the fact that Liu had endured exceptional sufferings in Chiang Kai-shek's jails was proof that he had been a secret member of the Kuomintang and not a true Communist. Maybe this reasoning did not convince everyone, but it effectively barred Liu's return to the political scene. Since the twelfth session of the Central Committee, his name is invariably accompanied by the epithets of "traitor, renegade, and strike-breaker," and the verdict can be regarded as definite.

Must we accept that in 1968 there was no other way to prevent this already battered man from making a comeback and that it was really necessary to baffle people by charges of this kind? Is it not true, in China as elsewhere, that what is exaggerated is therefore meaningless? For myself, I am inclined to believe that these enormities were required for the rehabilitation of the Party. The knocks it had taken in the Cultural Revolution were so many and so hard that it could recover at no lesser cost. This is not a value judgment but an observation based on what I saw and heard in China in 1971. As soon as anyone mentioned to me the name of a high official who had been dismissed, the explanation ended nine times out of ten with: "Inquiries have established that he deserted our ranks during the struggle against the Kuomintang," or that he had been a Japanese, an American, or sometimes a Soviet agent. In Shanghai, for instance, it was "established" that the former mayor, Ts'ao Ti-ch'iu, had deserted in 1934; in Peking, that Lu

Ning-yi, once a member of the Politburo and chairman of the trade unions, had been a Japanese agent, and so forth. It had even been "established" that Wang Kuang-mei, Liu's wife, was not a deviationist but simply a beautiful American spy. "In the class struggle, such infiltration by the enemy is just about inevitable," I was told, much as one might say, "Even the best families can't be completely immunized against certain diseases."

Of course, there was never any question of bringing these people before the courts and staging in China the witch-hunting trials for which the USSR had been attacked in the past. Except for Liu, the results of these inquiries were never reported in the official press, so that in some future time new inquiries—equally secret—could doubtless achieve a massive reduction in the number of Kuomintang agents and of Japanese, American, and Soviet spies. Once the prestige of the Party was restored, there would be no further need to make scapegoats and they could be taken back one after another. This was already happening in 1973; the former secretary-general, Teng Hsiao-p'ing, "the second high official who took the capitalist road," regained his position as vice-premier, and during the May Day festivities he calmly mingled with the crowds in Peking's parks. Other and lesser walking ghosts were also well received. But before reaching this stage, the Party had been obliged to endure a truly difficult period, and we should not be too astonished that it had recourse to what may euphemistically be called "exaggerations."

For it had been on a long voyage, so long that the homecoming seemed quite miraculous. In theory it had never lost respect in China, even during that period of unbridled criticism when all its organizations were described as "rotten" and almost all its cadres as "usurpers" infected with revisionism. But in reality no one could believe that a Party of rotten organizations and contaminated cadres could still be collectively good and be a solid mainstay of the dictatorship of the proletariat. It was remembered, too, that throughout this period the Chinese were shooting with live bullets at "the organizational line of Liu Shao-ch'i"— meaning the structural principles of a "normal" Communist Party. The use of this kind of device—a pretense of aiming wide of the real target—was very helpful. It was possible to avoid saying in clear terms, in a formal resolution which would be difficult to cancel later, that the creation of a new framework of institutions in China meant tearing up all the Party's rules and re-evaluating its role in society. The leaders spoke of this only in their private resolutions, and it was not by chance that the results of the inquiry of November 1967 were not published in the official press. So the point of no return had never been reached, and in the latter half of 1968 the leadership team knew that it had to retrace its steps, re-establish the old rules little by little—if possible with improvements—and restore the experienced cadres to enforce them again. But the way would be long and difficult, full of pitfalls and charged with bitterness. To follow it to the end, it was necessary to do no less than to convince people that the old Party organizations had never really been rotten, that the revisionist virus had by no means ruined the political health of the cadres, and that at worst they had suffered from a slight infection of which they had been well cured by mass criticism. To bring off such an operation, after laying bare the faults of the Party and allowing everyone to criticize it, was a gamble. But the Party center judged that it was indispensable; only thus could it emerge from the blind alley in which the movement had landed after two years of divisions "within the masses." And it was able to succeed in this operation by taking advantage of the artifices of the earlier period and by the tendentiousness of the new inquiries into the "real character" of the former leaders.

Yet the most ironical aspect was that this exploit was performed under the auspices of Lin Piao, the man who was least keen on getting the Party out of hock and had everything to lose from its strengthening. Perhaps he played the sorcerer's apprentice, blinded by his "religious" hatred of the "bourgeois general staff," because of his ideas—unification by doctrine and absolute, essential homogeneity of society and above all of its group of leaders. But it also seems to me that, given his position, all the contradictions of the period of consolidation were concentrated in him as an individual. His popularity was then at its zenith, and the mass inquiry of November 1967 was one proof of it among many others. In a sense, he was in training as a charismatic leader, and the masses saw him as the inspired defender of the correct interpretation of Mao's thought—that which gave them the right to "rebellion." But at the same time, Lin probably knew better than anyone that this right was becoming null and void, and that Mao himself had demanded that it should be limited in order to put an end to the tensions and begin the reconstruction on a firmer foundation. Essentially, this was what he had the job of explaining by announcing Mao's latest instructions and implementing them in practice, it being understood that the Chairman ought not, and did not want to, descend personally into the political arena. In short, it was Lin's task to justify the subjection of the movement to the direction of the Party, while this meant a disavowal on his own part and stained his image for the masses. Moreover, he had to settle problems of dissidence—such as that of Yang Ch'eng-wu—and thus take part in the infighting; he could not longer maintain his position above the battle. Those who now say that he was "a poor politician" must be pretending to be unaware that, faced with such a task, the most skillful politician would probably have been ruined.

Nevertheless, if it is true that Lin's chief aim was to obtain from Mao a guarantee against the ultimate comeback of those who represented in his eyes the spirit of the Party machine, and that he slowed down the rebuilding of the Party, he was doomed to defeat. If he gave priority to the issue of men as symbols, rather than to that of the structure of the institution itself, and pressed for irreversible expulsions, then he himself dug the pit into which he was to vanish. Moreover, by demanding a strictly homogeneous Party leadership, consisting solely of men convinced of the line that had been laid down, he deprived himself of any chance of staying in power, as a leader holding a minority view, after that line had changed. But these problems were not easy to foresee on the eve of the Ninth Congress; they would reveal themselves clearly only when the Party had been rebuilt in the aftermath of the Cultural Revolution.

In the course of the four main episodes of this period—the Yang Ch'eng-wu affair, the "hundred days' war" on the campuses, the creation of the May 7 schools, and the Central Committee meeting which expelled Liu—events turned decisively to the detriment of the line embodied by Lin Piao. And, throughout this year, the star of Chou En-lai was irresistibly rising—the more easily in that, as the "modest" number three in the hierarchy, he did not need to guarantee any definite rights to the masses or to be the high priest of Chairman Mao's gospel. The advantages of this position were in time to become very clear.

Postscript
Proletarian Education and
Rehabilitated Educators

After the mass exodus of the Red Guards, the universities reopened under the protection of Working-Class Mao Tse-tung Propaganda Teams and army teams. But they were greatly changed, and the old administrative or teaching cadres were the first to bear witness to this, with a mixture of enthusiasm and a certain type of unsubtle self-criticism. The student rebellion had dealt a deathblow to the teaching methods which they had used with excessive confidence for seventeen years, and they considered themselves to be among the main beneficiaries of a rank-and-file revolt which had at last opened their eyes to their errors. But, by stressing the contrast between their former bad behavior and what they had now adopted, they often gave a picture of the old university which did not altogether correspond to the picture presented to me by the same people or their colleagues in 1965. They even went so far as to give the impression that the old system had resembled that of the Soviet Union, and that it had allowed the professors to lead a life akin to that of Fellows of All Souls College, Oxford, concerning themselves only with their personal work and their academic prestige.[32]

---

[32] Thus, a former professor of history at Peking University (I prefer not to reveal his name) unblushingly told me that before the Cultural Revolution he had had no contact with his students and his one aim in life had been to publish books on ancient princes and princesses, to see his name printed in big characters on the cover. Sent into a railroad-engine plant during the Cultural Revolution, he saw that the workers, who were more meritorious than he was, did not sign their products (the engines); this gradually enabled him to realize his former vanity.

Such accounts, depicting the transformation of the "egotists" of yesterday into proletarian educators, utterly devoted to the cause, are doubtless the outcome of self-criticisms required during the Cultural Revolution, and presumably they will disappear in time. However, here and there in 1971 I found more balanced people in the universities. Their accounts, without contradicting those of the other type, were richer and more subtle, and helped me to understand both the genuine dead end which the old system had run into and the profound ambitions of that which is now being tried out.

Among the people I met who thus refrained from heaping ashes on their heads, the place of honor certainly belongs to Professor Chou P'ei-yüan, Vice-President of Peita (the Great New University of Peking) and a personal friend of his namesake Chou En-lai. Professor Chou is undoubtedly the most renowned intellectual of the Chinese Communist Party; his biography fills several pages of *Who's Who in China*. Believing, no doubt, that there was no need to refer to it, he was avoided the topic of his fairly celebrated personal adventures during the Cultural Revolution and confined himself to the problems of revolutionary education. But before describing his recent writings and my lunch with him in May 1971, I should first report on my interview with Madame Liu Chi at Futan University in Shanghai.

A woman in her sixties with a severe expression, Madame Liu is ten years younger than Chou P'ei-yüan. She has traveled abroad less than he has and has never held such high positions, but at Futan she ruled the roost in the decisive period from 1954 to 1966, and her encyclopedic memory enables her to recall the course of events perfectly. Though her idea of the university has changed a great deal since that time, she analyzes this change without distorting it by simplification. As a matter of fact, I am not sure that she intended at first to talk to me about it. During the collective information session at the beginning of my visit, she

---

Another professor, of philosophy this time, told me with a similar air of conviction that these words had formerly been written in big characters over the gates of his faculty: "Welcome, young student, come among us to become a famous man." When I said that I had visited his faculty in 1965 and the sign had not been there at all, he made an orderly withdrawal, implying that his account was intended for foreigners who had not been to Peking University before.

held somewhat aloof, allowing the former Red Guards to describe their battles in the Cultural Revolution and the working-class officials of Futan to explain the new teaching system, but they turned to her whenever they needed an item of information or statistical data. I was intrigued by this and decided to intrude a little into her discretion during a stroll on the campus. Not having caught her title, I asked her if she was not one of those "experts" whom the student rebels had found to be insufficiently Red.

"Me, an expert?" She was more amused than offended by the question. "I don't know whether my comrades think I'm that, but I'm certainly Red, and I have been for a good forty years. Perhaps some young people were not always aware of it, but were they so Red themselves?" She tidied her short-cut white hair—a sign of her dignified age—before telling me about her political education. A native of Shanghai, she followed in the footsteps of her father, a liberal murdered by Chiang Kai-shek's thugs, and went into underground work at the end of the 1920's as a fellow traveler of the Communists. This lasted for ten years, and in 1938 she joined the Party and enlisted in the New Fourth Army, which was fighting the Japanese in southeastern China. Through the ensuing sixteen years, she "educated herself in society" and in the ranks of the People's Liberation Army, which put into practice Mao's principle: "Commanders teach soldiers, soldiers teach commanders, all learn from one another." It was with this background that she returned to Shanghai in 1954 and was entrusted with a leading position in the Party organization at Futan University.

At that time it had many Soviet teachers, especially in the science faculties, which had come into existence only since the liberation.[33] It obviously followed the Soviet example and everyone took this to be a good thing, especially as the quantitative results appeared highly satisfactory: within five years, Futan achieved a tenfold increase in enrollment, from 400 students in 1949 to 4,000 in 1954, in twelve faculties instead of only four in 1949. Then the Russians departed, leaving their empty chairs but also leaving a structure which had its own force of inertia. At all

[33] Futan University was founded in 1905 by French Jesuits; up to the founding of the People's Republic, it was a private institution and specialized in the humanities.

costs, it had to be reformed and adapted to the Chinese conditions of development, "relying on our own resources." In short, the university faced the same problems of adaptation as other sectors of society, but it seems to have come up against greater difficulties in finding its "socialist path."

"Our reforms," said Madame Liu, "had three objectives: to politicize the teaching; to link it more closely to social practice and productive life; to change the social composition of the faculty and the students. It was a question of training graduates who were Red and expert—a formula with which you seem to be quite familiar—strengthening them against all mandarin tendencies, and putting them at the service of the people. Political courses were given a prominent place in the curriculum of all faculties, everyone was required to do at least two months' manual work a year, and a system of criticism and self-criticism among students was developed so that they would help one another and struggle against temptations of selfishness. Finally, supplementary facilities ensured that candidates of working-class origin could take their rightful place, and in 1966 they already represented 60 percent of the student body. But these overall results were deceptive, and we knew it. Why?"

Madame Liu paused to think a while, and this enabled me to sum up for her my interview on the same subject in 1965 with a director of a department in the Ministry of Higher Education, Hu Cha.[34] "All right," she said, "but since then we have come to understand the source of our difficulties better. The first reason was our insuperable obsession with numbers. We kept a very high percentage of graduates here to use them as new teachers and enlarge the faculties. This was particularly true in the sciences, where we started from scratch and we always had ten applicants for every available place. By trying to solve the problem in this way, we were bound to open the door to careers that were set apart. A lot of graduates were cut off from productive life for good, even if they did some intermittent manual work like everyone else. Because of this, the new teachers had no social practice worthy of the name and, far from becoming proletarian, they remained as bourgeois as the old ones. We criticized this

[34] See *China: The Other Communism* (New York: Hill and Wang, 1967), p. 298.

vicious circle, but we didn't know how to break out of it. The
second difficulty arose from our policy of recruitment to the Party.
I recognized it in hindsight, it's true, for at the time I did the same
as everyone and my first concern was to have as many Party
members as possible to balance the influence of bourgeois
academic celebrities inherited from the old regime. Our policy
toward them was to use them in their specialized fields and avoid
tangling with them over questions of teaching methods, but to be
vigilant on the political level and surround them with new
proletarian teachers and good militants. And here we suffered
enormously from the 'absurd ideas' of Liu Shao-ch'i, who invited
people to join the Party in order to become officials and declared
that every Party member was 'an additional cadre.' In effect, on
top of the special avenue for university careers, we had created
another avenue for official careers. When I came to Futan in 1954,
our Party organization had about ten members, all Communists
from before the Liberation; in 1966 we had a thousand members
and a great number of candidates getting ready to join in order to
become officials. Understand me," she went on, holding my eye,
"I'm not saying that all those who chose a university career were
'neo-mandarins,' or that all the new Party members were
careerists. There was nobody here who claimed that intellectuals
were destined to govern or that 'all you can learn from the people
is to be illiterate.' [35] But when the Red Guards declared that there
was a 'system of three gates' in China separating the intellectuals
from the people, they were right. In fact, a young man could pass
from school to university and then to an official job, and make
himself a distinctive life without even knowing the realities of
society. Once he had gone through the 'three gates,' he had no
further opportunity to integrate himself with the masses of
workers and could not benefit from their practical life or share his
bookish knowledge with them. We wanted to train the new
generation in the practice of the class struggle—which had been
ours—but we hardly ever succeeded."

"All the same," I said, "in 1965 Hu Cha told me about some

[35] She was making an allusion to the Red Guards (as it was later explained to
me), for they had accused teachers and cadres of saying that "all you can learn
from the people is to be illiterate."

very advanced experiments in 'half study, half work,' practiced for instance at the Institute of Technology for Those at Work in Shanghai, and said that by 1970 the Chinese universities would have no resemblance to those in other countries."

"That is true," Madame Liu confirmed, "but then it was a matter of isolated experiments and sometimes of mere intentions. The problem could only be solved when the working class took a hand. If Futan today is nothing like what it was yesterday, we don't owe that to Hu Cha or to people like me, but to the comrades from the Shanghai factories who have come here."

It seemed to me that she was dodging away from the role played by the Red Guards, so I asked her if they too did not deserve some credit for this great change. Rather than answering with a yes or a no, she started on her own story during the Cultural Revolution.

"The Party organization at Futan was headed by Yang Hsi-kuang, one of the Shanghai Party secretaries, and I was his deputy, responsible in effect for the administration of the university. My relations with the students had always been excellent. I lived on the spot, close to them, and from the first of June 1966, immediately after the broadcasting of the Peking University ta tzu pao, I began helping them to organize. It was necessary for them to make the best use of what we called the 'big four': big controversy, big discussion, posters in big characters, and big flourishing of ideas. We gave them the means to start a new paper, Red Spear, and all the space they needed to put up posters. Their criticisms didn't alarm me; on the contrary, I was the first to rejoice when many of them proclaimed that they wanted to be integrated with the workers and peasants and not to become officials.

"Then, on August 11 at ten o'clock in the morning, two students from Red Spear came and put up a poster on the door of my office, which called me a reactionary, a despot, a string puller, a twin sister of Yang Hsi-kuang, and I don't know what else. I couldn't control myself and, without even asking for an explanation, I went and put up my own poster here in the central avenue. I admit that it was violent too. I said that I'd been a Communist when my attackers were not born yet, and that at their age I'd fought in Chairman Mao's army against real enemies and not, like them, against the comrades who had given them the chance to learn and to live in freedom. The same evening, my poster had been signed by three thousand students, which means 95 percent of those who were present [it was August, so half of the student body were not on campus]."

Madame Liu's tone was firm, and for a moment I almost got the impression that the incident was a happy memory for her. But no; she recognized that she had reacted badly, had made an honest discussion with the rebels practically impossible, had "usurped" the prestige of the Party for her own advantage, and had implicitly covered Yang Hsi-kuang, who was not beyond reproach as a director. Once on the wrong track, she was led into staying on it through pride, and she even discreetly consulted the mayor of Shanghai, Ts'ao Ti-ch'iu, "the worst despot in the city." The rebels duly discovered this and drew the conclusion that they must redouble their attacks, since the Party committee at Futan was the weakest link in the system that they wanted to smash. After October 1966 they had a majority among the students, and some Party members (about 10 percent) joined their ranks and supplied them with a crushing dossier on Yang. He shut himself up at home on the pretext of illness and refused to have any confrontation with the Red Guards, who besieged the house for fourteen days and nights. Finally, at the end of November, he gave up, and his downfall was an irreparable blow to the "bosses of Shanghai."

"I stood beside Yang up to the end," Madame Liu said sadly, "but in the face of irrefutable facts I gave in without reservations. I told the rebels sincerely that I was ashamed to have been on the side of renegades like Yang against those who were ready to sacrifice everything for the revolution. I put myself at their disposal to make my self-criticism and struggle with them for our common ideals. Some were inclined to believe me, but others refused, not on my account but from hostility toward those who accepted me. So I had to rewrite my self-criticism to convince the second group, which offended the first group, and so it went on. Through the whole year of 1967 I did nothing but write and rewrite my record, and the more time went by, the less I knew what was required of me. I was questioned about people I had nothing to do with and on affairs I had never known about." All through this period, Liu Chi regularly drew her salary as a higher cadre—350 yuan a month[36]—but, except for an occasional spot of manual work on the upkeep of the campus, she did nothing that could remotely be regarded as useful. Discouraged, she decided to retire both from Futan and from active life.

"I no longer wanted to be an official or even a Party activist, and at my age, in this country, one has the right to retire. For me, the page had been turned. But in August 1968 the Working-Class Mao Tse-tung Propaganda Teams from nine Shanghai factories took control of Futan to get the university going again. They organized a provisional management committee with teachers and students, and one fine day they came and asked me to help them. I refused, pleading that I was very tired and wanted to be left in peace, and that maybe it was better for the new university not to have an adviser who had been criticized all over Shanghai. But they rejected these arguments and told me that, if I didn't pick myself up of my own accord, they would bring a big crane from their factory to get me on my feet. The students who had stayed at Futan also wrote me encouraging letters. So I came back, without feeling sure that I could help these comrades. It was not a question of injured pride, but of genuine doubt of my ability to make fresh suggestions. The workers and the soldiers understood my feelings and undertook a fundamental program of work with me. We discussed everything in a fraternal spirit, from my memories of the New Fourth Army to the defects of the 'three

[36] The salaries of cadres of the Ministry of Higher Education were the same as those of specialized teaching personnel, and therefore, oddly enough, much higher than those of cadres in industry and in particular of cadres in the administrative system and the Party. Though no official explanation has been given of this singular favoritism, it is presumably intended to protect the prestige of university administrators in relation to the scientists of whom they are in charge. In any case, and solely in the universities, a cadre of Madame Liu's status gets over 300 yuan a month while factory directors have a ceiling of 200. As for professors, they are even more pampered and their maximum salary can reach 560 yuan (the average worker earns 60–70 yuan). During the year when they were "in power" (1967) the Red Guards provisionally cut the salaries of faculty and cadres by 50 percent. But, according to Madame Liu, this measure was taken only in the fall of 1967, when she was already in the process of leaving Futan. The present position seems to be very vague. The system is being revised, but meanwhile the older professors and cadres are getting their former salaries, while new cadres have a right only to the salaries of their counterparts in industry.

gates' system, without any advance plan, simply to get to know one another and think things over together. Then we studied Chairman Mao's writings on the excessive length of schooling, the bad effects of exams and pure book learning, and also his directive of July 1968 commending the example of the No. 1 machine-tool plant in Shanghai, which trains its own engineers. After that, we had discussions with the workers from nine factories who had taken charge at Futan, and we organized conferences with workers' committees in the schools and the other universities in Shanghai. And, little by little, thanks to this mutual help 'by means of reasoning,' I understood what the revolutionizing of our teaching system should consist of and how I could contribute to it. In August 1970, when the Party committee in our university was formed again, I was again elected to the working executive."

Madame Liu repeated, "The new university is the product of the working class directed by the Communist Party, and the fruit of the historical experience of revolutionary cadres."

"And of the Red Guards?" I asked once more.

"They played a very positive role in the first phase of the Cultural Revolution," she admitted, "but then they succumbed to the factional spirit and to petty-bourgeois extremist ideas, because they were unable to integrate with the working class." This verdict, couched in the same words, was what I heard everywhere in 1971.

That seemed to be the end of the matter, but I was a bit surprised when, in the session which rounded off my visit to Futan, my hosts spoke about the forthcoming reabsorption of all the former staff and students without mentioning the young people who had "committed errors in the second phase of the Cultural Revolution." A working-class official named Tang, for instance, assured me that 107 professors, 235 heads of seminars, and 948 junior lecturers would be reabsorbed and employed in the new university. Answering a question about Party members, Liu Chi estimated that 98 percent or perhaps even more of the former members would be readmitted, since they had been completely re-educated by the Cultural Revolution. They had been "reformed" in the process of "struggle–criticism–transformation." The Party had carried through this kind of "rectification" of its members more than once and had always emerged strengthened with a minimum of human losses. I did not argue about this—anyway, she was speaking from experience—but I still found it rather strange that almost all of those who had joined the Party "to become officials" should have come through the test of the Cultural Revolution with flying colors, while most of the Red Guards, who could in no way be accused of careerism, had failed it. Had they really been given the same chance to "reform"? Would not the future of the new university have been better safeguarded if it had reabsorbed equal proportions of "old" and "new" people, of those who had in the past found a niche in the "three gates" system and those who had done the main job of destroying it? Two yardsticks were indeed being used "within the people," a procedure heavy with long-term consequences. Which brings us back to the sayings of Professor Chou P'ei-yüan.

Yenching University, where Edgar Snow taught in 1935, is now Peita (Peking University) and undoubtedly has the most beautiful campus in China. As large as Tsinghua and even greener, it looks like a huge park dotted with pavilions designed for rest and reflection. The place where Professor Chou received me might have been out in the country, and seemed to belong to the old China with its ample and richly colored architecture. My host, dressed in a light-colored "Mao" jacket, neatly tailored, shyly showed me his Little Red Book of quotations from Chairman Mao; he tried to use the customary catch phrases without always succeeding, and he forgot, for instance, to recite the epithets regularly attached to the name of Liu Shao-ch'i. Since I noticed this, he sometimes caught himself up and added "this scab" as an afterthought, with the air of saying, "We both know quite well that Liu was a traitor, a renegade, and a scab, don't we?" But this was done without embarrassment and even with a certain grace. This delightful old gentleman really had a great deal of charm.

However, what struck me most was that this learned man, educated in the United States in the 1920's—and by the best faculties of the California Institute of Technology[37]—talked about

[37] Born in 1902, Professor Chou completed his higher education in Peking and went to California in 1925 for four years of specialized study. He returned to the United States during World War II and took part in the American government's program of military research. In July 1949, he was back in Peking, where he became the first vice-president of Tsinghua University. He was well known to be a fellow traveler of the Communist Party.

science like the most far-out of young radicals in America or Europe. A former co-president of the World Federation of Scientific Workers, director of the first modern physics institute in China, and holding chairs at both Tsinghua and Peking universities (until the Cultural Revolution), he is recognized to be a scientist and not an ideologist (he has been a Party member only since 1959). However, he made use of his scientific authority to explain to me that "the bourgeoisie surrounds science with a veil of mystery to choose its acolytes, ensure a division of labor in society, and perpetuate the exploitation of man" and that there is no such thing as a neutral science governed by its own laws, nor are there "mysterious" sciences to which only an elite of specialists can gain admittance. "Some people in the West," he said, "have written that when we made the Cultural Revolution we sacrificed our scientific and technological progress. They don't understand that we haven't much interest in a race to acquire their science, because we are creating a society that will be at the opposite pole from theirs."

Professor Chou then gave me some examples of the scientific aptitude of the workers, especially the young ones. But as my knowledge in this field is elementary, the notes I managed to take were sketchy. Experience at the new university, he said, has already shown that a young worker, however unfamiliar with the technical innovations in his factory, can easily master integral calculus and spatial differential in a few months. Broadening the question to clarify the difference between the two lines that can exist under socialism, he went on: "The first, the bourgeois line, consists of admiring and imitating the science of advanced capitalist countries; the other, the proletarian line, aims to wipe out the barrier that stands between the people and the mastery of all the sciences, and to develop them in accordance with the needs of production. Liu Shao-ch'i's big idea was to import laboratories for pure research—this scab. On the other hand, Chairman Mao, in his letter to Vice-Chairman Lin Piao on May 7, 1966, wrote that the length of schooling should be reduced, that students should educate themselves on the industrial, agricultural, and military levels, and that we should revolutionize our education and not copy the bourgeoisie."

The discussion on the total incompatibility of these "two paths and two conceptions of the building of socialism" kept us busy for a long time; then we walked to the main library of the university. It has 2,700,000 books, of which 1,900,000 are in Chinese. Professor Chou was anxious to confirm to me that nothing had been destroyed and that Western rumors of a bonfire of old books during the Cultural Revolution were pure inventions. First we visited the section of the library devoted to old Buddhist texts and works dating from the ancient dynasties. My hosts handled illustrated books from the Ming period with pleasure, explaining to me the methods that had been in use for a long time to preserve the colors of the original designs. We returned to more contemporary topics in the department of scientific literature in Russian (almost 100,000 books) and I asked Professor Chou for his opinion of this material. His view was that it is useful to the extent that a good many teachers, having been educated after liberation, do not know any Western language except Russian. Aside from that, the Soviet literature is largely based on British or American publications and, except in a few details, reflects the same trend of scientific development.

Further defining his ideas on the usefulness of these books, Professor Chou declared that the proletariat should by no means ignore or minimize the importance of the discoveries of bourgeois science. These did indeed, over the last two centuries, provide a knowledge of the laws of nature. In China it is not a question of "excommunicating" this or that theory in physics or genetics—as the Soviet habit has been—but of looking at the problems of science from another viewpoint. The aim is to make scientific experimentation into a mass phenomenon, so that it becomes the handiwork of workers in the cities and the countryside and no longer a preserve of experts. As this process steadily develops, inventors will be able to go on to theoretical generalizations and make use of the knowledge derived from other societies, in their own way and profitably. In this dialectical process, the impulse must come from below: science, deeply rooted in social reality, will be enriched in a many-sided and original manner, far more fruitfully than in the past. For the universities, this poses in the first place the question: "Who should receive education?" To meet the needs of socialist development, it must be at the disposal of young people already engaged in scientific experimentation in production and capable, after studying at the universities, of pursuing this work and drawing the greatest possible number of their workmates into it. From this follows the choice of a certain type of worker-student and an entirely new method of teaching, which dispenses with courses delivered from a pedestal, qualifying exams, and lengthy secluded studies.

During lunch, with a tact for which I was grateful, Professor Chou illustrated his ideas by examples chosen from medicine rather than from his own specialty, dynamics. These examples, besides, were more striking. Before the Cultural Revolution, medical studies in China lasted for seven or eight years and, despite the efforts made over a seventeen-year period, the country had scarcely one doctor for five thousand people. Moreover, medical personnel were highly concentrated in the cities, which made the situation in the countryside more serious. But so long as Western medicine was taken as the model, there seemed to be no way of changing this state of affairs. Liu's adherents claimed that modern medicine could develop only in large hospitals, necessarily located in the cities. They put medical technique "in the command post" and consequently left vast regions with no medical care at all. Thanks to the Cultural Revolution, the proletarian policy won freedom from the dominance of bourgeois technique, and it was found that a "barefoot doctor"—the term is purely metaphorical—with two years of training was perfectly capable of caring for the sick and making progress through practice, even in remote regions, far from the hospitals. Besides, this allowed the masses to get involved in medicine—reserved until then for specialists—to enrich it with their traditional knowledge, and to raise the overall standard of hygiene and public health. Professor Chou concluded, "We call this relying on the human factor and concerning ourselves with the man who is ill rather than the technical nature of the illness."

From this we went on to acupuncture and Chinese traditional medicine, but my host stated that the present policy was by no means aimed at replacing costly Western-type medicine with ancient methods, even if these were improved. According to him, the two methods of the art of healing are complementary and not opposed, and he cited the use of acupuncture as an anesthetic in many hospitals, repeating that the real problem is the standard of health in the population at large, not the quality of a refined technique. It was the same in other branches of science, even though people find this hard to believe because of the traditional aura of mystery which surrounds scientific knowledge and makes it appear that access to it requires a prolonged initiation. For this reason, the struggle for the development of proletarian science was above all a political struggle against old ideas, to transform the popular attitude toward scientific experimentation. So it was necessary to use political standards in every field—"Western visitors seem unable to grasp this"—and to rely on the enthusiasm of young people unhampered by conservative ideas. For his own part, Professor Chou declared that he was delighted with the results gained in the first eight months of the new system with 2,700 students drawn from young workers (40 percent), young peasants (40 percent), soldiers (10 percent), and older workers (10 percent).[38]

These students, he went on to explain, were all volunteers and came from different parts of the country. Peita, despite its name, is no longer simply the great university of Peking; it aims to play a part in the cultural development of all China, and no longer wishes to be content with representing a big-city advanced sector. True, the level of knowledge among the new students is very uneven at the start, and this creates some problems for the teachers. "We had become used to being the kings of the university; we were at the center of everything that went on"—he was poking fun at himself—"and even if we didn't say so out loud, in fact we treated the students as geese who had to be crammed with our knowledge. Now our motto is: 'We all learn from one another,' and the first thing that we professors must learn is how to teach in a proletarian manner. To achieve this, each of us has to go to work in a big way on himself. For a start, we need to forget our old magisterial courses and lay aside all those specialist textbooks which were useful only for 'cramming.' Next, together with the students, we have to work out teaching outlines which include their kind of practical knowledge and help them to

[38] The older workers continued to draw their wages, while only the young students were housed without payment and drew 19.5 yuan per month for food and expenses.

progress. At the risk of repeating myself, I stress that all this is a dialectical process, political above all, through which everyone's level of ideological understanding is continually raised."

I asked how the students, especially in science, managed to learn at the same pace; inequalities of preparation at school must have some effects, notably in this sphere. Amused, he replied: "You are very superstitious on the subject of science if you imagine that our sphere is particularly vulnerable to these difficulties, more than the faculties of arts or letters for instance. My comrades in those faculties think just the opposite. We scientists have workshops on the campus which enable our students to continue the experiments that they started in the factory and to generalize from them. But for the humanities, the only factory is society itself, and their students have to adopt the method of 'going out and coming in'—that is, going away for prolonged inquiries and coming back to discuss the results. Besides, our students often have the satisfaction of seeing their innovations serving the needs of production, not only in our workshops but also in big factories. All the same, even with us, there are cases of backwardness for all kinds of reasons which have little to do with school preparation. How should we solve this problem? By setting exams and eliminating those who might later prove to be excellent, even better than the others? Or by giving them special attention and individual care to enable them to catch up with the general standard?"

As I had not been arguing in favor of exams, I didn't feel myself to be the target of the ironic thrust in my host's question. However, I admitted that I was, if not superstitious, at all events unqualified to follow a course in science and I would prefer to sit in on one in political theory or the history of the working-class movement.

Slightly disappointed by my request, Professor Chou answered that he did not know the program of the other faculties for that afternoon, and he suggested instead that we go to the student residence hall, to chat with the young people about their studies and the subjects that interested me. I was vaguely given to understand that I could return to Peita another day to attend classes in political science and that he would mention it to the faculty members concerned. Our meeting with the students was rather confused. What I got out of it was mainly information about their social background, their activity during the Cultural Revolution, and how they used their time. They made special mention of their "independent" studies, every morning from 7:30 to 8:30, in which they analyzed current events "in the light of the thought of Chairman Mao." One young worker from Liaoning Province seemed to be most at ease in these random exchanges, but he had only just arrived at Peita and he told me mostly about how he had been chosen to study by the three thousand comrades at his factory. It appeared that his two older brothers had been his main competitors. "They'll be able to come later," said Professor Chou, very happy with the way the meeting was going. However, directly after this, he apologized for being unable to stay with me and entrusted me to professors of philosophy Chao Kuang-wu and Ho Shu-lan. Would he have stayed if I had asked to visit the university workshops or the courses in integral and differential calculus? By changing the program, had I involuntarily cut short my discussion with this very learned despiser of traditional learning?

These doubts bothered me all the more because I had kept for the end of the interview the elucidation of certain points concerning fields in which generalized experimentation could not be undertaken, or did not arise in the sphere of applied science. I was trying not to be like those Westerners who have only one question to put when they hear about the "distinctive" development of science in China: "How about those hydrogen bombs—are you by any chance making them in scratch workshops through the scientific experimentation of the masses?" I had hoped that the general problem of the uneven level of productive forces in China, and of its consequences, would come up of its own accord, and without a controversial edge, in the session of "criticisms and suggestions." The absence of Professor Chou in this closing phase of my visit prevented me from hearing from his own mouth what he thought about these questions, which, if they did not invalidate the overall scheme of the new university, nevertheless called for special solutions.

A year and a half after this interview, in 1972, Professor Chou P'ei-yüan wrote an article for *People's Daily* which was discussed all over China: "Observations on the Revolution in Teaching in

the Faculties of Theoretical Science." In a certain fashion, it dealt
with the problems that I had unwisely kept in reserve. He based
his observations on two years' experience in the new faculties—
perhaps he would not have made the same remarks in 1971—and
made an attack on illegitimate simplifications such as "Theory is
useless" or "There is no difference between theoretical science
and applied science." Whatever the method by which one arrives
at it, he wrote, theory is not merely useful but indispensable.
Besides: "The link between certain abstract sciences and productive practice is not always very clear," but these sciences cannot
be neglected on that account. In short, while firmly defending the
principle of science rooted in the productive reality of society,
Professor Chou proposed that a fixed number of university staff
should devote themselves to pure science. He also declared that
specialization should conform to scientific disciplines and not to
the main sectors of production, and finally that, in addition to
their small factories, the universities were equally in need of good
laboratories.

Western scientific friends who know Professor Chou, and who
have read the notes I made in May 1971, see in this article a proof
that he has come to his senses at last and that China's universities
are reverting by degrees to "normal." I think they are mistaken.
The evidence is too slight to be conclusive, and in any case the
central problem of the new university system is not the place that
should or could be given to pure research in well-defined scientific
fields. Chou P'ei-yüan's proposals aim at an official restitution of
the rights of a small number of highly specialized researchers who
had anyway been sheltered by authority (the August 1966
resolution on the Cultural Revolution made an explicit demand
that they not be affected). Certainly, the Red Guards called for
the abolition of this "refuge" in the name of complete equality
and the right of everyone to have access to all knowledge. They
condemned all research which was not directly useful to the
people and took little interest in the relationship between pure
and applied science; they were not even very clear in their minds
that such a problem existed. But a society in the full flow of
development, such as China, cannot do without a certain
proportion of specialization, or neglect to invest in the "knowledge" of the future, even if this is not obviously accessible to

everyone or immediately profitable. I am convinced that Professor Chou never had any doubts about this. But that in no way prevented him from resting his hopes on a more speedy unification of the knowledge of the masses of workers by means of generalized scientific experimentation.

In other words, I believe that the egalitarian aspirations of the Red Guards have left a permanent mark on the whole of school and university education in China. What really counts is that the schools and universities no longer aim to select privileged elites of technocrats, or to ensure the social advancement of career officials. The methods of recruitment to higher education, the length and nature of courses, the obligation to return to one's original production unit—these suffice to guarantee that the overwhelming majority of students will remain workers. This should lead to a general raising of the cultural level, to a progressive mastery and modification of knowledge which will gradually wipe out the differences between intellectual and manual work. If being a graduate no longer means being privileged, if the relations between teachers and students are really changed in an egalitarian direction—in short, if the main features of the orientation of the Cultural Revolution are maintained—then Professor Chou's commonsense proposals can take their complementary place in the framework of a system which prepares and foreshadows a future society without hierarchies.

It is true, all the same, that discussion of this question is hampered by uncertainties concerning the significance of the current political period, following the Cultural Revolution and the fall of Lin Piao. Whatever one thinks of Professor Chou's latest intervention, at least it was public and clear. In contrast, other changes in the university system during its running-in phase have been made without explanations from Chinese sources. Thus, exams have been restored without any reason being given. We all remember that the abolition of exams was one of the battle cries of the Red Guards, who in this sphere were blazing a trail on an international scale. The symbolic significance of this restoration is, moreover, greater than its real importance, and one has every right to be worried by it. For many people, this even shows that, if a greater number of Red Guards had been allowed to stay on the campus, it would have done a world of good for those "re-educated educators" who did indeed adapt themselves to the system born from the Cultural Revolution, but who neither invented it nor pushed it forward. However, this problem cannot be isolated from the political context of China at the time of—and after—the Ninth Party Congress, which is the theme of the last chapter of this book.

CHAPTER SIX

The Fall of Lin Piao

Peril from the North

When the Russian tanks moved into Prague on August 21, 1968, Chou En-lai waited less than forty-eight hours before flaying the Soviet revisionist clique and calling on the Czechoslovaks to resist "in the name of their rich and glorious revolutionary tradition." Since he was speaking on the occasion of Rumania's national day, he added that Rumania and Yugoslavia were specifically menaced by Russian military expansion, "arising from American-Soviet cooperation aimed at a new partition of the world." [1] At the time, this prompt and irrevocable condemnation had a considerable influence on a whole section of the Left which tended to regard the Soviet invasion as half justified by the "rightist" excesses of the "new course" of Dubcek and his team. But observers did not seem vastly surprised by the violence of Chou's language and his warnings of future Soviet aggressions. No one, apparently, imagined that the Chinese premier could put his own country at the top of the list of eventual victims of Russian militarism.

Seventeen days later, *People's Daily* of September 7, 1968,

[1] See "Chinese Government and People Strongly Condemn Soviet Revisionist Clique's Armed Occupation of Czechoslovakia," *Peking Review*, supplement to No. 34 (August 23, 1968).

announced, on the home front, the victorious conclusion of the battle for the establishment of Revolutionary Committees in the provinces. "The whole country is Red," the editorial declared triumphantly, noting the creation on the previous day of committees in Tibet and Sinkiang, "the frontier outposts of the southwest and the northwest." [2] A mass meeting was at once held in Peking to celebrate this "total victory" of the Cultural Revolution, and Chou En-lai made another long and detailed speech. Directly after him, Chiang Ch'ing began her speech in a curious way by saying that she had been asked to speak "at the last minute" and had been a bit surprised by the compliment. Despite this unusual opening, the complete text of her speech was duly circulated by the New China News Agency and in special bulletins from Chinese embassies abroad.

Western commentators gained the impression that Chiang Ch'ing had been invited to give a left-wing endorsement to the rather hasty closing operation in the long debate on the installation of Revolutionary Committees in the provinces. No one, however, made a connection between this internal Chinese decision and the warnings of Soviet plans for military expansion. Nor was anyone surprised to see the special headlines which the Chinese press gave to the "condemnation of Soviet aggression against Czechoslovakia," while news of the development of the Cultural Revolution was becoming thinner. This even seemed to be normal, since the Chinese, according to their own statements, were to devote themselves from now on to "the building and consolidation of Party organizations," and it was well known that they had never been in the habit of discussing such topics in public.

But on March 3, 1969, the world heard, both from Moscow and from Peking, that "a blood-stained incident of extreme seriousness" had occurred on the Chinese-Soviet frontier, in the vicinity of the island called Damansky in Russian and Chenpao in Chinese. Moscow published its note of protest against the violation of its territory by Chinese frontier guards. Peking replied in kind and protested strongly against Soviet aggression. Each

[2] This editorial was reprinted in the information bulletin of the Chinese Embassy in Paris, No. 75 (September 20, 1968).

country loudly declared that this virtually deserted island in the Ussuri River came under its control and that frontier guards of the other nation had no business there. Each decided to make good its rights at any cost, and the battle on the Ussuri continued until it looked like it would escalate to a real war. The Soviet leaders, beating the patriotic drums for all they were worth, shouted that China was seeking to grab a million square miles of Russia's sacred soil, and published in the press pictures of Chinese prisoners which might have stirred the memories of anyone who had seen Bolshevik and Slavic prisoners depicted in the Nazi newspaper *Völkischer Beobachter* in World war II. The USSR declared that it would never yield to "these creatures devoid of critical power and totally indoctrinated," and showed films to demonstrate its "defensive" power in the Siberian east. These documentaries made a strong impression on the outside world. To see them was to recognize that the Soviet Army was probably the best equipped in the world, and that, in spite of Czechoslovakia, the bulk of its strength was still concentrated on the Chinese frontier—and had been for some time, for these countless launching pads for ultramodern rockets had not been built on the Ussuri in a hurry.[3]

Peking, nevertheless, continued to declare that the aggressors from the north had been "severely mauled by the frontier defense forces," and even showed photographs of weapons abandoned by Soviet troops in their "disorderly flight." [4] As for the origins of the dispute, the Chinese government stuck to its first version: China's title to Chenpao Island had never yet been disputed, even by Czarist Russia, which had, from 1850 onward, imposed unequal treaties on the old Imperial Chinese regime. According to Peking, Czarist Russia had in effect taken more than a half million square miles of Chinese territory—"roughly the equivalent of twelve Czechoslovakias"—but in spite of this historical fact, recognized by Lenin, China was not demanding the restitution of this territory. It proposed a negotiated agreement on all frontier disputes and, pointing out that China had always given full

[3] A Soviet documentary film was shown by most of the television networks of Western Europe. I saw it in Italy, in an RAI program on the Ussuri conflict.

[4] On March 21, 1969, the New China News Agency published five photographs of the battle for Chenpao Island. The fifth of these showed "part of the Soviet material seized by Chinese fighters."

publicity to Soviet diplomatic notes, invited Moscow to do the same and publish the Chinese government's statements in full in the Soviet press: "If you don't have a guilty conscience, if you are not cowards, if you are not trying to hide the truth from the Soviet people, then kindly do it." [5]

The guns were still thundering on the Ussuri when, on April 1, the Ninth Congress of the CCP met in Peking without any advance announcement. This time, the link between cause and effect was clear. It was easy to guess that the 1,512 delegates had been nominated (or in some cases elected) under the spur of urgency, and that a high proportion of the closed sessions was devoted to the military threat "coming from the north." In his programmatic report, published after the end of the Congress, Lin Piao stressed that "the Soviet government persists in its aggressive posture," but that it would never succeed in scaring the Chinese people.[6] Meanwhile the fighting on the Ussuri died down (though it was not known exactly who came out as master of Chenpao or Damansky Island), but the Chinese Communist leaders were clearly convinced that this was only a truce. They called on the nation to prepare for the possibility of war—"be it a small-scale war, a large-scale war, or a nuclear war." [7] Though they did not dot the i's, they gave the impression that they now saw the threat of war as coming from the USSR rather than from the United States. Indeed, the Americans appeared to be attempting to wind up the Vietnam War, and certainly had no intention of reversing this process to the extent of attacking China.

The events of the next three years were to show that the

[5] See "New China News Agency Note on the Soviet Government's Statement of March 29," circulated by the Chinese Embassy in Paris.

[6] To show clearly that the Peking government was "not afraid," Lin Piao mentioned this incident: "Our frontier guards, in their task of legitimate defense, have inflicted a well-deserved punishment on the aggressors. To get out of the mess, Kosygin asked on March 21 to speak to our leaders on the telephone. On March 22 our government replied in a memorandum: 'Given the present state of relations between China and the USSR, the use of the telephone for communication is not appropriate. If the Soviet government has anything to say, it is requested to address the Chinese government officially through diplomatic channels.'"

[7] This phrase accompanied the call for readiness in a large number of Chinese official statements.

outlook of the directing group in Peking had indeed changed. A discreet renewal of contacts between China and the United States led to "table-tennis diplomacy"; then Dr. Henry Kissinger made his unexpected trip to Peking, which enabled President Nixon, in February 1972, to make a personal visit to a country where there was still no American ambassador. The new departure in Chinese diplomacy was almost equally spectacular in other spheres of world policy. In September 1971 China made a triumphal entry into the United Nations. It received the prime minister of Japan and renewed relations with that country, as well as with a great many nations of Europe, Asia, Africa, and Latin America, avoiding so far as possible any discrimination.

In the light of these developments, many commentators reached the conclusion that the "great change of course" had started from the day of the Soviet invasion of Czechoslovakia. Events made it clear that Mao and Chou, obsessed by the "threat from the north," were impelled to call a halt to the Cultural Revolution in order to stabilize the home front and give themselves some diplomatic elbowroom (necessarily very limited in the preceding period because of the irruption of the Red Guards into national and international affairs). From then on, it seemed credible that this orientation would meet with strong resistance from Lin Piao and his supporters in the Party, not because they were pro-Soviet—that could be entirely ruled out—but because they did not accept the pace and the methods of the restoration of order which put a stop to the Cultural Revolution. Even Chiang Ch'ing's impromptu speech on September 7, 1968, assumed its full significance in hindsight; we now know that the speaker, with her "Left" reputation, has come to terms with Chou En-lai, and she is—with Chang Ch'un-ch'iao and Yao Wen-yuan—one of the three survivors of the old Central Group for the Cultural Revolution.

Of course, the theory based on this chain of events, from the entry into Prague of the Soviet tanks to Nixon's visit to Peking, by way of the Ussuri battle and the fall of Lin Piao, lays enormous stress on international events—of which we naturally have some knowledge—at the expense of internal politics, on which the Chinese are virtually silent. Nevertheless, it makes a good deal of sense and, as we have few keys to the deciphering of the final phase of the Cultural Revolution, we must be content with it—taking care, however, to place it in the larger context of relationships between China and the rest of the world before, during, and at the close of the Cultural Revolution.

The Vietnamese Ordeal

Even an outline account must go back as far as the Tonkin Gulf incident of August 1964, a decisive landmark in the Vietnam War. Up to then, it was well known that three successive American Presidents—Eisenhower, Kennedy, and Johnson—had given a decidedly unilateral interpretation to the Geneva agreements on the temporary division of Vietnam, and were bent on holding the southern portion, controlled by their allies in Saigon, for the "free world." But after August 1964 it had to be recognized that the Johnson administration was ready to raise the stakes beyond any foreseeable limit in the hope of winning by force of arms a battle that had been lost in the political sphere. Using as a pretext a Vietnamese attack on the *Maddox*—one of the U.S. Navy's biggest and least vulnerable warships—the President ordered the first bombing raids on the Democratic Republic of Vietnam and secured from Congress a blank check for all methods of waging war. From this moment, it was clear that the United States intended to use Vietnam as a global demonstration of readiness to crush any revolutionary war by force, and was indifferent to the political price to be paid in its relations with various nations and in world opinion. This challenge was made primarily to China, who had backed the Vietnamese from the outset, but also to the Soviet Union, standing outside the conflict but nevertheless obliged to react to this unprecedented violation of the frontiers of the Communist bloc.

Khrushchev, however, decided not to pick up the gauntlet. He confined himself to bringing the Tonkin Gulf incident before the United Nations, thus choosing to give the affair an "honorable" burial. Blinded by his hostility toward China, he seriously believed that North Vietnamese fishermen, manipulated by Peking, had tried to sink the *Maddox*.[8] This "mistake" certainly gave an

---

[8] It is noteworthy that the press in Eastern European countries waited several days before reporting the bombing of North Vietnam and that Communist papers

additional weapon—perhaps even a decisive one—to his comrades in the Kremlin who were out to get rid of him by any means at hand. In any case, directly after his fall on October 15, 1964, the new Soviet team decided to renew good relations with North Vietnam and to counter American aggression in a more energetic manner.[9] Chou En-lai was duly informed of this in Moscow at the time of his highly unexpected and very welcome appearance on the occasion of the forty-seventh anniversary of the October Revolution.[10] The American challenge had apparently restored the solidarity of the two nuclear powers of the East (China had achieved this status on the very day of Khrushchev's fall, perhaps celebrating this event by a fireworks display of several kilotons).

However, nothing halted the American drive, and in early 1965 it set new records in the assault on Vietnam. I was in Peking that February. Like other journalists, I heard that Kosygin had stopped off there on February 6 while on his way to Hanoi with a strong team of Soviet generals. The news of the resumption of the American bombing, which reached us next day, at first seemed incredible. Was it possible that the Johnson administration could take the risk of provoking the leaders of the Soviet superpower in this way? But the news was confirmed, and on the evening of February 7 a crowd of Chinese demonstrators shouted its indignation against "the crimes of Johnson, today's Hitler." This demonstration went on without a break until its climax three days later, on February 10, when all the columns converged in the late morning at a great meeting on T'ien An Men Square. In the afternoon, Kosygin was expected in Peking again, and this time the press was invited to the airport.

The welcoming ceremony was very simple—this was not a state visit—but the atmosphere seemed good, almost relaxed. In our presence, Chou En-lai chatted with Kosygin about the weather in

in the West took an equally cautious attitude. Forced to mention it at once, they were careful not to denounce it. No Western Communist Party organized the slightest demonstration of solidarity with the Vietnamese on the morrow of the Tonkin Gulf incident.

[9] For Soviet-Vietnamese relations in Khrushchev's time and after his fall, see Aldo Natoli's account in *Il Manifesto*, November 25, 1972, reprinted in *Le Monde*.

[10] See my interview with Chou published as an appendix to *China: The Other Communism* (New York: Hill and Wang, 1967).

Hanoi, and after shaking hands with all the Russian generals—and thus setting off a discreet tinkling of the shining medals which ornamented their ample chests—he took Kosygin to meet Mao. Next day, a photo in *People's Daily* told us that the Soviet leader had been received by the Chinese Chairman, surrounded by a full muster of his team. We learned nothing more; the paper gave absolutely no report of their discussion. There was not even the smallest or most Delphic phrase as food for speculation.

In early March, another set of photos in *People's Daily* told us that the Moscow police had brutally broken up an anti-American demonstration by Chinese, Vietnamese, and Korean students. The caption was terse but eloquent: "Who are your allies? Who are your enemies?" Then the Chinese students, victims of Soviet repression, began to return to Peking and the press broke this partial silence. The great polemic against the revisionists was vigorously renewed, in spite of the Vietnam War and no doubt even because of it.

On March 17, Chou granted me a long interview and unburdened himself on this burning subject. "The American aggression against the Democratic Republic of Vietnam," he said, "is an aggression against the Socialist camp in its entirety. This being so, all of us have the duty to help the N.L.F. of South Vietnam and the D.R.V., in accordance with the international engagements we have undertaken." The stress that he placed on "us" and on the duty of "all" implied that China and the USSR were learning to work together, forgetting their differences. Was the Vietnam War, then, reforging the unity of the bloc, or at least drawing China and the USSR nearer together? Chou replied:

> To talk of drawing nearer or farther apart is only a way of putting it. More important is to look at the roots of the question. If the Americans confine themselves to frightening people, some will allow themselves to be frightened, others not. This will produce disagreement, very great disagreement, between the first group, who fear imperialism, and the others, who are determined to stand up to it. But if the Americans are not content with threatening gestures and really want to provoke a wider conflict, then the Chinese and Russian people will close ranks. That is the truth. Remember that and you will see that history will bear it out.[11]

[11] See the *New Statesman*, London, March 26, 1965, and *China: The Other Communism*, p. 449.

However, after telling me with conviction that the Americans were "in for some surprises," Chou showed no concern for the feelings of his potential Soviet allies. He treated me to a complete indictment of Khrushchev and gave me clearly to understand that his successors were not much better. But it was only in appearance that this attitude was contradictory or undiplomatic. In fact, as Chou saw it, the Americans had already wiped out the frontier between the two Vietnams and, caught in the sweep of their escalation, were forced to widen the war and to offer further defiance to the Soviet camp and to world opinion. Like Japan and Germany in the late 1930's, by stepping up their expansion they would bring into existence a broad anti-fascist front in which the "social democrats" of Moscow would have to join. As for China, she intended neither to abandon the argument with the USSR on basic issues nor to decline a defensive alliance with her. The Chinese government, indeed, was evidently adopting a strategy born of its experience of "unity within struggle" with regard to the Kuomintang just before and during World War II.

These are not mere deductions. At the end of May 1965, Vice-Premier Ch'en Yi talked to me in even clearer terms than Chou En-lai: "The controversy itself [with the USSR] embraces above all a series of important questions of principle, one of which is to know if one can or cannot resolutely combat American imperialism. . . . All common and concerted action must be founded on a common understanding of the aggressors and on the common determination to combat them. If this basis were laid, common action would be possible. Otherwise, it would be impossible." [12] Ch'en Yi did not take "resolute combat" to mean that the USSR should declare war on the United States or send an expeditionary force to North Vietnam. No Chinese leader on any level ever spoke to me of a military counter-escalation on the part of the USSR as a condition of common action. All of them simply posed the political issue of the recognition by the Russians of the character of the Vietnam conflict—the acceptance of the principle that this new anti-fascist war ruled out any deal with the

[12] See *China: The Other Communism*, pp. 455–6.

enemy. In short, the USSR had only to endorse the slogan "Vietnam must win" and line up politically beside China, and the joint Sino-Soviet front would become possible.

On September 2, 1965, soon after I left China, the Peking papers gave great publicity to Lin Piao's essay on the twentieth anniversary of victory over Japan. In it, he drew a close parallel between the Chinese Communist strategy in the last war and that which ought to be adopted by the peoples of Asia, Africa, and Latin America in their national liberation struggle against American imperialism. Translated into a concrete political plan, this document urged the creation of "two, three, many Vietnams" in the Third World, under the leadership of Communist Parties, as the best way to help the Vietnamese by "encircling" the overextended American forces. The great lesson of the war against Japan, Lin Piao wrote, lay in its demonstration that a conventional army, however superior in equipment, was powerless when faced by guerrillas firmly rooted in the population. In China, for example, the Kuomintang's conventional forces, supplied and directed by the Americans, had been unable to resist the Japanese, whereas the Red Army had inflicted incalculable losses on them and had reached the point of virtually holding them hostage. The experience of Vietnam since 1960 confirmed this truth in new conditions, even though the Americans had employed an advanced technology undreamed of by the old Japanese militarists. Thus, everything went to prove that, by "relying on the human factor," putting "proletarian politics in the command post," and "basing oneself on the masses," the wretched of the earth could defeat the wealthy imperialists.

Until the time came when the peoples would relight the fires of revolutionary war, the question of material aid to Vietnam was sharply posed. It was the Russians who put it in the forefront of their renewed controversy with China. They were the first to give official publicity to the report of the talk between Mao and Kosygin, in order to show that the Chairman of the CCP was more interested in his struggle against revisionism than in concrete plans for the movement of Soviet material through China to Vietnam. In March 1965, Suslov and Ponomarev triumphantly showed a delegation from the Italian Communist Party, who were about to leave Moscow, a dispatch from their army men about the blocking of convoys to Vietnam by the Chinese.[13] This whispering campaign soon evoked a strong statement from Peking, accusing the Russians of deliberately failing to use special trains put at their disposal. Be this as it may, most of the Soviet material was sent by sea to Haiphong and did not touch Chinese territory. Moreover, the inability of the two nations to agree even on this apparently technical matter created an obvious uneasiness in left-wing opinion, even in Communist Parties sympathetic to China.

To put things right, the Japanese Communist Party sent a delegation to Peking in March 1966, led by its secretary-general, Miyamoto. According to its members—whose account has never been confirmed by the Chinese—they managed to convince the CCP (represented by Chou En-lai, Teng Hsiao-p'ing, P'eng Chen, Liao Ch'eng-chih, and Liu Ning-yi) of the wisdom of presenting the USSR and the Eastern European countries with a united plan for aid to Vietnam. The Japanese Communists were at that time very close to the Chinese and very unpopular in Moscow, and we may assume that this proposal was designed to put the Russians in the dock, deprive them of any excuses for stalling, and force them to step up supplies to Vietnam. The text of the Sino-Japanese statement has not come to light; but, according to the Japanese Communists, it was accepted in Peking and then torn up by Mao on March 29 at Tsunghua, a resort town near Canton where he received the negotiators. By their account, he poked fun at the ingenuity of his comrades and declared that, if the war in Asia were to spread, the USSR would indeed intervene, but on the side of the Americans and not against them. The Russians would simply take the opportunity to grab Manchuria and Inner Mongolia, for they were interested in carving up the world with the Americans and not in the struggle against imperialism.

These revelations were made only after the Japanese Communist Party broke with the Chinese and should be taken with a grain of salt. The fact remains that the attitude of the Chinese leaders changed in 1966, on the very eve of the Cultural

[13] I was given this information by a member of the Italian delegation, which was in Moscow for a meeting to prepare for the world conference of Communist Parties.

Revolution. That spring, the Chinese announced their conviction that the USSR was using its aid to put pressure on the Vietnamese—to oblige them to make concessions and, in fact, to surrender. They also accused the Russians of being in cahoots with the Americans in every respect, of regularly supplying the Americans with information, and even of telling them about Vietnamese defense plans. The great mobilization for the Cultural Revolution was accompanied by denunciations of every aspect of revisionism, at home and abroad, and equally systematic praise for revolutionary intransigence in China and throughout the world. Solidarity with Vietnam and appeals for revolutionary war all over Asia—these became, more than ever, the themes of China's internal and external policy.

However, there was no sign of any change in Chinese thinking about the consequences of American escalation in Vietnam. On the contrary, twelve days after the "incident" which is said to have occurred at Tsunghua, Chou En-lai made a formal statement on China's policy toward the United States. He reaffirmed that his nation always kept its promises and was ready to respond to any request from the Vietnamese. It was a warning that Chinese volunteers would intervene in Vietnam, as they had in Korea, should the Americans cross the 17th parallel. More, he advised the Americans not to put too much faith in their air and naval superiority, for in the event of a widening of the conflict "the war would take no heed of frontiers." "If you can come from the sky, why should we be unable to counterattack on the ground?" [14] he asked the strategists of the Pentagon, who could reasonably be expected to remember their experiences in Korea.

These statements gave the impression that China considered herself to be already at war with the United States and needed the Cultural Revolution—like the Yenan rectification campaign in the past—to be better equipped to face the enemy, by mustering a populace totally mobilized and shorn of weaklings. Edgar Snow, among others, took this view, and I think it is right. Among the many reasons which may have caused Mao to speed up events, a major role must have been played by his conviction that an

[14] See "Premier Chou's Four-Point Statement on China's Policy Towards U.S.," *Peking Review*, No. 20 (May 13, 1966).

American attack on China was likely or even imminent. All the evidence shows that the Vietnam War was a factor aggravating the break with the USSR and contributing to the launching of the Cultural Revolution.

It was in full swing in September 1966, when Ch'en Yi called a press conference in Peking to explain that China was now in a position to give more help to Vietnam and to face "aggression from north and south," thanks to her powerful mass movement. Maintaining this style of rhetoric, he wished the best of luck to invaders from any quarter and assured them that he was calmly waiting to give them the lesson they deserved. Moscow and Washington cried with a single voice that Ch'en Yi had threatened the USSR and the United States with all-out war. This chorus of hypocrisy was taken as confirmation that a "holy alliance" now existed in hostility toward China. The initiators and militants of the Cultural Revolution had not a moment's doubt of it and made it a favorite theme in their political campaigning. As we shall see, this left little room for diplomatic flexibility.

At the Hour of World Revolution

In contradiction to some theories, China during the Cultural Revolution showed no tendency to withdraw into herself. Official statements and the entire press, including the Red Guard papers, provide evidence that for the Chinese people these were years of great reaching out to the world, albeit in an unorthodox fashion. The very doctrines of the guiding hands of the Cultural Revolution explicitly linked the future of the "Commune of China" to the victory of the world revolution. Every militant had to realize that his efforts to "destroy the old order" would succeed only when foreign comrades did the same in their homelands. The phrase "world revolution" entered by degrees into current speech; after 1966, every practical or political achievement was the contribution of a factory or a rank-and-file group to the world revolution. The Chinese had no choice but to take an interest in what happened abroad, and they spoke of it a thousand times more than in the past.

This, indeed, was the outrage—obviously for the United States and the USSR, but also for other countries who were apparently less concerned. Reading Chinese documents, they gathered that Peking was giving strict effect to its new proletarian doctrine and seeking everywhere to stir up a "revolt against oppression," even in countries with whom China had diplomatic relations on the state level. Though they knew that China had no plans to organize a new International, and that her ideas of "independent popular struggle" ruled out attempts to "export revolution," yet they found this state of affairs intolerably shocking. Never since the early period of Soviet Russia had a nation thus beamed its voice to other peoples, calling on each of them to overthrow their own state. Besides, official notes from Peking's Ministry of Foreign Affairs recalled those that had come from the Bolsheviks in 1917, and fulminated in insulting terms against "running dogs of imperialism" or "revisionist vampires." Of course, these terms normally appeared only in "strong protests" or "grave warnings," not in invitations to discussion. But the fact was that the Ministry of Foreign Affairs sent out no other kind of notes, and had so little interest in negotiation that, from December 1966 onward, it recalled all its ambassadors (with the sole exception of Huang Hua in Cairo).

"Relations between states with different social systems" were pushed firmly into the background, while the Chinese leaders lauded "the armed struggles of the peoples" and "the mass movements abroad." The press gave ample space to news of guerrilla victories—in Vietnam naturally, but also in Burma, India, Thailand, Malaysia, and even the Congo and Colombia. Student exploits in Western Europe and the United States, and strikes in industrial nations, were hailed with the same enthusiasm, and special stress was laid on the "gigantic" demonstrations which, on every continent, roused the masses against American imperialist aggression in Vietnam. Big headlines regularly announced, "The revolutionary situation in the world is excellent," and the New China News Agency worked around the clock to prove it. Bad news, such as the Israeli victory in the Six-Day War, was played down, and the blame for these temporary setbacks was put on "the Brezhnev clique"—those "traitors doomed to end in the dustbin of history." For the Chinese militant, the whole world was on the move and total victory could not be far off.

The world really was on the move. The Cultural Revolution in

China coincided with a very powerful mustering of international public opinion against American aggression in Vietnam, with a turn to radicalism among young people, and with a renewal of working-class struggles in most industrial nations. Peking was making the most of a genuine phenomenon which had not been foreseen by existing governments and which was able to upset more than one assumption on the world scene. The Chinese had not brought about this situation and did not take credit for it—though the Cultural Revolution did, in various ways, stimulate the student revolt in the West—but, in their own style, the Chinese fitted it into their "line" and their vision of both the immediate and the long-term future. It can be assumed that at the outset of events, in 1966, they needed this international dimension for reasons of ideological consistency, to forge stronger links in every way with the great tradition of the Paris Commune. But it is unlikely that they put much trust in the mobilizing power of these slogans. In China, even more than in smaller countries, genuine passions are aroused and the "flames of revolutionary struggle are lit" mainly by domestic issues that directly affect daily life. Yet by attaching increasing importance to world events, the initiators of the Cultural Revolution showed that these had a special place in their hearts and that they had high hopes for future developments. Therefore, until the latter half of 1968, they relied more and more heavily on the unexpected but welcome progress of movements abroad. True, the leadership team of this period set out to "radicalize" every question and seldom bothered about subtle distinctions. But their deep conviction cannot be doubted; one can argue only about their capacity to influence events.

How was the Central Group's solidarity with foreign comrades shown in practice, bearing in mind that it refrained from direct intervention in their affairs? A careful reading of Chinese documents of 1967 and 1968 reveals the general outlines of the attitudes taken toward various categories of friends and enemies. Among the enemies, the United States held such a massively preponderant position that all others could be seen as accomplices or simply as "running dogs"—as shadows devoid of true personality. However, different degrees of complicity were distinguished, according to whether it was a question of capitalist nations, who were natural and sometimes reluctant partners of the Americans, or of non-capitalist countries (the USSR and its bloc), who were surreptitiously following the path of collaboration. In general, each was judged by its conduct with regard to Vietnam. Westerners who were cool toward American aggression showed by this token, in the Chinese view, that they wanted to free themselves from the American yoke and were creating "inter-capitalist" contradictions. As against this, denunciations were hurled at the hypocrisy of the Russians, who, while pretending to back the Vietnamese, gave repeated signs—swiftly highlighted by the Peking press—of their desire to come to terms with Washington.

But these standards were applied only so long as the internal situation in the countries concerned was relatively stable. When social conflicts or student struggles broke out anywhere, the solidarity which the Chinese felt obliged to show with the rebels took immediate priority over any concern to take advantage of inter-capitalist contradictions. A textbook example is the changed attitude toward Gaullist France in May 1968; the Chinese greeted the "working-class and student storm" with enthusiasm and held mass demonstrations to flay the "reactionary French authorities." As soon as the storm broke, the French government lost the tolerance it had enjoyed because of its earlier anti-Americanism and was depicted as "100 percent reactionary." The attacks were exceeded only by those made on the "Sato clique" in Japan when it too "ferociously" repressed the heroic struggles of workers, peasants, and students. As a general rule, strikers and rebel students were always faced by "reactionary authorities," so that the outbreak of a strike or a campus battle automatically evoked Chinese onslaughts on the government involved. That went for Italy from 1967 onward and also for West Germany, West Berlin, Norway, and almost every developed nation.

In the Third World the struggle took sharper forms, and governments were simply described as fascist. Up to 1967, only Indonesia had had the shameful distinction of ranking with the traditional fascist regimes of Spain, Portugal, and Greece. But when armed struggles broke out in Burma, President Ne Win was at once likened to Chiang Kai-shek and portrayed as "100 percent fascist." Other fascists included the Israeli leaders after the

Six-Day War, and the reactionary Indian government when it showed its true colors by forcibly smashing the peasant revolt at Naxalbari. As for Thailand, Malaysia, Mobutu's Congo, and various others, they qualified both as fascists and as running dogs of the Americans.

While supporting strikers and rebels, China was more cautious when it came to the efforts of Castro-type guerrillas. The Peking papers never mentioned Ché Guevara, even at the time of his death. It declared its opposition on principle—very clearly, though obliquely—to Castro's schemes by prominently reprinting an article in *L'Humanité Rouge* refuting the "sophistry" of Régis Debray, author of *Revolution Within the Revolution?* [15] It is known that pro-Chinese elements in Latin America refused to join in this type of struggle, which in their view had nothing in common with a true people's war.

Peking gave no space to these controversies, doubtless thinking that the question was of minor importance, and was apparently reluctant to cause bad blood between revolutionaries, to whom China's leaders paid great attention. In 1967 and 1968 admittance was granted almost exclusively to delegations of militant fighters or close friends; no individual visas were granted, even to men like Edgar Snow. Special consideration was shown to the "Marxist-Leninist" parties which emerged from the argument with Russia, and it was usual for Mao himself to receive their leaders. The Albanians, regarded as cast-iron ideological allies, were in a class by themselves. But the Chinese gave an equally warm welcome to delegations of students, even if they were not Marxist-Leninists of the true faith, and to "friendship associations" normally run by people who belonged to no party but were far out on the Left.

---

[15] Ché Guevara made his last visit to Peking in February 1965, and in all likelihood talked about his plan to leave Cuba and create guerrilla bases in Africa and Latin America. His idea of a struggle on the Cuban model obviously did not attract the Chinese, who were also distrustful of the close links between Castro and the Russians. In 1971, in private discussions about my book on Cuba, *Guerrillas in Power*, Chinese friends took me to task for my sympathetic view of Guevarism. According to them, it was doomed to defeat and was a distraction from mass struggle. The article against Debray, which was the only sign of an official stance, was published as "Marxism-Leninism, Mao Tse-tung's Thought, Is Universal Truth," *Peking Review*, No. 30 (July 26, 1968)—that is, well after Ché's death in October 1967.

In both these fields, the dividends were undoubtedly considerable. Despite the campaign of distortions concerning the Cultural Revolution, the prestige of China and of Mao grew steadily among rebels abroad, and, for the first time, a large segment of the "Old Left" began to recognize that China was not a latter-day copy of Stalin's Russia in the grip of suspect notions of state power. From late 1967 onward, student movements almost everywhere proclaimed their sympathy for China, and Maoism emerged as an idea which was perhaps still rather vague but capable of becoming a dominant force among the young people whose activities were causing so many things to happen and so many political realignments in their countries. Red Guard groups appeared even in the United States—remarkable, to say the least, when one thinks of where the American student movement had started from.

But, on the other hand, the international factor played a no less important role in the radicalization of Chinese youth. The "good news" from abroad, and the meetings with delegations of hopeful "friends," stimulated the ardor of the Red Guards and revolutionary rebels, who now began to take a keen interest in the international scene. The rank and file, of course, tended to take an uncompromising position and, by exerting pressure in this direction, it gradually became something of an embarrassment even to the very radical group which was then in power in China. Hence the importance attached to the incidents in the Ministry of Foreign Affairs in August 1967—and, a year later, to the less reported but apparently more dramatic events at Nanning, the main frontier town near North Vietnam.

The Nanning Incidents

Although firmly devoted to the doctrine of the "people's war," the Peking government could not altogether forfeit its non-ideological flexibility. Lin Piao's famous essay on "the encirclement of the cities by the countryside" in September 1965 did not quite dot all the i's, and, in particular, it was never laid down that the "countryside" was exactly the same thing as the peasant revolutionary armies. The phrase was a good deal more ambiguous, and Lin also gave an important role to "anti-imperialist peoples" in general, and notably to nations which resisted foreign oppression. It was thus possible to give credentials to certain progressive governments in the Third World, even to frankly bourgeois regimes. True, most of these governments were not keen to get involved with China; besides, the progressive category looked rather thin after the downfall of Sukarno, Nkrumah, and Ben Bella. Nevertheless, there were some countries in Africa and Asia which—either through conviction or for tactical reasons when they faced greater enemies—kept up good relations with Peking. The Chinese government did nothing to alienate them. Tanzania and Mali were among the "sympathetic" nations, Pakistan and Cambodia among the "opportunists"; others could be mentioned, but these certainly enjoyed "most favored nation" status in Chinese eyes.

This created no major problems so long as no rebellions broke out in these countries, and so long as the Red Guards stayed clear. Things became complicated in Cambodia, for instance, when the Samlaut peasant revolt erupted in 1967 and the "Khmers Rouges" was established. The friendly government of Prince Sihanouk embarked on counterrevolutionary repression (giving the task to General Lon Nol, who was later to expel the Prince) and, in Peking, the Red Guards began to stir up the crowds against the "fascists" of Phnom-Penh. The situation became yet more tricky when Sihanouk, while hostile to the "Khmers Rouges", proved himself very tolerant of the Vietnamese guerrillas who were in the front line of the anti-imperialist struggle. In these circumstances, much tact was required to keep all the balls in play—to keep Prince Sihanouk sweet in order to help the Vietnamese, without overtly abandoning the comrades in Cambodia (above all, the Chinese community in Phnom-Penh, marked down as a victim of the Prince's anti-Maoist wrath). But how was it possible to brave the risks of such delicate diplomacy under the eyes of the Red Guards, who moved into the Ministry of Foreign Affairs at this very moment? Could these intruders be allowed to find out that major concessions had already been made to the Cambodian government—for example, that the Little Red Book had not been published in the Khmer language? Last but not least, if the "seizure of power" took a firm hold, the uncompromising revolutionaries could not be prevented from soon treating Ayub

Khan, the dictator of Pakistan, as harshly as Ne Win of Burma, since the two regimes were as alike as two peas.

Chou En-lai's margin for maneuver had in any case been reduced to a minimum by the basic orientation of the Central Group for the Cultural Revolution and by the wholesale radicalization of public opinion. Such elbowroom as he still had—and to his mind it was vital—depended on one factor: the ignorance of the rank and file about the realities of the outer world. Hence the significance of the battle for control of the Ministry of Foreign Affairs, along with the fight to get Wang Li out of the Information Office. When Chou En-lai categorically refused to yield to the "seizure of power" in the Ministry of Foreign Affairs, it was because he could not allow the *whole* of foreign policy to be conducted in public, under the undisputed control of the rank and file with their all-or-nothing principles. In point of fact, the general line of Chinese foreign policy was unchanged after the "extremists" were cleared out of the Ministry of Foreign Affairs and the Central Group; one may search in vain for differences between Chinese communiqués in August 1967 and in the ensuing months. But the government's right to manage state affairs for itself was saved by the skin of its teeth.

However, as the months went by, the international situation underwent considerable changes—at first favorably from the Chinese viewpoint, then in an unexpected way—and the leaders in Peking had to recognize that, confronted by the masses whose political outlook was too single-minded, they no longer had enough room to maneuver. On February 2, 1968, the editorial in *People's Daily* hailed in lyrical terms the "brilliant victories of the North Vietnamese people in the Tet offensive." The news from the front surpassed the most optimistic forecasts; the exploits of the guerrillas, in the heart of Saigon and even in the American Embassy building, could indeed be described as splendid. The praise in the Chinese press was not exaggerated, and there was ample justification for the excited rallies which were held throughout China to celebrate the great Vietnamese victories. Indeed, similar demonstrations took place in many countries— notably in the United States, where the Johnson administration could not explain the astonishing attacking power of the small nation of Vietnam, under a hail of bombs from the world's most powerful air force.

On March 31, President Lyndon Johnson suddenly went on television to announce the partial suspension of the bombing of North Vietnam and his irrevocable decision not to run for office again. He promised to halt the bombing altogether if the North Vietnamese accepted the principle of talks aimed at a peaceful solution to the conflict. Johnson, who at times could not hold back his tears, appeared by his tone to provide confirmation that the bulk of the American establishment found the Vietnam War too politically expensive; the President was sacrificing himself to allow it to be ended. But Peking, without even waiting for Hanoi's reply, published a triumphant comment through the New China News Agency: "American imperialism has suffered an irremediable defeat. . . . It faces the collapse of its 'supremacy' in the capitalist world. In the United States itself, class contradictions are growing more acute day by day. The hostility of the American people toward the aggressive Vietnam War is increasing by leaps and bounds. The armed resistance of the black Americans is steadily spreading. The internal conflicts of the ruling clique are becoming more and more violent." [16] The enemy, in full defeat, was simply dodging to evade the disaster which, because of its scale, could not fail to bring about a historic global upheaval. Moreover, "all the signs show," the Agency commentary declared, "that the Soviet renegade revisionist clique has once again played the contemptible role of chief accomplice in Johnson's new plot." In conclusion, it quoted "President Ho Chi Minh, the great guide of the Vietnamese people, who has recently said, 'We are sure to win complete victory.'"

But Ho Chi Minh accepted Johnson's offer of talks, and Peking

[16] This commentary by a "correspondent of the New China News Agency" entitled "U.S. Imperialist Chieftain Johnson Tries New Fraud—'Partially Stopping Bombing' to Induce 'Peace Talks,'" *Peking Review*, No. 15 (April 12, 1968), seems to have been a final Chinese bid to forestall an affirmative reply by Hanoi to Johnson's offer. Some American experts state that the President made his speech only after having received assurances from the Vietnamese that they would agree to the Paris peace talks. If so, the Chinese must have been aware of these developments, but it seems that they still hoped to block the road by making violent attacks on Johnson's speech.

seemed to be caught off base. Chou En-lai's government and the official press refrained from criticizing the prestigious president of North Vietnam, but they had trouble in holding back the mighty anger of the rank and file. For the militants, the turnabout of the Vietnamese was quite inexplicable—nor was it explained—the more so as the "revolutionary storm" continued to gather strength, as was shown by the French crisis which exploded even before the peace talks opened. It seemed that the North Vietnamese, instead of taking advantage of this flood tide, wanted to check it in connivance with the "Moscow traitors." Passions suddenly broke loose and the ruling group had to use the greatest energy and skill to prevent the walls from being plastered with anti-Vietnamese posters. It was more or less successful; their existence leaked out abroad, but not their contents. Similarly, little is known of what happened at Nanning, where it was rumored that Vietnamese who were passing through were hooted by angry crowds in the streets.[17] It appears, indeed, that the "seizures of weapons" consigned to Vietnam in June 1968 were connected with this atmosphere.

The North Vietnamese, already aware through the New China News Agency statement of what official China thought of the peace talks, learned in this harsh fashion that Chinese public opinion was still more hostile. This surely had an influence on their internal unity and made it very hard for them to accept the American terms, which, according to certain official leaks, were more favorable than when the Paris agreements were signed four years later. But if Hanoi could not risk a break with Peking, the converse was also true. When North Vietnam agreed to take part in peace talks, the war entered a new phase and its stimulating effects on world opinion could not be maintained at the previous level. It became clear, too, that American strategy in Asia and in the world was undergoing a change. The Chinese government, having been the most loyal ally of the Vietnamese in the hours of trial, had no interest—to say the least—in being divided from them at a time when a new diplomatic game had to be played in the Far East. This would leave the Russians and the Americans

---

[17] In Hanoi, these painful incidents are always veiled in great discretion. Only recently have they been mentioned in private to foreign friends.

complete freedom to share out the Asian stakes. It was therefore a time for high diplomacy, and for this discretion was necessary. It was impossible to risk the continual interference of insistent and intolerant militants, of whom quite enough had been seen in the Nanning incidents. In any case, the prospect of a rapid growth of a powerful New Left throughout the world was already fading. In the fall of 1968, for a great many reasons, the Red Guards were sent off to the countryside. Slowly but surely, "relations between states with different social systems" regained the priority that they had enjoyed before the Cultural Revolution.

Czechoslovakia

The invasion of Czechoslovakia seems to have confirmed for the Chinese what they already believed: that the Russians had helped the Americans by putting pressure on Hanoi, in return for an "understanding attitude" toward their own efforts to stabilize and "modernize" their sphere of influence. From this viewpoint, the armed intervention in Prague merely showed to what lengths the Russians were ready to go. At all events, the Chinese press gave increasing space to events in Czechoslovakia and did not confine itself—as was thought in the West—to publishing formal government statements and the speech made by Chou En-lai at the Rumanian Embassy on August 23. It kept up a regular commentary on the Soviet-Czechoslovak negotiations in Moscow and their results; moreover, drawing on well-prepared material, it printed a number of studies, for instance on the "real character" of trade between the two nations. Dubcek and his team, of course, were blamed for having given in to the Moscow *diktat* in August and taking no account of the Czech people's will to resist. But Chinese comment laid more stress on this popular resistance than on the treachery of the leaders in Prague. It highlighted the slogans of Czech demonstrators: "Brezhnev—Hitler!" and "You have the tanks, we have the truth!" Taking these slogans as grist for its own mill, the Peking press depicted the Soviet leader as a new Hitler—an odious comparison hitherto reserved for President Johnson.

These details, unobserved at the time, assume significance in hindsight. Obviously, *People's Daily* could not announce in so many words that from this day onward the USSR was to be considered the main enemy. The Chinese government is not in the habit of unmasking its diplomatic batteries in this style; besides, in the fall of 1968 it was by no means confident of making deals in the West which would facilitate the creation of a defense system to ward off the threat from the new Enemy Number One. This change in the Chinese outlook was not made in a single day by a committee decision. It was linked with the great internal debates and influenced by changes in the world power game whose meaning became clear only later.

It must also be pointed out that, from the Russian viewpoint, China was already the main enemy, at least from the start of the Cultural Revolution. The Soviet leaders claimed that they were facing a threat and succeeded—as was seldom the case—in getting the population to share their feelings. Their entire propaganda machine was methodically directed against the Chinese menace; poets, normally less obedient, were mobilized to sound the alarm against the new "Tartar" invaders; servile journalists called on the West to build a unity of "white civilized nations." [18] The major theme was that China was demanding a half million square miles of Russia's sacred soil; in the grip of insoluble problems caused by Mao's madness, she had no way out except a drive for the wealth of Siberia. Everyone in Moscow worried about this forthcoming invasion—official circles and oppositionists, Stalinist diehards and pro-Western liberals. When I visited the USSR in 1970, the few people I met who had kept their heads assured me that the men in the Kremlin were carried away by their own propaganda and really were scared stiff of China. And yet, among the countless anti-revisionist diatribes produced in China, one may search in vain for a single one devoted to territorial demands, and the Kremlin's great fright appears on the surface to be absolutely baseless. To this, my informants in Moscow replied that the phobia had deep roots in the past, in the Russian inferiority complex with regard to China's ancient

[18] A commentator from the Novosti Agency, one Dadiantz, contributed to the discussion forum of *Le Monde* in such blatantly racist terms that the Communist press in Italy was moved to protest and to state that it had no intention of following the Russians in this brand of crusade against the "yellow peril." *L'Humanité*, the French Communist paper, was silent.

civilization, in a guilty conscience about Czarist annexations, and above all in the belief that time was on the side of the Chinese, who were destined to "overtake and surpass" the USSR.

To these explanations of the collective psychology of the Soviet leaders, one may add the humiliating and disturbing fact that events had repeatedly disproved their forecasts of developments within China. In 1967, the Russians seem to have believed that China was falling apart and that her nuclear tests were an act of desperation to gain possession of the only weapon that could prevent a breakup of the country.[19] Logically, if this was the case, Russia had little to fear; but logic was not the main element here. At all events, in 1968—well before the invasion of Czechoslovakia—the Russians were talking about an opportunity for a pre-emptive strike against the Chinese nuclear installations. In private, at meetings of the World Peace Council [sic], they even explained that they had the capacity to carry out this operation without causing too many human casualties and could thus save China from her own suicidal impulses.[20] After the invasion of

[19] The Chinese set off their first hydrogen bomb in July 1967, during the "hot summer" of the Cultural Revolution, when the outside world was least prepared for such an achievement. Moreover, Chinese scientists had reached this point in record time, two years and eight months after their first atom-bomb test in October 1964.

[20] The true father of this "surgical operation" on Chinese nuclear installations was undoubtedly John F. Kennedy. He talked about it as early as 1963, before the Chinese had conducted their first atomic test. Thanks to the indiscretions of writers close to the Pentagon, notably the Alsop brothers, we know that Kennedy, concerned about his good reputation in the world, would have liked the operation to be carried out half-clandestinely and by the use of conventional bombs only. The military chiefs replied that they could not guarantee the success of such a "clean" operation; in their estimation, the use of atomic weapons was absolutely essential to destroy the Chinese installations at a single blow and with complete certainty. President Kennedy was not ready to go to such lengths (though, in his speech of August 1, 1963, he clearly threatened China that he would). When his successor, Johnson, returned to the project, the American experts proved to be still more pessimistic. China already had her atomic bombs and might repay the American nuclear attack with a raid on American troops in Vietnam or even on the coast of California. When the Russians, some years later, took up in turn the idea of the "surgical operation," they seem to have counted on certain trump cards. Thanks to their long common frontier, they had not only built innumerable rocket bases aimed at China but also contemplated a military occupation of Sinkiang, where the Chinese nuclear installations are said to be concentrated.

Czechoslovakia and the challenge presented by the Chinese reaction, the Soviet leaders spoke of this punitive expedition (or preventive action, for the terminology varied) in such loud whispers that Peking could not ignore it. We may even guess that they displayed this "secret" in the hope of frightening China, perhaps even of inducing her to repent and bringing her back within the fold—in theory, China was still a part of the Soviet bloc and was subject to Brezhnev's doctrine of the "limited sovereignty" of Socialist nations. In any case, the special characteristic of a military threat is that its seriousness cannot be tested until it is put into effect. From the outside, the one certainty is that in the autumn of 1968 the Soviet fears were purely imaginary, while the Chinese were facing a real threat of tremendous gravity.

Whether the USSR was an "accomplice" of the United States or not, from early 1968 the Russians were openly seeking to create a *cordon sanitaire* around China. Tempting proposals in this vein were made to official allies of the Americans—in the first instance to Japan—and to other less committed nations, notably India. Premier Kosygin made several visits to New Delhi and promised to supply the Indians with Soviet supersonic fighter-bombers (which the Russians were refusing to give to the Vietnamese), while Suslov, the ideological pundit, went to Tokyo to meet the Japanese Communists and in particular to offer the Sato government a share in the development of that sacred soil of Siberia which had to be protected from the Chinese.[21] Less illustrious emissaries even slipped into Taiwan, Chiang Kai-shek's stronghold, and the Russians seem to have let it be understood that any enemy of Mao could be a friend of theirs, from the Indonesian fascists—famous for their massacres of Communists—to the Japanese, who had yearnings for rearmament and revenge. The Russians claimed that this sudden diplomatic activity had purely defensive purposes, but Peking had good reason to feel that it was in the sights of the big guns. It was urgently necessary to find some way, both military and diplomatic, to counter the schemes of a neighbor who was all the more dangerous because no trend of

[21] See the *People's Daily* commentary of February 5, 1968, "What Kosygin Was Up to in India," *Peking Review*, No. 6 (February 9, 1968); and "Soviet and Japanese Revisionists: Closer Collusion," *Peking Review*, No. 8 (February 23, 1968).

anti-war opinion could be discerned within the USSR. This was dramatically confirmed by the invasion of Czechoslovakia, when exactly eight individuals could be found in Moscow to make their protest on Red Square.

The Johnson administration, for its part, seemed to be resigned to "Soviet penetration" in Asia. It reckoned that only the USSR could get the Vietnamese to come to terms, thus enabling the United States to save face and thereafter to maintain a "reasonable peace" in Southeast Asia by agreement with the Russians. The Paris talks therefore produced some nasty surprises by showing that North Vietnam was not at Brezhnev's beck and call, and would sign nothing without the approval of her Chinese ally. In Washington, this disappointment even produced a surge of mistrust of the Russians, who were suspected of not playing the game through to the end and failing to put enough pressure on Hanoi. But, on the whole, Johnson's policy was trapped in its vicious circle of illusions, for which the price had to be paid in all kinds of ways. When the United States declined to put the invasion of Czechoslovakia on the United Nations agenda, or to condemn it even in formal terms, it was bound to be held morally responsible by world opinion for the "normalization" in Prague.

Paradoxically, Red China began to "exist" once more for Washington in November 1968, after the victory in the presidential election of the highly anti-Communist Richard M. Nixon. Even before moving into the White House, this former Red baiter and all-out supporter of Chiang Kai-shek started to sound out the possibilities of making contact with Peking. For various reasons, the new President had good personal relations with Rumanian President Nicolae Ceaucescu, one of the few leaders in Eastern Europe who was looked upon with favor in China, because he had always made difficulties for the Russians.[22] Nixon could have

[22] Ugo Stillo, the American correspondent of *Corriere della Sera* and one of the best-informed journalists in Washington, gave an account in July 1971 of the origins of the friendship between Nixon and Ceaucescu. It seems that in 1966, as a private citizen, Nixon decided to make a trip to Eastern Europe. The Polish government, regarding his visit as inopportune, refused him a visa; the USSR allowed him to come in but made not the slightest effort to give him a reception. Nixon spent a week in Moscow, knocking on every door and reminding people that he was a former vice-president of the United States, but failed to see anyone in the

found no better messenger to let Peking know of the unexpected intentions of the Republican administration now in power.

The Ninth Party Congress

On April 1, 1969, on the occasion of the Ninth Congress of the CCP, the leaders had to take up a position, on the one hand, on the Soviet attitude manifested by the invasion of Czechoslovakia and the local war along the Ussuri; and, on the other hand, on the American change of direction indicated by a certain de-escalation in Vietnam and by the offers to talk with China. The response had to be delicately balanced, and we can well believe what Chou En-lai has recently revealed about the top-level discussions while Lin Piao's programmatic report was being drawn up. According to Chou, the first version of this document, prepared by Lin and Ch'en Po-ta alone, was altered to such an extent that the final report should be regarded as a collective product.[23] The leaders of various Communist Parties often adopt this procedure in order to manifest their unity at a Congress. But, when he deprived Lin Piao of the sole fatherhood of the report, Chou by no means reduced its significance. On the contrary, he stressed—perhaps without meaning to—that this document, which has received little attention abroad, reflected the majority view of the entire Party center. It is therefore worth quoting some passages on foreign policy, the more so in that they benefit by being considered in the light of subsequent events. Here is what Lin Piao said about the United States and the USSR:

Kremlin. Giving up, he went off to Bucharest, where he expected nothing and was pleasantly surprised to be received with the honors normally reserved for heads of state. Ceaucescu met him in person at the airport and accompanied him throughout his stay in Rumania. He had the foresight to see that Nixon was by no means finished in American politics and that a suitable friend could win him an influential friend in Washington—perhaps the next President. Whatever his motives, it was a sound political investment. In November 1968, in thanking Ceaucescu for a telegram of congratulations, Nixon sent a particularly long and warm message. Some months later, in August 1969, he visited Bucharest again, this time as President. It is a safe bet that during this visit there was plenty of discussion about American-Chinese relations.

[23] Chou spoke of the changes in Lin Piao's report in October 1972 to Emmett Dedmont, vice-president of the *Chicago Daily News*. I am referring to the Italian version of this interview in *Corriere della Sera*, October 15, 1972.

American imperialism, the most ferocious enemy of the peoples of the world, is undergoing a rapid decline. Since he has been in office, Nixon has been faced with a colossal mess—an insoluble economic crisis, vigorous resistance from the peoples of the world and the masses in the United States, and a difficult situation in which imperialist countries are at loggerheads and the whip of American imperialism is proving less and less effective. Unable to find a solution to this state of affairs, Nixon, like his predecessors, can only fall back on a dual counterrevolutionary strategy: he gives himself the airs of a "man of peace" while stepping up the expansion of armaments and preparation for war on a vaster scale. Indeed, the military expenditure of the United States continues to increase year by year. . . . What is the purpose of all these aircraft, guns, nuclear bombs, and missiles, if not to intimidate, repress, and massacre whole populations and to dominate the world? But by these actions, American imperialism has aroused the hostility of the peoples and finds itself encircled and attacked on all sides by the proletariat and the broad masses throughout the world. This situation can only bring about ever wider revolutions all over the world.[24]

As can be seen, the viewpoint of the report is essentially—if a little more subtly—that of the New China News Agency commentary on Johnson's offer of peace talks on Vietnam. It would be hard to imagine a tougher statement, but perhaps it was not in this section that changes were made. Now let us look at the passage devoted to the USSR and its foreign policy:

Since Brezhnev came to power, the clique of Soviet revisionist renegades has seen its whip become more and more ineffective. The dispatch of hundreds of thousands of troops to occupy Czechoslovakia and the armed provocation in Chenpao Island are two grotesque displays recently staged by this clique. In an effort to justify its record of aggression and robbery, it peddles theories of "limited sovereignty," "international dictatorship," and "the Socialist community." What does all this nonsense mean? Simply that other people's sovereignty is limited while their own is unlimited. If you won't obey, then you are subjected to an "international dictatorship"—that is, a dictatorship exercised over the peoples of various countries to create a "Socialist community" dominated by new Czars, in other words colonies of social-imperialism on the model of Hitler's "New Order," the

[24] See "Report to the Ninth Congress of the CCP," in Collection of Important Documents of the Great Proletarian Cultural Revolution (Peking, 1970), p. 94.

"Greater East Asia Co-prosperity Sphere" of the Japanese militarists, and the "free world community" of the United States. . . . Lenin stigmatized the renegades of the Second International in these terms: Socialism in words, imperialism in reality, transmutation of opportunism into imperialism. Today, this could not be more applicable to the clique of Soviet revisionist renegades.

Later, having spoken of the Ussuri conflict, Lin Piao addressed himself to the relations between the USSR and other Communist Parties. He began by recalling that the CCP had always fought the "detestable great-power chauvinism" of the Russians and declared:

This clique [the Communist Party of the Soviet Union] indulges in endless talk about "brother Parties" and "brother countries," while in reality it regards itself as the "father Party" and behaves like a new Czar who occupies the territory of other countries just as he pleases. Not content with carrying on subversive and undermining activities against the CCP, the Albanian Workers' Party, and other Marxist-Leninist parties, it mounts ferocious attacks on all the parties as well as all the nations of its so-called Socialist community. . . . It abstains from no methods—repression, sabotage, subversion, and even the dispatch of troops to occupy its "brother countries" and the kidnapping of members of its "brother Parties." These fascist acts of banditry are dooming it to inevitable ruin.[25]

No profound analysis is needed to see that this document represents a major escalation in the charges against the Russians. Brezhnev and his colleagues are openly compared to Hitler and described as fascists, even though they are still, as hitherto, vaguely "social-democratic." If we add that Lin's warnings of a possible war follow immediately upon his remarks about the USSR, it is no strained interpretation to say that he sees the main military threat in 1969 as coming "from the north." What is equally striking is that he makes a tacit appeal to the "brother Parties" of the Russians and even seems to hope for a revolt within the traditional Communist movement in the Soviet sphere. For instance, he refrains from any criticism of the "members of brother Parties" kidnapped by the Russians, and there are no further allusions to the "treason of Dubcek's clique," or to

[25] See *Important Documents of the Great Proletarian Cultural Revolution*, p. 107.

"revisionists" who had lined up with the USSR or had uttered verbal condemnations to clear themselves with their constituencies. In Lin Piao's eyes, the invasion of Czechoslovakia was to produce in the pro-Soviet camp repercussions akin to those of the Vietnam War in the American sphere, and—in the one case as in the other—a revulsion against the excesses of Brezhnev and Nixon would inevitably lead to the collapse of the forces on which they had hitherto relied. Thus, taken as a whole, the report makes an optimistic analysis fairly similar to that of 1968, when the stirrings throughout the world were greater. The appearance of a grave threat on the northern borders and the continuance of the Vietnam War do not seem to be impelling China toward major diplomatic efforts. Priority is still given to relations with revolutionary forces, still seen as highly favored by world conditions. Moreover, for the first time, we note allusions to the prospect of a collapse of the pro-Soviet revisionist movement abroad. Since this had hitherto been regarded as the main hindrance to the progress of revolution, we must conclude that in 1969 political hopes were on the rise. Lin Piao's report leaves a very definite impression that diplomacy was the last thing that the Chinese leaders were concerned about.

Yet Chou En-lai could not have shared this view, either during the Cultural Revolution or—with greater reason—in the spring of 1969, when the guns were booming in the north and American peace offers were taking wing in the south. He subscribed to the collective report because he was not yet in a position to influence the dominant line, especially in face of the 1,512 Congress delegates, nominated or elected from among the militants of a movement which, though already on the ebb, had plenty of life left in it. In such a gathering, Mao himself would have thought twice before sowing confusion among his finest troops by preaching too much moderation. All the evidence shows that a renewal of diplomacy required first of all a stabilization of the home front, a gradual cooling of the ardor of the rank and file, and a more complete restoration of the decision-making power of the official Party organizations, which were then being rebuilt. The departure of the Red Guards and the "criticized" cadres to the countryside and the May 7 schools was not in itself enough to ensure a return to normalcy. It was also necessary to rebuild the machinery of recruitment and of "explanation," to restore the prestige of the Party and its leaders, and to elevate the leaders to a point where they would be above criticism—let alone more serious distrust—should their decisions, particularly in the sphere of foreign policy, depart temporarily from the pledges of the preceding period.

Thus, Chou's desire to get moving in diplomacy—apparently with Mao's support—was certainly not the only issue in the events that followed the Congress. Little is known of the twenty-three days of debates behind closed doors at the April 1969 gathering, but we know what emerged with regard to the composition of the new directing organs, and this is instructive. Lin Piao was constitutionally designated as Mao's successor and confirmed in his status as permanent guardian of the doctrinal purity of the Party, then being rebuilt. This was enough to show that he was in no sense in a minority and that the rank and file relied on him as in November 1967, at the time of the Party's famous opinion poll. In the new and limited Standing Committee of the Politburo, we find Mao (who by definition "guides the Party" but is not involved in day-to-day business) flanked by Lin Piao, Ch'en Po-ta, and K'ang Sheng, all known to be on the Left, face to face with Chou En-lai, the only moderate. In the entire Politburo, consisting of twenty-one full and four alternate members, only Li Hsien-nien, vice-premier in charge of finance, could be regarded as a close friend of Chou. Ch'en Yi and Ch'en Yün were no longer members, though Chou must surely have put them forward. Three veterans, almost ninety years old—Tung Pi-wu, Chu Teh, and Liu Po-ch'eng—kept their seats, but this could scarcely strengthen the position of the moderates; except for Tung, who was made interim Chairman of the Republic, they were prevented by their age from playing any political role. Even Yeh Chien-ying, another army veteran, was to occupy a purely honorific place. More than one foreign observer had the impression that the leaders clung to these old men through loyalty to tradition and to avoid bringing in too many young men belonging to the most radical wing.

Seven members of the new Politburo had never been in the Central Committee; thus they had skipped a rung of the ladder, as—to a lesser extent—had three former members or alternates of the Central Committee who were promoted without having held

ministerial posts. The Central Committee that emerged from the
Ninth Congress had 170 full and 109 alternate members, almost
twice as many as the old body. Another surprise was that only 27
percent of them were old Party cadres, while 28 percent were
representatives of mass organizations and 44 percent came from
the army. Emphatically, the balance of forces at the Ninth
Congress indicated a certain change—to the detriment of the "old
crew"—in the effect given to Mao's famous directive on the
"triple alliance."

Of course, the newcomers, whether civilian or military, had not
been chosen by Lin Piao with an eye to an internal struggle which
he could not have foreseen. They represented all the trends
manifested during the Cultural Revolution, but only within the
limited framework of a Communist movement strongly attached
to the "mass line" and with few links to the old machine. For
example, Chiang Ch'ing and her friends from Shanghai—Chang
Ch'un-ch'iao and Yao Wen-yuan—had been fairly open to
counsels of moderation in the period leading up to the Congress,
but in April 1969 it would have been distinctly premature to
connect them with the group of "moderates," still less with "old
directing cadres." In short, both in the policy line—strikingly
illustrated in the stance on international affairs—and in the
makeup of the leading organs, the Ninth Congress incarnated for
the last time the dominance of the men who had risen to power in
August 1966 on the wave of the Cultural Revolution.

But, before we come to the "back-tracking" of August and
September 1970, we may note that, according to some unverifi-
able leaks, Lin Piao wanted to prolong the existence of the
Central Group for the Cultural Revolution in order to demonstrate the permanence of the revolution itself, and on this point he
was not supported by a majority at the Congress. Mao came out
against this proposal, which amounted to creating a sort of
Politburo alongside the one that had just been elected. This
incident, so it is said, revealed a major disagreement between Mao
and Lin on the basic issue—the continuance of the Cultural
Revolution after the Ninth Congress. Together with Chou's
revelations about the changes made in Lin's draft report, these
details tend to show that the former vice-chairman was already
losing speed and that, despite appearances, he was not the victor

of the Congress. But this information, while it is plausible, simply confirms what we now know about the objective situation in China—that it was impossible to give fresh impetus to the mass movement which had carried Lin Piao to the peak of his power. Despite this handicap, it seems that the vice-chairman managed to maintain his rating at the Ninth Congress. There can have been few, at the time, who realized that he had no future.

The Aftermath of a Heated Central Committee Session

During the eighteen months between the election of the new Central Committee and its second plenary session, at Lushan from August 23 to September 6, 1970, no Party committees were formed at the provincial level. This tells us a great deal about how hard it was to rebuild the Party after the hurricane of the Cultural Revolution. Unfortunately, we have no trustworthy information about the causes of this delay or the discussions that it provoked at the top level. The resolutions of the Ninth Congress had set no timetable for setting up provincial organizations, so it was reasonable, both for foreign observers and within China, to assume that the delegates envisaged a slow process during which preparatory groups would have time to recruit new militants, check on the quality of old ones, and get them used to working together. Lin Piao's report spoke both of the "thousand and one tasks" awaiting the Revolutionary Committees, which were functioning everywhere since September 1968, and of the leading role of the Party. He said nothing precise about the relationship to be established between the existing committees and the Party organizations which had yet to be formed. One gathered that this problem had been intentionally left in suspense and would be gradually resolved "in practice." A year and a half later, the resolution of the Central Committee's second session, published on September 8, 1970, also failed to deal with this sensitive question, mentioning only a "heated" discussion of the matter.

But in October, barely a month after the Lushan meeting, the first provincial Party committee was set up in Hunan, Mao's home province, and nine other provinces followed suit in the next six months. This speed-up may have been planned well in advance, but it may equally well have been the outcome of a decision taken at Lushan, perhaps even accompanied by a severe rebuke to those responsible for the previous delay. According to recent revelations, the second guess is right; Mao is said to have dismissed Ch'en Po-ta and strongly criticized Lin Piao for failing to carry out the line of the Ninth Congress. In fact, the Chairman's break with his designated successor—and with the trend represented by Ch'en Po-ta—did indeed occur at this meeting, and on this very issue. But of course we have nothing in writing on this event, and the losers cannot tell us how they interpreted the line of the Ninth Congress on the rebuilding of the Party.

It is in the international sphere that we can most easily trace the divergence between the forecasts made by Lin Piao in April 1969 and the actual course of developments. In the period between the two sessions of the Central Committee, world trends were by no means favorable to "ever-wider revolutions." The storms of 1968, which had aroused such hopes in China, steadily died down, and the "reactionary authorities" appeared to have trimmed their sails effectively to the winds of revolt which now blew more and more feebly. The shock of Czechoslovakia had produced no breakup among the pro-Soviet Communist Parties, and in June 1969 they gathered in Moscow again for a world conference with no other aim than to manifest their loyalty (though with faint gulps of shame on the part of some of those present). Nixon's de-escalation in Vietnam, though partial and hypocritical—it was accompanied by intensified bombing and an incursion into Cambodia—evidently sufficed to break the protest front and defuse the explosion of moral revolt in the United States and elsewhere. The student movement was in the doldrums, while social struggles were now concerned with economic matters and were increasingly contained by the trade unions. So, instead of the strengthening of the revolutionary wave foreseen at the Ninth Congress, the movement was seen to be faltering. There was nothing extraordinary about this; a year and a half is too short a time to judge the overall trend of a revolutionary perspective, in which temporary setbacks are inevitable. But China was in no position to take an academic view of the situation; unless, in the near future, she could count on "ever-wider revolutions" and on a significant weakening of her American and Soviet enemies, she had to turn at once to a search for other methods of warding off the imminent dangers. No wonder, therefore, that the resolution adopted in September 1970 contained a formula that had been dropped since the Cultural Revolution: "In her efforts to practice peaceful coexistence between countries with different social systems, on the basis of the Five Principles and to combat the imperialist policy of aggression and war, our country is achieving victory after victory." [26] No doubt it would have been more in accordance with reality to say, "Our country hopes for victory after victory," for, in the recent period, China had devoted so little attention to relations with countries that had different social systems that she could scarcely have met with either victories or defeats. But the public revival of the principle of coexistence was of weighty significance—as soon became clear—even though the bulk of the resolution, from a desire for continuity, once again extolled the excellent revolutionary situation that prevailed in the world. The final statement also noted that this session, under Mao's chairmanship, had produced a very lively discussion; there is every reason to think that this had much to do with disagreements on foreign policy.

The atmosphere of this period in leadership circles has been portrayed by a privileged Westerner, Edgar Snow, who arrived in China with his wife at the beginning of August, three weeks before the opening of the Lushan session. At their first meeting, Chou En-lai talked to him about a dialogue with the United States and gave him to understand that his government had replied affirmatively to the United States' proposal to resume Sino-American discussions, merely stipulating that they should no longer take place in Warsaw. [27] The Nixon administration, having no particular love for Poland, had invited the Chinese to select the most

[26] See "Communiqué of the Second Plenary Session of the Ninth Central Committee of the Communist Party of China," *Peking Review*, No. 37 (September 11, 1970).

[27] Since the Geneva conference of 1954, the American and Chinese ambassadors had met more than 134 times in Warsaw to discuss questions of common interest, but these contacts had been broken off at the start of the Cultural Revolution. Another meeting was held in November 1969 and was the last to take place in the Polish capital.

convenient locale. Apparently, to demonstrate their good will and their desire to negotiate, the Americans had let it be known that they would be agreeable to a meeting place in China. One must admit that this was a big step; by suddenly sending emissaries to China, the United States took a risk of appearing to be "climbing down." Was this a journey to Canossa? That would depend on the status of the emissaries, on their reception, and on the timing.

The questions to be settled were innumerable, but the principle of entering a dialogue had been settled even before the Central Committee met. Such a decision could have been taken only by Mao, for he alone could secure the Central Committee's approval. Chou was in no position to risk such an adventure without being covered by the Chairman. Snow was quite definite about this when I talked to him after his return. However, he said nothing to me about any possible opposition from Lin Piao, the only top leader whom he had been unable to interview during his long stay in Peking. Nor was the eclipse of several leaders, directly after the Lushan session, interpreted to mean that they were opposed to Mao and Chou on this issue. It was indeed noted that from this time on Ch'en Po-ta, K'ang Sheng, Hsieh Fu-chih, and Li Hsüeh-feng—that is, a quarter of the Politburo[28]—no longer appeared in public. But, since these four great figures of the Cultural Revolution had never been directly involved in foreign policy, it seemed difficult to connect their disappearance with the sensitive question of private Sino-American talks or with the general revival of activity on the "front of peaceful coexistence."

Then, on October 1, 1970, during the anniversary parade of the People's Republic, Chou En-lai sought out Mr. and Mrs. Snow on their platform and took them to Mao for a short chat. However, the photos taken at this time of the Chairman and his American guests appeared in *People's Daily* only in December, on Mao's birthday, a week after the nine-hour interview which he granted Snow on December 18. It was in this talk that Mao indicated his desire that the coming dialogue with Washington should be on the

[28] K'ang Sheng and Hsieh Fu-chih made one or two more public appearances in 1970–1, but it was already known that they no longer held their former posts and there was no word of their being appointed to new ones. Hsieh died in 1972 and was given a ceremonial funeral. K'ang Sheng was not present, but made another appearance in 1973.

highest level; rather than receiving any American delegation, he
preferred that Nixon himself should come to Peking. "He will be
welcome," Mao explained, "for at the present time it is with him
that we should settle the problems between China and the United
States. If he is willing to come to China, it is of little importance
whether he comes as a tourist or as President." [29] This interview
was not intended for immediate publication—Snow expected to
include it in his book—and was to contain no direct quotations
from Mao; in accordance with custom, a draft of the text was
submitted to the Chinese authorities to be checked. Despite his
intention of returning to Europe for Christmas, Snow had to wait
all of six weeks before his notes were returned to him. What was
happening during this time? Was there some opposition on Lin
Piao's part to the invitation to Nixon, which could be understood
only by the administration in Washington because no one else
knew what was going on? Were steps being taken through
Rumanian or Pakistani channels to double-check that the American response would be favorable, lest Mao be made a laughing-
stock by a refusal from the sly American President? Be this as it
may, the one certainty is that these six weeks were not devoted
solely to a scrutiny of Snow's notes.

In April 1971, when the American table-tennis team, accompanied by American journalists, was received in Peking—to the
astonishment of the world—Snow sent a cable to the Chinese
Ministry of Foreign Affairs: "It is my understanding that I may
publish, without quotations, an account of my talk on December
18 with Chairman Mao." Twenty-four hours later, the reply came:
"Your understanding correct." The interview appeared in *Life* on
April 27, just when Dr. Kissinger was packing his bags for his
secret trip to Peking. At the same time, somewhere in China, an
enlarged meeting of the Politburo was held, in which—according
to recent leaks—Lin Piao and his friends made a final frontal
attack on the policy which, in their eyes, was an abandonment of
the Cultural Revolution. It is said that, failing to shake Chairman
Mao's determination, they decided to wage a factional struggle
against him and to embark on a "plot." All these charges are

[29] See Edgar Snow's interview with Mao in *Nouvel Observateur*, February 21,
1972, and in the London *Sunday Times*.

vague, but certain facts bear out the existence of an opposition of this kind to the Sino-American dialogue. At the end of July, two weeks after Kissinger's visit, and when the communiqué announcing the Nixon visit had already been published, the chief of the army general staff, Huang Yung-sheng, delivered a particularly violent anti-American speech. The New China News Agency surpassed itself on this occasion; its report was drawn up in Western style, with a headline and a summary which tended to make the story sensational.

The showdown came in September 1971. Lin Piao vanished. A list of the people who met their downfall along with him reveals the dimensions of the crisis. Out of twenty-one full members of the Politburo, only ten kept their positions, including the three aged veterans. Of the four alternate members, two disappeared. Foreign observers, attuned to the listening posts around China, could get no news about the great majority of the new members of the Central Committee elected at the Ninth Congress. More than sixty senior leaders of the Revolutionary Committees in the provinces lost their posts, including such national figures as P'an Fu-sheng, the key man in the model seizure of power in Heilungkiang; Wang Hsiao-yü, chairman of the Shantung Revolutionary Committee, and also cited as an example to the nation in 1967; Liu Ko-p'ing and Chang Jih-ch'ing, chairman and vice-chairman of the much-lauded committee in Shansi; and this list is not exhaustive. The ax struck at the chief of the general staff of the army, three of his deputies, and the majority of the top men in the air force, the infantry, the political department of the navy, and various commands in the provinces.[30] This tally, which is only provisional, indicates that the "plotters" were not short of supporters in most of the institutions created by the Cultural Revolution, and that these were drawn from the best activists— and probably also the rank and file—of the movement which, in previous years, had aimed at reaching "heights never yet conquered." In truth, if the notions of "majority" and "minority" can have any meaning in a situation in which no votes are taken, it

[30] Some valuable comments on the purge that followed the fall of Lin Piao are to be found in a study by Parris Chang, "Political Rehabilitation of Cadres in China: A Traveller's View," *China Quarterly*, No. 54 (April–June 1973).

must be admitted that the new international line was imposed by
a minority within the country.

The Drama of September 1971

"Plus ça change et plus c'est la même chose," we sometimes say in
the West when, despite the pompous oratory of our leaders, the
"new society" and other basic changes have yet to appear on the
horizon. In China a more apposite phrase might be: *"Même quand
ça change, on dit la même chose."* Once they have laid down a
"general line," as in 1958 or 1966, the Chinese leaders seek, at any
cost and regardless of what is happening, to prove that they are
strictly and faithfully implementing it without modifying it in any
respect, even to improve it. This being so, it is no use asking
questions in Peking about the "new" foreign policy, still less about
"changes" in internal strategy. Guests are loaded down with
documents concerning the establishment of the line—thus, I was
given the collection of documents on the Cultural Revolution and,
at my request, back numbers of *Peking Review*—and discussion
revolves around the correct interpretation of a document rather
than its implementation in practice.

My visit in 1971 took place three months before the fall of Lin
Piao. The reconstruction of the Party committees was then in full
swing, and "table-tennis diplomacy" was causing its first repercussions. The people I met in the factories told me that they owed
their productive or political successes to "the victory of the
proletarian line during the Cultural Revolution." Every piece of
news about the setting up of a Party committee in one place or
another was depicted as a fresh triumph for this line. When I
sometimes expressed my surprise at seeing the "triple alliance"
Revolutionary Committees eclipsed by those of the Party, and at
finding old cadres, much criticized in recent years, back in ruling
positions, I was promptly presented with point 5 or point 8 of the
sixteen-point decision of August 1966. "You see, it says here that
95 percent of the cadres are good or open to reclamation." When
I was concerned about point 9 of this decision, which proclaims
that the rank-and-file organizations should become "permanent
mass organizations, required to function for a long time," my hosts
answered either that "workers' conferences" in the factories had

replaced the trade unions in a permanent fashion, or else that "a long time" is rather more limited in Chinese and can mean a few years. Again, my guides said several times that they could not see why I was worried about the subordinate position allotted to young people who had emerged from the mass movement, or about the combining of jobs which very often ensured that the secretary of the Party committee was the same man as the chairman of the Revolutionary Committee.

Actually, there was no cause for surprise. By 1971 there was no longer any independent political rank-and-file movement; logically, therefore, there was no place for "representatives of the masses" distinct from the Party machine. The Party officials alone spoke with the authority that is conferred by real power, whereas the former activists from the masses had no future, it seemed, except to take their turn on the Party ladder. When an official recited his titles, he first introduced himself as secretary or deputy secretary of the Party organization, and added as a mere afterthought that he was also the chairman or vice-chairman of the local Revolutionary Committee. Why had he been elected to these key positions when he had been so harshly criticized by the rank and file? Might it not have been better to choose somebody who had "understood" the Cultural Revolution right from the start? "Chairman Mao teaches us that we must judge the cadres in the perspective of history and not from isolated incidents." Without any visible embarrassment, an effective reply came to every question, and one would have needed a magical degree of insight to guess that these very questions were causing a split at the top level and were about to lead to the dramatic "Lin Piao affair."

How many Chinese got wind of what was in the offing? Today, it is explained that the break between Mao and Lin occurred in August 1970 and became more acute in the spring of 1971, a situation that induced the Chairman to make a tour of the provinces in the summer in order to combat the pro-Lin tendencies. But, on the basis of the various contacts that I made, I can testify that everyone I met, even on a high level, behaved as if he were unaware of the extreme seriousness of the conflict, or as if he expected it to be resolved without any major crisis. Not only did the leaders fail to prepare public opinion by a judicious use of

their publicity network—they took advantage of it to convince
the masses that the policy of settling down after the Cultural
Revolution was endorsed by Lin Piao, by virtue of his position as
"the closest comrade in arms of our great guide, Chairman
Mao." [31] Ironically, the personality cult of Lin reached new
heights during this period. On May 2, 1971, his photo on the front
page of *People's Daily* was almost as large as Mao's, and he was
highly venerated amid the historic scenes of Chingkangshan (as I
will show in the postscript to this chapter). Indeed, this worship of
the crown prince was all the more noteworthy because the cult of
Mao was being played down; we know, thanks to Snow's
interview, that the Chairman was uneasy about the dimensions it
had assumed in recent years. One could well believe, from what
one saw and what one was told, that Lin Piao's personal position
was becoming stronger. He alone, it seemed, was perfectly
equipped to ensure the correct carrying out of Mao's line, which
of course had undergone no change despite the partial renuncia-
tion of the personality cult and the return to the dominance of the
Party.

When one takes a closer look at the plausible elements in the
"revelations" that were made after the event, one is tempted to
believe that these impressions were not so very false. It is simply
that, beyond a certain point, Lin Piao and his friends refused to go
on endorsing a policy that was not their own. The crisis came in
the fall of 1971, after Mao's swing around the provinces, when the
Party committees eclipsed—wholesale and without any formalities—the other mass organizations.[32] According to a document

[31] China has a system of spreading "unpublished" news through meetings in
schools and workplaces. Although it is difficult to estimate the scope and
effectiveness of this method of publicity on a national scale, it certainly reaches the
towns and the political activists whom the foreign visitor is likely to encounter.
Hence, I am convinced that in the spring of 1971 the best-informed cadres—who
had the task of informing others—knew nothing about the clash at the top and had
a cast-iron belief that Vice-Chairman Lin Piao, "the designated heir," was the most
trusted exponent of the "line of Chairman Mao" which they were following.

[32] In theory, "workers' conferences" were still functioning in the factories with
the duty of representing the rank-and-file organizations "adapted to the period of
reconstruction." The time was not yet ripe for reviving the extensively discredited
trade unions. Only in 1972, after the fall of Lin Piao, was it decided to rebuild the
trade unions and put an end to the "workers' conferences."

circulated among the cadres a year later, "Chairman Mao intended to return to Peking and meet with Vice-Chairman Lin Piao in order to persuade him to renounce his errors, on the principle of saving the sick man and curing the sickness." [33] This meeting could not take place because, according to the official account, Lin Piao fled in the direction of the USSR on September 12, 1971, in a civilian Trident aircraft, piloted by his son, after taking off from the seaside resort of Peitaho. The plane crashed in Outer Mongolia and Lin met his death, together with his wife, Yeh Ch'un (a member of the Politburo), and an unspecified number of accomplices. But this story flies in the face of all logic even in its details, and we have every right to assume that the crash of a Trident in Mongolia in September 1971 was linked to the fate of Lin Piao only several months later. In reality, after Mao's return, a meeting was held in Peking and attended by a great many leaders. It is not known whether Lin Piao and Ch'en Po-ta were present in person, but we may be certain that other leaders of the radical wing spoke for them and flatly rejected the Chairman's demand to conform to the new line and to pretend that it had not been changed since the Cultural Revolution. [34]

Certainly, this is only a theory. There is no real proof, for lack of evidence from the "rebel" side and of documents relating to the showdown of September 1971. But no other theory can explain the wholesale dismissals which occurred directly after-

[33] A fairly complete text of Document No. 12 on Mao's tour of the provinces, in August–September 1971, was given by Agence France-Presse in a dispatch from Hong Kong on September 10, 1972. In this document, whose authenticity is beyond question, these words were attributed to Mao: "What are we to do with all these people? . . . We must follow the policy of education: that is, make use of past errors to avert fresh errors, and cure the sickness to save the sick man. Lin Piao, therefore, must be preserved. No matter who is in error, it is always right to remain concerned for unity and for the line. After my return to Peking, I shall seek them out to hold a discussion with them. Perhaps they will refuse to come, but I shall look for them."

[34] About September 10, 1971, foreign correspondents in Peking noted the disappearance of all the leaders, including Chou En-lai, who postponed several appointments with Japanese and other visitors. They also observed a movement of limousines around the Great Hall of the People, which indicated a top-level meeting. Evidently it was not a Central Committee session, but rather one of those "working conferences" which were called at short notice, according to the customs of the CCP. But this was virtually all that could be discovered.

ward or the appearance ten months later of a fantastic account of Lin Piao's treachery. A moment's thought, in fact, tells us that in normal circumstances a group of leaders concerned to prove that they were pursuing the policy of the Cultural Revolution would not have dismissed from posts of responsibility most of the men who were most clearly identified with this policy in the eyes of the rank and file. If they did this, it can only mean that these men as a whole—rather than some isolated figures—refused to follow them. And if it was necessary, several months later, to mount a vast campaign against "crooks of the type of Liu Shao-ch'i"—that is, against Lin Piao and his friends—this means that it was absolutely vital to show that the departed chiefs did not represent (as people had hitherto believed) the spirit of the Cultural Revolution, and indeed that they had never represented it, because at that time, despite all appearances, they did not belong to the "proletarian camp."

The Triumph of Diplomacy

The right way to make a tit-for-tat reply depends on the situation. Sometimes, not to negotiate is to return tit for tat; sometimes, to negotiate is also to return tit for tat. . . . China's problems are complicated and our thinking must also be somewhat complicated. . . . We must constantly enlighten the people about the progress of the world and their gleaming future, to help them to have confidence in victory. At the same time, we must tell the people and our comrades that the road will make many twists and turns. There are still many obstacles and difficulties on the road of the revolution. . . . Some comrades would rather not think too much about the difficulties. But the difficulties are a reality and we must recognize them, analyze them, and combat them. . . . We must not imagine that one fine morning all the reactionaries will fall on their knees of their own accord. In short, the future is radiant but our road is tortuous.[35]

This warning, which Mao wrote in October 1945 with regard to the negotiations with the Kuomintang at Chungking, was recalled in the summer of 1971 in the context of the new Chinese foreign policy. At first, one might assume that this praise of diplomacy and

[35] Mao Tse-tung, *Selected Works*, Vol. IV (Peking: Foreign Languages Publishing House, 1965), p. 51.

tactics was intended simply to explain to the Chinese the reasons for Dr. Kissinger's surprise visit in July 1971 and to prepare them for the arrival of President Nixon. It could also be seen as an indirect retort on Mao's part to the uncompromising speech in which Huang Yung-sheng had demanded that the Americans clear out of the whole of Asia as a precondition for the opening of negotiations. At first sight, Huang had thus stated the position of Lin Piao and of many comrades who paid too little attention to the "difficulties," and Mao had unearthed his 1945 advice to persuade them to make their thinking more "complicated." That, apparently, was that.

But the editorial writers of Peking returned to the charge well after Lin's fall, and after Nixon's visit, calling on comrades to make a profound study of the essay "On the Chungking Negotiations" and to grasp "the general trend of the course of history." [36] Thus, this reminder of the past could no longer be regarded merely as an argument used at a given moment; it had to be seen as a justification, for a long period, of stressing "twists and turns in the face of obstacles." A theoretician on *Red Flag*, Hung Yuan, confirmed this clearly in August 1972: "China is still a developing country; we must keep on working hard to bring the revolution to fruition in the sphere of the superstructure, to consolidate and develop the economic basis of socialism, to add to the productive forces, and to make China a socialist country with a modern industry, agriculture, science, and culture. Many obstacles await us on the path of the revolution and we must therefore redouble our efforts." [37]

While awaiting this internal advance, China was obliged to contain her external enemies. As Mao advised, it was necessary to know how to negotiate. In fact, Chou En-lai's government used this method on a large scale and with great skill and—as Peking put it—the "revolutionary line in the field of diplomacy" enabled China to win "magnificent victories" within two years. Except for the Russians, who were extremely annoyed, foreign observers in general recognized the significance of these Chinese successes and

[36] See "Study Notes Relating to 'On the Chungking Negotiations,'" *Peking Review*, No. 34 (August 1972).
[37] Ibid.

agreed that they gave that country a leading position on the world political scene. How could it be disputed that China's entry into the United Nations in October 1971 was a triumph for her? How could it be denied that she became a rallying point for nations eager to escape from the domination of the two superpowers, which, as the Chinese said, were "trying to share out the world even while they quarrel?" And yet, it was also generally agreed, Chou En-lai's government won these victories only because it was converted to the doctrine of *Realpolitik* and no longer bothered about ideological prejudices. This had already been shown by its attitude toward the Bengali revolt in the spring of 1971 and toward the left-wing uprising in Ceylon.[38] Peking rejected this interpretation and kept repeating that China would never behave like a superpower; she would use all her weight on the international scene to advance the proletarian line of the Cultural Revolution by methods suited to the circumstances. In this field, as in internal policy, China's leaders were visibly concerned to maintain the principle of "continuity."

Nevertheless, to the outside observer, this continuity of China's "internationalist line" was not always discernible. In the short run, while it is easy to record the tactical maneuvers of Chinese diplomacy, it is much harder to see how they helped the perspective of world revolution which had been exalted in the

[38] The nationalist revolt of the Bengali people broke out in East Pakistan in March 1971; backed by India, it was repressed by the Pakistani Army with great ferocity but little success. At roughly the same time, Madame Bandaranaike's Center-Left reformist government in Ceylon was almost overthrown by a revolutionary movement of the far Left, described as "Guevarist." In both cases, the Chinese government wrapped itself in silence and maintained its good relations with the governments in power. This attitude amounted to backing the regimes against the rebels, who had no lack of legitimate grievances, whatever their precise political connections. Moreover, China's embarrassed identification with the repression in East Pakistan did not prevent the military intervention of India (backed by the USSR) later in the year and the creation of the pro-Indian state of Bangladesh. Only after the dismemberment of Pakistan in December 1971 did the Peking government publish a statement about the dangers that India—a multinational and not very united country—courted by encouraging and exploiting nationalist outbreaks among her neighbors. As for the events in Ceylon, the Peking press never uttered a word from beginning to end. In July 1972 Madame Bandaranaike was received in Peking with full honors by Chairman Mao, who is said to have favored her with the first "revelations" of the death of Lin Piao.

previous period. Doubtless, it is too soon to pronounce judgment on a strategy of great scope which aims at exploiting, over a long period, the inter-state contradictions both in the capitalist world and in Eastern Europe. But, without pronouncing a verdict on the two years of Chinese foreign policy that followed Lin Piao's downfall, we can raise certain questions about its manifestations, whose effects were felt within China. During the Cultural Revolution, the leaders encouraged the masses by presenting them with a very simplified picture of the "excellent revolutionary situation in the world," stressing their solidarity with the struggling peoples on every continent. Thanks to this sketchy outline of events abroad, the intervention of the rank and file in international affairs was naturally unsophisticated as well; and, as I have said, it more or less paralyzed Chinese diplomacy. The fact remains that, for the first time, the masses in China (even those who belonged to no movement) were made aware that their fate was linked to that of their comrades abroad; and, by taking an interest in happenings elsewhere, they broke out of the self-enclosed Chinese universe. Thus, I saw in 1971 that young people, even in remote country districts, were quite well informed. They put highly relevant questions to me, for instance, about the "May 1968 storm" in France. I had had no such experiences on my earlier visit in 1965, so the progress struck me as notable and promising. But it could be no more than a beginning; the maintenance of the line of the Cultural Revolution obviously required that the new curiosity of Chinese youth should be nourished by fuller information and deeper analysis, to strengthen their internationalism and develop their critical spirit.

Now, what strikes one about the Chinese press in recent times is that it flatly presents as evidence of the "excellent revolutionary situation in the world" events which have little in common with real progressive struggles—for example, Britain's entry into the Common Market—and makes no attempt to explain apparently curious invitations handed out to various foreign heads of state. I shall have more to say about Nixon's visit, which is a special case. According to private information, it was preceded and followed by a huge campaign of explanation. On the other hand, no similar effort was made, either in the press or through other channels, to justify the reception of the Burmese leader Ne Win, described not so long ago as "100 percent fascist"; or that of President Mobutu of Zaire, identified during the Cultural Revolution as "the murderer of Patrice Lumumba, the puppet of the Americans, the man who is drowning the struggle of the Congolese people in blood and sabotaging in a thousand ways the African liberation movement." [39] The memory of the Chinese people is not so short as that. *People's Daily* might have taken the trouble to explain how Burma and Zaire had changed, or how friendly relations with such states and such leaders could assist the cause of oppressed peoples. The examples may seem unimportant, since the fate of China does not depend on talking to Ne Win or Mobutu, but these unexplained contacts have a symbolic significance precisely because the necessity for them is not obvious. We must conclude that, having raised tactics to the level of doctrine, the Chinese government no longer feels obliged to find out what people are thinking or to convince anyone of the validity of its twists and turns. It may be suspected that secret diplomacy on a grand scale, justified by a few sententious phrases dating from 1945, will seem to the rank and file even more highhanded and even harder to understand than on the earlier occasion. No doubt the radicals of 1967-8 went astray in their efforts to arouse the masses by selective pieces of news about the advance of world revolution. But the current style of "making friends everywhere in the world" carries a risk of spreading confusion and political apathy.

Other questions arise from certain shadowy aspects of decisions—apparently more justified—such as the renewal of the dialogue with the United States. As in 1945, when the Kuomintang asked for negotiations, the Chinese Communists had good reason in 1971 to regard the American offer as a victory. In both cases, it was already a success to be treated on a footing of equality by an enemy who had hitherto refused such an approach. Besides, this time Nixon was coming to Peking, whereas Mao had been obliged to go to Chungking. In these circumstances, it was pointless to begin by making exorbitant demands; it is obvious, for instance, that General Huang Yung-sheng's policy could scarcely provide a basis for negotiations, since he wanted the Americans to

[39] See "Renegades and Flunkeys," a comment on the friendly talks between the Russians and Mobutu, in *Peking Review*, No. 16 (April 19, 1968).

surrender all along the line before the talks began. Nevertheless, there was a precondition which had to be demanded (perhaps Huang was trying to safeguard it by asking for "too much") and which arose both from internationalism and from China's own interests—namely, a change in American policy in Vietnam, where the war was still going on.

There was every indication that this condition had been met; the belief was widespread that the Chinese had agreed to receive Nixon only after obtaining Vietnamese approval and getting firm assurances that the United States would give up plans for military escalation in Southeast Asia. Chou En-lai's statements during this entire period indicated fairly clearly that China, unlike the USSR, would do nothing that might harm the fighting peoples of Indochina (Vietnamese, Laotian, and also Cambodian), with whom China alone had had a relationship based on unconditional solidarity.[40] From this stance, it could be deduced that the Peking government had agreed to ease the American withdrawal from Indochina—which the Vietnamese of course desired—by giving assurances that China would not move in there, as she had never had any intention of doing. It was also thought that the United States, like any other great power, preferred for reasons of pride to arrange its timetable of withdrawal with another great power, namely China, and thus to save face. So there were no grounds for thinking that China would go it alone in this sphere.

Great was the surprise, therefore, on August 17, 1972, seven months after Nixon's trip to China, when *Nhan Dan*, the central organ of the Vietnamese Workers' Party, published an editorial violently attacking "diplomatic treachery" aimed at isolating the Vietnamese and hampering their revolutionary task.[41] For the first

[40] Prince Sihanouk, the Cambodian head of state, was in Moscow in March 1970 when right-wing forces carried out a coup d'état in Phnom-Penh with American help. The Russians expressed their regrets but maintained diplomatic relations with the new Cambodian regime. Prince Sihanouk met with a better reception in Peking, where he was able to form a new government including the Khmers Rouges. China backed him without reservations or conditions, as he told me himself in Peking in 1971. Moreover, after Cambodia joined openly in the struggle against the United States and its puppets, representatives of the three Indochinese peoples held a conference near Canton in April 1970, attended by Chou En-lai, and thus publicly showed their solidarity with one another and with China.

[41] After his visit to Peking, Nixon went to Moscow in April 1972. The Russians, feeling that they were no longer outflanked by China, fraternized happily with

time since the foundation of the Democratic Republic of Vietnam in 1954, its government thus took issue in scarcely veiled terms with her "friends"—with the USSR certainly, but also quite obviously with China, who was also accused of dealing with the United States over the head of her Indochinese allies. The disclosure was painful and the affair was very serious; we can be sure that the Vietnamese, who had got used to measuring their words through long years of difficult cooperation with the Russians, would not have made such a forthright denunciation of "diplomatic treachery" unless it really threatened their vital interests.

But the worst was yet to come. In December 1972, before signing the peace terms already accepted in Paris, the Americans unleashed their super-bombers on the towns of North Vietnam, in the most cruel and cynical destructive operation of modern history. If there was ever a moment when the American President could be compared to Hitler, this was it; this way of extorting final concessions was a straightforward copy of Nazi methods. The American bombs were scattered over populated districts of Hanoi and Haiphong with a degree of barbarism hitherto unknown there.[42] But this time, in contrast to what had happened in 1965, no mass demonstrations were held in Peking (let alone Moscow) to denounce the crimes of imperialism. True, the Chinese press protested, and without mincing its words, but it gave no hint of a halt to the dialogue with Nixon and refrained from calling him a Nazi, the epithet so freely applied to his predecessor, Johnson. Had the Peking government never envisaged that its American guest would under any circumstances go to these lengths before he kept his promise to withdraw from Vietnam? Were the Chinese, taken by surprise, unable to make a gesture that matched what had happened? [43] Be this as it may, the whole world got the

him. They even signed a treaty on freedom of navigation, which does not lack a certain black humor when we recall that the Americans were then mining Vietnamese ports, contributing to the safety and freedom of navigation in their own style.

[42] Jean Leclerc du Sablon, the Agence France-Presse correspondent, earned the Polk Prize in the United States for his remarkable reports on the havoc wreaked by this bombing.

[43] In January 1973 Mao received Madame Binh, Foreign Minister of the Provisional Revolutionary Government of South Vietnam, and made a most solemn

impression that Nixon was able to resort to this unrestrained gangsterism only because he was confident of having neutralized both the Chinese and public opinion (including American opinion) thanks to "diplomatic treachery." Perhaps this impression was false, but world opinion was in fact shaken. Leaflets showing Mao and Nixon shaking hands had not shattered the morale of the Vietnamese, on whom they dropped from the sky together with fragmentation bombs. But Nixon's propagandists had succeeded in making effective use of this cozy photo, in the United States and in Western Europe, to show that the Chinese Chairman was no longer an enemy.

Of course, history is not made of ifs, and it is fruitless to wonder how the Vietnam War would have ended if Nixon had not gone to Peking and Moscow. But it is quite gratuitous to claim that there was no way of mobilizing opinion against the American war in Southeast Asia after the decline of the protest wave of 1968. What appears to be definite is that Peking, after a certain point, played down the importance of a political weapon which had neverthe-less shown itself to be effective in the earlier period. The decision was doubtless made that, in the face of the superpowers, it was wiser to take a short cut by "returning tit for tat" on the level of negotiation alone.

Did this new strategy succeed in warding off the Soviet and American threats against China? What exactly is the state of play in these famous governmental negotiations and what prospects do they offer to the Chinese? Can the Peking government manage to create a more reassuring image of China in official circles abroad, while maintaining for left-wing opinion its former reputation as a revolutionary country that refuses to compromise its principles?

Sino-Soviet negotiations were the first to make a fresh start in the fall of 1969. On September 11, on his way home from Ho Chi Minh's funeral in Hanoi, Kosygin stopped in Peking and had a long talk with Chou En-lai at the airport. This meeting doubtless prevented things from growing worse, and a phase of Sino-Soviet talks opened at the level of deputy foreign ministers. But no real

---

statement of solidarity: "We are of the same family, Vietnamese, Koreans, and Chinese." There was also a meeting in her honor in the Great Hall, attended by Chou, but no street demonstration.

détente appears to have ensued. The USSR continues to strengthen its military installations along the five thousand miles of its frontier with China and to show them cheerfully even to foreign visitors, confident of its right to "take precautions" in the face of a so-called threat of invasion. On the other side of the Amur River, the Chinese are hurriedly building an "underground Great Wall" for the whole country, in which they can take shelter in the event of a surprise attack. The construction of shelters and the accompanying mobilization of the masses are promptly denounced in Moscow as proof of Chinese belligerency. Peking retorts that this indignation is fraudulent; in his interview with Snow in 1970, Mao asked what harm it could do to Russia for the Chinese to get into bombproof shelters several yards under-ground. As for Chou En-lai, he has told visitors from various countries that he has had no reply to his approaches to the Soviet government on the subject of its military concentrations in the Far East. These create a certain nervousness in Peking, and no wonder; what government would not be nervous with a million and a half of another nation's best troops massed on its frontiers? American experts, who know something about preventive wars, which they themselves have urged, state that they would not be at all surprised to see a Soviet attack on China within the next three years.

But the Soviet leaders do not confine themselves to brandishing their weapons in the faces of the Chinese. They persist in efforts to create a "security system" in Asia, patently designed to encircle China. Moreover, some of their speeches—for instance, the one that Brezhnev made at Alma-Ata in August 1973—bring the Chinese out in a cold sweat because of their resemblance to the speeches that preceded the invasion of Czechoslovakia. What can be the meaning of these attempts at intimidation, while at the same time the USSR is all smiles for the West and is openly moving toward the integration of its economy with that of the capitalist world? These attitudes are not so contradictory as they seem. In order to succeed in their grand design of technological modernization for the USSR, Brezhnev and his team need to keep a tight hold on their "Socialist community" and guard against the possible political consequences of this new line within the bloc and in the USSR itself. Had China been weaker, she would long

ago have been "normalized" like Czechoslovakia. The dangers
that she faces are proportional to her stature; where tanks cannot
do the job, the need for a nuclear "surgical operation" presents
itself.

Most people regard these apocalyptic possibilities with incredulity, and prefer to think that the rumors of war will come to
nothing, as in the Cold War between East and West. But, in the
most hopeful view, we must not underestimate the damage that
can be caused by a long period of Sino-Soviet tension. (The Cold
War was a costly business both for the USSR and for the West.)
To begin with, it is certain that the USSR today gives China a
more acute encirclement complex than the United States did in
the recent past. Rightly or wrongly, Chinese leaders are convinced that in the event of American aggression they would find a
great many allies and defenders in the world, and notably in the
Soviet bloc. But they have few illusions about any help they might
get from the West if attacked by the Russians.

True, they have agreed to renew diplomatic relations with the
United States—by the exchange of information offices and not of
ambassadors—and they believe that the Americans have no
interest in letting the USSR become too strong in Asia. But from
this to relying on Washington is a jump that they are careful not
to make. They need other kinds of counterweight to Soviet or
American pressure (the latter has relaxed, but could be renewed
at any moment). Hence their desire to encourage the nations of
Western Europe to unite and hold their own with the superpowers. Hence, also, their appeals to the Third World, reinforced by
generous and disinterested economic aid. And hence, finally, their
interest in contradictions within capitalism or between the two
blocs, which has gradually replaced the former interest in the
development of proletarian forces abroad. All these changes
sometimes make us think that China has taken up the concept of
the "besieged Socialist fortress"; some decades ago, the imperiled
USSR also sought to buy time by dividing the front of its capitalist
enemies. This precedent tells us that such a policy, even if it is
inevitable, exacts a heavy cost from the nation that adopts it,
particularly in the field of internal progress.

Some of us view this eventuality with apprehension, even
though it is not a question of blaming the Chinese or impugning

their motives. Historical situations never take the same form twice, and analogies between the USSR in the past and China today may be highly deceptive. But these anxieties exist, and are increased by the clumsiness of Chinese propaganda. It is often disturbing to read the New China News Agency's dispatches, whose selection of documents and arguments reveals a preoccupation with state policy and makes no concession to China's friends abroad. Through the habit of praising anyone who is on cool terms with the USSR, even if for poor reasons, the Chinese seem to be encouraging a sort of *union sacrée*. And yet, in the past, they were the first to point out that "the class struggle must never be forgotten" and they always asked themselves the question: "What kind of people are your allies—and your enemies?"

In 1971, I saw a China that took great pride in having a social system that was absolutely "different." I am sure that this feeling did not die with the crisis of September 1971 and the elimination of Lin Piao. China has always vehemently rejected the values of the capitalist world and of the USSR. She asks the West neither for technical "aid" nor for advice, and refuses even the credits that she is offered. Those who imagine that she has "learned her lesson" and expect her to develop along Soviet lines will be much disappointed; they are mistaking their hopes for realities. However, the Chinese are less and less successful in making themselves understood by their real friends—certainly because they give priority to relations between states, but also because of their difficulty in explaining the ending of the Cultural Revolution and the dramas that followed it. Probably, without the internal clash of September 1971, they would have shown more sensitivity toward left-wing opinion at large, and would have held stronger cards in the difficult game of the diplomacy of a revolutionary nation.

But, since I have said a good deal about simplifications of history and about the dangers inherent in the current version of the fall of Lin Piao, I should like to end this chapter with an account of my journey in April 1971 to the historic places of Chingkangshan. To go by what we are now told, Lin Piao was already a "political corpse" then. But this merely lends pathetic overtones to the litanies recited at that time.

Postscript
The Houses of Mao and Lin Piao
in the Mountains of Chingkangshan

The past does not explain everything; but, in the Communist view, it illuminates the class struggle of the present day. Those who know the history of working-class battles are better armed for the battles that they themselves must wage. For this reason, opposite the Great Hall of the People in Peking, a large Museum of the Revolution has been set up. These two buildings in the same style, on T'ien An Men Square, symbolize the continuity of the Chinese Communist era. In documents recalling the recent history of his country, a Maoist militant should find the best explanation of his past sufferings and the new direction of his life.

But the big museum on T'ien An Men Square has been closed since the Cultural Revolution. No doubt the lessons that it taught were not considered to be effective enough, or perhaps the record of the Chinese Communist Party had been distorted. While we wait until the storm stirred up by these events calms down and an official version is established, we must be content with oral accounts which vary—true, within narrow limits—according to the speakers. We all know that revisions in this field must be made carefully. When a post-revolutionary society claiming to be the outcome of objective historical laws takes a fresh look at its past, there is a risk of causing its people profound anxiety. The Soviet example is definitive in this respect, but China too has not managed to spare the rank and file from "historical" surprises. I made this observation when I visited Mao's original Red base in the mountains of Chingkangshan. Here are my notes from this journey, made in April 1971, three months before the fall of Lin Piao.

With Mr. Chiang, my interpreter from Shanghai, I traveled in a small two-engined civilian plane to Nanchang, the capital of Kiangsi Province. From there we were to go by car to Mao's base, accompanied by two officials from the province. One of them, Comrade Wu, was the top man in the expedition; he wore thin spectacles on his emaciated intellectual face and asked politely after my wishes.

First we went to the Historical Museum of Nanchang, which stands in the middle of a square. We were welcomed by a team of charming young women wearing their Sunday best. Previously devoted to the uprising of August 1, 1927,[44] the museum is now divided into two sections: one deals with the battles of Ching-kangshan and the other with the struggles of the workers of P'ingh-hsiang District, more particularly the strike of the Anyuan miners in 1922. We visited only the latter section, since we were to see the Chingkangshan battles, so to speak, on the spot. The first two rooms showed, with the aid of photographs and statistics, the inhuman living and working conditions endured by the miners at the time, under ferocious exploitation by Chinese and Japanese capitalists. "But where there is oppression, there is resistance," concluded our guide. Another woman had the job of taking us around the room devoted to Chairman Mao's eight visits to the Anyuan miners in 1922. The absence of contemporary photo-graphs was redeemed by a large number of pictures showing the Chairman impeccably dressed in his long blue tunic. He arrives in the mining villages on foot from his native Hunan Province and holds meetings—each picture refers to a dated occasion—with comrades with determined faces who are evidently listening to his advice that they should move into action. He explains the importance of revolution in terms that seem remarkably up to date—"the working class must lead in everything," "dare to think and dare to act," etc.—and urges his hearers to make more far-reaching demands on their bosses. "In the light of the teachings of Chairman Mao," concluded the guide, "the level of understanding of the Anyuan workers rose considerably, and they prepared themselves ideologically and organizationally to launch the general strike of September 1922, famous throughout the world."

[44] The Chinese Red Army (later called the Red Army of Liberation) was born in Nanchang on this date, and it was in this first Communist armed rising that a whole constellation of future leaders, comrades of Mao from the outset, distinguished themselves. Some of them lost their jobs or went through difficult times in the Cultural Revolution, so I was curious to know what was said about them in recalling their feats of arms in 1927.

The fourth room recalled the sudden arrival, two days before the start of the strike, of Liu Shao-ch'i (though there was no picture of him). This renegade and strike breaker "furiously" creates obstacles to the plans made by Mao. He describes the strike as "adventurist" because, according to him, "conditions are not ripe and we cannot be sure of victory." The workers are not deceived, and Liu quickly changes his tactics; in the seventeen-point list of demands, he suggests omitting the four points which are least acceptable to the bosses. Thus, he already reveals that the interests of the capitalists are nearer to his heart than those of the workers, "that he is in the service of the oppressing class and not of the oppressed." The young woman tells us all this with animation, quivers her eyelids, grows angry, gets red in the face, and lowers her voice to stress the gravity of the situation. I don't dare to interrupt, for questions are invited only at the end of our visit.

We reach the famous date of September 13, 1922. The general strike breaks out all over the coal field and on the railways of the district. The capitalists at once ask the reactionary government for police and troops to suppress it. Seventeen thousand strikers, "inspired by the thought of Chairman Mao," are afraid of nothing and ready to fight to the end. But Liu is seized by panic and urges them to "wage a civilized strike and not to confront the enemy openly." At the same time, he asks the capitalists to negotiate, and when they threaten to arrest him, he hastens to declare, "I am not a worker, I have come as a mediator." Here our new guide takes up the lesson from the previous room: "It is necessary to choose. Which class should we choose—the proletariat or the bourgeoisie?" And she duly stigmatizes Liu's preference for the latter.

So to the climax. The workers, still inspired by Chairman Mao's thought, besiege the boiler house and put dynamite in the pits. The bosses, backs to the wall, are forced to accept the strike demands. But the "arch-traitor" Liu comes to the rescue, suggests a compromise in a legalistic spirit, sacrifices political demands to trade-union demands, breaks the revolutionary enthusiasm of the working class, and in return obtains from the bosses the right to start a "workers' club" at Anyuan. His line, which is opposed to that of Chairman Mao, cheats the Anyuan miners of their victory and in the long run paves the way to their defeat. Three years

later, in fact, on September 25, 1925, the hired thugs of the
capitalists attack this very club, and kill or arrest the best
militants, including its leader. "The facts presented here," our
guide sums up, "show clearly that Liu Shao-ch'i is a renegade, that
he unscrupulously betrayed the interests of the working class, that
he is simply a criminal who infiltrated the ranks of the proletariat."

Next we go to a room where tea is served, according to custom,
and where visitors have an opportunity to express their opinions,
criticisms, and suggestions. The guides, in full muster, are ready to
answer, for they have made a complete study on the spot, at
Anyuan, of the history of this strike which marked the opening of
the struggle between the two lines within the CCP. The
atmosphere is once again smiling and relaxed; I take advantage of
it to ask why Liu was not unmasked before the Cultural
Revolution, in view of the flagrant and long-standing nature of his
crimes. The women show a certain bewilderment—no doubt the
question had never occurred to them—but get out of it by
collective effort and in a friendly way through some general
remarks about the inevitability of the internal struggle in the
Party and on Chairman Mao's willingness to "cure the sickness
and save the sick man." The austere Comrade Wu cuts the
discussion short, for the car is waiting to take us to Chingkangshan.

Our last stop, after a road journey through rice fields, is the small
town of Yunghsin, which was part of the Red base several times
between 1927 and 1930. We spend some time there, because it
has a comfortable guest house, and also to study an event of July
1928 which is very rich in lessons. Interpreter Chiang, who is in
Chingkangshan for the first time, would prefer to visit these places
in chronological order, and so should I, but Comrade Wu makes
the decisions. We walk around the town, followed by schoolchil-
dren full of curiosity about the "foreign friend," and stop at an old
ancestral temple where we are awaited by the local team,
consisting of young men and women.

It is a cold gray day, and the temple, rather dark even in full
daylight, is far from inviting. But we are at the very place where
Chairman Mao had to struggle against the "bad line" in the Party,

and a subject like this cannot be taken care of in a few minutes. Chiang, however, maintains that explanations should begin from the event itself, instead of going back to the birth of the CCP in 1921 or the creation of the Chingkangshan base in 1927. So we plunge straight into the events of July 4, 1928. On that day, the delegates from the Party Committee of Hunan Province, supported by the higher organs of the CCP, give Mao and the command staff of the First Peasants and Workers Army orders to march toward southern Hunan. But Mao disagrees and gives his reasons in a long and well-argued reply, in seven points. Yes, he admits, most of the army consists of Hunanese men eager to return to their native province, but this is no reason to accept battle on terrain favorable to the enemy, who moreover is numerically stronger and better equipped. Besides, the Chingkangshan base provides a chance to fan out in the surrounding districts without too many risks and to strengthen the Red Army, which is not suited to positional warfare. He adds five less important arguments to these two main objections, but the Party delegates are very obstinate and don't allow themselves to be convinced. The order to march to southern Hunan remains in force.

Here the story becomes a little confused, because the speaker refers again to the desire of most of the soldiers to quit Kiangsi Province, so that it's not very clear whether Mao accepts the Party order through discipline or to bow to the will of the rank and file. What is clear, however, is that he takes part in this expedition reluctantly and solely to limit the damage. Events soon prove him right. After two defeats, in August 1928, the Red Army is forced to withdraw to its starting point. In a new meeting at Tunghsia, Mao triumphs politically all along the line. He takes advantage of this, not to say, "This is what happens when you don't follow me," but to draw general lessons on the strategy of the Chinese revolution: "We can destroy our enemies only by winning the people to our cause, by improving their lot through land reform, by giving them something more every day, and by mobilizing them for their war of liberation. We shall lose everything, on the other hand, if we seek a purely military victory over the militarists who oppress China."

Does this episode prove that Chairman Mao has always been

the one source of wisdom and that the Party, on the contrary, tended toward opportunism? Or that all those who oppose the Chairman end up badly? Or that the Chairman knows how to turn bad into good? Or all three at the same time? I am not to find out, for we are off again and soon in sight of Chingkangshan. Comrade Wu takes care to give me a thorough description of this famous zone. It includes about forty villages spread among the mountains and is inhabited by 34,390 people, belonging to three people's communes divided into twelve brigades and forty-six production teams. Two large villages, Maoping and Tseping, can pride themselves on being Mao's old capital. They are situated in the gorges of Huanyungchieh and separated by the pass of the same name, where a large monument was erected during the Cultural Revolution in honor of a battle which took place in 1928, soon after the disastrous expedition to southern Hunan. Maoping is better known because this is where Mao wrote his poem of sixteen words in Chinese, which is found in all the handbooks:

> The enemy advances, we retreat.
> The enemy halts, we harass him.
> The enemy is weary, we strike.
> The enemy retreats, we pursue.

Comrade Wu makes clear, however, that the Chairman lived at Tseping as much as at Maoping, and indeed had a slight preference for a hamlet midway between them, "the village of the big well," where he wrote his famous report "The Battle of Chingkangshan," [45] in November 1928. Our tour takes us first to Maoping, where we are to spend the night.

Two rectangular modern buildings, used as guest houses, have recently been built at this picturesque place, which consists of about thirty little houses clinging to the flank of the mountain. In the middle, the village square has been replaced by a rice field and the visitor can watch the process of rice planting from his window. Opposite, there is a disused ancestral temple which used to be a military hospital and where we begin our visit. This temple retains a beauty which our guides don't neglect to point out; we look particularly at a curious octagonal room (*pa tia lo*). But, here

[45] Mao Tse-tung, *Selected Works*, Vol. I.

again, the fame of the temple derives from a conference held on May 20, 1928, at which twenty-four delegates from the whole zone elected Mao as Chairman and laid down the main lines of their program. At the other end of the village, another graceful building maintained as a museum is also a historic spot; this is where, in April 1928, Mao met Lin Piao for the first time. Next we visit Mao's room in a third house, where in October 1928 he wrote his report "Why Red Power Can Exist in China"; and finally the command post of the 28th Division of the Red Army, commanded by Lin Piao, who also lived in it.

The people whom I meet at Maoping belong to the "May 7 Army of Chingkangshan," an organization in which the idea of May 7 (the date of Mao's letter to Lin Piao in 1966) counts for more than "Army." It is not a military unit, in fact, but rather a variety of the "May 7" schools for the cadres which function throughout China.

For a reason which I didn't get clear, another system too has been adopted in Kiangsi Province. The cadres and young intellectuals wishing to work in the country have been organized in detachments or battalions of the "May 7 Army" and distributed among already existing communes. Thus, they work in farm brigades like everyone else, but devote at least three mornings a week to studies and ideological discussions. The detachment of Ningkang District—to which Maoping belongs—is also responsible for the upkeep of the museums and instilling Mao's thought into visitors. Altogether, it consists of 460 former cadres and 698 young intellectuals—in reality, high school students coming mostly from Shanghai. How long do they stay in the countryside? Some, especially the cadres, have already returned to their duties after a year or a year and a half, but the period is not fixed. "We shall stay here until we are called to other tasks," the older ones generally answer, while the young intellectuals say that they have no objection to "serving the people to the end of our days in the communes of our glorious Chingkangshan."

The two generations seem to live together harmoniously, at least within the "May 7 Army." The young people receive and guide visitors, but their elders give them a hand when certain questions have to be answered. It appears that the same understanding exists during the farm work and the study sessions, and that the young people are not in an officially subordinate position. It was they, indeed, who described, in terms that were almost always identical in each of the Maoping buildings, the context in which Chairman Mao's struggle had to be seen. This preamble consists of quotations from the Little Red Book (which everyone waves as a greeting when we arrive and leave) and standard phrases about "the struggle between the two lines in the CCP." Ritual demands that these are repeated each time as if they were a novelty, that the interpreter has to translate them word for word, and often that a secretary has to note them in the record of the meeting. It all ends up with the obligatory statement: "Chairman Mao has waged a long and constantly renewed struggle against the notably reactionary line of the arch-traitor Liu Shao-ch'i. We must therefore state that, throughout the Chinese revolution, a bitter struggle has brought into confrontation, at every vital moment and on every important problem, the proletarian line of Chairman Mao and the bourgeois line of Liu Shao-ch'i."

Once this has been laid down, we come to the 1920's—when there was not much sign of Liu—to the "Autumn Harvest Uprising" in Hunan Province, directed personally by Mao, and to his arrival in the Chingkangshan Mountains with the remnants of his forces at the end of September 1927. "From this moment," I am told in solemn tones, "there began, at this very place, the rural revolutionary war, or second revolutionary war, which was to last until 1937, the date of the beginning of the war of resistance against Japan." The Following is a description of the special situation in Kiangsi Province and in the area with which we are concerned.

In these villages, still so devoid of riches, the European visitor has some difficulty in imagining the reign of mighty landlords exploiting the peasant masses. But the idea of wealth is relative, and the facts given to us seem to be unchallengeable. In 1927, 70 percent of the cultivable land belonged to a dozen families who oppressed the poor peasants and even had their own police force, recruited from "hirelings of the worst type." [46] Moreover, these

[46] Unlike other provinces, Kiangsi in 1927 had no war lord as governor and the administrative structure was vague, to say the least.

exploiters enforced an indescribable discrimination against a
national minority, the Hakkas, who were actually a majority in the
mountain zone. A few days after his arrival, on October 3, 1927,
Mao met with the Hakka rebels led by Yuan Wen-tsai and a tailor,
Wang Tso, and reached an agreement on united action. He
backed their demands and supplied them with arms, but also
explained to them that their enemies were all the rich, including
rich Hakkas. "Chairman Mao's method," continued the young
woman, "always consisted in uniting all forces against the main
enemy and exercising his predominance within the united front."
So, in the course of time, the Hakka rebels became an integral
part of the Red Army. But, in the words of a slogan of that time
faithfully repeated for us: "Without proletarian leadership, a
mainly peasant revolution can take the wrong road." Chairman
Mao needed a working-class element—supplied by the miners of
Anyuan, a coal field 180 miles from Chingkangshan—and above
all the absolute dominance of the proletarian ideology. He spoke
of this in his report to the historic meeting at Maoping in May
1928.

The third and most important theme concerns this event, and is
briefly explained by a former cadre, Comrade Sui. He stresses first
this quotation from Mao: "Without the People's Liberation Army,
the people have nothing," and then this one: "The Party must
command the guns"—exercise its authority over the army in an
absolute and unchallengeable manner. Not delving into theory, he
turns to the history of Chingkangshan. In 1927, when Mao's
soldiers arrived from Hunan, the peasants had fled to the
mountains, leaving everything behind them and seeking only to
save their lives. Having seen other armies, they distrusted all
soldiers. The Red soldiers, exhausted by a march which had been
marked by ceaseless fighting, were in great need of rest. But Mao
forbade them to enter empty houses and to touch anything in the
absence of the owners. Moreover, he ordered them to clean the
village streets and to do small urgent repair jobs. Perched on
the mountain, the peasants watched this, unable to believe their
eyes and even suspicious of a trap. Then the boldest among them
began to come down. Mao suggested that they call a big meeting
of poor peasants, and after some hesitation they all came. At the
end of this meeting, after explaining the aims of the rural

revolutionary war, he had weapons distributed to volunteers so that they could form their own Red Guards and defend themselves, under any conditions, against the return of the landlords and their hirelings.

"But Chairman Mao could not be the only one to make propaganda," Comrade Sui reasonably points out. Every soldier had to be able to put the mass line into effect; hence the priority given, from the start, to politics in the Red Army. "For Chairman Mao, there was no question of building an army in which the officers are educated and command while the soldiers are illiterate and obey. From the outset, our army regarded political work as its main driving force and required all its fighters to possess a high level of proletarian understanding. Thus, Party committees functioned in all units, in every regiment, every battalion, every platoon. Then the soldiers spread revolutionary ideas and mingled anew with the masses."

Comrade Sui goes on to the concrete resolutions of the Maoping conference. "It was decided that all members of the army should have equal pay. Chairman Mao himself got five fen, like the others. He refused the slightest privileges. When peasants brought him eggs and other foodstuffs as gifts, he always gave them to the hospital for our wounded and sick. He had a horse, but he was almost always seen walking in straw sandals, like those that are to be seen here, and lending his mount to anyone who was in a hurry or was tired. Of course, other leaders followed his example. As for the soldiers, they had 'two rights and five obligations.' The rights were to check the accounts of their regiments and to be informed on all problems. The obligations were to maintain discipline, to take part in administration, to contribute to material needs by work, to take charge of the education of recruits, and—the last and most important—to carry out political work among the masses."

Many little facts show how this line was put into practice and explain why Chingkangshan is regarded as a historic example, which forged a new type of people's army. "Our hospital had a minimum of three doctors and a maximum of eighteen," Comrade Sui tells us, "but very little medicine. When the peasants understood that this hospital was theirs too, that our doctors were at their service like our soldiers, they helped us to collect medicinal herbs in the mountains, and we set up a small drug industry together. We also started a school, first for children and then for adults." Comrade Sui would be happy to continue his account, but a messenger summons us to another house where a team is waiting for us.

We cross the village, passing peasants who are planting rice without paying much attention to us. Then we take a path leading to a wooded hill, on whose slopes we find the second famous spot in Maoping. "Yes," the young guide confirms, "it is the house of a landlord who fled in 1927. It was burned down during the white terror of the 1930's, but we have faithfully reconstructed it, copying every detail. Chairman Mao revisited it in 1965 and recognized it at once."

The two young women who welcome our group to the house and serve tea are wearing, on their black velvet jackets—very much in the Shanghai style—huge badges which depict Mao and Lin Piao smiling at each other. No doubt this is meant to show that, in this place where they met forty-three years earlier, they formed a friendship that was often to be recalled. The narrative goes back to the beginning, and we have to wait quite a while until Lin Piao appears; but, once on the scene, he never leaves it and stands faithfully at the side of Chairman Mao "on every occasion and on every problem." This is indeed the central point of two long accounts of the "meeting at Maoping" and its historic consequences: Mao always had a comrade-in-arms close to him, ready to uphold the proletarian line in all circumstances.

After the young intellectuals with their fixed smiles, an older cadre takes up the tale and expatiates on the collaboration of Mao and Lin, seen from the viewpoint of the class struggle. The main theme is that all the deviationists in the Party leadership—Liu Shao-ch'i above all—always tried to turn the revolutionary army aside from its task and sought every opportunity to change its customs and its style of work. "These pseudo-Communists turned a deaf ear to the rightful doctrines of Chairman Mao; sometimes they claimed that a Red Army could no longer exist in China, sometimes that it ought to launch big offensives and adopt the tactics of positional warfare. After the liberation, these strategists filled with bourgeois ideas made a furious attack on the mass line and the democratic traditions of our army. They declared that modern equipment is too complex and too scientific, that ordinary soldiers can't understand it, and therefore that it is impossible to have democracy in the People's Liberation Army. At their head was that political pickpocket and notorious careerist P'eng Teh-huai, who took part in the revolution to make personal profit out of it. But he was obviously protected by the arch-traitor Liu Shao-ch'i, for otherwise he would never have dared to speak of creating a professional and nonpolitical army in a country like China which lives under the dictatorship of the proletariat."

This tirade is greeted by a long outburst of laughter and approval from everyone present. Encouraged by his success, the cadre piles on the anecdotes about "the stupidity of the bourgeois clique obedient to the USSR, who thought that they could break the iron will of Chairman Mao and Vice-Chairman Lin Piao by advancing baseless pseudo-scientific arguments, when experience had already shown that the proletariat, with nothing but millet and rifles, had beaten an army of the class enemy armed to the teeth.

"Faced with these senseless challenges, Vice-Chairman Lin Piao laid down the 'four priorities' of our army: priority of man over equipment, of political work over other activities, of ideological work over other aspects of political work, and of living ideas over bookish ideas in ideological work. Finally, our style of work is inspired by the 'three and eight' [i.e., three points and eight characters in Chinese writing]. The three points are: to depend firmly on correct political orientation, to be industrious and flexible in one's work, to show flexibility in strategy and tactics. The eight characters convey four qualities: unity, dynamism, seriousness, and enthusiasm." The cadre lists these principles with the desired dynamism, seriousness, and enthusiasm, for he still has much to say about the role of the army and of Comrade Lin Piao in the Cultural Revolution. This new battle in the class struggle under the dictatorship of the proletariat was the direct prolongation of the struggle between the Communists and the Kuomintang, begun here at Chingkangshan. He concludes: "As you see, Vice-Chairman Lin Piao has always held high the red banner of Mao Tse-tung's thought, has implemented the proletarian line of Chairman Mao and defended it loyally and firmly, and has always been his closest companion."

Curiosity led me to ask why nothing had been said about the Nanchang rising of 1927, in which Lin Piao distinguished himself, and also why there was not a word about other illustrious participants in the battles of that period who—unlike P'eng Teh-huai—were not regarded as pickpockets and who were still in their posts (Chou En-lai, Chu Teh, Ch'en Yi, for example). I was also thinking of dead great men such as Yeh T'ing, honored as martyrs of the revolution. To avoid offending my hosts, I took the precaution of remarking that, in the *Six Military Writings of Mao Tse-tung*, published as a Little Red Book during the Cultural Revolution, the Chairman placed great importance on the Nanchang rising and spoke of several of its protagonists. The young guides went as red as the said book, but could think of nothing except to repeat what they had said before about the importance of the meeting between Mao and Lin. The cadre, having taken time to prepare a more elaborate answer, went into a dialectical analysis of the Nanchang rising and proved that fundamentally it was not "on the line," since in 1927 it was not correct to seize towns; the correct action was to arm the peasant masses and create revolutionary support bases, as Chairman Mao did.

At the risk of worrying my friends, I remarked that facts don't vanish from history because they were not "on the line." Anyway, isn't the first of August celebrated every year in China as Army Day, in memory of the Nanchang rising? Besides, if Vice-Chairman Lin Piao made the mistake of taking part in it instead of fighting in the countryside, his other comrades too should be forgiven and accorded their place in revolutionary history. Silence. No one seemed to understand what I was getting at, and I was accompanied to the guest house without a word spoken. Even the representatives of the "May 7 Army" who later came to see me appeared to be suspicious.

Next day, we climb to the pass of Huanyungchieh. A wonderful view of green mountains and gorges—the very ones celebrated in a poem by Mao—extends before us and helps us to overlook the hideous monument, in Soviet-Chinese style, surrounded by revolutionary flames in red stone. Suddenly another car arrives; we are joined by Comrade Ma, chairman of the Chingkangshan Revolutionary Committee. Thickset and jolly, with bushy black hair, he smiles at my compliments on his vigor. No, he says, he's not at all young, he has been a Party member for thirty-two years and a revolutionary cadre for at least twenty. This introduction, and our shared admiration for the countryside, make us friends. I take kindly to his way of talking, for he doesn't give any lectures, his account is not prepared beforehand, he jokes and improvises. The team of young guides rapidly withdraws; Comrade Ma himself will explain the battle of Huanyungchieh.

As a souvenir, he gives me a bamboo spike like those which the peasants used in 1928 to mine the ground and check the enemy's advance. Then he tells me the story of the Red Army's only mortar and its three shells—only one succeeded in going off, to the amazement of both sides, and was enough to frighten the attackers, who considered it wise to retreat. "Of course, it wasn't a battle like Hwai-hai in 1949 or Stalingrad, but all things considered, it may have been just as important," he says with a touch of irony. "Things were particularly chancy in August 1928 for the Red Army because, as you've already been told at Yunghsin, the mistakes which the Hunan Party Committee insisted on forced us to fight under the worst conditions, backs to the wall. The enemy had hopes of finishing us off and capturing our leaders. They were ten times stronger than we were in numbers and a hundred times in weapons, but we had the people with us, the human factor which counts for more than anything else. When you study the history of this battle, you understand the deep meaning of that saying of Chairman Mao's: 'Our heaven is the mass of the Chinese people.' " He tried to think of something to add to this, but his expression suggests, "You'll find the rest in the books." We return to the fields, the steep ravines, and the mountains which Chairman Mao loved so much.

"Take a good look, you'll see those 'great trees piercing the clouds,' making a sort of link between earth and sky. I'll show you the tree under which Chairman Mao rested during the battle; he recognized it, you know. Over there, on the horizon, it's Hunan. You see the difference in the colors? Our province is greener and lighter, not so hot, more cloudy." Comrade Ma has the soul of a poet and readily admits it, for China and Communism are indeed "the poetry of reality." My guides from Nanchang, especially the austere Comrade Wu, consider that we've stayed too long at Huanyungchieh and propose that we get on our way.

Comrade Ma gets into the car with me. He knows every stone in this neighborhood and talks about it along the road. "We're going toward the 'village of the big well'; the well may be big, but the village is very, very small. Chairman Mao probably stayed there for the sake of peace." A few miles farther on, he frankly opens up a delicate question. "I gather that you weren't pleased with the young people of the propaganda team yesterday and they didn't know how to answer your questions." I deny this, but Comrade Ma isn't convinced. "They came this morning to make a self-criticism and they're very worried about it. They don't want a friend of China like you, coming from so far, to take away a bad impression of Chingkangshan. There are some things they don't know because they're young and inexperienced, but maybe I can answer instead of them."

So I repeat what I had said the day before about the absence, in Chingkangshan, of a number of leading figures in the 1927 events. He has heard about this from the young people. I give an example: "There must be a house at Maoping where Chairman Mao met Chu Teh, since Chu was commander-in-chief of the Red Army throughout the Kiangsi period and later, whereas Lin Piao was only twenty years old then and obviously couldn't have been so important." He objects at once: "But everything was destroyed here, the white terror claimed more victims and ravages in Kiangsi than anywhere else. How do you think we can find the house now where Chairman Mao met Chu Teh?"

As on the day before, I speak of the Nanchang rising. "Why doesn't anyone say a word of Yeh T'ing, Ch'en Yi, Ho Lung, T'an Chen-lin, or even Chou En-lai? I know that some of these leaders were severely criticized during the Cultural Revolution—which to my mind shouldn't wipe out their earlier virtues—but others are still members of the Politburo. Why reduce such a rich and exciting history to the figures of Chairman Mao and Vice-Chairman Lin Piao alone?"

My neighbor's face clouds. He in turn takes refuge in silence and reflection, interrupted by our arrival at the "village of the big well." We make a stop in the house where Mao wrote "The Battle of Chingkangshan," but Comrade Ma lets the local team do the talking and looks anxious. I give up hope of an answer to my "criticism and suggestion." But at Tseping, when the whole group gathers for lunch, he finds his smile again and returns to duty.

"You are right in saying that our history is rich and exciting and that there have always been many valuable leaders who loyally followed Chairman Mao. We don't say that Vice-Chairman Lin Piao has been his only comrade-in-arms, although beyond question he is the best and closest. We always pay tribute to the memory of Yeh T'ing, we have great respect for Premier Chou En-lai and Comrade Chu Teh, who came here in 1965, and many others too. But you should know that before the Cultural Revolution, our history was 'manipulated' by the general staff of Liu Shao-ch'i, who put everyone retrospectively on the same level. He favored his protégé P'eng Teh-huai, made him the hero of Chingkangshan, and systematically reshuffled the cards. In the end, he rubbed out the truth about the struggle between the two lines. To bear out his theory of 'great peace' within the Party, he tried to make out that all Communists have always held the same ideas and upheld the same interests. His aim was to tie the hands of the masses, to prevent them from fighting the anti-proletarian ideas which he was smuggling in.

"This is exactly what we rose up against in the Cultural Revolution. You can't imagine what happened here at that time. I can't quote the exact figures, but I assure you that every day at least thirty thousand young people arrived here, as much as the population of the district. They slept in the open, even in winter, and held continuous meetings in favor of Chairman Mao's line. There was no way of checking this human flood. At the beginning of 1967, the Central Committee had to appeal to people to stop pouring into Chingkangshan, hindering production and disorganizing the district, but it wasn't obeyed. And, believe me, all those who came here wanted to study the line of Chairman Mao and defend it, not to bother about the history of Yeh T'ing or Chu Teh."

Comrade Wu, who is not an eloquent man, joins in. "Since 1935, the proletarian line of Chairman Mao has always had the upper hand in our Party, and there must be no misunderstanding on that subject." Comrade Ma expresses his agreement and reinforces this: "Otherwise, neither the liberation in 1949 nor the Cultural Revolution in 1966 could have happened." Then Comrade Wu again attacks Liu Shao-ch'i's theory of "great peace" in the Party. "Those who wanted this 'peace' really wanted the revolution to halt, which means that it would retreat; those who wanted a struggle represented the interests of the proletariat, and they alone were faithful to the line of Chairman Mao and the socialist road. In all the debates that our Party has known since 1927, Comrade Lin Piao always supported this point of view, defended it by his actions, prevented our army from losing its class character, and made it the best school of the thought of Mao Tse-tung. These are established facts. The Ninth Party Congress, in 1969, recognized them and chose Comrade Lin Piao to be the heir to Chairman Mao. Of course, our great leader and his comrade-in-arms have not been the only ones who defended the proletarian line, which has been predominant within the Party and in the country. Premier Chou En-lai and many other leaders always stood beside them. The main strength of the proletarian line has always rested in its implantation in the hearts of the masses, the true heroes of our history. Anyone who thoroughly studies our past finds the necessary facts in the works of Chairman Mao, as you observed yourself. Not a name has been struck out from his writings and everything is clearly explained there. But the young people who come here want to learn how to apply the thought of Chairman Mao today and carry the revolution forward. This is why they discuss, first and foremost, the lessons of the battle of Chingkangshan and of the struggle between the two lines in our Party."

I came back to Peking just in time to see the May 1 celebration of 1971, at which Mao and Lin Piao appeared together on the platform in T'ien An Men Square for the last time. In the capital, there was much talk of Mao's interview with Edgar Snow, which had appeared in *Life* at the end of April and which raised expectations that a brake would soon be put on the personality cult of Mao. But no one seemed to find in these statements a forecast of the coming fall of Lin, though everyone knew that he had stressed the unification of Chinese society by the mass diffusion of Mao's thought and favored an intensification of the cult of the Chairman for educational purposes. To suggest that there might be a disagreement on this subject—or on any other—between Mao and his designated heir would have been regarded in Peking as in very bad taste. In Chingkangshan it would have provoked a still stronger reaction.

I have tried in vain to imagine how my hosts and guides in Kiangsi reacted a few months later to the revelations about the "plot" of Lin Piao and Ch'en Po-ta. Did they manage to get their ideas into order again after this upheaval at the topmost reaches of the "proletarian line"? Then, exactly a year after my journey to Chingkangshan, a friend—Edgar Snow's son—went there too. At Maoping he was not shown the house where Mao met Lin, and Lin's name was never spoken. For that matter, the name of Lin Piao is never officially mentioned in the Chinese press; it speaks of "swindlers of the type of Liu Shao-ch'i" and one is left to guess that this refers, paradoxically, to Liu's greatest former enemy. But can anyone believe that such methods can restore to the history of the CCP its true collective character and put an end to the simplifications, naïvetés, and omissions of the current version, which can never be effective even as indoctrination?

CONCLUSION

When Will the Next Cultural Revolution Occur?

The spokesman of the Soviet Union's China experts, Krivtsov—who has also been a diplomat in Peking—has been saying lately that China, having rebuilt the system favored by the former Vice-Chairman of the CCP, now has "Liu Shao-ch'i-ism without Liu Shao-ch'i." [1] Similar judgments, sometimes more cautiously formulated, can be found in the press of pro-Soviet Communist Parties, who are also hailing what they believe to be "the re-establishment of healthy norms of administration" in China. "Look for yourself," they suggest. "The Party again holds supreme authority, the trade unions have been rebuilt and are used as transmission belts for the Party's directives to the workers, the disorderly Red Guards have been replaced by a well-disciplined Communist Youth League, and the 'great adventure' of the Cultural Revolution was no more than a brief aberration, successfully overcome." According to them, the great upheaval that shook China from 1966 to 1969—which they described at the time as a "Nasser-type coup"—really changed nothing, for the simple reason that nothing can be changed in "the logic of the development of a post-revolutionary society on the road to industrialization." Once again, the theorists of these Communist Parties are patting themselves on the back by claiming to have

[1] See Gianni Corbi, "Mao è ancora Mao?" *L'Espresso*, Rome, August 19, 1973.

been right all along. They are forgetting slightly too soon that, not long ago, they thought the great Chinese social upheaval was part of a military action, which turned out to be nonexistent. And they are in grave risk of being caught out again; what acrobatics will they stage next, while continuing to claim that they were "right all along"?

As I see it, revolutions that change nothing are an impossibility, and with regard to the one that China went through between 1966 and 1969, anyone who thinks that it has left no deep marks or that it is now forgotten must be naïve indeed. True, the Tenth Congress of the CCP, held in late August 1973, has formalized the re-establishment of an institutional system based on the total dominance of the Party, whereas one of the chief aims of the Cultural Revolution had been to develop a sharing of power between the Party and the mass organizations. But is this Party a Communist Party like any other? And can it really expect, after the terrible shock waves of recent years, to manage society in the "traditional" way?

Let me say at once that the resolutions of the Tenth Party Congress reveal a certain number of persistent strains from the Comintern tradition, which are bound to cause us sharp anxieties. The indictment of Lin Piao, presented by Chou En-lai and Wang Hung-wen during the session (which lasted for four days and was held behind closed doors), bore enough resemblance to other notorious indictments made in various Communist countries to suggest alarming comparisons. Not that it came as a surprise; official versions of the "Lin Piao affair" had fully prepared us for this climax, and the "revelations" of the Congress have not required me to change a comma in what I wrote in earlier chapters. Chou himself said at the Congress that, since everyone was "in the know" regarding this affair, it was "unnecessary to discuss it in detail." [2] Sooner or later, however, at some future Congress, it will be necessary to revise these details and to replace the rituals of exorcism with a political analysis of the great crisis at the end of the Cultural Revolution.

A study of the origins, the course, and the provisional ending of

[2] See Chou En-lai, "Report to the Tenth National Congress of the Communist Party of China," *Peking Review*, Nos. 35–36 (September 7, 1973).

the Cultural Revolution leads us, nevertheless, to conclude that the CCP is not like any other Communist Party, and that it is somehow destined to follow a radically different policy from that which was pursued by Stalin in his day—and from that now adopted by the Communist movement which is loyal to the USSR. Now that we stand at a certain remove from these events, it is easier for us to see them clearly and to draw the lessons, thus getting rid once and for all of the superficial ideas formerly spread in the West.

The first lesson, of course, concerns the role of Mao. Everyone seems to recognize today that the charismatic leader of Chinese Communism has dominated his Party and his People's Republic, without an equal and without a break ever since the Yenan days. The myths about his being outvoted or even dismissed in the 1950's have collapsed of their own weight. It is admitted that, at the most, there were certain periods when the Chairman—no administrator by inclination—tended to withdraw into his library, as he is apparently doing again now, and to hand the reins to assistants who faithfully implemented his line. No one today would seriously claim that he had to make a revolution to regain his lost power or to take revenge on his rivals. This is one step forward; everyone now accepts the idea that the causes of the Cultural Revolution are immensely deeper.

We can also bury another myth, which depicted the Cultural Revolution as a struggle of men in uniform against civilians, a coup staged by the army to install its dictatorship. On this question too the experts have revised their ideas, and the highly prestigious *China Quarterly* has explained with its customary erudition that the army men were involved in events just like other Communist militants, without hidden purposes or private ambitions, and that their actions had nothing to do with the old Chinese "war lord" tradition.[3] Indeed, the course of events showed repeatedly that in China the army is not a distinct body, concerned with its privileges and capable of playing its own political game. We will not insult the People's Liberation Army by comparing it with the Chilean Army or any other conventional

[3] See Ellis Joffe, "The Chinese Army after the Cultural Revolution: The Effect of Intervention," *China Quarterly*, No. 55 (1973).

"loyal" army.[4] Those who tried to make such absurd comparisons now have plenty of thinking to do; in China, the men in uniform behaved throughout the Cultural Revolution like Party stalwarts, often shouldering the most unrewarding tasks, sometimes making mistakes and disagreeing among themselves, but never—even in the trying times when they could not accept the "new line"— dreaming for a moment of imposing their arguments by using their guns. The climax of the Lin Piao affair suffices to show that this commander-in-chief of the army never considered forcing a military dictatorship on the Chinese people. So it must be agreed that the Cultural Revolution was not the outcome of a contest between army and civilians. Another step forward.

Finally, the most significant fact that can be deduced from this story: no clear line, no simple division between darkness and light, distinguishes "utopians" dedicated to the development pattern conceived during the Great Leap Forward from "realists" in the Party who favored the Soviet model. Had this been the case, China would now be following the "Soviet road," since it is generally agreed that the "realists" have won the day and that their ideas of the Party's role in society have triumphed. But, despite the victory of the so-called "Liu Shao-ch'i-ism without Liu Shao-ch'i," the Chinese are renewing in the most heartfelt style the "general line of the Great Leap" and applying it with even more consistency and logic than in the past. From all the evidence, the concept of the dominance of the Party does not necessarily go together with a determined policy of enforced industrialization; it does not inevitably mean the adoption of the entire Stalinist doctrine (now still in force in Eastern Europe) of giving priority to a certain method of "the development of productive forces." To understand this, one may turn to the documents of the Tenth Party Congress, for they are most explicit on this point; all the slogans and all the quotations from Mao about economic progress are drawn from the period of the Great Leap, and they run like a red thread through the speeches on the tasks of the Party. Besides, among those entrusted with imple-

---

[4] The Chilean Army was renowned for its loyalty to the constitution—until it carried out the putsch of September 1973 to overthrow the perfectly legal government of President Salvador Allende.

menting this line at the level of the Central Committee and in particular the government, we meet again a good many of the old "high officials" such as Teng Hsiao-p'ing, secretary-general of the Party in 1966, and T'an Chen-lin, the most vigorous defender of the old "headquarters" and the man most denounced during the Cultural Revolution. Can we seriously imagine that these men represented a pro-Russian group, now that they are being hoisted back into the saddle to consolidate and develop a totally anti-Russian pattern? If Mao is now entrusting the controls of economic power to an almost complete muster of the old team (Liu Shao-ch'i is one of the few not qualified for rehabilitation, and we have seen why), it must be because he knows perfectly well that the team shares today, as it did yesterday, his views concerning the "different development" of productive forces under socialism.

So the "second Chinese revolution" is now cleared of the three myths that hid its real face. The final scene takes us back quite naturally to its true origins, which in my view are enshrined in the sixteen-point decision of August 1966. This shows that, in Mao's eyes, the building of socialism extends through a long historical period and depends basically on the class struggle, on the political and productive action of the workers themselves. In 1966—which, by the way, was a year of economic boom and not of crisis—Mao considered that the Party, while remaining a vital instrument in the service of the working class, had to be balanced by other rank-and-file organizations and subjected to a wholesale rectification in the framework of "broad democracy." To his mind, only this new "form and method" of mass mobilization could prevent the arteries of the Party from hardening and allow a renewal of the "line of the Great Leap" which was required to speed the material progress of society. It is a certainty that this venture was bound to clash with all the Party's habits; it is obvious that it could not succeed "100 percent," as the Chinese say; it is more than likely that errors of leadership contributed to the difficulties. All the same, we must not fail to see the forest for the trees; the Cultural Revolution was the by-product of China's "different" development pattern and is entirely—I should even say inevitably—part of the logic of Chinese ideas about the building of socialism through the class struggle. So, when all the platform speakers at the Tenth Party Congress called for another Cultural Revolution, and even a series of future revolutions, they were by no means trying to please Mao by copying his style. The same causes produce the same effects; they were well aware that the needs which had led to the explosion of 1966 had not disappeared, and therefore that other explosions were bound to come "according to the laws of the class struggle," which—as the Chairman had reminded them—are "independent of the human will."

In terms of theory, it is not hard to see why this should be so. For classical Marxism, as for Mao, the concepts of equality and freedom are indivisible. A society that seeks to abolish social distinctions and hierarchies is bound to pose the question of the initiative and decision-making power of the producers as a whole. It must inevitably look forward to a system in which institutions are no longer based on a permanent delegation of power to administrators who, even if they are well-intentioned and "at the service of the people," are nonetheless divided from the people by the logic of facts. It remains to be seen whether these basic questions—the concern of all real socialists—were not raised precipitously in the China of 1966. That, indeed, is the one genuine issue which could divide the leaders of the CCP, and the issue that mainly concerns us today.

In this book, I have tried not to clog the narrative with too many reflections on the various episodes of the Cultural Revolution. In the overall context, they can stand without commentary. They show, certainly, that the social structure of China is still far from homogeneous and remains deeply marked by the exploitation—colonial, capitalist, and feudal all at the same time—which it endured in the past. The revolution, as Mao promised, did indeed give "something more every day" to the formerly disinherited, but these "somethings" did not add up to enough to free the Chinese people from the multitude—hard for us to imagine—of the material deprivations under which they suffered. It was not enough to convince them all that the only way out was through a collective effort, through renouncing all selfishness and all schemes to secure individual advantages in the meantime. The support and devotion given by the majority already constituted a unique success, on which no other socialist revolution could pride itself. But was it possible to cross this frontier in a single spurt, relying on the youngest and the most dedicated to drag the more backward along—those who were still hampered by "old ideas, old customs, old manners, and old habits"?

"A master who is too strict has no disciples; water which is too pure has no fish." Mao quoted this line from an old Sung poem to reprove (as we are now told) the conduct of Lin Piao and Ch'en Po-ta during the Cultural Revolution.[5] He rebuked them for trying to impose on everyone standards of behavior that did not correspond to the real possibilities of society. In other words, a country like China may set up a Lei Feng as the model of an altruistic outlook—and may be greatly strengthened when this example is followed by a large number of soldiers, workers, and young people—but it cannot reasonably demand from everyone such a degree of heroism and sainthood. Such an exorbitant demand would drive a section of the population—unable to respond to it for material reasons—into sterile conformism and living in a "double truth," a contradiction between outward appearance and inner conviction. This, in fact, is what Mao was cautiously telling Edgar Snow when he said that the "cult of his thought" appealed to three categories of people: "First, those who are sincere; second, those who swim with the current and shout 'Long live Mao!' because everyone is doing the same; and third, the hypocrites." [6]

In an essay published in *Red Flag* a year after the fall of Lin Piao (whose name was not yet mentioned in it), the problem is attacked from another angle through the question: "Why study political economy?" [7] The writers reaffirm, in Mao's fashion, that the transformation of production relationships is an absolute and long-term priority for post-revolutionary society, but they stress that it cannot be achieved by purely voluntarist action which ignores the objective foundations of Marxist political economy. The struggle must not be postponed while waiting for "maximum economic achievements with minimal production costs"—a formula attributed to Soviet revisionists—but, on the other hand, it can be won only "little by little," through the progressive

[5] According to a dispatch from Serge Romensky, Agence France-Presse correspondent in Peking, dated July 6, 1973.

[6] See Snow's interview with Mao in *Nouvel Observateur*, February 21, 1972.

[7] See *New China Notebooks*, September 1, 1972.

elimination of "capitalist factors in production relationships." This is not "reformist gradualism," because, in attacking the heritage of the old relationships, reliance must be placed only on "the class struggle, the struggle for production, and scientific experimentation on the mass level." Anyone who departs from this "correct line," whether by yielding to simple gradualism or by forcing the pace of feasible changes, adopts "mistaken ideas either of the Right or of the ultra-Left."

Stripped of its rhetorical and inquisitorial trappings, this document (like many others published during the same period) expresses in sober terms the real dilemma of the second Chinese revolution. That revolution was, on the one hand, "absolutely indispensable"—to use the approved phrase—to allow the masses to "free themselves from the remnants of capitalism" and thus achieve a qualitative jump in their manner of living and working; and, at the same time, incapable of solving the problem because of the insuperable material restraints imposed by the level of productive development. However, is it true that men like Lin Piao and Ch'en Po-ta failed to understand this truth, or refused to recognize it even when the course of events showed that certain limitations could not be exceeded?

At the risk of repetition, I must again recall that we do not know the losers' version. Thus, we cannot know how they looked at the situation that had come about and what measures they advocated. The knowledge summarized in earlier chapters enables us, at best, to venture some general conclusions. It appears, in the first place, that closely identifying Lin and Ch'en with each other is somewhat arbitrary. Although they belonged to the same wing of the Maoist movement, the two men were active in different spheres during the Cultural Revolution and did not necessarily take up the same positions on immediate issues. The first and the most unhappy of these issues, which had to be faced after the middle of 1966, was the scale of the hostility between the masses and the Party cadres. It was an unexpected phenomenon, for—once again—the conduct of most of the cadres had been regarded as quite acceptable by Maoist standards, and it had been supposed that the governed, on the whole, took the same view. It is indeed quite possible that 95 percent of the cadres really were "good or open to reclamation," and that the bitterness of the criticisms aimed at them can be ascribed chiefly to a sort of collective frenzy—to the desire to find a scapegoat for grievances stored up, by sheer necessity, through years of laborious toil in a country that is still so poor. When you spend your life pulling levers in a factory, eight hours a day, six days a week, and with no holidays, you may appreciate your job security and the "simplicity" of your well-meaning superiors, but when the lid is taken off you are naturally tempted to lash out at the nearest target, especially when you are encouraged to express your criticisms and your profound feelings.

However, when things became so explosive that the masses were divided and all rational debate was intensely difficult, was it not necessary to calm down the movement before it went beyond the limits set out by the sixteen-point decision of August 1966? Was it not necessary to stop this wave of criticisms, designed to help the masses to form their own organizations, from utterly submerging the Party and creating a power vacuum? No simple answer can be given to these questions; that would be to forget the atmosphere prevailing in China at a time when Mao himself was repeatedly and explicitly attacking "the authoritarianism of the center" and any kind of action from the top downward. Yet, according to the present leaders, Ch'en Po-ta bore an especially heavy responsibility for pouring oil on the flames at the critical moment. As chairman of the central group, he had given key jobs in the field of propaganda to his old colleagues on *Red Flag* (notably Wang Li), who were particularly inclined to "upset everything" and to forgive the former leaders for nothing. He also refused to check in the slightest degree the activities of the Red Guards—who, as we know, had been instructed not to interfere in industry and agriculture—and allowed their organizations to merge with those of the "revolutionary rebels" in the mines and factories. In short, he removed all the barriers that might have canalized the movement, and hurled against the cadres an uncontrolled and uncontrollable destructive force in search of "proletarian power." It is a fact that the rehabilitated cadres now show far more resentment against Ch'en Po-ta than against Lin Piao, though Lin is designated today as "Guilty Man number one." [8]

[8] The animosity of the rehabilitated cadres toward Ch'en Po-ta did not arise solely, it is said, from his tendency to identify all holders of responsible posts with

In fact, if we can at a pinch describe Ch'en as an extremist (though no more so than Chiang Ch'ing and other members of the Central Group), the same does not seem to be precisely true of Lin Piao. He adhered very strictly to the directives of the Chairman in the crucial phase of the Cultural Revolution; his speeches, taking an essentially moral tone, preached the collectivist virtues and warned against recourse to violence. The *Documents of the Great Proletarian Cultural Revolution*, which I have often quoted, contain most of Lin's public speeches and are highly instructive in this context. But a careful reading also indicates that he persisted in his belief that everything could be settled by a profound study of Mao's thought, and therefore that he was not at all inclined to put the brakes on the movement because of the many injustices suffered by the cadres. This "master who is too strict" seems to have taken his own textbooks too literally, especially the chapters about the "excellent revolutionary situation in China and throughout the world." Hence, he was opposed to compromises and in the final phase of events he naturally backed the "hard-liners" against the "tacticians." By doing so, did he betray the policy and the hopes of Mao?

The part played by Mao is just what is most baffling for the analyst on the outside. He alone, it appears, had the power to stop the excesses by a direct intervention—witness the effect he had produced in the opposite direction when he put up his personal poster on the door of the Central Committee on August 5, 1966. He took no such action in 1967 to put the movement into reverse, although by that time he recognized that China was not Shanghai, and that even in Shanghai it was impossible to create a true commune. From then onward, his attitude can be explained only by his conviction that a huge political debate, no matter how chaotic, was the best conceivable social experience for the masses, and must be allowed to continue for as long as possible. When all is said and done, the best summary of what the Chairman was thinking is doubtless to be found in the words he uttered in September 1967, which I have already quoted:

the *ancien régime* that had to be destroyed. It was caused also by the fact that he had in the past been a theoretician of the Party organization, so that he was seen as a "traitor," a man who had switched sides, choosing the right moment in the hope that his past would be forgotten. But these are explanations given after the event.

There has never been such a broad and deep mass movement as this. In the factories and the countryside, in the schools and the army units, in the whole nation, everyone is talking about the Cultural Revolution and feeling involved in national affairs. Before, when families came together, they wasted a lot of time in small talk. Now, everything is different. As soon as they meet, they talk of great problems; fathers and sons, brothers and sisters, husbands and wives, even adolescents and grandmothers, all join in the discussion.

So, in Mao's eyes, the Cultural Revolution had shaken up the whole Chinese people more than any of the other events—dramatic though they were—in their recent history, such as the war against Japan and the civil war which led to the first revolution of 1949. For the first time, a movement had genuinely and deeply stirred this vast country and everyone, in truth, had been lifted above the limited horizon of family or neighborhood affairs. However, this situation could not last forever because of the clashes it was causing between too many one-sided truths, and because there were too many demands that could not be satisfied. But the experience, albeit transitory, would leave its mark as a qualitative jump in consciousness, and for most people that precedent would never be forgotten. Nothing in the future would ever be the same as before—human relationships, the reconstructed Party, the attitudes of young people toward authority, would all bear an indelible stamp and, Mao believed, would lead to the understanding of the truth that the right to rebellion is inseparable from Marxism. The Cultural Revolution did not solve China's problems, and Mao had not hoped for so much. That it had transformed the conditions of the problem, he took to be a highly satisfactory outcome. After his return to Peking in the fall of 1967 from his last big tour of the provinces, he was opposed under all circumstances to efforts to start the mass movement up again and to look for miraculous solutions in a country which still needed to "develop the economic foundations of socialism, build up its productive strength, and equip itself with a modern industry, agriculture, science, and culture." When the time came for the great reconciliation that followed the great upheaval, it was (as we have seen) much more difficult to achieve at the top than halfway down.

That should not surprise us. In a sense, right from the start, the confrontation had been tougher among the leaders, because it divided men who had lived and worked together for decades—responsible men who were fully aware of the scope and gravity of the conflict. And then, the fears of those who were skeptical in the final phase of a too hasty rebuilding of the Party were clearly not without foundation. Have they not been accused since then—with a certain logic, if we take the words literally—of being anti-Party? Experience has shown once again that a Communist Party machine has a long memory and can soon reassemble its "black files" on nonconformists and heretics, as K'uai Ta-fu well knows. Finally, it is now clear that no balance between the Party and the mass organizations could be established in quiet times after the ebbing of the tide, and that the Party was certain to end up holding all the strong points in the institutional structure of China.

All this is now on the record, and the Tenth Party Congress has even written into the statutes a new definition of the Cultural Revolution; its main purpose, we are told, was "to consolidate the Party." [9] To judge by the size of the membership—twenty-eight million—the outcome on this level is completely convincing. To be sure, however much it is "consolidated," all is not calm in the Party; the way in which it called this Congress, half secretly and subjecting the delegates to repeated scrutiny, speaks for itself. Besides, while it has achieved a great success in getting the old cadres back into harness, it prefers not to talk about this subject, which it seems to find particularly embarrassing. Teng Hsiao-p'ing appeared at a banquet one day at the end of April 1973 and then strolled around the parks of Peking on May Day in carefree style, as if everyone were in a fit of amnesia, as if no one could remember that not long ago he had been "China's second Khrushchev." In August, on the occasion of an international table-tennis tournament (in China this sport is linked eternally with maneuver and diplomacy), T'an Chen-lin took his place in the VIP stand with the bland confidence of an old leader who had never gone astray—a revolutionary whose record is unstained and unbroken. Many other old "high officials" came back, on tiptoes

[9] See "Constitution of the Communist Party of China" and Wang Hung-wen's "Report on the Revision of the Party Constitution," *Peking Review*, Nos. 35–36 (September 7, 1973).

and without a word being spoken. How can this silence be justified? Either these men had been unjustly and overharshly criticized, in which case amends were due; or else the criticisms were accurate and the former deviationists should now be explaining why they made their mistakes and how they achieved their comeback. Silence is surely the worst solution, for it allows all kinds of people to think all kinds of things about these leaders who are now back at the high table.[10] But in the summer of 1972, when Professor Parris Chang of the University of Pennsylvania asked why rehabilitated provincial secretaries were almost always sent to provinces other than those where they had ruled before the Cultural Revolution, he received this disarming reply: "In their old provinces they had been so much criticized that for them to take up their former posts would have been embarrassing for them, for the Party, and for the masses." [11]

"Embarrassing," indeed, is a nice euphemism. The problem is fundamental rather than merely awkward; the Party cadres had been absolutely stripped naked during the great upheaval, and it was impossible to restore their old prestige without disavowing the Cultural Revolution. Now, Mao and his team were careful to disavow nothing. Not for a moment did they intend to announce that the second Chinese revolution had only been a kind of counterrevolution after all. Moreover, they have refrained from accusing Lin Piao and Ch'en Po-ta of "leftist extremism," having grasped in time that such charges might cast doubt on the wisdom

[10] Alain Bouc, correspondent of *Le Monde* in Peking, has been alone in his lyrical and enthusiastic reaction to the return of Teng Hsiao-p'ing. "A precious asset," he writes in his journal, *La Nouvelle Chine.* "Think of it—such a distinguished personality coming around to the new line, what a source of support! It is like Fouché supporting Robespierre, or Kautsky changing his mind and supporting Lenin." (*La Nouvelle Chine*, No. 13, June 1973.) The more you think of it, as Bouc rashly urges, the less you can imagine Lenin's delight if he had seen Kautsky offering his support without saying a word, just by appearing in a Moscow park like a ghost.

[11] See Parris Chang, "Political Rehabilitation of Cadres in China," *China Quarterly*, No. 54. Professor Chang put this question at Changsha, on learning that Chang P'ing-hua, Party secretary for Hunan Province, had been given the same position after his rehabilitation, but in Shansi. According to Professor Chang's notes, only one rehabilitated provincial secretary got his old territory back; this was Chao Tzu-yang of Kwangtung, who seems to have returned with the whole of his "much-criticized" team from before the Cultural Revolution.

of the Cultural Revolution itself. True to their principle of "turning bad things into good" and reducing the "struggle between the two lines" to didactic simplicity, they have chosen to defend the entire Cultural Revolution at all costs, and to lump Liu Shao-ch'i, Lin Piao, and all the "deviationists" together as adherents of a "pro-Soviet line" opposed to the class struggle and to the rights of the masses to self-emancipation. As for those who returned to the fold, whether from common sense or from the need to use their competence again, no doubt they bear witness by the very ambiguity of their position that Party officials are only human—fallible, open to criticism, capable of being dismissed, and of being rehabilitated when required.

Far be it from me to sing the praises of this procedure, taken as a whole, or to claim that it can be reconciled with Mao's theories on the "deep wisdom of the masses." I have maintained the contrary throughout this book; to my mind, the only way to educate the masses and advance their critical awareness is to tell them the truth about everything and inform them fully, by speaking to them in political terms and not by telling them stories about "traitors," "snakes," "scabs," and "super-spies." Rightly or wrongly, I believe that the Chinese workers were perfectly capable of understanding why Liu Shao-ch'i was not the right man for the situation of 1966 and why Lin Piao could not be retained in power in 1971. It is more than likely that the inspirational effect of such explanations would have been far greater than what has now been achieved by turning every dissident into a "Soviet agent" or a champion of the restoration of capitalism and, for that matter, of feudalism—the charge made today against Lin Piao after he had fought as a Communist for fifty years.[12] But I need

[12] Chou En-lai has involuntarily shown how scanty is the evidence of Liu Shao-ch'i's and Lin Piao's alleged complicity with the USSR. As the only proof of Liu's "treason," he cited Brezhnev's speech in March 1967 regretting the overthrow of the former vice-chairman and a *Pravda* article a few days later on the same topic. As for Lin Piao's illicit relations with the Russians, which are said to have been of long duration, the least one can say is that he covered his tracks, since the Chinese people have not been offered an atom of proof. We may note finally, in an almost comical vein, that (according to *Le Monde* of September 5, 1973) the government has evidence of Ch'en Po-ta's treachery: in March 1969, he went to speak to the troops on the Soviet border. Doubtless he used the opportunity to chat with his Russian accomplices across the Ussuri River through a bullhorn. What can we say of an indictment made up from such items?

not belabor the point; I have already pointed out that such tales injure China's political development, blacken her reputation in the eyes of her friends abroad, and thus hinder the application of her international policy.

Having said this, one must understand what is meant by "good" and "evil" in China today, even though one is affronted or disturbed by the way in which these concepts are put forward. In this respect, the Tenth Party Congress is instructive because of its simplicity. Even before it met, on August 18, 1973, there was a sudden commemoration of the seventh anniversary of the famous rally on T'ien An Men Square, which opened the series of meetings between Mao and the eleven million young Red Guards who had flocked to Peking in 1966. *People's Daily* abruptly devoted three articles to these events (doubtless to make use of a three-year backlog) and renewed its praise of the Red Guards as if nothing had happened. By this account, the young militants had always been "excellent" and 100 percent loyal to the line of Chairman Mao, although some bad shepherds—"crooks of the Liu Shao-ch'i type"—had vainly attempted to lead their movement astray. What will be the practical results of this wholesale rehabilitation of the Red Guards on the eve of the Congress? We cannot yet be sure, but I think that this action set the tone for the meeting of August 1973.

The leitmotif of the speeches by Chou En-lai and Wang Hung-wen, in fact, was loyalty to the Cultural Revolution and continuity from the Ninth Party Congress. Following this tack, they reaffirmed that the most blameworthy theory (or rather "absurdity") for a Chinese Communist was to stress the contradiction "between the advanced socialist system and backward forces of social production" in China. The adherents of this "absurdity," among whom Lin Piao was included, drew the conclusion that the backward production forces must be developed before anything was done about the "advanced socialist system"; in other words, they adopted the old Soviet principle of priority for economic growth. Nobody in China had been heard to defend the Soviet pattern since 1958, but the leaders considered, not without justice, that such temptations were inevitably present in the Party, which not only has the inspiring but arduous task of initiating fresh experiments, but also must manage society on a day-to-day basis and may thus be seduced by a "quieter" type of policy. To show that there must be no question of letting things slide in that direction, these leaders solemnly declared that the main contradiction, after the revolution as well as before, is between the proletariat and the bourgeoisie, between those who have an incentive to change everything and those who defend the old order or new privileges.

More than this, in 1973, just as on the eve of the Cultural Revolution, the Party leaders gravely warned the nation that the danger of a "usurpation of power" in China could come only from within the Party's own ranks. Repeating, almost word for word, the arguments advanced before the "great wrath of the masses," they now made use of Liu Shao-ch'i and Lin Piao in a glorious didactic effort to show that the really dangerous traitors had been "concealed" in the "headquarters," and that vigilance must be maintained because still others might be lurking there. Emphatically, this Chinese Communist Party, barely rebuilt after the shock of the Cultural Revolution, seemed to be lighting the fires of opposition once more and doing its best to supply its challengers with theoretical and historical footholds for future struggles.

Of course, neither Chou En-lai nor Wang Hung-wen imagined that imitators of Miss Nieh and K'uai Ta-fu were on the point of taking up the torch again with the backing of Chairman Mao. The time was not ripe for a new nation-wide agitation, and the leaders even seemed to be worried by the dead calm that blanketed the masses since the end of the Cultural Revolution. The two keynote speakers at the Congress went so far as to deplore this political passivity of the "governed" in the face of dangerous tendencies on the part of some rehabilitated "governors" who—in Wang's words—"are intolerant of statements coming from the masses, and go so far as to stifle criticism and resort to reprisals." But on this extremely delicate issue the CCP does not always have the right answer ready. It can demand, as in the past, that its comrades behave better and follow the noble Chinese Communist tradition of criticism and self-criticism, but since 1966 it is well known that appeals to cadres to correct their own course often have limited results.

Chou En-lai, therefore, came closer to grips with the situation in the mass organizations. "The leadership of these organizations must be strengthened," he said, "so that power is really in the hands of Marxists, of workers, poor peasants, and other toilers, and the task of consolidating the dictatorship of the proletariat is carried through in every rank-and-file unit." And Wang Hung-wen reminded his comrades that "a true Communist must act without any selfish considerations and dare to go against the current, unafraid of being dismissed, expelled from the Party, thrown into prison, forced into divorce, or subjected to violence." These appeals, which clearly echo the slogans of the great upheaval, may sound very surprising (or pathetic, depending on how you look at it) in the mouths of leaders who were concerned to "stabilize the situation." In reality, I believe, they reflect that profound belief on the part of the leaders of Chinese Communism to which I have referred—that the transformation of the institutional framework of their society is inevitable and that future Cultural Revolutions will be necessary in the very name of their chosen doctrine and pattern of development. For Chou En-lai well knows that real mass organizations, on the model of the Paris Commune, have yet to be created, and that in the meantime it is useless to expect the existing trade unions and associations to play a decisive role in "consolidating the dictatorship of the proletariat." As for Wang Hung-wen, who belonged to the Shanghai rebels in 1966, he is well equipped to know how hard it is to challenge the established machine, and he cannot reasonably urge isolated Party members to take on the job by themselves.

So everything hangs together in this Congress, which drew a heavy line through the "Lin Piao affair" and nevertheless preserved the principles and the promise of the Cultural Revolution. Even the choice of new leaders testifies to the desire—if not the necessity—to cling to the line of "a series of revolutions" (or of "the continuous revolution," if we prefer that older term). The supreme positions in the Party were given only to men who incarnated the old tradition of revolutionary war and to those who belonged to the "proletarian headquarters" during the Cultural Revolution or made their mark during that period. No position at the top level was given to those who had been rehabilitated or who had been less active. In the Presidium of the Politburo, Chairman Mao is surrounded by five vice-chairmen and three other leaders. Four of these members of the inner circle need no introduction—Chu Teh, Chou En-lai, Yeh Chien-ying, and Tung Pi-wu, all veterans and founding members of the CCP and the Red Army. It is widely known, moreover, that Chu Teh and Tung Pi-wu are symbolic figures, whereas Chou and Yeh by contrast are very active and continue to be in charge of the Party and of the army respectively.

When we look at the four other members of the Presidium, two at least bring an element of surprise. The position of number three in the Party hierarchy, with the title of vice-chairman, goes to Wang Hung-wen, scarcely thirty-six years old and a mere Central Committee member after the Ninth Party Congress. Thus, he has received the most dramatic promotion in the record of the Party since the era of the Long March. But, young as he is, Wang is also a symbol. In 1966, when he was a Shanghai textile worker and an ordinary Party member, he was one of the organizers of the Shanghai Workers' Revolutionary Rebel General Headquarters on the eve of the "January storm" which led to the proclamation of the Shanghai Commune in February 1967. Since then, he has distinguished himself as the best of the young cadres who emerged from the movement, and in 1970 he became Party secretary for the great city. The purpose of whisking him to the summit at the Tenth Party Congress was doubtless to dispel the impression that the best rebels had lined up with Lin Piao and had been swept aside at the same time as he was. Wang Hung-wen's career demonstrates that, under the dictatorship of the proletariat, a Communist who dares to go against the stream can still reach harbor.

Another surprise was the reappearance of K'ang Sheng in the number-five position, which he had held at the time of the Ninth Party Congress. This veteran Maoist, a Politburo member since 1936 and formerly a vice-chairman of the Central Group for the Cultural Revolution, had made very, very few public appearances since the "hot" session of the Central Committee at Lushan in the fall of 1970. His reputation as a man of the far Left and his links with other vanished figures, including Ch'en Po-ta, had led to an immediate belief that he had found difficulty in adjusting to the "new line" and had left the political scene for good and all. There is no proof that this belief was altogether baseless; as we know, illnesses are sometimes diplomatic. In any case, K'ang Sheng has regained his place in the inner circle elected at the Tenth Party Congress, completely re-established or drawn in as a symbolic figure like Chu Teh. In his person, the Central Group is restored to full dignity in the eyes of the masses.

Finally, two other promotions went to Chang Ch'un-ch'iao of Shanghai and Li Teh-sheng of Anhwei, who had made their names particularly during the events of 1966–9 and, though no longer young, can legitimately be taken to represent the new generation emerging from the Cultural Revolution. But, all things considered, can there be any other kind of new generation in China? When we weigh up the factors for and against the ultimate eruption of another Cultural Revolution, we must ask first of all how the old guard could find successors who are not, first and foremost, marked by the experience of a Cultural Revolution. We have seen that in the CCP, as in all Communist Parties born of the Third International, the personalities of the old guard combined in varying proportions their own tradition and that of the Comintern. Thanks to Mao, the element of originality has always been very powerful, incomparably greater than in their comrades in other countries; but, even in their language, we recognize elements common to all Communists. Besides, everything is not Stalinist in the heritage of the Comintern, which has made so deep a mark on the history of the working-class movement. But it is a certainty that this tradition elevates organization at the cost of spontaneity, that it is more "Jacobin" and more concentrated on the vanguard than the tradition which stresses the "mass line" and defends the right of the masses to political self-determination. Now, the thought of Mao Tse-tung, which was already an original extension of the doctrine common to all Communists, has enriched it since the Cultural Revolution—really, since the Great Leap Forward—with astonishing innovations. The old balance can change only in this direction because the heirs of the Chinese revolution—sorry, revolutions—have been trained and are being trained, in theory and in practice, in the school of this latter doctrine. And it is a doctrine, I need not repeat, which does not ask anyone to respect hierarchical law and order or to be content with small improvements handed down from above by leaders, however enlightened they may be.

Since so many factors, from the development pattern of society to the political training of the young, herald a third Chinese revolution, should we conclude that it is virtually inevitable? That would be contrary to the teaching of Mao himself, and he understands better than anyone how to analyze the situation in his country and the great revolutionary currents. According to him, all mechanistic determinism is likely to be either an excuse for or the result of mere intellectual laziness. Nothing in history is decided in advance, whether in China or elsewhere. The class struggle, he teaches, is not an operetta, before the revolution or afterward. It touches heights and depths over a long period, in the course of which men battle to emerge from their prehistory and to create at long last a truly free and equal society. Instead of peering into the crystal ball, let us simply bear in mind that every aspect of this struggle is of direct concern to us, influences our future, and teaches us as much about ourselves as about the faraway Chinese. Reader, this is your history. The author has never doubted that for a moment.

INDEX

Index

467

First Congress, 348
First Peasants and Workers Army, 431
Five-Year Plan, 52, 60, 63, 65, 86, 97, 148
Foreign Language Institute, 268, 282
Fours, the, 331–2, 334
Fourth Army, 323–4, 356, 361
Fu Ch'ung-pi, 319–20, 323–4, 330
Further Education College, 248
Fushun, 293, 300–2
Futan University, 214, 355–62

General Political Department, 257
General Strike of September 1922, 428–30
Great Leap Forward, 7, 10, 13, 16, 26, 68, 72, 74, 90–2, 94–101, 107, 114, 121–3, 143, 148–9, 152, 164–5, 208, 220, 232, 261, 305, 314, 346, 448–9, 463
Group of Five, 139–40, 155–6, 158, 275
Guevara, Ché, 389

Hakkas, 435
Han Ai-chin, 248, 330, 332, 334
Hanoi, 379–80, 422–3
Harbin, 215, 226–7
Harbin Red Rebels United Headquarters, 226
Headquarters of the Revolutionary Revolt of Shanghai Workers, 209, 211–12, 215, 228, 264
Heilungkiang, 226, 247, 338, 411
"Historical Experience of the Dictatorship of the Proletariat, On the," 70
Ho Chi Minh, 104, 393, 423
Ho Lung, 182, 279, 348, 441
Ho Shu-lan, 369
Hong Kong, 267–8, 281–2
Hopson, D. C., 281–2
Hot Summer, 290–1, 293, 300, 311, 315
How to Be a Good Communist (Liu Shao-Ch'i), 117–18
Hsiao Hua, 257, 283, 286
Hsiao Wang-tung, 140
Hsieh Fu-chih, 231, 270–2, 274–6, 279, 287, 318, 323, 348, 409

Hsü Hsiang-ch'ien, 251–2, 257, 271, 279
Hsu Yen, 267
Hu Cha, 357–9
Hu Chuang, 163
Hu Feng, 136
Hu Shan-ch'u, 295, 298, 301–2, 305
Huang Hua, 386
Huang Yung-sheng, 318, 323, 411, 417, 420–1
Huanyungchieh, 432, 439–41
Humphrey, Hubert, 98
Hunan, 12, 117, 219, 340, 406, 428, 431–2, 434–5, 440
Hunan Party Committee, 440
hundred days' war, 316, 326, 330, 353
Hundred Flowers campaign, 58, 71–2, 136–7, 156, 176
Hung Yuan, 417
Hurley, Patrick, 46
Hydroelectric Institute, 272

Incident of May 20, 239–41, 243
Inside Story of Ch'ing Court, 259–60
Institute for Agricultural Science, 249
Institute of Geology, 248, 264
Institute of Technology for Those at Work in Shanghai, 359

January Storm, 209, 216, 250, 253, 274, 290, 311, 317, 462
Johnson, Lyndon, 378–9, 392–3, 395, 399, 401, 422

K'ang Sheng, 156, 189, 225, 314, 404, 409, 462–3
Kao Kang, 111, 304
Keng Chin-chang, 211, 228
Kennedy, John F., 378
Khrushchev, Nikita, 11, 19, 37, 52–5, 57–9, 64–5, 74, 77, 97–9, 101–5, 116, 121, 144, 181, 268, 296, 278–9, 381
"Khrushchev's Phony Communism and Its Historical Lessons for the World, On," 102–3
Kiangsi, 33, 39, 110, 173, 269, 332, 340, 427, 431, 433–4, 441, 444